The Treatment of the War Dead in Archaic Athens

Also available from Bloomsbury

Funerary Epigrams of Ancient Greece, Marta González González
Greek Warfare, Hans van Wees
Homer's Iliad and the Trojan War, Jan Haywood and Naoise Mac Sweeney
The Trojan War in Ancient Art, Susan Woodford
War and Violence in Ancient Greece, edited by Hans van Wees

The Treatment of the War Dead in Archaic Athens

An Ancestral Custom

Cezary Kucewicz

BLOOMSBURY ACADEMIC
LONDON • NEW YORK • OXFORD • NEW DELHI • SYDNEY

BLOOMSBURY ACADEMIC
Bloomsbury Publishing Plc
50 Bedford Square, London, WC1B 3DP, UK
1385 Broadway, New York, NY 10018, USA

BLOOMSBURY, BLOOMSBURY ACADEMIC and the Diana logo are trademarks of Bloomsbury Publishing Plc

First published in Great Britain 2021
This paperback edition published 2022

Copyright Cezary Kucewicz, 2021

Cezary Kucewicz has asserted his right under the Copyright, Designs and Patents Act, 1988, to be identified as Author of this work.

For legal purposes the Acknowledgements on p. viii–ix constitute an extension of this copyright page.

Cover image: Greek civilization, 6th century BC. Krater depicting the fight for the body of Patroclus. From Farsala, Greece. Detail. (Photo by DEA/G. DAGLI ORTI/De Agostini via Getty Images).

All rights reserved. No part of this publication may be reproduced or transmitted in any form or by any means, electronic or mechanical, including photocopying, recording, or any information storage or retrieval system, without prior permission in writing from the publishers.

Bloomsbury Publishing Plc does not have any control over, or responsibility for, any third-party websites referred to or in this book. All internet addresses given in this book were correct at the time of going to press. The author and publisher regret any inconvenience caused if addresses have changed or sites have ceased to exist, but can accept no responsibility for any such changes.

A catalogue record for this book is available from the British Library.

Library of Congress Cataloging-in-Publication Data
Names: Kucewicz, Cezary, author.
Title: The treatment of the war dead in archaic Athens : an ancestral custom / Cezary Kucewicz.
Description: London ; New York : Bloomsbury Academic, 2020. | Includes bibliographical references and index. | Summary: "Exploring the representations of the war dead in early Greek mythology, particularly the Homeric poems and the Epic Cycle, alongside iconographic images on black-figure pottery and the evidence of funerary monuments adorning the graves of early Athenian elites, this book provides much-needed insight into the customs associated with the war dead in Archaic Athens. It is demonstrated that this period had remarkably little in common with the much-celebrated institutions of the Classical era, standing in fact much closer to the hierarchical ideals enshrined in the epics of Homer and early mythology.
While the public burial of the war dead in Classical Athens has traditionally been a subject of much scholarly interest, and the origins of the procedures described by Thucydides as patrios nomos are still a matter of some debate, far less attention has been devoted to the Athenian war dead of the preceding era. This book aims to redress the imbalance in modern scholarship and put the spotlight on the Athenian war dead of the Archaic period. In addition, the book deepens our understanding of the processes which led to the establishment of first public burials and the Classical customs of patrios nomos, shedding significant light on the military, cultural and social history of Archaic Athens. Challenging previous assumptions and bringing new material to the table, the book proposes a number of new ways to investigate a period where many 'ancestral customs' were thought to have their roots"– Provided by publisher.
Identifiers: LCCN 2020024464 (print) | LCCN 2020024465 (ebook) | ISBN 9781350151543 (hardback) | ISBN 9781350151550 (ebook) | ISBN 9781350151567 (epub)
Subjects: LCSH: War and society–Greece–Athens–History–To 1500. | War casualties–Greece–Athens–History–To 1500. | Burial–Social aspects–Greece–Athens–History–To 1500. | Funeral rites and ceremonies–Greece–Athens–History–To 1500. | Greece–Civilization $y To 146 B.C. | Homer–Criticism and interpretation. | Mythology, Greek.
Classification: LCC DF275 .K83 2020 (print) | LCC DF275 (ebook) | DDC 399–dc23
LC record available at https://lccn.loc.gov/2020024464
LC ebook record available at https://lccn.loc.gov/2020024465

ISBN:	HB:	978-1-3501-5154-3
	PB:	978-1-3501-9163-1
	ePDF:	978-1-3501-5155-0
	eBook:	978-1-3501-5156-7

Typeset by RefineCatch Limited, Bungay, Suffolk

To find out more about our authors and books visit www.bloomsbury.com and sign up for our newsletters

Contents

List of Figures	vii
Acknowledgements	viii
Notes to the Reader	x
Introduction: The War Dead in Ancient Athens	1
Sources and outline	4

Part One

1 The Homeric War Dead — 13
  Homeric society: Elite vs commoners — 15
  Fighting over the dead — 18
  Despoiling the dead — 21
  Protecting the dead — 24
  Common dead — 30
  Mutilation of the dead — 34
  Mutilation by animals — 37
  Afterlife — 39

2 The War Dead in the Greek Mythological Tradition — 43
  Early Greek mythology — 45
  Battlefield truces: Seven Against Thebes — 49
  Mutilation of the dead: Eurystheus' decapitation — 56
    Eurystheus and the children of Heracles — 57
    Amphiaraus and the Seven Against Thebes — 62
    Menelaus and the *Little Iliad* — 67
    Achilles and Hector — 70
  Greeks vs Barbarians – The Persian Wars — 73

Part Two

3 The War Dead in the Early Greek Iconographic Tradition — 79
  Archaic iconography of war — 81

	The war dead in Archaic Athenian art	86
	Iconography of change?	97
4	Archaic Monuments for the War Dead	101
	Elite burials	102
	The war dead and Archaic Greek warfare	112
5	Ancestral Customs in the Classical City	119
	Towards public burials	120
	A *patrios nomos*	124

Part Three

6	War, State and Society in Archaic Athens	135
	Early Athens	138
	Solon's reforms	149
	Peisistratus' tyranny	157
	Agricultural revolution?	164
	Cleisthenes and democracy	169

Conclusion	177
Notes	181
Bibliography	251
Index	275

Figures

1	West frieze (part), Temple of Athena Nike, Athens	50
2	Red-figure terracotta bell-krater, unattributed, *c.* 440–430 BC	65
3	South frieze (part), Temple of Athena Nike, Athens (plaster cast)	74
4	Black-figure amphora, attributed to the Lysippides Painter, *c.* 520–510 BC	89
5	Exterior of black-figure cup, attributed to Exekias, *c.* 530 BC	90
6	Exterior of black-figure cup, attributed to Exekias, *c.* 530 BC	91
7	Exterior of red-figure cup, attributed to Oltos, *c.* 515–510 BC	92
8	Black-figure amphora, attributed to Exekias, *c.* 540–530 BC	94
9	Black-figure amphora, attributed to Exekias, *c.* 540–530 BC	95
10	Grave *stele* of Aristion (plaster cast)	111
11	Red-figure loutrophoros, attributed to a painter of the Group of Polygnotos, *c.* 440 BC	125
12	White-ground lekythos, attributed to the Thanatos Painter, *c.* 435–425 BC	126

Acknowledgements

This book, as the title indicates, deals with how the Archaic Athenians treated their war dead. More specifically, it looks at 'ancestral customs', the particular ways in which the Athenians talked about their past, both recent and distant, real and imagined. This process of telling stories about the past was expressed in a rich variety of artistic forms and cultural discourses, which worked on the level of the individual, family, community and *polis*, helping to make sense of the present by rooting it in the traditions of the past. And while the intention of this book is to shed some light on this process, it has itself been part of my own story of curiosity and fascination with ancient Greece. In the more distant past, it began with my mum reading a watered-down, child-friendly version of the *Iliad* to me (with particularly nice pictures) when I was little, followed by the compulsory reading of Sophocles' *Antigone* in secondary school, which first made me notice the dichotomy between the importance ascribed to the proper treatment of the dead in Greek tragedy compared to Homer's epic, as I vividly remembered the drawing of Achilles dragging the body of Hector behind his chariot. In the more recent past, it has taken the form of many years of academic research, first during my graduate studies at Cardiff and UCL, then as part of a postdoctoral project funded by the National Science Centre, Poland (project number 2018/28/C/HS3/00418), of which this book is the result.

A two-sentence summary of my own story, however, hardly does it justice, just as merely listing the names of the people who have been an essential part of this journey feels unfair and inadequate. But it will have to do. Beginning with the more recent past, I would like to thank my doctoral supervisor, Hans van Wees, whose guidance has been invaluable since the day I first walked into his office as a struggling undergraduate from Poland. My intellectual debt to him will undoubtedly be clear throughout the chapters of this book. I am also grateful to my postdoctoral supervisor at Cambridge, Robin Osborne, who examined my thesis and has since constantly challenged me to approach the ancient evidence ever more critically. The book has also benefited greatly from the advice, comments and discussions I have had with a number of brilliant academics, including Paola Ceccarelli, Nick Sekunda, Bogdan Burliga, Josho Brouwers, Joshua Hall, Roel Konijnendijk, Matthew Lloyd and Owen Rees. Although their help has been enormous, any errors which remain are, of course, my own. Furthermore, my work on this project has been made significantly easier due to the support of the intellectual community at Wolfson College and the Faculty of Classics in Cambridge, where I conducted the final stages of my research. In particular, I would like to thank Susanne Turner, Meg Westbury and Ed Johnson. Similarly, I am grateful for the administrative support of the staff at the University of Gdańsk, especially Grażyna Stasiłowicz. Last but not least, the publishing process was facilitated greatly by the team at Bloomsbury (Lily Mac Mahon, Georgie Leighton, Alice Wright), who helped and encouraged me at every step, and by Sophie Gillespie, who copyedited the final manuscript.

Moving to the more distant past, this book owes a great deal to the love and unwavering belief in me from my parents, Ewa and Leszek, who not only introduced me to the *Iliad* but also enabled me to pursue the uncertain academic path. I cannot thank them enough for everything they have done for me. I have also been blessed with the support of my brother Michał and his wife Karolina (dziękuję!), as well as my Welsh in-laws, especially Eric Bye, who proofread the final manuscript (diolch!). For his lecture on the conquests of Alexander the Great, which sparked my own anabasis into the study of the ancient Greeks, I will forever be indebted to my high school history teacher, Łukasz Skupny. Even though it has nothing to do with Alexander, I hope this book will live up to his standard.

Finally, despite the generous help of all these people, this book would not have seen the light of day without one person in particular. While the boundless patience, encouragement and kindness of the person that is closest to you helps beyond measure, it does so even more when that person happens to be the most brilliant academic and original thinker you know. Words truly cannot express how grateful I am for sharing this story with you, Caroline.

Notes to the Reader

Throughout this book, I follow the convention of using Latinized (or Anglicized) versions of familiar Greek names. Where names are less familiar or are found on *stelai*, I maintain the transliterated Greek form. The original Greek is given in transliterated form in the main text where its inclusion is crucial to the argument; longer excerpts are given in the footnotes for significant passages.

All translations of ancient texts are taken from the Loeb Classical Library unless otherwise indicated. The exception to this rule is Homer. Richmond Lattimore's translations of the *Iliad* and *Odyssey* are used unless otherwise stated. I am grateful to the University of Chicago Press for granting me permission to use Lattimore's translation of the *Iliad* (© 1951, 2011 by The University of Chicago. All rights reserved). I will refer to passages from the *Iliad* in Arabic numerals, and will use Roman numerals for the ones from the *Odyssey*.

The names of ancient authors, texts, scholarly databases and journals are abbreviated according to the conventions found in the *Oxford Classical Dictionary*. The only exception to this is the Beazley Archive, the entries of which I will prefix with the abbreviation BA.

Introduction

The War Dead in Ancient Athens

The war dead were granted special significance in the cultural imagination of Classical Athens. If a man died fighting for the *polis*, his body had to be identified and recovered under a formal truce and brought home, regardless of geographical distance, his social standing or military skill. He and the fallen fellows of his tribe would be cremated and later honoured in Athens with a public burial ceremony, held in the winter of any year the city found itself at war. The remains of the dead, divided into ten cypress coffins according to tribe, were first laid out for two days for the Athenians to pay their respects and bring offerings; they were then carried in an official funeral procession, together with an empty bier for those whose bodies were lost or irretrievable, to be laid in the Kerameikos, the most prestigious urban cemetery in Athens, where marble casualty lists were erected recounting the names of those who died in the course of the year. The burial ceremony was concluded with a funeral oration (*epitaphios logos*) in praise of the fallen, given by a distinguished citizen chosen by the city, as well as funeral games (*agon epitaphios*) with competitions in athletics, horse-racing and music.

The customs and ceremonies concerning the retrieval, treatment and burial of the war dead at Athens were described in some detail in ancient accounts, most prominently by Thucydides, who provides us with an outline of the procedures in his account of Pericles' funeral speech for the war casualties of the first year of the Peloponnesian War (2.34). The fundamental premise behind the Athenian customs, famously referred to by Thucydides as 'the law of our forefathers' (*patrios nomos*), was based on the absolute moral obligation to respect and bury the dead, ostensibly felt by all ancient Greeks, and often still used as an archetypal paradigm for military forces in the modern day.[1] In addition, the Athenian ceremonies of *patrios nomos* were inseparably linked with the democratic nature of the *polis* and its army, as each fallen warrior was granted similar treatment and commemoration in honour of his sacrifice for the community. The inherent egalitarianism of the procedures meant that all men were rendered equal upon their death, leading Socrates to remark in Plato's *Menexenus*, a dialogue devoted entirely to the subject of funeral oration, that:

> (…) to fall in battle seems to be a splendid thing in many ways. For a man obtains a splendid and magnificent funeral even though at his death he be but a poor man; and though he be but a worthless fellow, he wins praise, and that by the mouth of accomplished men who do not praise at random, but in speeches prepared long beforehand.
>
> *Menex*, 234c

Despite scholarly interest in the significance of the war dead in Classical Athens, not to mention their burial, commemoration and their symbolic role within wider ideological discourses of the city, far less attention has been devoted to the Athenian war casualties of the Archaic period. The origins of the rules regarding the retrieval of the dead from the battlefield, described simply by Isocrates as the 'ancient custom and immemorial law' (*Paneg*. 55), as well as the Athenian ceremonies of *patrios nomos*, are often traced back to the Archaic era, with little or no discussion of the customs which they replaced or were modelled upon. The chief reason for the latter lies in the scanty nature of the surviving evidence for burial practices in the Archaic period, with only few examples of pre-500 BC battlefield *polyandria* in the wider Greek world (none in Attica), and some occasional references scattered among the authors of later periods, which often projected the experience and procedures of war in their own times onto accounts of the distant past. As a result, the main scholarly assumptions concerning the treatment of the war dead in early Athens are often based on larger historical models concerning the development of warfare in Greece. By far the most influential among them, known as the 'hoplite revolution' model, postulated that the rules regarding the proper treatment of war casualties and their common battlefield burials arose as a by-product of a major restructuring of citizen militias which took place around 700 BC. This change, as scholars such as Victor Davis Hanson, Gregory Viggiano or Josiah Ober maintain, was introduced by an emerging class of small farmers who began to influence and eventually dominate the political and military affairs of their *poleis*.[2] In time, the organization and practices of war were redefined, as old elite ideals of the past were replaced with a new civic spirit, embodied most profoundly in the introduction of a hoplite phalanx formation, but also in the crystallization of new Panhellenic conventions of war, in which the control of the battlefield and the war dead played an important role in determining the victors and losers of a military encounter.

Despite the marked impact of the 'hoplite revolution' model on the few studies of the Archaic Athenian war dead, another influential way to approach the subject was proposed in Nicole Loraux's famous study of the funeral oration in Classical Athens.[3] According to her, the discourses surrounding the commemoration of the war dead in Athens, along with the whole institution of the *patrios nomos*, were drawn from aristocratic traditions and ideals of the Archaic era. The choice of themes employed in the speeches given to glorify the deeds of the Athenians who died on behalf of their *polis* emulated the values and heroic code of epic poetry, as the praise previously ascribed only to the Athenian nobility was made available to all who sacrificed their lives in defence of their community. Loraux's work, which profoundly influenced all subsequent studies of the war dead in Athens, focused exclusively on the Classical period and confined itself primarily to the realm of ideology. The question of the retrieval and burial of the dead in early Athens was left untouched, because Loraux, following a seminal article by Felix Jacoby and a monograph titled *Greek Burial Customs* by Donna Kurtz and John Boardman, assumed that the ancient Athenians buried the dead communally on the battlefield.[4]

A similar assumption was adopted by William Kendrick Pritchett, who in the fourth volume of his monumental *The Greek State at War* gathered all evidence, archaeological and literary, for the burial of the war dead by ancient Greek armies.[5] As part of his discussion, he maintained that Athenian practices of *patrios nomos* broke with the Archaic and wider Greek tradition of burying the dead on or near the field of battle.[6] Likewise, in her most recent book on the war memorials in Archaic and Classical Greece, Janett Schröder further echoed Pritchett's conclusions, stating that the tradition of *patrios nomos* 'does not go back to Archaic times' when the Athenians buried their dead on the battlefield.[7] This notion – since Jacoby's article, often adopted without question – has been indirectly challenged in studies by Christoph Clairmont and, more recently, Nathan Arrington on the Athenian war dead in the Classical period.[8] Both begin their investigations with a short section on the burial customs of the Archaic period, noting that the limited evidence of sixth century BC gravestones of Kroisos and Tettichos, who died in battle and were buried by their families in individual graves at home, indicated that the Athenian armies of the era could have brought the bodies of the fallen warriors back home. War burials in the Archaic period, they both concluded, were predominantly in the hands of private families, who buried and commemorated their fallen sons at home. Their discussion of the implications and wider significance of these conclusions, however, were relatively limited and served only as an introduction to their detailed treatment of the Athenian practices of the Classical period. Despite challenging the view of the majority, their work followed the larger pattern characteristic of modern scholarly work on the war dead at Athens, which tends to focus only on the much-celebrated customs of the Classical *polis*, to the exclusion of any earlier practices.

The main rationale of this book, therefore, is to address the imbalance in modern scholarship and put the spotlight on the Athenian war dead of the Archaic period. In essence, the investigation carried out over the following six chapters builds on the work of previous authors dealing with the customs of *patrios nomos* at Athens, but instead of taking their conclusions forwards in time, it looks back to an age when public burials and commemoration in the form of casualty lists and funeral orations were not yet set in place. In addition, the purpose of this study is to extend the scope of current debate to other topics related to the subject of the war dead in Greece, such as the practices of combat despoliation and mutilation, widespread in the early literature and artistic representations of the era. The evidence of the latter, which has so far attracted little scholarly attention, offers striking insights into the early ideology surrounding combat and its development from the Archaic to Classical periods. In particular, it highlights significant shifts in the expectations of Athenian audiences in the early decades that followed the introduction of democracy, which reflected the unique ways in which the *polis* attempted to create a new self-identity. The latter process resulted in the establishment of new customs and traditions, the legitimacy of which was often deliberately traced back to the ancestral past.

As such, the present study aims to complement the seminal works of Loraux and Clairmont, but, more importantly, to pave the way for new areas of research with potentially important ramifications for our understanding of early Athenian war, society and culture. To achieve this, a wide range of sources is employed and discussed, including poetry, mythology, gravestones, epitaphs, pottery and literary accounts, which, considering their often-controversial nature and dubious historical value, deserve a few words of introduction.

Sources and outline

At its core, this book attempts to trace fundamental shifts in the practice and procedure of war from Archaic to Classical times. The first two parts (Chapters 1–5) build upon each other to help us establish a narrative of these changes, by introducing multiple forms of complementary evidence. The final part (Chapter 6), in contrast, seeks to explore the implications of this evidence in light of the broader history of the period. As to the sources themselves, the first part of the book explores the representations of the war dead in early Greek mythology, particularly the Homeric poems and the Epic Cycle. In their final form from around the mid-seventh century BC, the relevance of the *Iliad* and the *Odyssey* for the mortuary customs of the Athenians may not be immediately clear, but the poems remain the richest literary source for the burial customs and social attitudes to death in early Greece. Their many passages on the treatment (or maltreatment) of the war dead, as we will see in Chapter 1, provide us with detailed accounts of the norms and expectations held by Homeric society surrounding the despoliation, recovery and burial of fallen warriors. These ideals, despite the fictitious and heroic nature of the poems, were drawn from customs meaningful to contemporary audiences, which had to be kept within the limits of the experience and knowledge of the Greeks in the seventh century BC.

The challenges of using works of epic poetry for a historical study of early Greece, let alone Archaic Athens, are nonetheless multifaceted and many. Being a product of a long oral tradition spanning across many centuries back to the Mycenaean era, the Homeric poems have often been seen as an amalgam of ideals and traditions, combining a number of different, and often incompatible elements. Furthermore, reading the *Iliad* as a historical account or a military treatise runs counter to its purpose as a work of art, governed by its own rules and logic, and, at times, unresolvable contradictions. And while both of these factors have discouraged some scholars from using the Homeric epics as evidence for early Greek social, political or military history, the central premise of this book is that certain historical realities can be grasped from the poems, especially when these refer to consistent and coherent customs embedded in the core of Homeric societies. These customs, as it will be shown throughout this book, were representative of its era and the way in which the Greeks practised and thought about war for most of the Archaic period. Considering the enormous influence of the *Iliad* and the *Odyssey* in Greek culture in subsequent centuries, and especially their impact on the ideology of combat, a study of the war dead in the Homeric epics is essential for our understanding of early Greek attitudes to the treatment of the combat fallen. The 'hierarchical' standards which defined the post-mortem fate of the war dead in the poems were reflective of, and determined by, the high importance ascribed to social status by the Homeric elites, whose conspicuous burials asserted their superiority over the masses. The latter reinforced the high stratification of heroic society enshrined in the epic poems, which in many ways resembled the social realities of the Attic communities during the Archaic period.

The elite ideology of the Homeric poems is also investigated in the dynamics surrounding the practices of mutilation and deliberate exposure of the dead, which constituted an important theme in the battle narratives of the *Iliad*. The high prominence of both subjects in the story, which famously culminates in Achilles' maltreatment of the body of Hector, stood in radical opposition to the ethical norms held by the Athenians of the Classical period, who categorically condemned such practices as loathsome and befitting only the barbarians (Hdt. 9.79). The prevalence of mutilation episodes in the *Iliad*, described in an often surprising amount of detail, points to the different moral and cultural discourse present in early Greek representations of war. This discourse, far from being criticized or at odds with the values celebrated in the epics, is consistent with the heroic code ascribed to the poem's heroes and arguably also its early audiences.

The relevance of mythological stories for Athenian attitudes towards the war dead is investigated further in Chapter 2, which takes as its focus the mythical episodes concerning burial truces and the mutilations of the dead that feature in the vast body of early Greek mythology. The stories of Theseus' recovery of the Argive dead in the aftermath of the Seven Against Thebes campaign, as well as the gruesome episodes of Eurystheus' decapitation or Menelaus' mutilation of Paris, often recorded in the now lost Epic Cycle poems, give us an important insight into the popular discourses that surrounded the treatment and mistreatment of the war dead during the Archaic period. The episodes in the surviving fragments of the Cyclic myths, scattered throughout the accounts of later mythographers, provide a new and valuable source of evidence previously overlooked by scholars studying early Greek war and society. In most cases, the ideals they depict supplement and enrich the picture of combat, including its practice and ideology, enshrined in the Homeric epics, thus confirming that the treatment of the war dead portrayed by Homer was drawn from similar customs and standards across all early mythological accounts. Even more importantly, tracing the development and reception of these stories in the Classical period reveals major changes in the attitudes and ideology of the war dead and their proper treatment. This phenomenon, as the chapter will go on to demonstrate, took place in the first decades of the fifth century BC, during which the Classical authors and artists, such as Aeschylus, Pindar and Euripides, attempted to censor mutilation episodes from the mythical past and introduce new versions of traditional stories which highlighted the moral duty and righteousness behind the respectful treatment of war casualties. Such editorial activities were especially strong among the Athenians of the Classical period, who used the mythical accounts of Theseus' civilizing actions at Thebes, or the military help given to the children of Heracles pursued unjustly by Eurystheus, in order to glorify their past and justify their political and moral leadership in the wider Greek world.

The second part of the book shifts the attention away from the early mythical accounts dealing with the war dead and looks towards the evidence for retrieving and burying combat casualties in the Archaic era. Compared with the detailed picture given to us by the *Iliad* and early mythology regarding the war dead, the availability of other sources for the period is relatively small, which has hindered previous scholarly studies of the subject. One body of evidence which deserves special attention, not least because of its enormous richness in both quality and quantity, consists of iconographic representations on Athenian black- and red-figure pottery. The study of Archaic war imagery, often dismissed by military historians for its lack of realism and heroic subject matter, forms the subject of Chapter 3. In an effort to move beyond previous scholarly biases, a case is made to reintegrate the images of combat into studies of early Greek warfare as a valuable portal into popular discourses on war and death in combat. The latter, represented in dramatic portrayals of fights over and retrievals of the fallen, formed a major part of all combat representations in Attic art for most of the sixth century BC, suggesting, as it will be demonstrated, that such themes were not only meant to depict heroic episodes from myth, but also reflected the perception and experience of war by the Athenians fighting in the citizen armies. The dramatic decline in these representations towards the end of the Archaic period further accentuates the significance of the themes for earlier generations, as well as the arrival of new modes of warfare in which combat retrievals and fights over the dead were far less relevant.

The other body of evidence indispensable in any study of pre-Classical Athenian history is of a funerary nature. While it would be natural to expect that an investigation into the treatment and burial of the war dead has to devote most of its focus to graves and bones, such an assumption has proven futile in the case of Archaic Athens. No examples of battlefield burials, known as *polyandria*, survive before the end of the sixth century BC, directing any investigations instead to the graves of private Athenians, which underwent a number of transformations during the Archaic era. A study of the funerary monuments adorning the tombs of the Athenian elites, including elaborate and highly conspicuous grave *stelai* and *kouroi*, together with their accompanying inscriptions, is the subject of Chapter 4. These monuments were often raised specifically for Athenian casualties of war, among whom Kroisos and Tettichos were not isolated cases. Accordingly, they hold a potential to shed important light on the post-mortem practices of Athenian armies of the period, while also illuminating how the families of the deceased wished to remember and commemorate their fallen sons. Taken together with the evidence of iconography from the previous chapter, it is argued that the fate of the war dead was fundamentally defined by highly elitist principles and a mentality which, in turn, influenced the contemporary practice and ideology of war, recalling the norms represented in the mythological accounts of the Archaic era.

In Chapter 5, the discussion continues into the final years of the sixth century BC and the early decades of the democratic city, which witnessed the emergence of the institution of public burials for the war dead. The usual scholarly conundrum about when the latter was first established, which many archaeologists tend to refer to as the 'million dollar question', is nonetheless given second place to an investigation of how the Athenians reacted to the changes in the custom and, more importantly, how the state attempted to facilitate this transition. With the physical absence of the bodies of the fallen, new ways to commemorate and honour the dead had to be established. In the years following the reforms of Cleisthenes, the decision on what to do with the war dead was under negotiation, both on the battlefields and in the houses of Athenian families. The result of this dialogue was a custom which deliberately blended the public and the private, drawing from the epic commonplaces of the past in order to glorify the civic values of the present. As such, the institution, rooted in elite ideals on the level of both ideology and practice, became the symbol of the city's self-identity.

The conclusions drawn from the investigations of Archaic grave monuments, pottery and Classical burial ceremonies are subsequently set in the wider context of early Athenian political history, presented to us by a number of later authors, most importantly Herodotus, Aristotle and, to a lesser extent, Plutarch. Since the reliability of their accounts is often questioned by modern scholars due to their often all-too-clear personal agendas and the distance which separated their works from the events of the Archaic period, the combination of evidence discussed in the previous chapters of this book is used to illuminate and supplement their narratives of early Athens. Applying the evidence of mythology, iconography and grave monuments is particularly useful in a study of the social and institutional developments of the Athenian citizen army, which, according to most scholars was largely underdeveloped or altogether non-existent during the Archaic era. In the final part of the book (Chapter 6), therefore, we will look at the structure and organization of the Athenian military force by attempting to find new ways to interpret the major political events in the city, including Cylon's failed *coup d'état*, the legislation of Solon, the rule of the Peisistratids, the democratic reforms of Cleisthenes and their relation to the practice and ideology of war in the sixth century BC. The treatment and burial of the war dead, as will be suggested, offers important new insights into the nature and composition of Archaic Athenian armies, illuminating a number of social and cultural shifts largely overlooked in previous scholarship, which transformed Athens towards the end of the Archaic period.

Part One

1

The Homeric War Dead

The *Iliad* is littered with corpses and gory depictions of death in battle. Men die from fatal blows to nearly every part of the body, including the eyes, mouth and bladder. Warriors are decapitated and mutilated, heads and armless torsos are sent 'spinning like a ball' (13.204) or rolling 'like a log down the battle' (11.147).[1] The *Iliad*, as Moses Finley summarized, 'is saturated in blood', whilst the 'poet and his audience lingered lovingly over every act of slaughter'.[2] According to one estimate, there are no fewer than 274 men killed in the *Iliad*. Some of the most famous and memorable scenes of the poem concern the deaths of the main heroes Sarpedon, Patroclus and Hector.[3] The centrality of death and dying as the leading theme of Homer's epic poem is undeniable, and would go on to provide a source of inspiration for all ancient Greek writers. 'The *Iliad*', as Emily Vermeule concluded, 'put dying, though not death itself, in stage center and shaped the tradition of subsequent literatures, that death is not the enemy of achievement or creativity but its cause, since the contemplation of death is the single factor which makes us long for immortality'.[4]

For Homeric warriors, however, not all deaths were equal. The social status of elite heroes, or the *aristoi*, required them to receive lengthy and lavish funerals after their deaths in battle. Achilles' obsequies, for instance, lasted for seventeen days; Hector's funeral took nine and Patroclus' two days, concluded with glorious funeral games.[5] The fate of the dead bodies of the common warriors in the *Iliad*, on the other hand, is markedly different. Most end up unburied and exposed to scavengers. This contrast is especially evident when one compares the opening and closing lines of the poem:

> Sing, goddess, the anger of Peleus' son Achilles and its devastation, which put pains thousandfold upon the Achaeans, hurled in their multitude to the house of Hades strong souls of heroes, but gave their bodies to be the delicate feasting of dogs, of all birds, and the will of Zeus was accomplished . . .
>
> 1.1–5

> They piled up the grave-barrow and went away, and thereafter assembled in a fair gathering and held a glorious feast within the house of Priam, king under God's hand. Such was their burial of Hector, breaker of horses.
>
> 24.801–4

The radical difference in the treatment of the bodies of elite and non-elite warriors – the one exposed and mutilated, the other buried and glorified – seeps through a number of similar passages in the *Iliad*, which provide an important insight into the social world depicted in the poem. The double standard governing the retrieval and burial of the dead, however, has rarely been considered in the numerous studies of Homeric society, which usually tend to focus either on the political and economic status of the poem's kings and nobles (*basileis*), or the historical authenticity of the communities portrayed in the *Iliad* and *Odyssey*.

In this chapter I will explore the ideals and norms surrounding the retrieval and treatment of the war dead, as depicted in the Homeric poems. I will analyse epic scenes involving fighting over corpses, mass and individual burials, as well as despoiling and mutilating the dead. What were the reasons behind the contrasting treatment of the bodies of elite and common warriors? Can they throw any meaningful light on the ideals and structure of Homeric society? Finally, did the Homeric poems reflect or provide an archetype for the Athenian standards governing the treatment of the war dead of the Classical period? The Homeric epics are our richest literary source for burial customs in the early Greek world, on the levels of practice, ideology and social and religious attitudes to death.[6] This richness, as we will see in this chapter, also manifests itself in the way the poems depict the war dead, their recovery, treatment and commemoration. The historicity of the latter practices, firmly embedded within the poetic depictions of combat, belong to a wider debate on the relation of the fighting scenes from the epic to the realities of war in early Greece. Despite obvious difficulties in trying to assign a precise time frame to Homeric warfare, recent scholarly studies tend to highlight the similarities between battles depicted in the *Iliad* and the type of fighting portrayed in the poetry and art of the seventh century BC, in particular the songs of Callinus and Tyrtaeus.[7] The poems, according to these interpretations, bore a clear resemblance to early Archaic warfare, while at the same time providing enduring military ideals for generations of Greek audiences. The relation of these ideals, especially those surrounding the treatment of the war dead, to the historical realities of Archaic battlefields will therefore be a common thread throughout the chapters of this book. Homer, as

Plato remarks in the *Republic* (606E), was the 'educator of Hellas', and his influence was nowhere stronger than in the matters of the military ethos and war.[8] Any study of Greek attitudes towards the war dead, therefore, has to begin with the *Iliad*.

Homeric society: Elite vs commoners

The traditional view that permeates most studies of Homeric society emphasizes the class boundary which separated the *aristoi* and *basileis* from the multitude of commoners.[9] The iron curtain which divided the Homeric princes from the rest of the people was strictly adhered to and rarely crossed in both the battle narratives of the *Iliad* and the depictions of household and community life in the *Odyssey*.[10] The most common example used to demonstrate the rigid class ideology of the poems is the famous episode of the Achaean assembly in Book 2 of the *Iliad*.[11] After Agamemnon's plan to order a mock retreat of his army to test the Achaean morale fails, Odysseus, prompted by Athena, restores order by speaking to both kings and common warriors:

> Whatever king or man of note he met, to his side he would come and with gentle words seek to restrain him, saying: 'It is not right, man, to try to frighten you as if you were a coward, but sit down yourself, and make the rest of your people sit'... But whatever man of the people he saw, and found brawling, him he would drive on with his staff, and rebuke with words, saying: 'Sit still, man, and listen to the words of others who are better men than you; you are unwarlike and lacking in valour, to be counted neither in war nor in counsel. In no way will we Achaeans all be kings here.'[12]
>
> 2.188–203

Odysseus' speech has an immediate effect and the Achaean army unites once more, with the exception of a commoner Thersites, who disrupts the assembly by abusing Agamemnon. Odysseus, however, immediately scorns him ('you shall not lift up your mouth to argue with princes, cast reproaches into their teeth' 2.250–1) and strikes him with a royal sceptre, much to the approval of the rest of the army.

The whole episode reveals a clear class-division between the Homeric nobles and commoners.[13] The first were men of influence; respected and politely spoken to, leaders of men in combat and council. The others were cowards of no account in battle or assembly, kept in check with harsh words and, if necessary, violence.

As such, the social world depicted in the *Iliad* and *Odyssey*, according to traditional interpretations, was rigidly stratified into classes and centred primarily on the actions of the *basileis* and *aristoi*, who held an unquestionable monopoly in war and politics. The lives and exploits of the common people, on the other hand, were consequently downplayed by the poet. 'Throughout the poems', as Ian Morris remarked, 'the *basileis* are glorified, and the *demos* ignored to the point of total exclusion'.[14] The poems, therefore, have been widely seen as products of an elite ideology, composed and informed by an elite perspective and written for an elite audience.[15]

The Homeric *basileis* stand out from the crowds on account of their wealth, noble birth, superior fighting skills and physical beauty.[16] They occupy the highest political positions in their respective communities, while at the same time continually striving to enhance their social rank and reputation in the eyes of the fellow *aristoi* by performing outstanding deeds on the battlefield, in the assembly or, indeed, in any other competitive environment. In times of peace, the *basileis* act both as heads of their households (*oikoi*), which consist of a large estate in town and a sizeable amount of land in the countryside, and rulers of their communities.[17] During war, they recruit men among their followers, retainers and dependants and lead them in battle. Altogether, the Homeric *basileis* form a cohesive and highly competitive group, defined by shared social norms and values, and led by the paramount *basileus* whose position is usually inherited and based on superior wealth and numbers of followers.[18]

Furthermore, the Homeric princes enjoy a number of privileges assigned to them by their communities. As Sarpedon, the paramount *basileus* of the Lykians, explains in his famous speech to Glaukos, the *aristoi* are honoured by all people with 'pride of place, the choice meats and the filled wine cups in Lykia, and all men look on us as if we were immortals, and we are appointed a great piece of land by the banks of Xanthos, good land, orchard and vineyard, and ploughland for the planting of wheat' (12.311–14).[19] These honours, as Sarpedon adds, are given to them because of their military leadership and martial excellence:

> 'Therefore it is our duty in the forefront of the Lykians to take our stand, and bear our part of the blazing of battle, so that a man of the close-armored Lykians may say of us: 'Indeed, these are no ignoble men who are lords of Lykia, these kings [*basilēes*] of ours, who feed upon the fat sheep appointed and drink the exquisite sweet wine, since indeed there is strength of valor in them, since they fight in the forefront of the Lykians'.
>
> 12.315–21

The battle narratives of the *Iliad* confirm the supremacy of the Homeric *basileis* in combat, as the action focuses nearly exclusively on the individual exploits of a small number of leading heroes.[20] The long episodes of the martial feats (*aristeia*) of Agamemnon, Diomedes or Achilles, lend further support to the class-division in the poem, as the nameless masses of warriors (*laoi*) appear to play no significant part, aside from being helpless lambs to the slaughter. Recent studies of Homeric warfare, however, emphasized the role of the *laoi*, who despite rarely taking the centre stage in the many combat scenes of the *Iliad* are nonetheless much more than idle spectators.[21] A number of passages in the poem stress the primacy of mass fighting, as well as the superiority of close-order formations composed of rank-and-file warriors, which according to some scholars may even provide the first literary examples of the Greek phalanx formation.[22] Although often ignored in the combat narratives, the masses, therefore, seem to play a far bigger role in Homeric warfare than often assumed, operating quietly in the shadows of their superiors, the *Iliad*'s *basileis*.

The iron curtain theory of Homeric society has nevertheless had a number of critics, beginning with George Calhoun's 1934 *Classical Philology* article. Calhoun questioned the radical class-division interpretation of the poems, suggesting instead that Homeric society was homogenous and structured around the principles of a tribal monarchy. There was no distinction, according to him, between nobles and commoners, as the poet was hardly 'acquainted with well-defined social classes'.[23] Consequently, Homer's *basileis* did not inherit their positions by birth but rather by their qualities and characteristics; there were no specific terms for nobility of birth and relatively little attention was paid to family ancestors or genealogy, as the Homeric kings and leaders appeared to 'come of the same stock as the generality of the folk'.[24] Furthermore, Calhoun argued, the vocabulary used by the poems to describe the lower classes and commoners was very limited, especially when compared to later Archaic and Classical sources. This lack of technical words and phrases for both the nobility of birth and the inherently inferior masses demonstrates, therefore, a general lack of awareness of class-based divisions, in turn indicating a society based on the principles of a simple tribal organization, led by the strongest and most capable men. According to Calhoun, such a society corresponded historically with the Dark Age tribal monarchies which preceded the early Archaic aristocracies.

Although initially rejected, Calhoun's argument found a number of supporters in more recent scholarship who threw further doubt on the concepts of class and class-division within societies depicted in the *Iliad* and *Odyssey*.[25] The bulk of their arguments followed and elaborated on the criticisms raised by Calhoun.

Anne Geddes, for instance, put further stress on the relative absence of the lower social orders in the 'technical vocabulary, in the social attitudes of the people of the poem, or in any visible economic category. As far as Homer goes, they hardly exist at all.'[26] John Halverson, in his study of the *Odyssey*, stressed the lack of any 'real class-tension or even class-consciousness' in the story; there is, he argued, no nobility or monarchical kingship in the poem, as the society is largely homogenous, with the exception of slaves, beggars and hired workers.[27] According to Tracey Rihll, the only actual division in Homeric societies was between the few *oikos*-heads and leaders (*basileis*), and those being led, who comprised of 'any and everybody who defers to someone else's judgement whensoever a decision is required'.[28] For this reason, she concluded that there were 'no 'commoners', 'masses', 'multitudes' or any other 'lower orders' distinguished or distinguishable as a 'class', nor are there 'aristocrats', 'chiefs' or 'kings' *qua* 'classes'.'[29] Finally, concerns were raised over the supposedly superior position of the Homeric *basileis*; notions of hereditary nobility and kingship were questioned, as well as the extent of the actual political power wielded by Homeric princes.[30]

The focal point of most critics of the 'class-division view' is the near-total exclusion of the lower classes, or commoners, from the narratives of the *Iliad* and *Odyssey*.[31] Since their existence is rarely mentioned in the poems, and is never accompanied by any technical terms or consistent social attitudes, it is argued that there was no established, class-based, difference between the elite and the commoners.[32] As Geddes observed, even though 'Homer might wish to exclude' the latter 'from the story (although it is not clear why he should have done), as he wished to exclude iron, even so one would have expected them to creep back into the poem in small ways, in the similes for example.'[33] Apart from the Thersites episode, which, according to her and other critics of the class-division model, has been credited with far too much social and political significance, there are very few other cases of the radical class inequality usually assumed as the *status quo* by the majority of scholars.[34] A closer look at the conventions concerning the retrieval and treatment of the Homeric war dead, however, reveals that there are numerous instances of seemingly class-driven norms and practices which have so far gone largely unnoticed in scholarly debates on Homeric society.

Fighting over the dead

The usual course of events after the death of any Homeric warrior follows a clear pattern, described well in the very first scene of mass-fighting in the *Iliad*:

> Antilochos was first to kill a chief man of the Trojans, valiant among the champions, Thalysias' son, Echepolos ... As he dropped, Elephenor the powerful caught him by the feet ... and dragged him away from under the missiles, striving in all speed to strip the armor from him, yet his outrush went short-lived. For as he hauled the corpse high-hearted Agenor, marking the ribs that showed bare under the shield as he bent over, stabbed with the bronze-pointed spear and unstrung his sinews. So the spirit left him and over his body was fought out weary work by Trojans and Achaeans, who like wolves sprang upon one another, with man against man in the onfall.
>
> 4.457–72

As the sequence demonstrates, following the death of a warrior, the killer, or an enemy who happens to be closest to the victim (in this case Elephenor), attempts to strip the armour of the corpse. The comrades of the slain, on the other hand, feel obliged to protect the body and prevent the enemy despoiling it. This, in turn, leads to an intense struggle over the dead which later, after the death of Elephenor, escalates as more warriors join in the fight on both sides.

Fighting over the fallen, referred to by German scholars as *Leichenkämpfe*, constitutes one of the vital and most frequently recurring elements of Homeric battle descriptions.[35] The scenes depicting *Leichenkämpfe* are, in fact, so numerous that they provide a way for the poet to weave the battle episodes together, as the focus moves from individual duels to group fighting. According to one estimate, one in every four killings in the *Iliad* is followed by an attempt at despoliation by the killer.[36] The scenes of fighting over the dead involve some of the most elaborate and dramatic episodes in the whole of the *Iliad*, especially when they follow the deaths of Homeric *aristoi*. The importance and fierce nature of such fights is especially evident in the struggle for the body of Sarpedon, which takes up 181 lines of the poem (16.502–683), and the famous fight over the corpse of Patroclus, which forms the subject of Books 17 and 18, for a staggering total of 999 lines (17.1–18.238). Moreover, the level of detail in the *Leichenkämpfe* scenes serves to highlight the unusual intensity of such fights within the battle narratives of the *Iliad*. Among the most graphic episodes are the fights over Kebriones and Patroclus, which depict individual (Kebriones) and group (Patroclus) efforts literally to pull the corpse back to one side:

> So above Kebriones these two, urgent for battle, Patroclus, son of Menoitios, and glorious Hector, were straining with the pitiless bronze to tear at each other; since Hector had caught him by the head, and would not let go of him, and Patroclus had his foot on the other side, while the other Trojans and Danaäns drove together the strength of their onset.
>
> 16.759–64

> As when a man gives the hide of a great ox, a bullock, drenched first deep in fat, to all his people to stretch out; the people take it from him and stand in a circle about it and pull, and presently the moisture goes and the fat sinks in, with so many pulling, and the bull's hide is stretched out level; so the men of both sides in a cramped space tugged at the body in both directions; and the hearts of the Trojans were hopeful to drag him away to Ilion, those of the Achaeans to get him back to the hollow ships. And about him a savage struggle arose.
>
> 17.389–98

The widespread nature of fights over the dead in the *Iliad* is, to a large extent, a product of the mechanics of heroic combat. Despite occasional similarities to the phalanx warfare of the Classical period, Homeric battles are rarely fought in massed formations, combining instead both fighting at close range and missile warfare.[37] The armies fight in relatively open formations, which consist of small and mobile groups of warriors that move freely around the battlefield. Moreover, the bulk of Homeric armies is nearly always divided between a minority of warriors who operate near the frontline, known as the 'foremost fighters' (*promachoi*), and the majority, or the 'multitude' (*plethos*), who hang back behind them. Every warrior is expected to join the *promachoi* at some point in the battle, but the main burden of fighting in the frontline falls on the Homeric elite, the *aristoi* and *basileis*, who lead their own groups of friends (*hetairoi*) and followers (*therapontes*). The combat between the opposing *promachoi* most often takes the form of single blows ('hit-and-run' attacks) as warriors dash forward to fire an arrow, throw a spear, or engage the enemy at close range, before quickly retreating back into the multitude.[38] The fighting occasionally intensifies when more men feel impelled to join the frontline fighters, usually as a response to a particular crisis (e.g. defending the ships) or, more often, to despoil a corpse or to protect and retrieve the body of a fallen comrade.

The general openness and fluidity of Homeric battlefields allows the poem's leading warriors, the *aristoi*, to perform their highly conspicuous acts of martial prowess, as the poet shifts his focus from one heroic feat to another; at the same time, it provides the perfect environment for fights over the dead, thus accounting for their prevalence in the battle descriptions of the *Iliad*. The next question that we have to ask, therefore, is: what are the motivations of the Homeric warriors who fight over the slain? Why do men risk their lives trying to take hold of enemies' armour; and, in turn, why do they feel obliged to protect their slain comrades at all costs?

Despoiling the dead

Despoliation during combat was the bread and butter of Homeric warfare. As we have already seen, attempts to despoil a slain enemy follow one in four killings in the *Iliad*. The practice is, in fact, so widespread in the poem that even a god may take part: Ares strips the Aetolian Periphas (5.842–4).[39] There are two main strategies for plundering the bodies during the battle: a quick dash forward to snatch the armour on the spot (e.g. 11.579; 13.550–1; 15.582–3); or dragging the body behind the lines of the *promachoi* to plunder at leisure (4.465–6; 16.780–2; 17.316–8). Stripping the enemy dead of their armour and weapons in the heat of the battle was, nonetheless, a very risky venture, as demonstrated by the example of Elephenor. Five men, according to Hans van Wees' count, are killed during an attempt at despoliation, while four are wounded and several warriors are forced to retreat or to fight for their lives.[40] The obvious danger involved in despoliation, however, did not discourage Homeric warriors, as the spoils acquired during the fighting were considered a source of pride and a testimony to one's bravery and martial skill. Idomeneus' hut, for instance, had its own special display of the items taken from the slain Trojans by the Cretan leader:

> 'You will find one spear, and twenty spears, if you want them, standing against the shining inward wall in my shelter, Trojan spears I win from men that I kill, for my way is not to fight my battles standing far away from my enemies. Thereby I have spears there, and shields massive in the middle, and helms and corselets are there in all the pride of their shining.'
>
> 13.260–5

Weapons and armour obtained during combat, as Idomeneus' speech suggests, serve as a proof of a warrior's involvement in the fighting among the *promachoi*, thus testifying to his courage before his peers and contributing to his social status. Any spoils acquired in this way were treated as trophies – symbols of military success – which Finley saw as the Homeric equivalent of head-hunting.[41] Stripping the armour of a dead enemy provided both glory (*kleos*) and honour (*timē*), and the higher the status of the slain warrior, the bigger the glory.

The armour of leading enemy warriors was deemed particularly desirable. Despite its high material worth, the armour of the *aristoi* was primarily sought for its symbolic value as a trophy.[42] The Homeric elite were, as a rule, clad in shining bronze armour, often unrealistically extravagant, which set them apart from the rest. The fame of Nestor's shield, for instance, 'goes up to the sky now, how it is all of gold, the shield itself and the cross-rods' (8.192–3). Diomedes' corselet, 'wrought with much toil' by the god Hephaestus, was also no less impressive (8.195). But the most extravagant of all is Achilles' shining new armour, also wrought by Hephaestus, the description of which takes up the entire third of Book 18 (468–616). Capturing such armour provided an immediately recognizable mark of military success which, in turn, accounts for the unusual intensity and lethal nature of some fights over the corpses of Homeric *aristoi*. The Trojans, for instance, are especially eager to despoil the body of Patroclus, who, during his *aristeia* of Book 16, wore the armour of Achilles, which was to bring a 'great glory' to whoever captured it (17.16, 130–1). In the end, the armour is won by Hector, who withdraws in order to put it on and later triumphantly wear it in battle (17.186–7). Wearing the armour of the slain enemy hero was in no way an uncommon practice. In a story told by Nestor, Lykourgos, and later his henchman Ereuthalion, carried the armour of the famous 'club-fighter' Areïthoös, which the former won after killing his enemy in a duel (7.136–49).

As we learn from the duel between Hector and Ajax, which concludes the first day of fighting in the *Iliad*, the victor of an arranged duel was under normal circumstances expected to strip the armour of the fallen opponent – which served as a mark of his victory – before returning the body for a funeral.[43] The rules are clearly laid out by Hector:

> 'Behold the terms that I make, let Zeus be witness upon them. If with the thin edge of the bronze he takes my life, then let him strip my armor and carry it back to the hollow ships, but give my body to be taken home again, so that the Trojans and the wives of the Trojans may give me in death my rite of burning. But if I take his life, and Apollo grants me the glory, I will strip his armor and carry it to sacred Ilion and hang it in front of the temple of far-striking Apollo, but his corpse I will give back among the strong-benched vessels so that the flowing-haired Achaeans may give him due burial and heap up a mound upon him beside the broad passage of Helle.'
>
> 7.76–86

The armour of the leading enemy men slain in battle was highly valued by Homeric warriors, who were nearly always ready to put their lives at considerable risk in order to obtain it and win glory among their comrades.[44] Some of them, like Hector or Lykourgos, would triumphantly wear it in battle to remind their followers and enemies alike of their heroic feats. Others, like Idomeneus, would display the spoils in their huts before bringing them back home to delight the hearts of their mothers (6.481) and hang them on the walls of their dining halls as trophies.[45] Such displays were no doubt intended to impress visitors and confirm the martial excellence of the host. Hector's duel arrangements with Ajax also suggest that the vanquished enemy armour and weapons could be dedicated in a god's temple; the arms of Dolon, captured by Odysseus and Diomedes, are similarly offered to Athena (10.457–63, 570–1).[46] Finally, the armour of elite enemy slain could be given out as some of the most prestigious prizes at funeral games. Sarpedon's 'far-shadowing spear', shield and helmet, and Asteropaios' 'magnificent silver-nailed sword', are offered by Achilles to the winner of combat in full armour at the funeral games for Patroclus (23.798–809); Asteropaios' bronze corselet is also awarded as a special prize in the chariot race (23.560–2). It is quite clear, therefore, that the variety of potential uses of armour obtained from leading enemies, all of which were intended to raise the social status of the successful despoiler, helps to explain the eagerness of the Homeric warriors to obtain them at all costs.

The other common way to acquire battlefield spoils was to collect them during a pursuit of the enemy's army, or indeed after the fighting had finished. Despoiling the bodies during pursuit provided a much safer way to obtain enemy armour; van Wees notes that 'all 25 instances of despoliation during pursuit are successful, whereas during steady battle no less than 13 of 34 attempts by individuals fail'.[47] Spoils acquired in such way, despite being less prestigious, were still highly desirable. And so Nestor forbids the Greeks to stay behind with 'eye on the plunder', encouraging them to keep pursuing the Trojans: 'let us kill the men now, and afterward at your leisure all along the plain you can plunder the perished corpses' (6.68–71). In a similar fashion, Hector urges the Trojans to 'make hard for the ship' and 'let the bloody spoils be'; the practice of plundering corpses is so common that he has to threaten his soldiers with death and exposure:

> 'Make hard for the ships, let the bloody spoils be. That man I see in the other direction apart from the vessels, I will take care that he gets his death, and that man's relations neither men nor women shall give his dead body the rite of burning. In the space before our city the dogs shall tear him to pieces.'
>
> 15.347–51

Some warriors may go so far as scavenging for spoils in the dead of night. In their reconnaissance mission in Book 10, Odysseus and Diomedes encounter the Trojan scout Dolon, whom they suspect (albeit wrongly) of stripping the armour of perished corpses (10.342–3, 386–7). Enemy spoils obtained in pursuit or after battle did not serve as a mark of individual bravery for the *promachoi*, and so could hardly have contributed to honour or social status among his peers. Moreover, the armour acquired in such a way would virtually never be that of the slain *aristoi*, as their bodies would normally receive immediate attention upon their death, whether from those who attempt to despoil or retrieve them. That meant most of what was available after the battle must have consisted of weapons and armour that belonged to common warriors, which none of the *promachoi* felt the need to plunder or protect. The main reason for this was most likely its low material and trophy value, especially when compared to the expensive and shining armour of the *aristoi*. Homer devotes very little attention to any descriptions of common men, which considering the poem's elite focus is hardly surprising. But it does seem natural to assume that their equipment was categorically and economically inferior and so not worth fighting for during the combat.[48] Since it did not belong to the Homeric *basileis* and *aristoi* – the warriors *par excellence* – such armour was no symbol of military prowess and so of interest only to the common soldiers. We must, therefore, assume that the accumulation of spoils during pursuit and the aftermath of battle had a predominately materialistic motive. Such spoils could be reused or potentially sold, but had little value as trophies or symbols of military success.[49]

Plundering the fallen during and after battle was, in conclusion, a fully legitimate and important practice in the warfare depicted in the *Iliad*. Homeric *promachoi* fought and repeatedly risked their lives to obtain the armour of leading enemy warriors, which provided symbolic proof of their courage and augmented their status as superior fighters and leaders of men. The trophy value of plundered equipment, however, depended on the social, or class, status of the victim, as the armour of the elite was depicted as superior and categorically different to that of the common warrior. The main motivation behind the Homeric practice of combat despoliation lay, therefore, primarily in the desire of the *aristoi* to increase their honour and status among their peers. On the other hand, the driving factor behind the post-battle despoliation was the common man's eagerness to acquire extra wealth outside the normal channels of booty distribution, which normally included other plunder (i.e. livestock, slaves, mobile goods) from raiding expeditions and the sacking of villages and towns.[50] All this, in turn, helps to explain the unusual eagerness of Homeric warriors, especially the *aristoi*, to plunder the corpses of their enemy counterparts. Their success, however, was often limited, as their efforts were constantly undermined by the friends and followers of the slain.

Protecting the dead

Upon the death of any Homeric hero in combat, it was the duty of his friends and companions to protect his body from the enemy and to retrieve it. Fighting over the body of one's comrade was one of the highest moral obligations for all Homeric warriors, and led to some of the most impressive displays of martial prowess in the whole poem. Some men, in fact, feel compelled to defend the corpses of their friends on their own, whilst greatly outnumbered by the enemy. The Trojan hero Aeneas, for instance, offers such protection to the fallen Pandaros, until he is knocked unconscious by a stone thrown by Diomedes:

> But Aeneas sprang to the ground with shield and with long spear, for fear that somehow the Achaeans might haul off the body, and like a lion in the pride of his strength stood over him holding before him the perfect circle of his shield and the spear and raging to cut down any man who might come to face him, crying a terrible cry.
>
> 5.297–302

The obligation to protect and retrieve a fallen or wounded comrade was particularly strong when the men concerned were leading warriors in the army.[51] As already noted, the fights that ensued over Sarpedon and Patroclus form some of the longest and fiercest combat scenes in the *Iliad*, involving an unusually large number of men (by Homeric standards). In a similar way, when Hector is wounded by Ajax in Book 14, the brief struggle that follows immediately draws the bravest Trojans, both from among the *aristoi* and *laoi*, who ensure he is retrieved and carried back to the city:

> Screaming aloud the sons of the Achaeans ran forward in hope to drag him away, and threw their volleying javelins against him, yet no man could stab or cast at the shepherd of the people; sooner the Trojans' bravest gathered about him, Aeneas, and Poulydamas, and brilliant Agenor, Sarpedon, lord of the Lykians, and Glaukos the blameless; and of the rest no man was heedless of him, but rather sloped the strong circles of their shields over him, while his companions caught him in their arms out of the fighting and reached his fast-footed horses, where they stood to the rear of the fighting and the battle holding their charioteer and the elaborate chariot, and these carried him, groaning heavily, back toward the city.
>
> 14.421–32

The driving force of obligation to protect the bodies of slain comrades lies in the power of the Homeric concept of shame (*aidos*).[52] The society depicted in the *Iliad* and *Odyssey* was structured around what Eric Dodds famously referred to as 'shame-culture', in which every Homeric leader negotiated his identity and social status in the eyes of his fellow elite.[53] All men competed throughout their lives for honour and glory (*timē*), a constant supply of which was always available to them on the battlefield. At the same time, such men also fought to avoid shame, which lowered their social status among their peers. Failure to protect the corpse of a relative or friend was widely seen as a common source of shame, as it dishonoured both the dead warrior, whose armour would normally be stripped by the enemy, and his runaway comrades. Consequently, appeals to avoid shame and moral indignation (*nemesis*) from the rest of the army are omnipresent in the *Iliad* and serve as a means to inspire courage and stir the warriors to join in the fighting to protect their reputation.[54] Sarpedon's last words are spent urging Glaukos to gather his men and 'stir them up to fight' for his body, 'for I shall be a thing of shame and a reproach said of you afterward, all your days forever, if the Achaeans strip my armor where I fell by the ships assembled' (16.496–500).[55] Shortly afterwards, Athena, likening herself to Phoinix, encourages Menelaus to protect and retrieve the dead Patroclus, as it 'will be a thing of shame, a reproach said of you, if under the wall of the Trojans the dogs in their fury can mutilate the staunch companion of haughty Achilles. But hold strongly on, and stir up all the rest of your people' (17.556–9). The fear of shame in the eyes of their peers, therefore, provided a strong motivation for Homeric warriors to defend the bodies of their fallen friends and companions, sometimes even at the risk of serious injury or death.[56]

Another factor which inspired men to protect the corpses of the slain was the general sense of comradeship which characterized both the Achaean and Trojan armies. The death of a companion on the battlefield usually inspired a range of negative emotions among his comrades, such as sorrow (e.g. 13.402, 581; 16.508, 548), pity (5.561, 610; 17.346, 352) and anger (13.660; 16.553, 585).[57] The strength of these emotions is often matched by the elaborate phrases used to describe them in the poem. Koön, seeing his brother Iphidamas killed and stripped by Agamemnon, is overcome by 'the strong sorrow' which 'misted about his eyes for the sake of his fallen brother' (11.248–50). Similarly, the Trojans are 'taken head to heel with a sorrow untakeable', upon hearing about the death of Sarpedon (16.548–9), while soon later, 'the dark cloud of sorrow closed over Hector' when he is told of the death of his companion Podes (17.591). The death of Patroclus in particular inspires strong feelings in Antilochos, who 'stayed for a long time without a word, speechless, and his eyes filled with tears, the springing voice was held still within him' (17.695–6); and Achilles, who fouls his own body with dust and ashes, and tears his hair in grief over the death of his closest friend (18.23–7).

The binding sense of loyalty and comradeship among the warriors, which these passages clearly convey, was, to a large extent, a product of the organization of Homeric armies. The army contingents in the *Iliad*, as mentioned before, consisted of many small and highly fluid bands, each comprising a leader (*basileus*) – on whom the battle descriptions usually focus – followed by his retinue of friends, companions (*hetairoi*) and retainers (*therapontes*).[58] Each contingent consisted of no more than a few dozen men, most coming from the same community and tied by a variety of bonds, such as family, friendship or economic dependence.[59] The bands were generally divided into those who fought at the frontline with the leaders (*promachoi*); those who stood back to support the frontline by carrying the spoils and the dead and wounded away from combat; and those staying behind, who either retreated from the melee to gather their strength and courage, or took care of the wounded.[60] The small-scale nature of such units allowed for the creation of a strong feeling of comradeship, perhaps no different, as van Wees suggested, to the modern military 'buddy' relationships.[61] Loyalty was largely based on mutual trust and support in combat, as well as a fair share of the rewards and booty distributed after a successful battle or sacking of a settlement, which, apart from its immediate material value, increased each warrior's honour and respect in the community.[62] The Homeric *aristoi* were always surrounded by a number of warriors who followed them around the battlefield, assisted in combat and despoliation and retrieved their bodies in the case of injury or death.

Finally, the retrieval of the bodies of leading warriors from the battlefield was ascribed special significance in the *Iliad* as it allowed the *aristoi* to receive individual and highly conspicuous funerals later. The funeral rituals of the greatest Homeric warriors provided an opportunity to express the social status of the deceased and to confirm their place among the heroes of his community.[63] The event itself, which could take as many as seventeen days depending on the status of the deceased, consisted of a number of customs and ceremonies which included the washing of the corpse (XXIV.189–90), the ritual lament (XXIV.293–6), the cutting of mourners' hair (23.135–7), burning on a funeral pyre and gathering of bones (24.786–98), and the erection of a mound and gravestone (16.674–5), concluded by a funeral feast (24.802–3) and games (23.257–897). The scale and lavishness of heroic funerals were meant to reflect proportionally the honour that the slain warrior accumulated in his life, thus enshrining his glory in the memory of men to come.[64]

According to an influential notion of Jean-Pierre Vernant, throughout his life every Homeric hero aspired to a certain kind of death, referred to as 'beautiful death' (*kalos thanatos*).[65] Such death, suffered ideally at the time of full adulthood on the battlefield, honoured the hero with eternal fame and 'imperishable glory' (*kleos aphthiton*). Heroic death, as Vernant explained, seizes the warrior in the fullness of youth and beauty, as 'it raises him above the human condition and saves him from common death by conferring sublime luster on his demise'.[66] A lavish funeral, in turn, provided a fitting end to the life of a heroic warrior, marking and symbolizing his beautiful death to the fullest extent.

The importance of death in battle followed by a heroic funeral is repeatedly commented upon by the Homeric heroes. Odysseus, lamenting the hardships of his journey home from Troy, regrets that he had not died on the battlefield:[67]

> 'Three times and four times happy those Danaäns were who died then in wide Troy land, bringing favor to the sons of Atreus, as I wish I too had died at that time and met my destiny on the day when the greatest number of Trojans threw their bronze-headed weapons upon me, over the body of perished Achilles, and I would have had my rites and the Achaeans given me glory. Now it is by a dismal death that I must be taken.'
>
> V.306–12

In a similar way, when Achilles meets Agamemnon in Hades he pities the manner of his death at the hands of Aigisthos and Clytemnestra, wishing instead that he had died in Troy:

> 'How I wish that, enjoying that high place of your power, you could have met death and destiny in the land of the Trojans. So all the Achaeans would have made a mound to cover you, and you would have won great glory for your son hereafter. In truth you were ordained to die by a death most pitiful.'
>
> XXIV.30–4

As already observed, the normal procedures following an arranged duel required the victor to return the body of the vanquished for a funeral. The existence of such rules, however, indicates that in other circumstances this was not always the practice. The denial of burial and exposure to animal mutilation, as well as other forms of maltreatment, were all common themes in the *Iliad* and *Odyssey*, representing an ever-present threat that loomed over all Homeric *aristoi*. Being denied a funeral, and left unburied and forgotten, stood as the radical opposite of the ideal of the beautiful death, forming a terrifying prospect for the main heroes of the poems.[68] The horror of such treatment is made apparent in the plans of the river god Skamandros, who intends to kill and prevent the burial of Achilles:

> 'I will whelm his own body deep, and pile it over with abundance of sands and rubble numberless, nor shall the Achaeans know where to look for his bones to gather them, such ruin will I pile over him. And there shall his monument be

made, and he will have no need of any funeral mound to be buried in by the Achaeans.'

21.318–23

The humiliation involved in the practice of deliberate exposure and animal mutilation is, however, almost never the fate of the Homeric *aristoi*.[69] Although Hector's body is initially mistreated and denied burial by Achilles, it is eventually returned for a full and glorious burial with the help of the gods. The gods also famously intervene after the death of Sarpedon, whose body is rescued from the battlefield by the divine messengers Sleep and Death, and carried to Lykia, 'where his brothers and countrymen shall give him due burial with tomb and gravestone. Such is the privilege of those who have perished' (16.667–75). These episodes further highlight that the beautiful death, followed by a lavish funeral, was the rightful due of the Homeric *aristoi*, even if their bodies could not be recovered by their mortal comrades.[70]

All in all, the main motivations behind the numerous attempts to protect and retrieve the bodies of the slain warriors in the *Iliad* stemmed from Homeric notions of shame and comradeship. The central concern of every Homeric man was to avoid the shame of failure in the eyes of his community and comrades. Abandoning the corpse of one's friend or relative on the battlefield, to be despoiled by the enemy and mutilated by scavengers, was widely regarded as one of the biggest sources of shame and detrimental to a warrior's honour and status. The nature of Homeric armies, on the other hand, which consisted of small bands of men, enabled close bonds of friendship and loyalty within each contingent, which in turn encouraged individual warriors to put their lives on the line for their comrades. Such units, built largely on trust and fair distribution of booty after successful campaigns, were structured around the Homeric princes, the *aristoi* and *basileis*, whose martial feats and superior military prowess were central to the unit's success in battle. The protection and retrieval of the bodies of leading men upon their deaths was consequently of utmost importance and nearly always drew all available warriors to the frontline. Finally, retrieving the corpses of the Homeric elite enabled personal and highly conspicuous funerals. A heroic death suffered in battle, followed by a lavish funeral, is presented in the poems as the rightful due of the *aristoi*, which opens a path to ultimate fame and glory.

To sum up, the prevalence of Homeric fights over the dead in the *Iliad* is hardly surprising, as the determination of warriors to despoil the bodies of their slain enemies was more than often matched by the obligation felt by the defenders to protect their fallen comrades and carry their bodies to safety. A study of the *Leichenkämpfe* scenes helps to reveal the importance of Homeric concepts of honour and shame, highlighting the competitive nature of the social world depicted in the poems, where men constantly strive to enhance, or at least maintain, their status in their respective communities. In addition, the many episodes of fighting over the dead provide further evidence for the underlying division between the Homeric *aristoi* and the masses of common warriors. The former, distinguished by their bravery, martial skill and shining armour, led the masses to combat and fought among the *promachoi*. They competed among themselves for battlefield glory, continually putting their lives at risk to capture the armour of enemy counterparts which testified to their military and social status. The common warriors, on the other hand, dutifully followed the *aristoi* to battle, supporting them in combat, assisting in despoliation, protecting when needed and retrieving their bodies in case of injury or death. After battle, they occasionally plundered the countless abandoned corpses for any remaining spoils, most of which were of little trophy or prestige value other than their material worth. The poem's main focus, however, was firmly on the exploits of the elite; the bronze-clad warriors, whose superiority and military excellence was reaffirmed with every successful despoliation, and whose 'imperishable glory' was to be completed with a glorious funeral. Homeric *aristoi*, both living and dead, stood at the centre of the world depicted in the *Iliad*. The procedures for the retrieval and treatment of their bodies further confirm their special importance in the battle narratives of the poem.

Common dead

The procedures for retrieving and burying the bodies of common warriors are far less apparent, especially when compared to the treatment of elite soldiers. This is understandable, considering that the poems are nearly exclusively concerned with the exploits of the *basileis*, and devote far less space to the fates of the non-elite. A closer reading of a number of passages from the *Iliad*, however, grants us a glimpse of the treatment of the bodies of common Homeric warriors, which, unsurprisingly, appears to be very different to that received by the poem's *aristoi*.

In a famous passage from Book 7 which concludes the first day of the fighting, the Trojans send their herald, Idaios, to the Achaeans proposing a peaceful resolution of the conflict and to ask for a truce to collect and dispose of their dead: 'They told me to give you this message also, if you are willing; to stop the sorrowful fighting until we can burn the bodies of our dead. We shall fight again afterward, until the divinity chooses between us, and gives victory to one or the other' (7.394–7). The Achaeans refuse the offer of peace, but Agamemnon agrees to the request concerning the burial of the bodies: 'But about the burning of the dead bodies I do not begrudge you; no, for there is no sparing time for the bodies of the perished, once they have died, to give them swiftly the pity of burning. Let Zeus, high-thundering lord of Hera, witness our pledges' (7.408–11). The dead on both sides are subsequently washed, lifted onto the wagons, burned and buried, all in a single funeral mound, 'a common grave for all stretching back from the plain' (7.423–36).

At first glance, the mass burial scene of Book 7 seems to indicate that the corpses of non-elite warriors were picked up and buried in a common grave after each day of fighting. The burial truce agreed between the Achaeans and Trojans may further remind us of the Classical practice of *anairesis*, which involved the sending of a herald to retrieve the dead following a battle.[71] The episode, however, is an exception. The burial truce of the first day is the only one mentioned in the whole of the *Iliad*; there are no similar agreements after the second, third or fourth day and so the practice does not appear to be the standard.[72] More importantly, the passages describing the *Iliad*'s only mass burials are considered by some scholars to be a late, post-Homeric addition to the poem.[73] According to Denys Page, the latter part of Book 7, which includes Nestor's speech, the burial truce and the building of the Achaean wall, was most likely a fourth century BC Athenian insertion. Page's argument is based primarily on the reading of a passage from Thucydides, which implies that the Achaeans built their wall shortly after their initial landing in the first year of the war, and not in the tenth year as suggested by the latter part of Book 7.[74] As a result, he argued, 'the *Iliad* current in Thucydides' day did not include the extensive passage in the Seventh Book of which the building of the wall in the tenth year is the principal theme.'[75] In addition, in his proposal to build the wall, Nestor recommends that the Achaeans should burn the bodies of the slain, 'so that each whose duty it is may carry the bones back to a man's children, when we go home to the land of our fathers' (7.334–5). The practice of bringing the ashes of the slain back home is nowhere else mentioned in the *Iliad*, nor, in fact, in any other early epic poem.[76] Moreover, Nestor also suggests building a single corpse-pyre and raising a tumulus over it (7.336–8), in turn providing foundations for the defensive ramparts, which the Achaeans do shortly after (7.434–7). These actions, as we will see later, reflected the standard Greek *polyandria* burials, while making

Nestor's earlier proposal of bringing the bones back home incompatible. Nestor's recommendation at 7.334–5 has, therefore, been rejected by a number of scholars, as early as Aristarchus, as a later interpolation.[77] And since the custom of bringing back the ashes of the fallen was practised in Classical Athens, Page concluded that the lines, along with the latter part of Book 7, must have been a post-Thucydidean Athenian insertion.[78]

All in all, although the exact dating of Page's late insertion may be doubted, his argument does help to explain the contrast between the mass burials of Book 7 and the lack of any similar agreements throughout the rest of the poem. But while it seems inevitable that Nestor's proposal at 7.334–5 was a later Classical insertion, there is no need to reject the genuineness of the entire episode. The collective burial scene may instead provide us with a rare glimpse into the procedures concerning the recovery and burial of the bodies of common men, which stood in radical opposition to the 'normal' treatment of elite warriors.

As we have already glimpsed while looking at the instances of post-battle despoliation, some corpses of fallen warriors appear to be left on the battlefield after each day's fighting, providing a source of cheap plunder for profit-driven enemy men. The episode involving the Trojan scout Dolon, for instance, clearly suggests that it was not unusual for warriors to return to the battleground, sometimes in the dead of night, to strip the armour of the enemy slain (10.342–3, 86–7). This general impression of the unburied scattered across the battlefield is, in fact, constantly reinforced throughout the poem.[79] As we learn from the very first lines, the *Iliad* is not only a story of Achilles and his anger towards Agamemnon, but also that of the 'strong souls of heroes, who gave their bodies to be the delicate feasting of dogs, of all birds', all according to Zeus' will (1.1–5). The motif of the fallen warrior left exposed, and prey to dogs and vultures, which we will explore later in this chapter, is very common in both the *Iliad* and *Odyssey*, and often serves to highlight the contrast between the fates of common warriors and those of leading Homeric men.[80] Other passages which convey the notion of unburied corpses are brought up in the context of both the Trojan and Achaean battlefield assemblies. When the Trojans gather in an assembly by a river, we are specifically told that they choose a 'clean ground, where there showed a space not cumbered with corpses' (8.489–91). Similarly, a Greek assembly in Book 10 also takes place in an area specifically said to be free of the fallen (10.199). Finally, during Diomedes and Odysseus' night raid on the Trojans, we read that the heroes had literally to force their way 'through the carnage and through the corpses, war gear and dark blood' in the no man's land (10.298). Eventually, both of them hide among the corpses in order to ambush Dolon (10.349).

It seems inevitable, therefore, that the bodies of Homeric warriors, unless rescued and retrieved during the fighting, were normally left on the battlefield for an indefinite amount of time. This impression of unburied corpses conveyed throughout the *Iliad* may further suggest that the mass burial scene of Book 7 was indeed a later, Classical insertion to the poem, as proposed by Page. The lack of any similar scenes throughout the *Iliad*, however, could also be explained by the elite focus of the poem. Mass burials of common warriors were of little consequence or interest to the *aristoi*-driven narrative of the story. The building of the Achaean wall, important for the later developments in the poem, nonetheless provided an opportunity for a brief mention of the usual procedures regarding the treatment of the common dead, which normally do not merit the poet's attention. The bodies of common men would, accordingly, be buried in a mass *polyandrion* under a formal and temporary truce, agreed occasionally by the opposing forces during a longer conflict, such as the ten-year-long Trojan War. The exact frequency of such truces is impossible to determine, but they are rare enough to make the motif of unburied bodies appear in Homer's offhand and casual remarks concerning post-combat despoliation, assembly scenes and mutilation by scavengers. Initial exposure, animal mutilation and enemy despoliation was all that a slain common warrior could look forward to, before eventually – often after a number of days – his body would be burned alongside all other 'commoner' corpses in a mass grave. The contrast with the post-mortem treatment received by the *aristoi* could hardly be more profound.

We may conclude that the procedures regarding the retrieval and treatment of the war dead in the *Iliad* reflect and reinforce the class-division between elite and common warriors in Homeric society. The poem's main focus is firmly on the *basileis* and *aristoi*, their exploits in life and their heroic deaths. The common, non-elite warriors receive only an occasional mention, most often to fill the *aristeiai* of the Homeric princes or to emphasize the latter's political and martial superiority. Their presence, however, and social inferiority, is firmly reflected in the poem in the treatment (or lack of it) they receive upon their deaths. Looking at the many scenes of *Leichenkämpfe*, the practice of despoliation, and the contrasting burial procedures, which all provide a consistent part of the *Iliad*'s narrative, one can get a clear glimpse into the stratified social structure of Homeric society. The common warriors make brief, often indirect but nonetheless constant appearances in the story. Or, to use Geddes' words, they 'creep back into the poem in small ways', whether through their loyalty to their leaders, their arms and armour, or indeed their abandoned corpses.

The *Iliad*, therefore, presents us with what we could refer to as a 'hierarchical' model for the recovery of the war dead. The bodies of the elite fighters, the *aristoi*, are normally dealt with and rescued *during* the fighting. Their positions as leaders of men, in both military and political sense, required them to receive an individual and highly conspicuous burial upon their deaths on the battlefield, which confirmed their status as heroes and assured their 'imperishable glory' in people's memory and in the epic songs to come. The corpses of common soldiers, on the other hand, are not retrieved during the battle but are instead left on the battlefield, exposed to animal mutilation and despoliation by profit-driven enemy men. Their bodies, if we accept the authenticity of the only mass burial scene of the *Iliad*, are burned together and buried in mass graves only when a rare truce is agreed. The contrast between the elite and common slain – the one glorified and remembered, the other mutilated and forgotten – serves to highlight the superior status, both in life and death, of the Homeric *aristoi*.[81] As such, the *Iliad*'s 'hierarchical' model of the retrieval and treatment of the war dead stands in a clear opposition to the Classical Athenian 'egalitarian' custom of *patrios nomos*, according to which *all* warriors were to be retrieved and provided with similar funeral honours *after* a battle. But before we can ask whether these 'hierarchical' standards bore any resemblance to the historical reality of early Athenian warfare, we must first look at one other aspect of Homeric war dead 'etiquette', namely the practice of the mutilation of the dead.

Mutilation of the dead

The countless and often brutally realistic acts of slaughter in the battle scenes of the *Iliad* reach their apogee in the Homeric descriptions of the mutilation of the dead. The theme of the mutilation of the corpse (*ton nekron aeikizein*) was well-embedded in Homeric epics, with numerous instances in the *Iliad* and a few mentions in the *Odyssey*.[82] Its prevalence in the poems is already implied in the opening lines of the proem (1.1–5), where hints of exposure and mutilation by animals are no less frequent than the gruesome mutilations carried out by men.[83] Grim spectacles of heads rolling like balls (13.204), and armless torsos spinning like logs (11.147); of bodies dragged in the dust (22.401), and kidney fat nibbled upon by eels and fish (21.203–4) testify to what Vermeule described as the 'baroque magnificence in the physical ruin of Homer's heroes.'[84] The episodes mentioning successful mutilations usually appear at the end of a fighting sequence between small groups of warriors, and much like the scenes depicting *Leichenkämpfe*, they serve to intensify the battle episodes, while at the same time highlighting the brutal nature of epic warfare. Compared to the Classical

Athenian norms governing the treatment of the war dead, which radically condemned any form of maltreatment as befitting barbarians rather than Greeks (Hdt. 9.79), the sheer presence of mutilation acts, as well as their importance as narrative tools in the *Iliad*, has baffled scholars since antiquity.[85] Far from being a mindless act of savagery, however, the Homeric practice of mutilating enemy corpses, known as *aikia*, provided an extreme but seemingly acceptable way to exact revenge and has often been explained as a product of the agonistic culture and the competitive ethic of Homeric warriors.[86]

There are six examples of mutilations carried out on the dead in the *Iliad*.[87] The most famous concern the mistreatment of the body of Hector, whose corpse is initially stabbed by multiple Achaean warriors, who mock the softness of his body (22.369–75), before being dragged by Achilles behind his chariot at random over the next twelve days (22.395–404; 23.21–2; 24.14–18, 416–17). Other post-mortem mutilations come in the earlier parts of the battle narrative. Agamemnon is responsible for the first two which occur during his *aristeia* in Book 11: he kills Hippolochos and cuts away 'his arms with a sword-stroke, free of the shoulder, and sent him spinning like a log down the battle' (11.145–7); moments later, Agamemnon is stabbed by Koön but manages to retaliate and fatally wound the latter, upon which he 'came up and hewed off his head' (11.259–61).[88] Corpse decapitation features also in Books 13 and 14. First, while the two Aiantes strip the fallen Imbrios of his armour, the 'son of Oïleus ... hewed away his head from the soft neck and threw it spinning like a ball through the throng of fighters until it came to rest in the dust at the feet of Hector' (13.202–5).[89] Then, in perhaps the most vividly gruesome episode, Peneleos drives his spear clean through the eye and neck of the Trojan Ilioneus and cuts the head off at the neck, which he subsequently lifts 'high like the head of a poppy', with Ilioneus' eyeball still on the point of the spear, in order to boast to the terrified Trojans (14.493–507).[90] Apart from these examples, there are several instances of warriors intending to mutilate the bodies of their enemies, which further confirm the prevalence of the theme in the context of the battle narratives of the *Iliad* (16.559–60; 17.39–40, 126; 18.177, 334–7).

As is evident in the case of Peneleos' grisly decapitation of Ilioneus, conspicuous acts of mutilation terrified enemy warriors and might have been on occasion performed as a type of psychological warfare. But as I have argued elsewhere, such incidents cannot be seen as random acts of brutality but were instead the product of Homeric dynamics of honour and vengeance. The latter, in fact, is the driving factor behind all instances of mutilation in the *Iliad*, as is immediately obvious in the case of Achilles' maltreatment of Hector in revenge for the death of Patroclus.⁹¹ Agamemnon explicitly declares that Hippolochos' 'mutilation shall punish the shame of your father', who advised the Trojans to kill Menelaus when he came to Troy as an envoy (11.138–42). Similarly, the Lokrian Ajax beheads Imbrios 'in anger for Amphimachos', slayed moments earlier by Hector, at whose feet he throws the head of Imbrios (13.202–5). Even Peneleos' mutilation of Ilioneus is committed as a result of the death of Promachos and the vaunting speech of his killer Akamas, which 'stirred the anger in wise Peneleos' (14.486–7). Indeed, the association of mutilation and vengeance is best demonstrated by the remarks of Euphorbos, who wishes to behead and despoil Menelaus in revenge for the death of his brother Hyperenor:

> 'Then, lordly Menelaus, you must now pay the penalty for my brother, whom you killed, and boast that you did it, and made his wife a widow … and left to his parents the curse of lamentation and sorrow. Yet I might stop the mourning of these unhappy people if I could carry back to them your head, and your armor, and toss them into Panthoös' hands, and to Phrontis the lovely.'
>
> 17.34–40

Spectacular as they often are, Homeric mutilations are rarely motivated by a sense of audience or a 'desire to demonstrate or advertise performance *per se*'.⁹² And while anger plays an important role, the main factor driving attempts to maltreat the bodies of the enemy derived from the Homeric cycle of vengeance. Homeric men, and in particular the *basileis* and *aristoi*, were expected to respond with force and aggression when offended or wronged. As already established, all Homeric *aristoi* competed throughout their lives for honour (*timē*), for which there was a limited potential in their respective communities.⁹³ In effect, the main social motivation for Homeric men was to aspire to gain more honour, most often via outstanding deeds on the battlefield, and at the same time to defend their social status which was perceived to be under constant threat. The death of a friend or relative imposed shame (*aidos*) on both the slain and his comrades, as their *timē* was thus reduced and transferred to the killer. Successful retaliation, in turn, directed at either the killer or his kin or follower, enabled the *aristoi* not only to display their anger and martial prowess, but also to restore the balance of *timē* disturbed by the initial killing.⁹⁴ Within such system, mutilating the body of one's enemy provided the ultimate means to retaliate and shame the victim in cases where the restoration of honour demanded more than a conventional killing. As such, only vengeance killings result in mutilations, confirming that such acts were deeply rooted in the ideals of vengeance in Homeric society.⁹⁵

Acts of mutilation are almost never condemned in the poems.[96] Far from being ethically or morally wrong, they appear to have been a perfectly justifiable form of revenge within the social world of the Homeric *aristoi*, necessary to restore and reinforce the balance of *timē*.[97] Homer's fastidious commitment to detail in descriptions featuring mutilations indicates that they formed an entirely acceptable, if slightly unusual, feature of heroic battles. There are, furthermore, no hints that the Homeric gods criticized or disapproved of the acts of deliberate mutilation or maltreatment of the dead. The only instance of mutilation which does seem to be morally criticized in the poem is Achilles' maltreatment of Hector, twice described as 'shameful treatment', or *aeikea erga* (22.395, 23.24), and also condemned in a speech by Apollo who accuses Achilles of having lost pity and shame (24.44–54). As I have demonstrated elsewhere, however, the use of the phrase *aeikea erga* put no moral blame on Achilles, but instead emphasized the fullness of his vengeance for the death of Patroclus, as well as the shame imposed on Hector.[98] The cycle of vengeance, nonetheless, should have ended with the funeral of Patroclus and it was Achilles' consistent maltreatment of Hector *after* the funeral which Apollo condemned as excessive, based both on the moral norms of Homeric society and the social standing of Hector.[99] The disapproval of the gods did not apply to the act *per se*, which, as we saw earlier, was widely regarded as a legitimate way to exact revenge 'within reason' by the Homeric *aristoi*. All in all, the overwhelming majority of the intended and successful mutilations are considered morally acceptable by Homer and the Homeric gods.[100] They are presented as part of the vengeance system of Homeric society, and as such constitute a consistent and significant part of Homeric warfare.

Mutilation by animals

The grim examples of warriors hacking apart the bodies of their dead enemies do not constitute the most dominant theme of corpse mutilation in the Homeric epics. Far more numerous are mentions of animals feeding on the bodies of the fallen, which altogether comprise the most common of all mutilation themes in the poems. As already noted, the mention of dogs and birds feasting on human flesh appears in the very first lines of the *Iliad*:

> Sing, goddess, the anger of Peleus' son Achilles and its devastation, which put pains thousandfold upon the Achaeans, hurled in their multitudes to the house

of Hades strong souls of heroes, but gave their bodies to be the delicate feasting of dogs, of all birds, and the will of Zeus was accomplished . . .

1.1–5

The 'delicate feasting' of scavenging animals, whose presence is repeatedly evoked in the *Iliad* and *Odyssey*, is the spectre that haunts the Homeric warriors;[101] the numerous appearances of scavengers in the epics provide, according to Vincent Rosivach, 'a stereotyped expression related to death in battle'.[102] Among the ways in which the theme of animal mutilation functions in the poems, the most common take the form of vaunting over the enemy ('you will glut the dogs and birds of the Trojans with fat and flesh' 13.831–2; 'on you the dogs and the vultures shall feed and foully rip you' 22.335–6); disciplining insubordinate or cowardly warriors ('any man whom I find . . . to hang back by the curved ships, for him no longer will there be any means to escape the dogs and the vultures' 2.391–3; 'may that man who this day wilfully hangs back from the fighting never win home again out of Troy land, but stay here and be made dogs' delight for their feasting' 13.232–4); or lamenting about one's future ('my dogs in front of my doorway will rip me raw' 22.66–7), or the fate of one's relatives ('for him, the dogs and the flying birds must by now have worried the skin away from his bones' XIV.132–4). Expressed in countless similar threats, taunts and mockery, the motif of animal mutilation formed a consistent and important part of Homeric psychological warfare.[103]

Rather unsurprisingly, the fear of animal mutilation was meant to be felt especially by the Homeric *aristoi*. The heroic code of the latter, as we observed earlier, placed special emphasis on the 'beautiful death' (*kalos thanatos*) in battle followed by a conspicuous funeral, both of which were crucial in cementing the fame of an outstanding warrior for future generations. By contrast, the prospect of being left unburied and feasted on by dogs and birds was a 'sinister obverse' of the 'beautiful death', accurately described by James Redfield as the 'antifuneral'.[104] Being left unburied and forgotten – abandoned by family, friends and followers, and prey to scavenging animals – annihilated the social status of the Homeric *aristos*, obliterating his life's honour (*timē*) and glory (*kleos*), and degrading him to the status of a commoner, whose unburied bodies were scattered over the Trojan plain. In this way, animal mutilation was a terrifying vision for any member of the elite, which in turn helps to explain the recurring nature of threats and insults concerning dogs, birds and the post-mortem fate of a slain enemy. Such fate was to be avoided at all costs, and so Hector's dying words, for instance, were to beg Achilles to not 'let the dogs feed' on him, but to return his body to his parents for 'the rite of burning' (22.338–43). The constant fear of exposure and animal scavengers, combined with the importance ascribed to protecting and retrieving the bodies of the *aristoi* in battle, testifies to the ever-present reality of animal mutilation on the Homeric battlefield.

Nonetheless, the prospect of animal mutilation is rarely fulfilled in the poems, as the practice of deliberate exposure and denial of burial, despite the many threats, almost never affects the poem's *aristoi*.[105] Even when men fail to rescue the body of an elite warrior, the Homeric gods intervene in order to provide their favourite mortal *aristoi* with full burial ceremony. Achilles' maltreatment of Hector is accordingly cut short by the gods who ensure that he gets the burial his status requires. Hector's body, moreover, is protected continuously over the twelve days after his death by Aphrodite and Apollo, who 'drove the dogs back from him by day and night' and 'guarded his body from all ugliness', until Achilles finally concedes to the order of Zeus and returns the body to Priam (23.185–7; 24.18–21). Similarly, Sarpedon's body is rescued by the gods from the battlefield and carried to Lykia, where his countrymen give him a full 'burial with tomb and gravestone' (16.667–75).[106] Animal mutilation and exposure seem, therefore, to be reserved mainly for the common warriors whose post-mortem fate, mentioned in the opening lines of the *Iliad*, is juxtaposed with that of the poem's main heroes, the *aristoi*, whose treatment, by contrast, is encapsulated in the *Iliad*'s closing lines and the glorious funeral of Hector.

The motif of animal mutilation, we may conclude, was used consistently throughout the *Iliad* and *Odyssey* as a powerful symbol of complete social humiliation and military defeat, reflecting the competitive and status-driven nature of Homeric warfare. In addition, the theme helped to reinforce further the division between the *aristoi* and commoners which permeates the poems, reminding the audience that exposure on the battlefield was the height of shame and horror for the former, while at the same time a grim reality for the majority of the latter.

Afterlife

Another potential explanation for the practices of mutilation and deliberate exposure in the *Iliad* and *Odyssey* can be sought in the Homeric ideas concerning death and the afterlife. According to the common belief enshrined in the poems, upon the death of any living person the soul (*psyche*) would immediately leave the body to begin its descent to the Underworld.[107] The journey, however, as a number of passages suggest, was completed only with the burial of the body, which served 'as a rite of passage for the dead into an afterlife.'[108] The souls of those who did not receive a proper funeral following their death were, on the other hand, denied entry into Hades and forced to occupy the outskirts of the Underworld until their bodies received burial in the upper world. The liminal and unhappy state of the 'unburied' souls in the afterlife was most explicitly brought up by the ghost of the dead Patroclus, who appeared to Achilles complaining about his fate and asking for his body to be buried:

> 'Bury me as quickly as may be, let me pass through the gates of Hades. The souls, the images of dead men, hold me at a distance, and will not let me cross the river and mingle among them, but I wander as I am by Hades' house of the wide gates.'
> 23.70–4

In a similar way, during Odysseus' *nekyia* in Book 11 of the *Odyssey*, one of the first souls he encounters is the ghost of his companion Elpenor, who died falling off the roof of Circe's palace and was left behind unburied (X.552–60). Elpenor begs Odysseus to:

> '... remember me, and do not go and leave me behind unwept, unburied, when you leave, for fear I might become the gods' curse upon you; but burn me there with all my armor that belongs to me, and heap up a grave mound beside the beach of the gray sea, for an unhappy man, so that those to come will know of me. Do this for me, and on top of the grave mound plant the oar with which I rowed when I was alive and among my companions.'
> XI.71–8

As these episodes demonstrate, the fate of the body of a deceased man had a clear impact on his soul's successful transition to the Underworld. The souls of both Patroclus and Elpenor are unable to settle in Hades, as their bodies have not been provided for by their living companions, Achilles and Odysseus respectively.[109] Deliberate exposure by Homeric warriors might have been likewise motivated by a desire to harm an enemy *after* his death. In addition, taking a step further and mutilating his body could have an adverse effect on a soul's well-being in the afterlife. The very first souls to approach Odysseus during his *nekyia* are those of the brides, virgins, unmarried men, and 'long-suffering elders', but also the spirits of 'many fighting men killed in battle, stabbed with brazen spears, still carrying armor upon them' (XI.34–41).[110] The physical appearance of the latter, still dressed in their armour and bearing the mortal wounds which they received in battle, suggests that any damage done to a warrior's body would normally remain with his soul after his death.[111] Such beliefs may also be reflected in some of the battlefield vaunts, as Poulydamas, for instance, exclaims after killing Prothoënor: 'I think this javelin leaping from the heavy hand of Panthoös' high-hearted son was not thrown away in a vain cast. Rather some Argive caught it in his skin. I think he has got it for a stick to lean on as he trudges down into Death's house' (14.454–7). It seems, therefore, that the practice of the exposure or mutilation of a corpse had serious implications on the victim's fate in the afterlife, since, as Sarah Iles Johnston concluded, it 'forces the ghost to enter the Underworld completely dishonored'.[112] Instead of being only an attack on a man's social status, the Homeric acts of *aikia* might have been motivated by further factors, since the vengeance of the killer could at times go beyond the grave.

The eschatological explanation for mutilation and deliberate exposure in the poems is, nonetheless, problematic, as the post-mortem fate of a victim's soul is never mentioned by those who commit the acts. The emphasis is nearly always on vengeance and social humiliation, and there are no hints that the maltreatment of the corpse was specifically aimed at harming one's soul in the afterlife. Although an eschatological motivation could be read into such practices, it seems that the main point of describing tormented souls in the Underworld was to stress the importance of proper funeral rites, and thus to reinforce the obligation to retrieve and bury the corpses of companions, no matter the circumstances. The duty to provide for the burial of one's friends and followers was not only a human moral code for the Homeric *aristoi*, but was also believed to be safe-guarded by the gods, who are often depicted as the protectors of the dead in the poems.[113] Elpenor, as we saw earlier, makes it clear to Odysseus that should his body remain unwept for and unburied, he might become 'the gods' curse' upon him. The same threat of a divine curse is echoed in Hector's dying plea to Achilles, if the latter should fail to give his body to the Trojans for his 'rite of burning' (22.338–60).[114] The motif of the 'unburied' soul, suffering in the afterlife and denied entry to Hades, was, therefore, used primarily to emphasize the necessity of burial, on both human and divine levels. Since its association with the Homeric practices of mutilation and denial of burial is never made explicit in the poems, it is highly doubtful that these acts had any clear eschatological motivation. The main purpose behind the Homeric practice of *aikia* was always vengeance and the restoration of social status; its scope, accordingly, was limited to the world of the living.

*

The story of the Homeric war dead parallels the social divides depicted in the *Iliad* and *Odyssey*. Divisions between the commoners and the elite, or the *aristoi*, prevalent in both poems, are mirrored in the ideals and procedures governing the recovery of fallen warriors, as well as their burial after the battle. The 'hierarchical' model enshrined in the Homeric tradition was consequently far removed from the 'egalitarian' norms governing the treatment of the dead that formed one of the defining features of Classical Athenian *polis* and its self-identity. Similarly, the practices of mutilation and mistreatment of the dead, radically condemned by the Athenian writers of the fifth century BC, were not uncommon and were entirely acceptable within the honour-driven society of Homeric *aristoi*. As such, the customs surrounding the war dead in the poems, including their recovery, burial and proper treatment, could not have provided a mythical archetype for the conventions of *patrios nomos* of the Classical era. Indeed, it is perhaps most revealing that the practice of *aikia*, according to Herodotus one that befitted only the barbarians, is successfully committed only by the Greeks in the *Iliad*. Before we can examine whether Homeric ideals were present on Archaic battlefields, however, we must first turn our attention to depictions of the war dead in other early Greek mythological accounts, which, despite their often fragmentary nature, provide important insights into the developments that took place in Athens between the Archaic and Classical periods.

2

The War Dead in the Greek Mythological Tradition

The impact of the Homeric epics on the Greek practice and ideology of war was profound. The *Iliad* provided a universal exemplar and military ethos for all men to learn from, emulate and aspire to. Even though the mythical world of Homeric battlefields – dominated by extraordinary feats of larger than life heroes and frequented by an array of deities eager to support their favourite mortals – was in obvious ways removed from the military realities of Greek warfare, its influence over the Greek experience and perception of combat was undeniable.[1] Among the many timeless ideals enshrined in the epics, however, those related to the treatment, and indeed mistreatment, of the war dead were far less suited to the battlefields of the Classical period. The hierarchical standards of Homeric armies, which retrieved the bodies of leading men during combat and left the corpses of the nameless masses unburied and untended often for long stretches of time, coupled with the practice of mutilation carried out in revenge on the fallen enemies, stood in a radical opposition to the egalitarian ideals of the Classical era. As the latter began to seep into the ideological discourse of war, all those who sacrificed their lives in defence of the *polis* were rendered equal, retrieved *en masse* under a formal truce after a battle, and given a public burial at home, which eventually became one of the symbols of Athenian democracy. In time, the conventions regarding the retrieval and proper treatment of the war dead were commonly referred to as the 'laws of the gods' and the 'laws of all Greece' (Eur. *Supp.* 19, 311), forming an 'ancient custom and immemorial law' (Isoc. *Paneg.* 55) universally adhered to by all Greek armies.

Despite the supposed antiquity of the customs concerning the proper treatment of the war dead, their historical origins remain largely unclear, mostly due to the scanty and unreliable nature of the evidence for warfare in the Archaic period. The traditional explanation favoured by scholars who support the 'orthodox' model for early Greek warfare maintains that battlefield truces for the retrieval of the dead (*anairesis ton nekron*) were a by-product of the introduction of the phalanx and the so-called 'hoplite revolution' of the late-eighth and early-seventh centuries BC.[2] According to this view, such customs formed one of the unwritten 'agonistic' laws of hoplite war, which aimed to limit and regulate the extent of war damage on the Greek *poleis*, and was introduced by an emerging class of *georgoi*, or small farmers, who came to dominate and shape the practice of Greek warfare in the period from roughly 700 to 450 BC.[3] The existence of any formal laws of war has, nonetheless, been subsequently questioned by 'revisionist' historians, who argued that most of the unwritten rules of war are not actually attested in our sources until the latter half of the fifth century BC and the works of Euripides, Thucydides and Xenophon.[4] The early date for the introduction of the conventions regarding the proper treatment of the war dead was similarly challenged; the question of its origins, however, has been left largely unexplained.[5] This is surprising considering the importance of the custom in Classical warfare.

With this in mind, the purpose of the present chapter will be to bridge the gap left by orthodox and revisionist scholars and to trace the shift in the ideology and customs surrounding the treatment of the war dead in Archaic and Classical Athens. Considering the seeming lack of any firm evidence for early discourses of the war dead, which hindered most previous studies on the subject, we will turn our attention to different source material, largely unexplored and overlooked by scholars studying early Greek warfare. The vast body of Archaic mythology, as this chapter will demonstrate, offers an important insight into the attitudes and beliefs which influenced the practice of war in early Greece. In addition to supplementing and putting the epic poems of Homer in context, the reception of Archaic myths in the Classical period can be revealing of the changing perceptions and ideals held by later Greek audiences. As myths were retold and reinterpreted, their meaning constantly changed, providing new generations of artists and politicians with a fertile ground to engage with and discuss the most important issues of the day. This process was arguably at its strongest in Athens in the Classical period, and the stories concerning the treatment and mistreatment of the war dead were often at the forefront of such discussions, whether in the plays of Aeschylus, Sophocles and Euripides, the carved reliefs of the Athenian temples, or political speeches of the later orators. The special nature of such stories, adaptable and flexible, occupying a space somewhere between past and present, allows us a glimpse into the changing ideology of war in ancient Athens, implying that the shift of attitudes towards the treatment of the war dead took place much later than is usually assumed.

The temple of Athena Nike, built on the Acropolis in the late 420s BC, is one of the most evocative examples of Athenian engagement with the war dead in its mythological past.⁶ A common ideological thread running through its friezes concerns the battle dead, their sacrifice, recovery, and proper treatment.⁷ On the west frieze, displayed in the British Museum, a fierce fight to recover the dead is represented, commonly identified with the famous episode from the myth of Seven Against Thebes: Theseus and the Athenians help to recover the bodies of the fallen Argives who attacked Thebes, providing the mythical precedent for the custom of battlefield truces for the recovery of the war dead in Greece. The north frieze depicts another glorious scene from the city's mythical past, when the Athenians sheltered the children of Heracles and fought against the Argive king Eurystheus; among the many dead on the battlefield, Eurystheus is captured by two Athenians who hold him by the beard, alluding to a tradition which had the Argive king killed and decapitated after the battle. Finally, on the south frieze, which represents a more recent historical episode, the Athenians fight the Persians (at Marathon or Plataea), who disregard the corpses of their comrades littered over the battlefield, in stark contrast to central Hellenic values.⁸

The three battles depicted on the friezes clearly symbolized Athenian moral superiority and leadership, both past and present, befitting a temple to Athena Nike. Victories over the Thebans, Eurystheus and the Argives, and the Persians were emblematic of the city's glorious military history and its long-standing concern for the virtue and justice among the Greeks. The artistic focus on the proper treatment of the war dead, accordingly, played a key role in this political and ideological image, placing the Athenians as the just protectors of time-honoured Greek customs and traditions. And while these three narratives provide us with a powerful example of the Athenian self-image in the Classical period, the temple of Athena Nike, as we are going to see in this chapter, can be also seen as a microcosm of a long and changing tradition concerning the treatment of the war dead in Athens. Before we focus on each of the stories depicted in the friezes of the temple, however, a brief introduction to the world of Archaic Greek myths, including their potential uses and limitations, is needed.

Early Greek mythology

Greek mythology comprises a substantial corpus of myths embodied in a large collection of narratives (both poetry and prose) and representational arts (vases, statues, architecture) which reflect the cultural, religious and political attitudes of the ancient Greeks. The definition of a myth itself, however, is problematic, since myths never constituted a category native to Greek thought.⁹ Myth, according to modern scholarship, is a traditional story of gods and heroes, dependent on a framework of comprehensive thought which comments upon important issues in the culture in which it is told.[10] Greek myths were born in a predominantly oral environment, with the *Iliad* and *Odyssey* being its first known literary products. Their traditional nature endowed them with a fluid and adaptive character; an ability to respond, adapt to and explain new and changing circumstances. Greek myths were, as a result, continually told and retold, first by epic bards and poets, and later by artists, tragedians and politicians, constantly changing in the process of retelling.[11] Successful survival of individual myths depended on their cultural relevance, as remarked already by Telemachus in the *Odyssey*, who asserted that: 'People, surely, always give more applause to that song which is the latest to circulate among the listeners' (I.351-2). The fluid character of Greek myths was often exploited and used to express powerful, ideological messages, which derived their authority by drawing on a stable and widely recognized repertoire of symbolic resources. As Jonathan Hall observed, Greek myths 'constituted what structural linguists call a *langue* ("language") or universally comprehensible system of symbols, from which a particular conjunction of symbols – a *parole* or "speech" – could be assembled, deconstructed, and reassembled to achieve a particular ideological aim'.[12]

One of the most famous examples of such an ideological manipulation of mythological material occurred as part of the Spartan military expansion in the mid-sixth century BC.[13] The Spartan efforts to resurrect the mythical tradition that associated Agamemnon, the legendary king of Mycenae and the leader of the Achaean expedition against Troy, with their city have been widely seen as an ideological attempt to legitimize the Spartan expansionist policy in the Peloponnese (Hdt. 1.67–8). Agamemnon was a mythological figure capable of validating their political claims of leadership, despite being a hero more naturally associated with Argos, Sparta's main rival in the region. The story of the bones of Agamemnon's son Orestes, 'discovered' by the Spartans in the earth of their long-hated adversaries Tegeans, has been even described as 'a propaganda coup worthy of Goebbels himself'.[14] A few decades later, a similar initiative to resurrect and claim a mythical superhero was also well underway in Athens, where Theseus was being raised to the exemplary figure of the new Athenian democracy on account of his civilizing role in the mythological past.[15] His remains, as Plutarch tells us, were also 'found' and brought back with 'great pomp and ceremony' to his 'native' land of Athens (*Cim.* 8.5–6). The manipulation of mythological stories in both of these instances is very clear, demonstrating the ideological power of Greek myths.

The *Iliad* and *Odyssey*, as noted earlier, provide us with the first literary expressions of the Greek mythological tradition. They were written in a formulaic style, which reflected a long process of oral transmission in bardic poetry behind their origins, as demonstrated by the pioneering work of Milman Parry and Albert Lord.[16] The date of their composition is not certain, but most scholars place them no earlier than mid-eighth and no later than early seventh century BC. Despite their undeniable fame and influence over Greek culture, the mythological story of the Trojan War and its aftermath was, however, by no means limited to the Homeric epics. The whole tradition of the Achaean invasion of Troy formed the core of the so-called Trojan Cycle, which comprised of eight separate epics, including the *Iliad* (dealing with the last year of the siege) and *Odyssey* (relating Odysseus' journey home). The other six works (*Cypria, Aethiopis, Little Iliad, Sack of Ilion, Returns, Telegony*) related the rest of the long Trojan saga, although none have survived but for a few fragments and plot summaries in late authors. The other mythological tradition roughly contemporary with the Trojan Cycle was that of the Theban Cycle (*Oedipodea, Thebaid, Epigoni, Alcmeonis*), narrating the tragic story of the city of Thebes (including the life of Oedipus and the myth of the Seven Against Thebes). Taken together these two cycles, the Trojan and the Theban, along with a few other potential poems (*Titanomachy, Heraclea, Theseis*), are commonly referred to as the 'Epic Cycle'; its poems, which in their entirety cover Greek mythical history from the beginning of the world to the end of the heroic age, emerged from the same oral performance culture as the *Iliad* and *Odyssey*, based on the mythical stories circulating in early Greece.[17]

The extent of the popularity of the Epic Cycle poems in the Classical period is unclear, though we will see that their influence on Athenian artists and writers must have been considerable. But the first widely attested interest in the collection as a whole came in the Hellenistic era.[18] The structure of the Epic Cycle familiar to us was most likely produced in this period, but despite the renewed interest of Alexandrian scholars in the Archaic poems, not much of them has survived to our times. Apart from a number of quotations and indirect references in the works of later ancient writers, our most important source of information for the poems of the Epic Cycle are summaries excerpted from the work of a certain Proclus, preserved in an MS of Homer's *Iliad* as background information for readers not familiar with the story of the Trojan War.[19] In addition, the close resemblance between the subject matter included in Proclus' work with the earlier mythological compendium of Apollodorus has led scholars to suspect that the two texts must have been intimately related. And while Proclus may have used Apollodorus' *Bibliotheca* in his account, it seems far more likely that both authors derived their accounts separately from the same compendium of the Epic Cycle poems originating from the Hellenistic period, as suggested by Martin West.[20]

Apollodorus' *Bibliotheca* (or *The Library of Greek Mythology*), dated by modern scholars to the mid- or late-first century AD, is arguably the most valuable and comprehensive mythographical work that has come down to us from antiquity.[21] We do not know much about the author but one feature that characterizes his account is his frequent consultation of Archaic sources that are otherwise lost, usually at the expense of more recent works.[22] The authors he uses and occasionally cites are the Archaic/Classical mythographers Pherecydes, Acusilaus and Hecataeus. His other sources include the Archaic poets Hesiod, Pindar and Simonides. Furthermore, in line with his preference for early mythological material, Apollodorus' account of the Trojan War is largely, if not entirely based on the Epic Cycle tradition.[23] The accuracy with which he reproduced and/or summarized the accounts of these early sources (most of which survive only in fragments) inspires us with confidence in accepting some of his statements as genuinely Archaic and thus representative of the early mythological tradition in Greece. Apollodorus' *Bibliotheca*, combined with Proclus' summary of the Epic Cycle, provide us with enough material to reconstruct the basic storylines of myths circulating in the Archaic period, even if their nature is often fragmentary and infused with a dose of later Classical and Hellenistic editorship.

Due to their fragmentary and mostly anecdotal nature, the poems of the Epic Cycle have rarely featured in scholarly works on early Greece, which often tend to focus exclusively on the *Iliad* and *Odyssey*. The surviving Cyclic material, in addition, has been traditionally considered to be artistically and historically inferior to the Homeric epics, further discouraging scholars from any concerted historical engagement with the Epic Cycle.[24] Recent decades, nonetheless, witnessed a growing interest in early, non-Homeric mythology, spurred on initially by the so-called 'Neoanalysis' approach. 'Neoanalysis' questioned the primacy of the *Iliad* and *Odyssey* within the Archaic mythological traditions, positing that both epics drew extensively from earlier Cyclic material, as shown by numerous traces left in the narratives of the poems.[25] At the same time, a number of studies emphasized the dominance of non-Homeric scenes (most of which featured in the Epic Cycle) in early Greek art, demonstrating their importance and cultural significance among early Greek communities.[26] As 'Homer-centrism' is gradually waning in studies of early Greek myth, the Epic Cycle poems are increasingly seen as valuable windows into Archaic culture and society.

There are naturally certain limitations and difficulties in using the Cyclic material for any studies of early Greece. The surviving verse of the Epic Cycle contains less than 150 lines and Proclus' summary has been questioned with regards to the seemingly neat boundaries created around individual poems, which in their Archaic versions likely overlapped and did not form a continuous narrative.[27] The tampering and manipulation of the poems must have occurred at some later stage of their literary transmission, carried out in order to enhance their presentation as a single, unbreakable unit. There is no reason to suspect, however, that any of their main contents were extensively changed or omitted. An awareness of the key Cyclic storylines, in turn, gives us a better idea and appreciation of the changes introduced by later authors who constantly engaged with traditional Archaic myths, providing us with a valuable insight into the cultural discourses of the Classical period. Considering the marked presence of Atticisms and thematic accretions of Attic provenance in the surviving fragments, the prominence of the Cyclic epics was particularly strong in Athens, as recently noted by Marco Fantuzzi and Christos Tsagalis.[28] It is also important to bear in mind that the Epic Cycle poems were most likely not the only ones of their type in the vast body of early Greek mythology. Most of the original tradition concerning the Trojan and Theban Wars is now lost, and the Homeric and Cyclic poems represent only the tip of the iceberg. This tip, nevertheless, must have been seen as the most important and representative of the tradition by later Greeks, and thus worthy of preservation and continuation. Finally, every scholar studying the reception of myths in ancient Greece has to be constantly aware of the fact that myths in Greece functioned on both local and Panhellenic levels. Both levels, however, as will be demonstrated below, are equally important, revealing the various stages of the manipulation and reinterpretation, which can in turn shed some valuable light on the political, religious or indeed military life of Greek societies. And some of the most revealing cases of the remodelling of early Archaic myths in the Classical period concern the traditions of the treatment and maltreatment of the war dead.

Battlefield truces: Seven Against Thebes

The west frieze of the Athena Nike temple depicts the Athenian recovery of the Argive war dead at Thebes, the finale of the Seven Against Thebes saga (Fig. 1). The myth was very popular in antiquity and was described by Hesiod (*Op*. 161–3) as one of the two greatest exploits of the age of heroes, second only to the siege of Troy.[29] Forming the main subject of a number of tragedies, the myth of the

Seven Against Thebes concerned the war between the sons of Oedipus, Polyneices and Eteocles. After Oedipus' tragic departure as the king of Thebes, the story goes, his sons were unable to divide the rule between themselves and resorted to war. Enlisting the help of the Argive king Adrastus and several other heroes, Polyneices attacked Thebes and Eteocles' army. He was, nevertheless, unsuccessful, and died in a duel with Eteocles which proved fatal for both brothers. After the battle, according to the tradition, the new Theban king Creon forbade the burial of the Argive dead, which in turn led Adrastus, the sole survivor on the Argive side, to supplicate the Athenian king Theseus to help him recover the bodies of his dead comrades. The fallen were subsequently recovered, either by diplomatic or military intervention, and buried in Eleusis and/or Eleutherae.

The retrieval of the Argive dead, which from our perspective forms the central part of the story, is related to us in more detail by Plutarch in his *Life of Theseus*. The legendary Athenian king, Plutarch summarizes,

> (...) aided Adrastus in recovering for burial the bodies of those who had fallen before the walls of the Cadmeia, not by mastering the Thebans in battle, as Euripides has it in his tragedy, but by persuading them to a truce; for so most writers say, and Philochorus adds that this was the first truce ever made for recovering the bodies of those slain in battle, although in the accounts of Heracles it is written that Heracles was the first to give back their dead to his enemies. And the graves of the greater part of those who fell before Thebes are shown at Eleutherae, and those of the commanders near Eleusis, and this last burial was a favour which Theseus showed to Adrastus. The account of Euripides in his 'Suppliants' is disproved by that of Aeschylus in his 'Eleusinians,' where Theseus is made to relate the matter as above.
>
> *Thes.* 29.4–5

Plutarch, quoting Aeschylus' lost play *Eleusinians*, states that in the traditional version of the myth, Theseus recovered the dead by persuading the Thebans to

Fig. 1 *Athenians recovering the Argive war dead (Seven Against Thebes)*. West frieze (part), Temple of Athena Nike on the Athenian Akropolis, marble relief. The British Museum, London, No. 1816,0610.160.

agree to a truce, and not by a military action portrayed famously in Euripides' *Suppliants*. He also suggests, referring to the Atthidographer Philochorus (*FGrH* 328 F 112), that this was the first ever truce concluded for the purpose of recovering the bodies of the dead, setting a moral exemplar for subsequent generations to follow.[30] Theseus' diplomatic actions in the finale of the Seven Against Thebes provided, therefore, a mythical archetype for the Greek convention of *anairesis*, which in turn formed an essential part of Greek warfare in the Classical period.

The convention of *anairesis* consisted of a set of strict procedures which governed the aftermath of any military encounter in Greece. The usual order of events required the defeated army to send heralds to the victors requesting a truce for the retrieval of the dead. Such a request was regarded as a formal admission of defeat, and entitled the victors to set up a battlefield trophy made of the enemy's captured arms and armour, erected at the spot where the enemy turned to flee. Under the custom, the victor could not honourably refuse to grant the truce for the recovery of the dead, which, once agreed, was traditionally sealed with libations which marked the official end of battle.[31] The procedure was based on the fundamental obligation to respect and bury the dead, commonly felt by all ancient Greeks. The sending of heralds by the defeated side was an admission of powerlessness and the inability to retrieve the fallen warriors, stripped of their armour and weapons by the enemy. The mastery of the battlefield dead, therefore, was the ultimate criterion of victory. As such, the rules of *anairesis* provided a way to determine the winner of a battle in a quick and decisive way, reflecting, at the same time, the moral and religious importance ascribed to the proper treatment of the dead. Any deviations from the *anairesis* procedure, such as denial of burial or maltreatment of enemy's corpses, were extremely rare and always viewed as a serious transgression and an offence against the gods.[32]

The conventions of *anairesis* constituted an important and regular part of Classical Greek warfare, and were mentioned on numerous occasions by Thucydides in his battle accounts of the Peloponnesian War.[33] Interestingly, however, the procedure receives no mention at all in Herodotus, and appears to be completely absent from the few accounts of battles from the Archaic era.[34] Despite the seeming lack of any clear-cut early evidence, the prevailing assumption among most modern scholars, in particular those following the 'orthodox' model of Greek warfare, is that the custom of battlefield truces for the recovery of the dead originated sometime in the Archaic period. The sole basis for this claim, in turn, is usually found in Greek mythology and the story of the

Seven Against Thebes, which as Pritchett and a number of other scholars maintain, testifies to the antiquity of the battlefield truces, whatever their origin.[35]

The mythical recovery of the Argive dead, and especially the Athenian involvement in the process, undoubtedly gives us a very clear expression of Classical Greek attitudes to the treatment of the war dead. In our most detailed account of the story, Euripides' *Suppliants*, we are explicitly told that the rules regarding the retrieval and proper burial of enemy soldiers were the 'laws of the gods' (19) and the 'laws of all Greece' (311). The myth, which highlighted Theseus' civilizing role and concern for justice, formed a patriotic commonplace between a number of Classical Athenian writers and orators, including not only Aeschylus and Euripides, but also Herodotus, Lysias, Isocrates, and Demosthenes.[36] It held a special place in Athenian folklore and public discourse, becoming a mythical paradigm of Athens' self-image as the protector of the oppressed and the guardian of Panhellenic customs. Its appearance on the temple of the Athena Nike was, therefore, no coincidence. One problem, however, which a closer study of the finale of the myth of Seven Against Thebes reveals, is that the origins of the Athenian involvement in the story are very unclear and problematic.

In his comprehensive study of early Greek mythology, Timothy Gantz observed that the tradition of Theseus' retrieval of the Argive dead, either by negotiation (Aeschylus) or war (Euripides), does not appear in our sources until the Attic drama of the fifth century BC, where in fact, according to him, it might have conceivably begun.[37] In a similar fashion, Bernd Steinbock suggested that Athenian intervention on behalf of the fallen Argives emerged in the mainstream tradition only in the last decade of the sixth century BC.[38] The myth of Seven Against Thebes formed the central subject of the Cyclic poem *Thebaid*, but there is no evidence for either Creon's refusal of burial for the Argive soldiers, nor for the subsequent Athenian recovery of the dead as playing any part in the lost epic.[39] These events are similarly never mentioned by Homer or Hesiod, further suggesting that Theseus' much celebrated act of statesmanship, as well as the first burial truce, were either absent or much less popular in the early mythological tradition.[40]

Our earliest testimony for the post-battle events mentioned by Plutarch in his account of Seven Against Thebes is the aforementioned lost play *Eleusinians* by Aeschylus, composed in the late 470s BC. The source for Aeschylus' version of events is uncertain, but Steinbock speculates that the story 'almost certainly' predated Aeschylus' play and originated from local traditions. According to him, the evidence of dual burials at Eleusis (leaders) and Eleutherae (common warriors) related by Plutarch, indicates that both sites might have been initially connected to the burial of the Seven, with each community identifying a local landmark linking it to the epic past.[41] The early importance of such traditions would have been initially marginal and confined only to the community itself and its immediate vicinity. As the Greek *poleis* developed over the Archaic period, these local hero cults provided an opportunity to root their identity in the great mythological past, as well as to forge a common and unique civic self-image, often in opposition to other Greek *poleis*. In time, the local stories surrounding the burial of the Seven were crystallized with the play of Aeschylus, who claimed the burial site for his hometown in Eleusis, thus 'spreading a local tradition to the entire polis community'.[42] The local stories concerning the fate of the fallen Argives, if accepted as genuine, would confirm that their burial did not take place at Thebes; they do not, however, contain any obvious hints of military intervention by the Athenians or an official burial truce as part of the early versions of the story.

The initial small-scale nature of such local accounts connecting the burial of the fallen Argives to Eleusis and Eleutherae is also confirmed by an alternative tradition expressed most prominently by the Theban-born Pindar. In his account of the myth in the *Ninth Nemean*, written most likely in the mid-470s BC, Pindar speaks of the fallen Argive heroes feeding seven funeral pyres by the banks of the river Ismenos at Thebes, suggesting that the bodies were buried following the battle at Thebes, and not in Eleusis or Eleutherae:

> (...) and on the banks of the Ismenus
> they laid down their sweet homecoming
> and fed the white-flowering smoke with their bodies,
> for seven pyres feasted on the men's young limbs.
>
> *Nem. IX* (22–24)

The seven funeral pyres indicate, in all probability, a peaceful and uncontested burial for all dead warriors from each of the seven invading contingents, as if, as Gantz observed, 'there was no question of the bodies ever being denied burial or reclaimed by relatives'.[43] This interpretation is favoured by the Vatican scholiast (ΣO. 6.23d Drachmann), and further implied by the wording of another reference to the myth in the *Sixth Olympian*, where Pindar also speaks of the 'seven pyres of the dead' (*Ol.* VI 15).[44] In both cases, Pindar's likely source for the Argive burials at Thebes was, according to the scholia citing Asclepiades of Myrlea, the Cyclic poem *Thebaid* (Fr. 6 West).[45] The antiquity of Pindar's version of the story is also confirmed by a statement from the *Iliad*, which speaks of Tydeus, one of the seven invaders, being buried 'under the heaped earth in Thebes' (14.114).[46]

Again, there is clearly no mention of Tydeus ever being denied burial, which here also takes place at Thebes and not Eleusis. Pindar's account, therefore, most likely reflected a local Theban tradition, according to which the burial of the Argive dead took place after the battle in Thebes and did not necessitate any intervention from Athens. His explicit mentions of the myth in his *Ninth Nemean* and *Sixth Olympian* odes were most likely a response to the Athenian version depicted in Aeschylus' *Eleusinians*, which brought the Athenians and Theseus onto the stage and accused the mythical Thebans of flouting Panhellenic laws by withholding funeral rites for the defeated Argives. This conflict of mythical traditions, referred to by Steinbock as a 'memory war', most likely originated from three different local variants of the story (Eleusis, Eleutherae, Thebes), which coexisted side by side for most of the Archaic period until the production of Aeschylus' play.[47] The latter, based originally on an Eleusinian tradition, introduced Theseus and the Athenians to the narrative, thus elevating the myth to a 'national' level and establishing it as one of the timeless mythical paradigms of Athenian virtue and concern for justice.

The final question that we ought to answer is: why would Aeschylus and the Athenians modify the story? As we saw earlier in this chapter, due to their flexible character, Greek myths were often reshaped and reinterpreted by ancient authors to suit the changing political and social needs of their audiences. This process was arguably at its strongest at Athens in the fifth century BC, and tragedies were often among the most conspicuous examples of mythical reinvention at work. The dramas of the Athenian playwrights, as Ian Storey summarized in his study of Euripides' *Suppliants*, provided an opportunity 'to re-invent the traditional myths, to add Athenian themes and characters to existing stories, to create for themselves a picture of Athens as the greatest and the noblest city in Greece, a sanctuary for the oppressed, (...) a home for heroes of other myths'.[48] Aeschylus' *Eleusinians*, focusing on Theseus' heroic involvement in the aftermath of the Argive invasion on Thebes, was most likely such an attempt to reinvent the traditional, Cyclic mythological material, adding new characters, new plots and new meanings.[49] Aeschylus' play has been often seen by scholars as part of the Athenian political programme of the Cimonian period, which aimed to transform Theseus into a national hero in order to justify the growing imperialism and hegemony of Athens in the first half of the fifth century BC.[50] In addition, the denial of burial by the Thebans, which was conceivably also introduced for the first time by Aeschylus, offered a good opportunity to glorify the Athenian past at the expense of Thebes, which in the 470s BC was a prime target of Athenian animosity for 'medising' during the second Persian invasion.[51] The mythical narrative of the *Eleusinians* fits perfectly, therefore, with the political and cultural scene of Athens in the early Classical period.

While we may assume with relative certainty that the story of Theseus' intervention on behalf of the fallen Argives emerged only in the early Classical period, the exact origins for the Theban denial of burial to the fallen Argives, as well as the subsequent burial truce, may be impossible to determine. Aeschylus' play could have drawn most of its narrative from a local Eleusinian tradition, although a number of scholars suspect that the introduction of Athens and Theseus to the story was simply a creative invention on the part of the tragedian. Storey, for instance, concluded that there is 'nothing in the remains of the early epics that suggests an Athenian presence in the [Seven Against Thebes] story. In fact the appeal to Athens and the response of Theseus is very likely the creation of the Athenian dramatists of the fifth century'.[52] It is perhaps conceivable that the early Attic traditions surrounding the burial place of the Argive dead (Eleusis and/or Eleutherae) led the Athenians to assume that the fallen were specifically denied burial in Thebes, which never featured in any of the early versions of the myth, nor in the Cyclic poem *Thebaid*.[53] This, in turn, added a new dimension to the story, allowing the Athenian intervention to take place – first diplomatic (Aeschylus), later military (Euripides) – and depicting Theseus as the archetypal champion of Panhellenic customs.

We may conclude that the finale of the Seven Against Thebes testifies to the multiplicity and flexible nature of Greek myths, used and reinvented by Greek authors in accordance with the changing political and cultural environment of their respective *poleis*.[54] The stories surrounding the burial place of the fallen Argives reveal at least three different local traditions (Eleusis, Eleutherae, Thebes), each of which placed the tombs of the dead heroes within the confines of its own *polis*. By the beginning of the Classical period, however, the myth took on a new significance, spurred on by the production of Aeschylus' *Eleusinians*. The play presented, potentially for the very first time, a new version of the events, which introduced Theseus and the Athenians to the story and accused the Thebans of denying burial to the fallen Argives. This version, despite the best efforts of Pindar, was backed and elaborated by a number of Athenian writers, artists and orators, eventually becoming one of the emblematic mythical paradigms of Athens' virtue and moral superiority. Within a few decades, its wide-ranging popularity led to the myth's appearance on the west frieze of the Athena Nike temple on the Acropolis, where it served as timeless testimony to the Athenian respect for the so-called *patrios nomos*, which governed the proper treatment of the war dead.[55]

The burial truce concluded by Theseus, which according to Plutarch and Philochorus was the first of its kind in Greek warfare, was in all likelihood an important part of the new Athenian tradition, brought into prominence by Aeschylus and continued throughout the Classical period. But its significance in the earlier, Archaic versions of the myth, including the Cyclic poem *Thebaid*, was far more limited, if not altogether absent. While the stories concerning the burial of the leading Argive heroes were contested by local communities, eager to claim their final resting ground within their own geographical confines, the fate of the mass of the war dead was of a far lesser interest. The initial lack of concern for the latter in early Greek mythological traditions, compared to the later depictions of the Argive war dead in the Athenian art and drama of the Classical era, could be taken as further evidence for the 'hierarchical' standards which governed the battlefields of the Homeric epics, where the post-mortem fate of the leading warriors overshadowed that of the masses.

While the myth of the Seven Against Thebes, as featured in the plays of Aeschylus, Euripides, and the Temple of Athena Nike, provides us with a powerful example of Classical Greek attitudes towards the recovery and treatment of the war dead, it cannot be taken as the ideal and symbol of earlier Greek, let alone Athenian, attitudes. Any modern scholarly assumption which sees the post-battle conventions established by Theseus in the myth as a testament to the antiquity of the procedures of *anairesis*, therefore, cannot stand. The origins of these customs must be sought elsewhere. But before we can move on to the possible date and historical circumstances behind the new attitudes towards the war dead at Athens, we must first look at the darker side of early Greek mythology and the stories of deliberate maltreatment of the fallen dead in battle.

Mutilation of the dead: Eurystheus' decapitation

On the north frieze of the temple to Athena Nike, we find another story which offers a unique insight into the mythical reinterpretation carried out by the Athenians in the Classical period. The scene depicts an episode from the famous myth of Eurystheus' pursuit of the children of Heracles: as the Argives are defeated in combat, Eurystheus is held by two Athenians, one of whom may be preparing to strike his neck and cut off his head.[56] The last detail, Eurystheus' decapitation, although not explicitly represented in the frieze, alludes to an older mythological tradition which had the Argive king killed and beheaded after the battle. And while such practices bear a close resemblance to the combat narratives of the *Iliad*, where mutilating the dead provided the ultimate way to exact revenge upon one's enemies, they were radically condemned by the authors of the Classical period. Mistreating the dead was widely considered to be the most outrageous and unholy of acts, more suitable, as Herodotus states, for barbarians than Greeks, 'and even in them we find it loathsome' (9.79).[57] The example of Eurystheus' decapitation, however, indicates that stories involving mutilation were by no means limited to Homeric epics only, and were a recurring theme in the mythological traditions of the Archaic era. Tracing the early origins of these stories, which include episodes from the Theban and Trojan Cycles, as well as their reception in the Classical period, can shed an important light on the changing Greek attitudes towards the war dead. This, in turn, may give us a better understanding of the reasons behind the striking difference between the ideals enshrined in the *Iliad* and those championed by the Athenian writers of the democratic era.

Eurystheus and the children of Heracles

The story of the children of Heracles and Eurystheus was well-known in antiquity, and its scope and popularity extended well beyond Athens. According to the myth, after the death of Heracles, his children were pursued through Greece by Eurystheus, the king of Mycenae. Having been refused protection by a number of cities, the Heraclidae arrived in Athens where their appeal as suppliants was accepted. This, in turn, led Eurystheus to declare war on Athens, during which he was defeated and killed while attempting to flee from the battlefield. Apollodorus, relating the full story, states that he was then decapitated by Hyllus, one of Heracles' sons, and had his eyes gouged out by Heracles' mother Alcmene:

> Being pursued, they came to Athens, and sitting down on the altar of Mercy, claimed protection. Refusing to surrender them, the Athenians bore the brunt of war with Eurystheus, and slew his sons, Alexander, Iphimedon, Eurybius, Mentor and Perimedes. Eurystheus himself fled in a chariot, but was pursued and slain by Hyllus just as he was driving past the Scironian cliffs; and Hyllus cut off his head and gave it to Alcmene; and she gouged out his eyes with weaving-pins.
>
> Apollod. 2.8.1

The story of the return of the children of Heracles formed an important part of early Spartan mythology, legitimizing the historic Dorian invasion. The Athenian appropriation of the myth was most likely a slightly later development intended to bolster the city's connection to Heracles and his children, and to strengthen its political image.[58] The oldest attestable source relating the story was, as later works tell us, an early Classical Athenian mythographer Pherecydes (Fr. 84 Fowler):

> This is told by Pherecydes: (...) The Athenians did not refuse war and Eurystheus invaded Attica and, after a line of battle had been established, he himself died in battle. Most of the Argives were put to flight. With Eurystheus dead, Hyllus and the other Heraclidae and their allies re-established themselves in Thebes.[59]
>
> Ant. Lib. *Met.* 33

Pherecydes, who as we noted earlier was one of Apollodorus' main sources, composed an extensive work on Greek mythology, comprising as many as ten books.[60] The work, known as *Historiai*, or *Researches*, is unfortunately lost but the surviving and often extensive fragments (180 arguable quotations; 13 from Apollodorus) allow us to reconstruct the main contents of his books.[61] The myths concerning the Heraclidae were most likely covered in the third volume of his work, and we can confidently assume that the story of Eurystheus' defeat at the hands of the Athenians was related in some detail. The surviving fragment that we have comes from a second century AD grammarian Antoninus Liberalis, whose primary interest in the story was the later metamorphosis of Alcmene and her shrine in Thebes.[62] Accordingly, he had no need to mention the manner of Eurystheus' death and any potential maltreatment of his body; the latter, however, considering Pherecydes' preference for Archaic sources and the general nature of his work, was almost certainly mentioned by the Athenian mythographer, later finding its way to the account of Apollodorus.[63]

The first source that does explicitly mention the manner of Eurystheus' death is Pindar. In his *Ninth Pythian* ode, composed between 478 and 474 BC to celebrate a victory in a hoplite race of Telesicrates, he briefly mentions that Iolaus, a Theban national hero and nephew of Heracles, decapitated Eurystheus:[64]

> Seven-gated Thebes
> once recognized that Iolaus too did not dishonor him.
> After he cut off Eurystheus' head with the edge
> of his sword, they buried Iolaus beneath the earth
> in the tomb where his father's father lay, the charioteer
> Amphitryon, a guest of the Spartoi after migrating
> to the streets of the Cadmeans with the white horses.
>
> *Pyth. IX* (80–3)

Iolaus' involvement in Eurystheus' death was an important part of the Theban version of the story according to which he was to be miraculously rejuvenated or brought back to life for the duration of the battle between the Argive and Athenian armies.[65] Pindar's work has often been seen by modern scholars as an intermediary between the social and aesthetic worlds of Archaic and Classical Greece.[66] The Theban-born poet relied extensively on the traditional body of mythological stories (including the Epic Cycle) not only to glorify his patrons, but also to teach important lessons and even to edit and correct certain versions of myth which he found unsuitable or morally questionable, as we saw in the story of the Seven Against Thebes.[67] His decision to include Iolaus' decapitation of Eurystheus, therefore, clearly shows that he regarded it as a heroic act, bearing no ethical connotations whatsoever.[68] Iolaus' actions were certainly not condemned by the Thebans, who gave him a public burial in the tomb of his grandfather Amphitryon. It is interesting to note, however, that Pindar's use of the myth would highlight the fact that Iolaus performed a great deed by decapitating Eurystheus, thus coming to the rescue of the children of Heracles. The mutilation detail (killing Eurystheus and *then* cutting his head off) was omitted by the Theban poet, as it might have been seen as less glorious, if not altogether morally questionable. Whether the latter was true or not, Pindar is the only Classical source that explicitly mentions Eurystheus' decapitation, which subsequently disappears from our evidence for more than 400 years.

By far the most important work dealing with the myth is Euripides' *Heraclidae*, written most likely between 430 and 428 BC.[69] The play is our most detailed source for the story of Eurystheus' pursuit of the children of Heracles; it explores a number of themes important for the Athenian audience of the fifth century BC, including the rights of suppliants, the treatment of prisoners of war, the tensions between individuals and the state, and the moral limits of vengeance. The concluding lines relate the final fate of Eurystheus:

> **Alcmene** Why then, hearing these words, do you delay to kill this man, if it is fated to win salvation for your city? For he indicates the safest course: the man is an enemy, and his death brings benefit. [*To the slaves guarding Eurystheus*] Take him away, servants, then you must kill him and give him to the dogs. [*To Eurystheus, as he is led away*] For do not hope that you will live to expel me again from my native land!
>
> **Chorus Leader** This seems right to me. On your way, servants. For our actions will be free from pollution to our rulers.
>
> Heracl. 1045–55

The manner of Eurystheus' death in the play is problematic. Euripides is the first source to attribute the killing of Eurystheus to Alcmene, who sentences him to death and instructs her servants to throw his body to the dogs, in bold defiance of Athenian law regarding the treatment of prisoners. The end of the play, however, is ambiguous, because Alcmene's initial proposal was to kill Eurystheus and give his body to his relatives, which she appears to have forgotten moments later.[70] The unclear nature of this passage has led some scholars to put a lacuna at the end of the play, even though it is impossible to determine how large it was, or what exactly it contained (or indeed whether it was there or not).[71] Interestingly, Euripides does not mention Eurystheus' decapitation at all. The Argive king is instead captured by Iolaus in battle and brought to Alcmene who orders her servants to execute him – a sequence of events commonly seen by modern scholars as the poet's own invention.[72] This omission is perhaps surprising, since Euripides was often regarded by his contemporaries as a controversial writer who undermined the traditional religious and moral beliefs of Athenian society, and did not abstain from graphic descriptions of violence and cruelty.[73] Alcmene's conduct in the final scenes of the play, if we accept the inconsistency of the ending as genuine, would have certainly been disturbing to a fifth-century BC audience, but a further mutilation detail would have no doubt increased the shocking impact of the play even more.[74] It seems, however, that a 'softer' or 'censored' version of the story, which purposely omitted the decapitation tradition, was prevalent by Euripides' time. This is confirmed by other Classical evidence, including the frieze of Athena Nike, which depicts the capture of Eurystheus but not his execution or beheading.

Other Classical authors who mention the myth include Herodotus (9.27.2), Thucydides (1.9.2) and Xenophon (*Hell.* 6.5.47). All of them talk about Eurystheus' death but significantly none of them goes into any detail about it. As Herodotus' and Xenophon's passages show, the story of the flight of the children of Heracles and the protection of them by the Athenians has been gradually incorporated into Athenian political mythology, with an intention to glorify Athens as the mythical avenger of the feeble against the strong, who fight for justice in the face of oppression.[75] This idea was subsequently adopted and developed more fully in the political speeches of Lysias (*Funeral Speech* 11–16) and Isocrates (*To Philip* 34; *Paneg.* 58–60). The traditional manner of Eurystheus' death, known from Pherecydes, Pindar and earlier Archaic traditions, is again never mentioned. If anything, Isocrates in his *Panathenaicus* appears to follow Euripides' version suggesting that Eurystheus became an Athenian prisoner after the battle:

> For our country was invaded (...) by the Peloponnesians, led by Eurystheus, who not only refused to make amends to Heracles for his ill-treatment of him

but brought an army against our ancestors with the object of seizing by force the sons of Heracles, who had taken refuge with us. However, he met with the fate which was his due. For so far did he fail of getting our suppliants into his power that, having been defeated in battle and taken captive by our people, he became the suppliant of those whom he had come to demand of us, and lost his own life.

Panath. 193–4

The omission of the mutilation detail is perhaps hardly surprising, because such detail would no doubt damage the image of justice and lawfulness that the Athenian orators wanted to champion through the mythical story. And there is every reason to suspect, as William Allan observed, that the early fourth-century BC patriotic speeches of Lysias and Isocrates reflected the expectations of a fifth-century BC audience too, thus falling in line with Euripides' *Heraclidae*.[76] The available evidence, therefore, appears to suggest that the decapitation of Eurystheus ceased to be a part of the children of Heracles myth from the mid-fifth century BC onwards.

The myth is also mentioned in a number of later sources, including Diodorus (4.57), Strabo (8.6.19) and Pausanias (1.32.6). But the mutilation detail is described only in Strabo, which, considering Iolaus' involvement (noted also by Pausanias) suggests that the Theban version of the story must have become the dominant one in Attica.[77] The separate burial places of Eurystheus' body and head were likely a local tradition, probably forgotten by the time of Pausanias, who speaks only of a single tomb by the Scironian Rocks. Our latest ancient sources relating the myth are Apollodorus (2.8.1) and Zenobius (*Proverbs* 2.61) who, considering their similarities, most probably consulted the same work as Apollodorus.[78] They both clearly go back to the early Athenian version of the story, placing Hyllus as the one who killed and decapitated Eurystheus. The detail of Alcmene's gouging out Eurystheus' eyes, mentioned only in these two works, seems to have originated from an early Archaic version as well, potentially derived from the very same source. And as Heracles' mother was mentioned by Pherecydes in relation to the story (as related by Antoninus Liberalis), Apollodorus' and Zenobius' accounts would have been most likely based on the work of the Athenian mythographer.

All in all, the late, post-Classical writings relating the myth and decapitation of Eurystheus seem to highlight the editorial attitudes of Classical Athenian authors. The Archaic story of the mutilation of the Argive king, likely drawn from the Cyclic tradition and later related by Pherecydes, has been reinterpreted and modified from the first half of the fifth century BC onwards, demonstrated most clearly in the works of Euripides and Isocrates, and in the north frieze of Athena Nike. Other mythical maltreatments of the war dead, as we shall see, confirm this pattern.

Amphiaraus and the Seven Against Thebes

The second example of a mythical mutilation of the war dead takes place in the context of the now familiar story of the Seven Against Thebes and the infamous conduct of Tydeus. The relevant episode, which concerns the death of Tydeus and the decapitation of Melanippus, constitutes perhaps the most gruesome example of mutilation and cannibalism in the entire corpus of Greek war mythology.[79] As Apollodorus relates, during the final battle between the Argives and the Thebans, a Theban Melanippus wounded the Aeolian hero Tydeus, but was himself killed by the Argive warrior-seer Amphiaraus. The latter then cut off Melanippus' head and handed it to Tydeus, bidding him to consume the brains; Tydeus did so, thereby disgusting Athena who had planned to save his life and grant him immortality:

> But Amphiaraus hated Tydeus for thwarting him by persuading the Argives to march to Thebes; so when he perceived the intention of the goddess he cut off the head of Melanippus and gave it to Tydeus, who, wounded though he was, had killed him. And Tydeus split open the head and gulped up the brains. But when Athena saw that, in disgust she grudged and withheld the intended benefit.
>
> Apollod. 3.6.8

Unlike Eurystheus' example, we know from the scholiast on the *Iliad* that this story was covered by Pherecydes and that it formed a part of the Cyclic poem *Thebaid* (Schol. D *Il.* 5.126). The myth, however, never featured in the Homeric epics, despite the prominence of Diomedes in the *Iliad* and the repeated mentions of his noble father Tydeus. This is most likely due to the extreme nature of the story, depicting both mutilation and cannibalism, as reflected in the surviving fragment of the *Thebaid*:

> Tydeus the son of Oineus in the Theban war was wounded by Melanippus the son of Astacus. Amphiaraus killed Melanippus and brought back his head, which Tydeus split open and gobbled the brain in a passion. When Athena, who was bringing Tydeus immortality, saw the horror, she turned away from him. Tydeus on realizing this begged the goddess at least to bestow the immortality on his son.[80]
>
> *Thebaid* Fr. 9

Judging from the surviving fragment, we can be almost sure that Apollodorus drew on the account of Pherecydes, who himself must have taken the story directly from the Epic Cycle, thus providing us with an authentic account of an Archaic Cyclic myth. The story featured in the *Thebaid*, however, differs in small details from Apollodorus' version, which not only adds a justification for Amphiaraus' actions (hatred for Tydeus) and also implies that the latter did not kill Melanippus. This divergence, as we will see, points to an alternative tradition which sought to dissociate Amphiaraus from the macabre episode in the Theban saga.

Early awareness of the gruesome events from the *Thebaid* is indirectly displayed by Bacchylides and Pindar.[81] The first, according to the scholiast on Aristophanes' *Birds* (1536), mentioned Athena's intention to give immortality to Tydeus (Fr. 41), but we do not know whether this included the full account of the story. In a similar way, Pindar briefly refers to Athena bestowing immortality on Diomedes in his *Tenth Nemean* (7), which can be also plausibly ascribed to the Cyclic story of Tydeus' dying request to the goddess.[82] We may assume that the latter's cannibalism is here simply taken for granted, but it is nonetheless noticeably absent from Pindar's other allusions to the story of the Seven Against Thebes in his poems. This, as some scholars suspected, was most likely because of the violent and savage character of the episode, since Pindar would certainly have been aware of the Cyclic version of the myth.[83] Whether his omission was deliberate or not, the Theban poet certainly did not devote any space to Tydeus or Melanippus in his works. He did, on the other hand, write about Amphiaraus, who was in fact one of his favourite heroes. In the full version of the myth, shortly after killing Melanippus, Amphiaraus was swallowed by a chasm in the earth opened by Zeus' thunderbolt. Pindar mentions the story on three occasions, in his *Ninth* (24–7) and *Tenth Nemean* (8–9) and in his *Sixth Olympian* (14) odes. In these fragments he shows the highest regard for Amphiaraus, whom he describes as 'twice excellent, prophet and champion with the spear' (*Ol. VI* 17), demonstrating that the Argive seer was an important and influential figure in his time.[84] This is further confirmed by Amphiaraus' status as a 'saving hero' in Boeotia which is attested from the late-sixth century BC onwards (and briefly related by Herodotus), and his oracle at Oropos, in the northwest of Attica.[85] Interestingly, Pindar never mentions (or deliberately omits) the Archaic mutilation detail in relation to Amphiaraus, which would certainly have brought discredit on the Argive seer's reputation in Classical times. But, in fact, apart from Pherecydes, no other Classical or Hellenistic source does.

In Aeschylus' *Seven Against Thebes* (467 BC), our most extensive Classical source dealing with the myth, Amphiaraus is also described as an ideal seer and warrior, 'a virtuous, upright, courageous and pious man' (610) – well worthy of his heroic status in Greece and certainly not capable of maltreating the bodies of his enemies.[86] His mutilation of Melanippus is again not mentioned, and neither is Tydeus' subsequent cannibalism. Aeschylus must have known the myth well, as Gregory Hutchinson observed, but it is unlikely that he meant for 'the audience to remember it'.[87] It seems, therefore, that decapitating Melanippus had been completely erased from Amphiaraus' mythical CV from the early Classical period onwards.[88] This assumption is further supported by a fragment of an unknown play by Sophocles, which refers directly to Tydeus' cannibal feast, but importantly adds that it was the Aeolian hero who decapitated Melanippus, seemingly absolving Amphiaraus from any responsibility for the events:

> **Odysseus** (*to Diomedes*)   I shall say to you nothing dreadful, neither how you were driven out as an exile from your father's country, nor how Tydeus spilt the blood of a kinsman and settled in Argos as a guest, nor how before Thebes he made a cannibal feast off the son of Astacus, after cutting off his head.
>
> Soph. Fr. 799

The allusion to cannibalism and decapitation in Sophocles' play is striking;[89] Odysseus includes both details among the dreadful things committed by Diomedes' father, which matches Tydeus' reputation for extreme brutality depicted in the *Thebaid*, and also his character depiction in Aeschylus, who described him as 'mad, with lust for battle, like a snake shrieking at noon, belabours with abusive shouts ... like a fierce chariot-horse that snorts against the bit' (*Sept.* 380–94). Equally striking, however, is the fact that Sophocles puts the sole blame for the death and mutilation of Melanippus on Tydeus. The latter might have been his innovation but some scholars proposed that the storyline may have appeared already in the late-Archaic poems of Stesichorus or Bacchylides, who intentionally innovated on the events narrated in the *Thebaid*.[90] Although Sophocles' account is not reflected in the main Classical plays dealing with the myth of Seven Against Thebes (e.g. Euripides' *Suppliants* and *The Phoenician Women*), which avoid any depictions of the manner of Melanippus' death or the immediate fate of his body, the iconographical evidence confirms that from the Classical period onward Tydeus became the focal point of the story.[91]

The first piece of relevant evidence comes in the form of a pedimental relief from a temple at the Etruscan city of Pyrgi. The Pyrgi Columen Plaque is a large-scale Etruscan monument built around 470 BC.[92] The relief represents two scenes from the Seven Against Thebes myth: Tydeus biting Melanippus' head with Athena looking on; and Zeus striking Capaneus with a thunderbolt. The iconography is undoubtedly striking, but interestingly the detail of Melanippus' decapitation has been clearly omitted. The plaque depicts Tydeus attacking the head of his still-living adversary; Amphiaraus is not present at the scene at all, very much in accordance with the literary sources of the Classical period. The second example is a badly broken bell-krater now in New York, painted between 440 and 430 BC (Fig. 2). The vase illustrates Tydeus sitting at the foot of a tree and resting his head on his hand. At his feet lies the head of Melanippus. A young girl labelled *Athanasia* (immortality) approaches him, but Athena, whose owl hovers in front of the seated hero, draws her away from behind. Although the nature of the evidence here is more conjectural, the story of Tydeus' cannibalism has been recognized by the majority of scholars as the subject of the vase.[93] If the latter is accepted, the portrayal of Tydeus is strikingly different to the one depicted in the literary sources. In both Pherecydes' and Aeschylus' accounts he

Fig. 2 *Athena withdrawing Athanasia from Tydeus*. Red-figure terracotta bell-krater, unattributed, *c.* 440–430 BC. The Metropolitan Museum of Art, New York, No. 12.229.14a,b,f,g,i,j,k / Rogers Fund, 1912.

is described as a war-crazy madman, whereas on the krater he is presented as a gloomy, mournful and heavy-hearted individual. His act of cannibalism is, of course, not depicted, as the main focus of the scene is Athena's withdrawal of immortality, echoing the theme from Bacchylides and Pindar; while the act of cannibalism is undoubtedly taken for granted, the artist's depiction of the episode provides a fresh take on the story, encouraging the viewer to move beyond immediate moral repulsion and consider the motivation behind Tydeus' actions, depicted as a tragic and emotionally complex figure. Needless to say, Amphiaraus is nowhere to be seen; his dissociation from the entire episode is complete.

Apart from these two representations, the story of Melanippus' decapitation and Tydeus' death disappears from our sources for a long time. It comes back a few centuries later in Roman literature, first meriting a brief mention in Ovid's *Ibis* (427, 515), and then in Statius' *Thebaid* (8.751–6). The latter is our most detailed account of the incident (which later inspired Dante to include it in his *Divine Comedy*), but in Statius' account it is now Tydeus who asks his comrades for the head of Melanippus.[94] Finally, the story is briefly noted by Pausanias (9.18.1–2) – who, for the first time since Pherecydes (500 years earlier!), acknowledges the involvement of Amphiaraus, but does not mention his beheading of Melanippus; the aforementioned Apollodorus (3.6.8) – who, in an attempt to give a comprehensive account, likely combined the Archaic Cyclic version with later Classical sources; and finally, Libanius (*Progymnasmata* 9), who does not name the killer of Melanippus but includes Tydeus' cannibalism.

To sum up, the story of Amphiaraus' decapitation of Melanippus and Tydeus' cannibalism, which formed a part of the Theban Cycle and the Archaic myth of the Seven Against Thebes, was markedly modified by Classical authors. Amphiaraus' act of mutilation was related only by Pherecydes, whose main source was the Archaic *Thebaid*, and otherwise altogether erased from the ancient mythological tradition. Tydeus' cannibalism, linked to the story of Athena's withdrawal of immortality from the Aeolian hero and its conferral on Diomedes, was, on the other hand, initially preserved (and potentially reinterpreted) in the late-Archaic poems of Bacchylides and Pindar, later finding its way to an unknown play by Sophocles and the iconographical tradition of the Classical period. The few fifth-century BC representations of the gruesome scene, although limited in number, suggest that the story of Tydeus' cannibalism exerted some cultural significance throughout the early Classical era; it nonetheless fell out of favour by the end of the century, eventually reappearing with a renewed power in Roman literature.

Menelaus and the *Little Iliad*

The popularity of the *Iliad* and *Odyssey* in the Greek world meant that the most familiar examples of the mutilation of the dead, including Achilles' maltreatment of Hector, would have been associated with the Homeric poems. Such stories, judging by their relative prominence in the epics, were nonetheless spread over the entire saga of the Achaean invasion of Troy, referred to as the Trojan Cycle. One such example concerns the death of the Trojan prince Paris, known also as Alexander. Our oldest version of this myth comes from the Cyclic poem known as the *Little Iliad*. This late-seventh century BC poem, ascribed to a certain Lesches from Pyrrha or Mytilene, dealt with the events of the Trojan War after Achilles' death up to, and including, the sack of Troy.[95] According to Proclus' summary, after the initial story of Ajax's suicide, the *Little Iliad* described Odysseus' capture of Helenus, the son of the Trojan king Priam. Helenus, who possessed prophetic skills, predicts that the city of Troy could not be taken without the help of Philoctetes, the keeper of the bow of Heracles, whom the Achaeans left on the island of Lemnos on their way to Troy (because he was bitten by a snake). Diomedes, therefore, sails to Lemnos and brings Philoctetes back, who is then:[96]

> (...) healed by Machaon, and fights alone against Alexander and kills him. His body is mutilated by Menelaus, but then the Trojans recover it and give it burial.[97]
> *Little Iliad* Arg. 2c–d

Considering the popularity of the Cyclic poems, we may assume that the story must have been well-known in early Archaic tradition. The pattern of the mutilation here follows very closely many similar incidents in the *Iliad*: after a duel, Menelaus takes an opportunity to exact immediate vengeance on the body of Paris, who dishonoured him by abusing his hospitality and taking Helen away to Troy. As an ensuing battle develops over the body of Paris, the Trojans manage to recover it from the battlefield, and give him a fitting funeral later. The *Little Iliad*, therefore, provides us with a clear mutilation story which fits within the larger framework of the events of the Trojan War;[98] it is, however, the *only* ancient source that mentions Menelaus' mutilation of Paris.

The Classical authors took as their focus the story of Philoctetes, and especially the Achaean envoy sent to bring him back from Lemnos. Pindar, in his *First Pythian* ode, composed around 470 BC for Hieron of Syracuse, alludes to the myth, emphasizing Philoctetes' physical suffering caused by the snake-bite wound:[99]

> Just now, indeed,
> after the fashion of Philoctetes,
> he has gone on campaign, and even one who was proud
> found it necessary to fawn upon him as a friend.
> They tell that the godlike heroes came to fetch him
> from Lemnos, wasting from his wound,
> Poeas' archer son,
> who destroyed Priam's city and ended
> the Danaans' toils;
> he walked with flesh infirm, but it was the work of destiny.
>
> *Pyth.* I (50–55)

Philoctetes' involvement was further mentioned in a dithyramb by Pindar's contemporary Bacchylides.[100] According to the scholiast on Pindar's *Pythian* 1.52, the poet agrees with the story 'that the Greeks removed Philoctetes from Lemnos in accordance with a prophecy of Helenus, since it was fated that without Heracles' bow Troy would not be sacked' (Fr. 7 Campbell). The myth, or at least the part of it leading up to the duel between Philoctetes and Paris was, therefore, very much in circulation in the early Classical period.

The tragedies of the Classical period follow the poetic representations and concentrate on the events at Lemnos. Sophocles' *Philoctetes* (408 BC), the only surviving play dealing with the story, describes the attempts of Odysseus and Neoptolemus to bring Philoctetes back to Troy.[101] The latter is finally persuaded to go by Heracles, who miraculously appears at the end of the play, foretelling that Philoctetes will find release from his disease and then conquer Troy and slay Paris (1421–31). Unfortunately, Sophocles' other play, *Philoctetes at Troy*, which most likely dealt with the events following the hero's arrival at Troy, is now lost.[102] Both Aeschylus and Euripides also wrote plays on the same subject, and again both of them were centred on the events happening on the island of Lemnos (the choruses of both plays consist of men of Lemnos).[103] In short, it seems that the death of Paris was not a popular subject among Classical authors at all.

The episode on Lemnos was also featured in Classical art. The earliest appearances of Philoctetes are dated to the mid-fifth century BC and concern both his wounding by a snake on the way to Troy, and the Achaean embassy to Lemnos. Until the end of the fifth century BC, there are as many as ten representations of these stories in Greek art. Furthermore, the healing of Philoctetes in Troy is twice depicted in Etruscan art (both around 450 BC). There are, however, no surviving representations of Philoctetes fighting at Troy (or indeed killing Paris), further confirming that this part of the myth was less appealing to the Classical Greek audiences.[104]

The duel between Philoctetes and Paris reappears in a number of later sources. It was briefly mentioned by the Hellenistic poet Lycophron (*Alex.* 62ff. and 912ff.), and the Augustan grammarians, Parthenius (*Erotica Pathemata* 4) and Conon (N. 23 – Oinone). Our most detailed accounts, however, come from the fourth-century AD writers Quintus Smyrnaeus (*The Fall of Troy* 10.206–58) and Dictys Cretensis (4.19–20). Rather surprisingly, none of these texts mention Menelaus' mutilation of Paris, further suggesting that the *Little Iliad*'s version of events was completely erased from the Classical period onwards. Even Apollodorus, who as we saw in other fragments often followed early versions of mythical stories, simply states that Philoctetes 'killed Alexander with an arrow' (*Epit.* 5.8). His version of the story, nonetheless, reveals an important tradition regarding Paris' death, which may explain the absence of the *Little Iliad*'s mutilation detail in our sources.

According to Apollodorus, before abducting Helen, Paris was married to Oenone, the daughter of the River Kebren. His wife, instructed in the art of prophecy from Rhea, warned Paris not to go after Helen. After failing to convince him, she told him that he could seek her help if ever wounded, for she alone could heal him. And so when Paris:

> (...) had abducted Helen from Sparta and Troy was under attack, he was struck by an arrow that Philoctetes had shot from the bow of Heracles, and made his way back to Oenone on Mount Ida. But she was bitter at the wrong she had suffered and refused to cure him. So Alexander was carried off to Troy, where he died; and when Oenone had a change of heart and brought the remedies for his cure, she found him already dead and hanged herself.[105]
>
> Apollod 3.12.6

The story of Oenone and Paris completely omits the *Little Iliad*'s mutilation detail. Here, Paris is badly wounded by Philoctetes, only to die later when refused help by Oenone. The story could not, therefore, have been a part of the Epic Cycle (where Paris dies on the battlefield), and it similarly does not appear in Homer. Its origins can be traced to the early Classical period.[106] The earliest source for Oenone's attempt to cure Paris has sometimes been identified with a fragment of Bacchylides, restored by Lobel:

> ... from high above the comely wife of (Paris), Oen(one), hastened along her final (path).[107]
>
> Fr. 20 D

Lobel's restoration, as a number of scholars have pointed out, cannot be taken for granted, since the poem might refer to Althaea, the mother of Meleager.[108] The fragment, nonetheless, could have concerned Oenone's story which may, in turn, be confirmed by its presence in Hellanicus' mythographical work *Troica*. Hellanicus, who flourished in the latter half of the fifth century BC, was cited in the manchette of Parthenius' *Erotica Pathemata* (34) as a source for the story of Corythus (Fr. 29 Fowler).[109] According to it, Corythus, the son of Paris and Oenone, came to Troy and made trouble between Helen and Paris, who killed him in a jealous rage. This action, combined with Paris' initial choice of Helen over Oenone, further motivated the latter's refusal to heal Paris after his duel with Philoctetes. The origins of this story, again, are unclear, but its subject matter (nymph falling in love with a faithless mortal), combined with its supposed mention in Hellanicus has led modern scholars to assume that the myth may have been as old as the early Classical period.[110] The absence of the mutilation story of the *Little Iliad* among Classical authors may not be due to a lack of evidence or deliberate censorship, but might instead reflect the growing popularity of a new tradition which included Oenone (and excluded Menelaus' mutilation), eventually coming to dominate our sources, suppressing the earlier Cyclic version.[111]

To sum up, despite the overwhelming lack of evidence concerning the myth of Paris' death in Classical tradition, it seems that the early Archaic version described in the *Little Iliad* was replaced, never to return, at some point during the Classical period. The tragic love-story of Paris and Oenone, which could no longer accommodate Menelaus' mutilation of the Trojan prince, took its place and became gradually dominant in later mythological tradition. Our earliest literary sources reflecting this process are Hellanicus, and potentially Bacchylides, placing it in the first half of the fifth century BC, together with the examples of Eurystheus and Amphiaraus. The myth, therefore, provides us with another example of an Archaic story involving war mutilation being reinterpreted and suppressed in the early Classical period.[112]

Achilles and Hector

While tracing the development of mutilation stories in early Greek mythology has been possible and indeed very revealing – despite the often-fragmentary nature of the evidence – the afterlife of the mutilation episodes in the *Iliad* is surprisingly harder to follow.[113] The monumental form of the Homeric poems became highly canonical in Greece, most likely from the last decades of the sixth century BC onward, which in turn meant that most writers were reluctant to engage with the story again, preferring instead to focus on the events beyond the *Iliad* and *Odyssey*, or other stories of the Epic Cycle.[114] Consequently, the mutilation episodes involving Hippolochos, Koön, Imbrios and Ilioneus are not treated by any artist or playwright of the Classical or later periods.[115] The story of Achilles' maltreatment of Hector, however, forming a central part of the poem's events, did occasionally feature in other artistic genres, confirming the general pattern which we witnessed in other cases of mythological mutilation.

The scene of Achilles dragging the body of Hector behind his chariot appears first in the Athenian black-figure art, with the earliest surviving representations dated to *c.* 540 BC. In her article on the subject, Emily Vermeule counted up to 18 clear depictions of the episode, which must have provided a significant source of inspiration for the artists of the latter half of the sixth century BC.[116] More importantly, however, the theme suddenly disappears from Greek art towards the end of the Archaic period, with no surviving representations in red-figure. This disappearance, although not uncommon in the Greek art of the period, is still striking and may point to a different attitude of the Athenians of the early Classical era.

The Athenian dramatists of the fifth century BC, who as we saw throughout this chapter had often been at the forefront of editorial activity in the realm of the mythological past, did not engage with the episode of Hector's mutilation at any substantial length. Aeschylus may or may not have covered the story in his now-lost Achilles' trilogy (*Myrmidones, Nereides, Phryges*), but the surviving fragments are too scanty to reconstruct detailed plots of the plays.[117] The only mention of Hector's mutilation in Athenian drama, in fact, comes from Sophocles' play *Ajax*, where Teucer, addressing the corpse of Ajax, reveals a slightly different tradition concerning Hector's death:

> **Teucer** Consider, I beg you, the fates of two mortals! Hector was lashed to the chariot rail with the belt that this man had given him and mangled till he breathed out his life; and this man, who had this gift from him, fell dead, perishing by this weapon.
>
> *Aj.* 1028–33

In this version, which Gantz suspected was a 'Sophoklean invention', Hector is still dragged by Achilles behind his chariot, but this time the latter uses a belt that Hector received from Ajax.[118] In addition, it is clear that Hector was dragged to death, which indicates that Achilles' revenge was not, at least in the initial stages, performed on Hector's dead body. And while such a small change to the wider tradition of Achilles' mutilation of Hector may appear insignificant, it might provide us with an early indication of the disbelief experienced by the Classical Athenians regarding Achilles' actions, who viewed any maltreatment of the dead as morally repugnant and shameful.[119]

The most explicit expression of moral indignation at Achilles' mutilation of Hector was supplied by Plato, who as part of his discussion on the education system of the ideal city-state, has Socrates suggesting that a number of Homeric stories should be eliminated from the curriculum, being unsuitable for the citizens of a just city:

> Then again there is the dragging of Hector around the grave mound of Patroclus and the slaughter of the captives at the pyre: we shall say that none of these stories is true and we shall not allow our people to believe that Achilles, son of a goddess and Peleus, the most temperate of men and grandson of Zeus, and brought up under the eye of the most wise Chiron, was so fully distraught as to have within him two opposing afflictions: meanness with his greed for possessions, and, on the other hand, contempt for gods and men.
>
> *Resp.* 3.391b–c

Plato's condemnation of the Homeric episode is perhaps most indicative of the new attitude of the Athenians towards the proper treatment of the war dead.[120] The process of censorship and the reinterpretation of traditional mythological stories which he envisioned for his ideal city-state was, as we saw throughout this chapter, already underway in Classical Athens, as the city's dramatists, poets and artists constantly engaged with the past in order to modify the often well-known in line with the beliefs, norms and ideals of their own time.

One area affected by this process was the mythical stories depicting the mutilation of the war dead, which underwent a major change from Archaic to Classical times. The Archaic mythical episodes that included maltreating the dead were clearly objectionable to later audiences, which often led Classical Athenian authors to suppress or modify the traditional versions of these myths. This change of attitudes had most likely taken place sometime in the first half of the fifth century BC, during which some authors, with a more traditional, Archaic approach (Pherecydes) could still mention the mutilation stories; others (Aeschylus, Pindar) could decide deliberately to suppress and/or reinterpret them. The new versions of the myths were, in turn, fully established by the second half of the fifth century BC, being expressed most clearly in the plays of Sophocles and Euripides. Athenian tragedy, therefore, as the most important medium of myth in the Classical period, seems to have been at the forefront of this process.[121]

The Classical tragedians were undoubtedly aware of the existence of mutilation episodes in the earlier mythological tradition, since they often based their plots on the Epic Cycle stories. The broad tradition of the Epic Cycle provided an enormously rich narrative vein for the Classical authors to use and experiment with. And so Sophocles, according to Athenaeus, 'took great pleasure in the Epic Cycle and composed whole dramas in which he followed the Cycle's version of myths' (277 C).[122] In a similar fashion, Aristotle in his *Poetics* states that the Cyclic poems *Cypria* and *Little Iliad* supplied the plots for more than eight tragedies, including *Philoctetes*, *Sack of Troy*, and *Trojan Women* (1459a37–1459b7).[123] The tragedians' familiarity with the mythical mutilations depicted throughout the Epic Cycle was, therefore, undeniable, as was their decision to omit or re-interpret these episodes to suit the expectations of their audiences.

The disappearance of the mythical traditions of Eurystheus' decapitation or Menelaus' mutilation of Paris, coupled with the increased prominence given to the story of the burial of the fallen Argives in the Seven Against Thebes, hints at the changing attitudes and ideals of the Athenians in the early Classical period. And while this ideological change occurred gradually and over a long period of time, the south frieze of the temple of Athena Nike stands as a monument to the shift in mentality on the treatment of the war dead.

Greeks vs Barbarians – The Persian Wars

The south frieze of Athena Nike broke with other images in the panel by depicting a story from the recent past. The frieze, now in the British Museum, portrays a fierce battle between the Athenians and Persians, commonly associated with either Marathon or Plataea. Among the many fallen warriors we find four dead Persians, enfolded in their native garments, and a few more defeated Persians. Interestingly, there are no casualties on the Greek side, as the gloriously naked Athenians heroically battle and defeat their enemies.[124] Even more strikingly, however, the Persians pay no attention to their dead comrades, making no attempts to recover their bodies. Compared to the other friezes on the Athena Nike temple, and in particular the west frieze which depicted the Athenian rescue of the Argive dead from Thebes, the difference between Persian and Athenian attitudes towards the war dead could not be any more profound. As Evelyn Harrison pointed out, the message behind the frieze is very clear: 'Hellenes honor their dead, barbarians do not. Hellenes who do not honor their dead are no better than barbarians'.[125] As such, the friezes provided a powerful symbolic

Fig. 3 *Athenians fighting the Persians*. South frieze (part), Temple of Athena Nike on the Athenian Akropolis, plaster cast. Museum of Classical Archaeology, Cambridge, No. 158 (Original: The British Museum, London, No. 1816,0610.159).

response to the events of Delium in 424 BC, condemning the 'barbaric' acts of the Thebans who forbade the retrieval of the fallen Athenians for seventeen days. At the same time, however, the juxtaposition of the Hellenic norms and customs with the 'barbaric' ways of the Persian invaders hints at the potential origins of Athenian, and indeed wider Greek, ideology and self-image, which placed a strong emphasis on the proper and respectful treatment of the war dead.

The mythological evidence discussed in this chapter suggests that the first signs of a new attitude concerning the war dead occurred in the first decades of the fifth century BC. The editorial activities of Pindar, who began the process of rewriting the mutilation stories of the mythological past, coupled with Aeschylus' *Eleusinians*, arguably the first written work to make a strong statement about the inherent righteousness of the custom of *anairesis*, provide the first strong indications of a marked change in the artistic evidence of the 470s BC. Since the development of such new cultural ideals would not have happened overnight and must have been spurred on by a significant event, we should suspect that the experience of the Persian Wars played a crucial part in this process. The Persian Wars were a defining event for Greek warfare and the Greek world in general, one which has been widely acknowledged by modern scholars as instrumental in the creation of a new identity, both cultural and military, defined in extreme opposition to the 'otherness' of the Persian enemy.[126] A new ideology which championed the proper respect and treatment of the war dead would have been a small but nonetheless important part of that identity, reflecting the egalitarian ideals of Classical Greek armies, and standing in a symbolic contrast to the 'barbaric' customs of Persian mutilation and the denial of burial.[127]

The new cultural ideal which arose in opposition to the Persian mistreatment of the dead is perhaps best illustrated by an anecdote from Herodotus, who in his work often highlighted the lack of regard for the dead displayed by the non-Greek people he discussed.[128] According to his account, following the Greek victory over the Persians at Plataea, Lampon, one of the leading men of Aegina, suggested that the Spartan general Pausanias should decapitate the corpse of Mardonius in revenge for the latter's similar treatment of Pausanias' uncle Leonidas (9.78). Pausanias categorically refused, on the grounds that such practices 'befit barbarians rather than Greeks, and even in them we find it loathsome' (9.79). The mere fact, however, that Lampon suggested the idea of mutilating an enemy's corpse in the first place indicates that such practices could still have been regarded by some as a viable way of exacting revenge, as was once the norm in the mythological stories of the Trojan and Theban wars.[129] Within a few decades the latter were erased, suppressed and abandoned by Classical Athenian dramatists, artists and orators, in favour of the new ethical standards which became the very essence of Greek virtue and moral superiority.

Finally, the formal custom regarding war dead retrieval must have taken its form soon after the Persian Wars, or perhaps even *during* the Persian Wars. The famous and highly controversial oath reputedly sworn by the Greeks on the eve of the battle of Plataea in 479 BC does include a vow to bury the dead, immediately after the vow to fight bravely and loyally:

> [23] I shall fight while I live, and I shall not put life before being free, and I shall not desert the taxiarch nor the enomotarch, neither while they live nor when they are dead, and I shall not depart unless the leaders lead the way, and I shall do whatever the generals command, and I shall bury in the same place the dead of those who were allied, and I shall leave no one unburied.[130]

The oath, which might be a later invention, has created a lot of controversy among scholars, but there is no reason to deny the possibility that the mention of the burial of the dead could hint at an actual agreement that the Greek forces established before the battle, which later became an established, Panhellenic procedure.[131] The rules regarding the retrieval of the war dead, then – essential to the practice of Classical Greek warfare – may have begun as a pre-battle oath. Fifty years later, they came to be widely known as the 'immemorial' laws of all Greece, as the Athenian authors tampered with and reinterpreted their mythological past, presenting themselves as the ancestral champions and protectors of age-old Hellenic customs. These roles, adopted in order to justify Athenian hegemony and political leadership in the Greek world of the fifth century BC, were most powerfully illustrated by Theseus' actions in Thebes, sheltering the Heraclidae from Eurystheus, and defeating the 'barbaric' ways of the Persians, all of which they proudly depicted in the frieze programme of the Athena Nike temple.

*

The mythological traditions of the Homeric poems and the wider Epic Cycle, as this and the previous chapter have shown, provided the Athenians with powerful cultural and ideological models to perceive, think about and question the status of the war dead in the *polis*. As such, they can be used as valuable sources to explore the attitudes and beliefs surrounding the treatment of war casualties, which underwent a significant change towards the end of the Archaic period. Considering the paradigmatic role played by myths in Athens and Greece, we should suspect that the effects of this cultural shift, which took on a Panhellenic significance after the experience of the Persian Wars, were far-reaching and left a mark not only on the artistic evidence which dealt with the city's mythological past, but also on the actual norms and practices accompanying the retrieval, disposal and commemoration of the war dead in Athens.[132] The investigation of the latter, therefore, forms the central subject of the second part of this book.

Part Two

3

The War Dead in the Early Greek Iconographic Tradition

Following the naval victory at Arginusae against the Spartans in 406 BC, the Athenian generals were confronted with a difficult decision: either to capitalize on their success and sail with all speed to besiege Mytilene, or to retrieve the fallen, 'since the Athenians are incensed at those who allow the dead to go unburied' (Diod. Sic. 13.100). In the event, they were able to do neither. The sudden outbreak of a storm forced them to put in at Arginusae. Upon their return to Athens, Diodorus tells us (13.100–2), the victorious generals faced the wrath of the community, outraged that they had not recovered the corpses of their fellow citizens who sacrificed their lives on behalf of their country. After a public trial, the generals were duly condemned to death and all of their property was confiscated, even though they had won 'the greatest naval battle that had ever taken place of Greeks against Greeks' (13.102).[1]

The story recounted by Diodorus provides clear testimony of the special status granted to the war dead in Classical Athens. Their retrieval, normally guaranteed under the Panhellenic convention of *anairesis*, was of paramount importance.[2] It is no surprise, therefore, that failure to follow such procedures was very rare and always presented as an indication of calamity and utter moral collapse, as was the case during the disastrous Athenian retreat from Syracuse in 413 BC (Thuc. 7.75). Following every battle, it was the duty of the general to obtain a truce for the retrieval of the dead, the request of which depended on the outcome of the battle. Once the truce was agreed, the casualties would be picked up, identified, assigned by tribe, cremated and finally transported back to Athens. Despite the logistical difficulties involved in this process, perhaps most strongly apparent after naval battles like the one above, the procedure was said to form an integral part of the city's 'ancestral custom' (*patrios nomos*) – the annual public funeral for the war dead.[3] The latter, described in some detail by Thucydides (2.34), consisted of a funeral procession and oration, followed by a collective burial in the 'most beautiful quarter' of the city in Kerameikos, with one coffin for each tribe, and the common grave surmounted by a casualty list inscribed with the names of the fallen.[4] The whole procedure was intended to be inherently egalitarian and thus emblematic of Athenian democracy, as all who sacrificed their lives for the *polis* were equally celebrated and glorified by the citizens. The *patrios nomos* was the symbol of Classical Athens, even though, as Nicole Loraux demonstrated in her influential study of the funeral oration, the discourse it employed was often structured and built upon the elite ideals of the Archaic period.[5]

The presence of the war dead in Classical Athens, both physical and symbolic, had a profound impact on its citizens. Various forms of commemoration, verbal (funeral oration) and visual (public ceremony and graves), provided an ever-present reminder of the sacrifices made on behalf of the city, endowing casualties of war with a special, heroic status in the political and cultural spheres of the *polis*. But the origins of the *patrios nomos* in Athens are paradoxically rather unclear, and have been debated by scholars ever since antiquity. Some place them as early as the legislation of Solon; others look towards Cleisthenes' democratic reforms, while some assign them to the years following the Persian Wars and the figures of Cimon or Ephialtes.[6] While the controversy is still very much ongoing (and may never be definitively resolved), the continuing difficulties in tracing the beginnings of the public funeral in Athens stem from, and emphasize, our limited knowledge of the practices surrounding the burial of the war dead in the Archaic period. Despite the overwhelming presence of the war dead in Classical Athens, the war dead of Archaic Athens are often overlooked.

It has been commonly assumed that the Athenian war dead of the Archaic period were normally buried in a *polyandrion* on the battlefield.[7] With the exception of Classical Athens, according to a number of scholars, such custom dominated in Greek warfare and was 'presumed to reach back to the dark centuries before 600 BC'.[8] But there are significant problems with this argument, especially when compared to the evidence that survives for early war burials in Athens and wider Greece. These problems are essentially of a twofold nature: a) there are at present no surviving remains of any Athenian *polyandria* before the reforms of Cleisthenes, and very limited evidence for *polyandrion* burials in the wider Hellenic world;[9] b) the practice of mass battlefield burial stands in a radical opposition both to the 'hierarchical' ideals depicted in the Homeric epics, and the more egalitarian Classical custom of *patrios nomos*, which (in spite of their differences) were built on the tradition of bringing the ashes of the dead back home. The purpose of the second part of this book will be, therefore, to revisit the limited evidence for early Athenian war dead and uncover the roots of

Classical *patrios nomos*. Echoes of the Archaic traditions of the elites, it will be shown, went far beyond the funeral oration. Although trends in iconography and burial archaeology indicate that the treatment of the war dead underwent major changes between the Archaic and Classical periods, in some sense the elite ideals of the Archaic period were merely repackaged to suit the sensibilities of a Classical audience. But in the broader shift in ideology and practice, as this and the next two chapters demonstrate, it builds upon the arguments made earlier in this book. As we will see, for example, just as mutilation stories were gradually removed from the mythological tradition, so too the popularity of images of fighting over the fallen faded over time.

Any study of Archaic Athenian, or indeed Greek, burials has traditionally relied, to a greater or lesser extent, on the evidence preserved in the Homeric epics. The *Iliad* and the *Odyssey*, as we saw in Chapter 1, provide a wealth of information concerning early Greek burial practices, including the customs and expectations surrounding the recovery and treatment of the war dead. The precise relation of the latter – which form a consistent and coherent part of the Homeric fighting scenes – to the actual realities of combat in early Greece continues to be a matter of some debate. In what follows I aim to concentrate on only one aspect of Homeric warfare most relevant to our study: namely the practice of *Leichenkämpfe*, fighting to retrieve the bodies of the most prominent of the dead while battle is still in progress. The motif, essential throughout the combat episodes of the *Iliad*, and reflective of the social and political ideals championed in the poems, stood in fundamental opposition to the collective retrieval of all fallen warriors alike after the end of battle that was the Classical Greek norm, and to the egalitarian collective burial of the war dead that was established by the Athenian custom of *patrios nomos*. It is perhaps rather surprising then that the Homeric practice is clearly reflected in Archaic Athenian depictions of war, providing one of the leading combat themes in Attic black-figure vases, to which we now must turn our attention.

Archaic iconography of war

Although the black-figure technique of vase painting was first invented in Corinth around 700 BC, its revolutionary effect on Greek art was fully exploited – artistically and commercially – by Athenian painters in the course of the sixth century BC, by the end of which Athens monopolized the pottery markets of the Greek world. The visual imagery of Attic black- and early red-figure pottery is indisputably among our richest sources for Archaic Athens.[10] Its historical significance lies predominantly in the multifarious nature of scenes depicted on the vases; the latter, distributed across a variety of pot shapes serving different functions, illustrated a range of mythological episodes, including those containing famous heroes, monsters and gods, but also images relating to everyday life, such as drinking parties, athletics, religious ceremonies or war. In addition, the continuous production of large quantities of Athenian black- and red-figure pots suggests that they stood at the forefront of popular cultural discourses of the day, being affordable and disseminated broadly across the social strata of the *polis*. Since the preferences of the vase consumers, who looked for both function and imagery in their purchases, influenced the artistic choices of the manufacturers, the iconography of Attic pots provides us with a unique gateway to the cultural, social and religious worlds of Archaic Athens.

The extraordinary popularity and success of Athenian pottery throughout the Greek world is best reflected by the number of surviving pots, which according to the Beazley Archive, amounts to tens of thousands for the Archaic period alone. Apart from Athens and Attica, the vases have been found in large quantities in mainland Greece and the Aegean, as well as Sicily, north Africa and, most importantly, Etruria; such wide geographical spread of Attic pottery across the Mediterranean indicates the extensive appeal and demand for the work of Athenian artists.[11] The resulting wealth of historical material available to us, however, does not come without its drawbacks. For instance, despite the large number of pottery finds, it has been estimated that the surviving evidence contains a meagre quarter of 1 per cent of all pots manufactured by the Greeks; in other words, only one in four hundred vases survive.[12] This means, in theory, that any generalizing theories about the uniqueness, or indeed popularity, of certain scenes depicted on pottery will to some extent always remain speculative, even more so since black- and red-figure vases were not mass produced but individually made, occasionally as part of specific commissions. Furthermore, the prominence of Attic vases outside of mainland Greece introduces the question of foreign markets and their impact on the production of painted pottery in Athens. Most of the best preserved examples of Athenian pots, and indeed many of the ones which we will discuss in this chapter, come from Etruria, which has led some scholars to posit that their iconography does not necessarily represent messages relevant only to Athenian society; in some cases the images specifically catered to other markets.[13]

While these issues, along with the more obvious challenges of precise identification of the scenes depicted on pottery, should be borne in mind by anyone studying the iconography of Athenian black- and red-figure vases, the potential rewards of engaging with such a broad evidence base are too great to be passed over. Considering that most of our historical sources for ancient Athens (and the ancient world in general), tends be either lacunose or biased by the agendas of their authors, Attic pottery, when carefully approached, offers us an opportunity not only to understand the dominant cultural discourses current in Archaic Athens, but also how they developed and changed over time.[14] Even though the amount of pottery available to us falls well short of what the manufacturers produced, it still provides a working sample of the whole; the artists' focus on certain themes and episodes, repeated on pots found in the contexts of domestic, religious and public use, can be particularly rewarding, indicating wider trends and interests of the consumers. And while the latter did not have to be limited to Athens and the Athenians alone, it seems plausible to assume that such imagery could have been and was sufficiently attractive for buyers in Etruria and elsewhere. As Robin Osborne argued in his recent book, the weak correlation between vase images and the markets in the Mediterranean indicates that Athenian potters 'did not feel the need to create new iconographies in order to satisfy ... specific markets'; the Etruscans were no doubt frequently well-acquainted with the iconographic themes of Attic vases, but would often have bought them regardless of whether what was painted on them 'observed their particular local preferences or reflected a world with which they were familiar'.[15] The different provenances of pots can certainly play a role, but there is no reason to doubt that in most cases Athenian painters catered first to the Athenians, especially in iconography which matches artistic records preserved in other Attic media, such as gravestones or temple reliefs. Scenes of war and combat dominant in black-figure art are one example of this, providing us with an Athenian perspective on the subject, in turn appreciated and potentially shared by the Etruscans and other non-Athenian consumers.[16]

Shifting our focus to the early Greek depictions of combat, nonetheless, brings with it a plethora of different problems; the field of Archaic war iconography is a minefield of scholarly controversies.[17] Since the publication of Hilda Lorimer's influential article in the late 1940s, the prevailing assumption among scholars has been that the majority of early vase portrayals of battle showed either 'archaic' or 'heroic' scenes: some images were deliberately meant to recreate the customs and habits of the past ('archaising'); others were based solely on epic poetry and exploits of its heroes.[18] The 'archaic' and 'heroic' depictions of war were accordingly distinguished by a number of 'non-historical' elements, supposedly used by early artists to label their combat scenes; these included, for instance, the presence of Boeotian shields, chariots, archers, nudity of warriors, addition of mythological names or depictions of duels between individual warriors. Such an interpretation stemmed predominantly from the scholarly assumption that battles in Archaic Greece were fought by heavy-armed hoplites arranged in close phalanx formations and only the vase images illustrating these formations, such as the famous Chigi olpe, could be taken to correspond to the reality of Archaic warfare.[19] Any vases depicting combat in duels, which formed one of the favourite subjects of early Greek painters, were accordingly discarded as anachronistic idealizations of aristocratic warfare designed to refer back to the Homeric epics, bearing no resemblance to the actual realities of combat and having consequently little value for the study of Archaic practices of war. As a result, the study of Archaic iconography of war became an exercise in identifying 'archaisms' and/or items 'inconsistent with hoplite equipment' and the phalanx formation, as recently remarked by Fernando Echeverria.[20]

Despite the dominance of the 'myth vs reality' model in studies of early Greek war iconography, questions began to be raised about its simplistic categorization and *ad hoc* dismissal of a vast number of painted vases based on their supposed unrealism. These came first from the art historians, who challenged the scholarly division between scenes of myth and scenes of everyday life, emphasizing the interrelationship between the two in ancient Greek culture and thought. Modern attempts to separate and categorize these, as Mary Beard argued, crudely oversimplify vase images, which meaning usually depends 'on the subtle interplay of both registers: myth and "real life". We are not just dealing with a figure who is *either* Hector *or* an Athenian hoplite; we are dealing with a figure who can be and is *both*'.[21] Early scenes of combat, focused predominantly on individual actions, should be therefore seen as artistic and ideological constructions of the Archaic *polis*, expressing the ideals of the time and imbued, as François Lissarrague demonstrated in his influential study of warriors in Athenian art, with a strong social and political meaning.[22] According to Tonio Hölscher, it is consequently misleading to ask whether the 'heroic' combat scenes of Archaic art are faithful evidence of contemporary warfare:

> The well-known answer that they present an idealizing stylization of warfare in terms of Homeric concepts of heroic valour does not address how such representations were compatible with the reality of contemporary wars. Since these depictions *must be* evidence of how fighting was actually conceived and also at some level how it was experienced, we should rather ask *how* these representations relate to military practice and *how* we should explain the fact that fighting in war was experienced in this form.[23]

One answer to such questions was that the dominance of duels among early vase depictions, was deliberately meant to reflect the personal experience of war and fighting, emphasizing the warrior's loneliness.[24] At the most basic level, any Greek battle, regardless of formation, consisted of encounters between individual warriors. The use of the Corinthian helmet, as Hölscher himself suggested, heightened the experience of isolation, severely limiting its wearer's hearing and vision so that nothing beyond the one-on-one encounter with the enemy would be perceived. 'This was surely', as he concluded, 'a dominant experience of early Greek warfare – in spite of the conceptual coherence of the phalanx'.[25] The Archaic artistic illustrations of single duels should be accordingly interpreted as 'neither correct nor incorrect versions of military reality', but treated instead, together with the rare depictions of mass combat in phalanx-like formations, as 'complementary views of the same reality' and 'legitimate representations of real experiences'.[26]

At the same time as the 'constructionist' approach of art historians offered a way to look beyond the supposed 'archaisms' of early combat scenes, a different approach was pioneered by military historians working on Archaic warfare. Scholars like Peter Krentz and Hans van Wees challenged the orthodox theories of early Greek warfare, positing that Archaic battles were not, for the most part, fought in phalanx formations. Instead, early Greek armies operated in relatively open and fluid formations, reminiscent of those described in the *Iliad*. As a result, the small-group clashes and duels depicted in early iconography were, they argued, stylized but not wholly unrealistic close-ups of combat, essential to our understanding of the Archaic practice of war.[27] Accordingly, the overwhelming prevalence of the latter in early Greek art was not without its basis in contemporary war practices, but rather offers artistic reflections of actual modes of fighting. This new approach, in turn, held the potential to bring back iconographic evidence to studies of Greek warfare and, as Echeverria noted, liberated 'a vast pool of information from the chains of the phalanx, making it accessible for historical interpretation on the light of the new approaches to Greek warfare'.[28] Taking a similar position, Echeverria further problematised the previous interpretations of 'heroic' elements on Greek vases, such as the Boeotian shields, archers and nudity, also noting that the overwhelming majority of warriors tend to be anonymous, with no visual hints of their identity. This, as he proposed, allowed ancient audiences to engage with the images on a personal level: 'Sharing largely the same weapons and fighting styles, it was always possible for the viewer to identify with the figures depicted, and to equate the warlike deeds in the scenes, real or imaginary, with their own.'[29]

The notion that combat scenes depicted on pots bore no relation to the contemporary experience of war and instead reflected – almost exclusively – previous modes of 'heroic' fighting preserved in epic songs can no longer stand; even more so when we consider that many of the users of such vases would have had direct experience of war.[30] 'Merely to spell out the possibility', as Osborne remarked, that men serving in Archaic armies would have reflected 'only on the stories they had been told and never on the military life they had led . . . is to spell out its grossly improbable nature'.[31] But while we should move beyond the previous scholarly biases concerning the phalanx and the issues of 'myth vs reality' in iconographic representations of war, it is clear that a number of Athenian vases did depict combat scenes featuring mythical creatures, gods, or fantastic episodes drawn for the epic songs. These, of course, may have still contained valuable information about contemporary ideals of combat, but studies of individual scenes, rewarding as they are, can contribute only so much to any broader understanding of what the Greeks valued and wanted to see. A quantitative approach to vase imagery, on the other hand, increasingly adopted in studies of Greek iconography, can be equally revealing on the level of wider patterns and schemes of war representations.[32] Putting figures on pots, in addition, tells us stories of change in subject matter; these, as we saw in the last chapter, often reflect other ideological and cultural shifts – the disappearance of scenes of Achilles maltreating the body of Hector in red-figure vases being one example. Choosing a defined theme, such as fighting over corpses or retrieving fallen warriors from the battlefield, and tracing its artistic representations over time, should therefore allow us to access an important cultural discourse on the war dead, which pre-dates the Classical institution of *patrios nomos*. As it happens, both themes were much favoured by black-figure artists and their continuous presence in early iconography holds the potential to give us a significant insight into the actual experience and practice of Archaic combat.

The war dead in Archaic Athenian art

The earliest depictions of warriors retrieving the dead from the battlefield appear in Geometric art towards the end of the eighth century BC. Gudrun Ahlberg-Cornell identified three representations of an individual warrior carrying over his shoulder the body of a dead comrade.[33] The subject of these early images has been commonly associated with the famous episode of Ajax rescuing the dead Achilles as recounted in the Epic Cycle poem *Aethiopis*. This interpretation is based on compositional similarities to the later black-figure depictions inscribed with the names of the Achaean heroes, particularly the François vase painted by Kleitias. In addition, the enormous size of the fallen warrior, whose hands and feet almost reach the ground, may also be seen as a deliberate mark to emphasize the godlike stature of Achilles by the Geometric artists. Rather importantly, however, none of the earliest representations of the scene identifies the protagonists, and in most cases the fallen warrior appears to be nude.[34] Other mythical candidates for the scene are difficult to find, although the appearance of Ajax and a certain Aristodamos in a series of sixth-century BC shield bands from Olympia indicates that the composition was not exclusive to Ajax and Achilles.[35] Interestingly, two of the scene's earliest representations are impressions from a single mould; one is on an East Greek amphora found in Ischia, the other on a terracotta plaque from the Samian Heraion. This may imply that similar imagery of warriors retrieving the dead had a bigger presence in the Geometric era. The composition subsequently continues throughout the Greek art of the seventh century BC, with four representations in Ahlberg-Cornell's catalogue of the Orientalizing period, becoming extremely popular, as we will see, in Attic black-figure.[36]

Artistic representation of duels over a fallen warrior begins a little later on Protoattic and Protocorinthian pottery of the seventh century BC.[37] The scenes most commonly depict a general melee, which consists of pairs of opposing warriors in hoplite equipment, of whom some may fight over the body of a dead or wounded man.[38] The duelling warriors are occasionally accompanied by comrades, who either try to rescue the fallen fighter or to despoil the enemy corpse. Such a scene, familiar from the fighting sequences in the *Iliad*, is represented on a Protocorinthian aryballos from Louvre attributed to the Chigi group, where one warrior attempts to snatch the fallen warrior's helmet (or indeed to drag his body away in order to plunder at leisure); while the comrade of the slain holds on to his leg and tries to pull him back.[39] The prestige and glory involved in stripping the armour of the slain foe is clearly conveyed in these early representations, as the resolve to rescue the fallen is evenly matched by the attacker's desire to despoil the body, in spite of the risks involved.

Lorimer, who collected and studied all early artistic representations of duels over a fallen warrior, dismissed their historical relevance, asserting that the images are based on an epic commonplace, and could hardly have been a feature of hoplite tactics and fighting.[40] Van Wees, on the other hand, argued that early Corinthian depictions of fighting over the dead and wounded, reminiscent of Homeric warfare, indicate the actual combat practices of the seventh century

BC.⁴¹ Any similarities between artistic images and the *Iliad* stem, according to him, from the fact that 'real-life battles continued to be fought under essentially the same conditions, which accommodated the whole range of 'duelling', small-group combat, and occasional massed confrontations'.⁴² The continuous presence of a variety of fighting modes in Greek art since the Geometric period appears to support Van Wees' interpretation; among the scenes, the depictions of fights over the fallen constituted a significant part of the early artists' repertoire. But the full prominence of the latter in Archaic art becomes unmistakably clear in the sixth century BC during the floruit of the black-figure technique; as more combat imagery survives, the portrayals of fighting over and rescuing the dead substantially multiply.

The Beazley Archive at Oxford records no fewer than 260 representations of fighting over the fallen in late Archaic Athenian art (Table 1).⁴³ The majority of them fall within the 550 to 500 BC period, which also shows the highest number of all combat depictions in the Archive records. The sheer quantity of these scenes indicates the exceptional popularity of the subject of duelling over the dead, which, as Susanne Muth noted, dominates all combat imagery of the second half of the sixth century BC.⁴⁴ An additional survey of the pot shapes indicates that amphoras were heavily preferred for these representations (65 per cent), followed by lekythoi (10 per cent) and hydriai (10 per cent).⁴⁵

Most representations consist of a single duel between warriors over the dead, an example of which is provided by a black-figure amphora from New York (Fig. 4). The body of the fallen is usually placed in the centre of the composition, flanked on both sides by individual, and most often unidentifiable, heavy-armed warriors engaged in a duel; no other combatants are present, though spectators on either side, consisting of women, old men, and/or youths are often depicted.⁴⁶ The addition of the latter may have further highlighted the individual aspect of

Table 1 Images of fighting over the fallen in the online Beazley Archive

Date Range	600–550	575–525	550–500	525–475	500–450	475–425	450–400
Number of records	3	36	151	65	5	0	0
Number of all combat depictions	51	402	901	867	217	74	45
Number of all archive records	1,899	5,456	13,138	18,748	13,043	12,464	8,435

Fig. 4 Black-figure amphora, attributed to the Lysippides Painter, found in Vulci (Etruria), *c.* 520–510 BC. The Metropolitan Museum of Art, New York, No. 58.32 / Gift of Colonel and Mrs Lewis Landes, 1958.

early battles, emphasizing the importance of retrieving the fallen from the perspective of their absent families.[47] This message is especially clear on vases that depict, on one side, the scene of a warrior's departure from his household – also very popular in the sixth century BC – and the fight over a corpse on the other.[48]

Depictions of fighting over the dead within the melee are also fairly popular and, unlike in the Protocorinthian and Protoattic art, usually form the central subject of the scene. Likewise, combat in small groups is also common, as is collective defending of the fallen, with some warriors dragging the body to safety, and others chasing away the enemies.[49] Among the most famous examples of fights involving multiple warriors is the Exekias cup from Munich (Figs 5 and 6). Depicted on the exterior of the latter under the handles are two battle snapshots featuring a confrontation between groups of three hoplites each struggling for possession of a dead warrior separating them. No inscriptions identifying any of the figures are included; instead, the main focus of the scenes

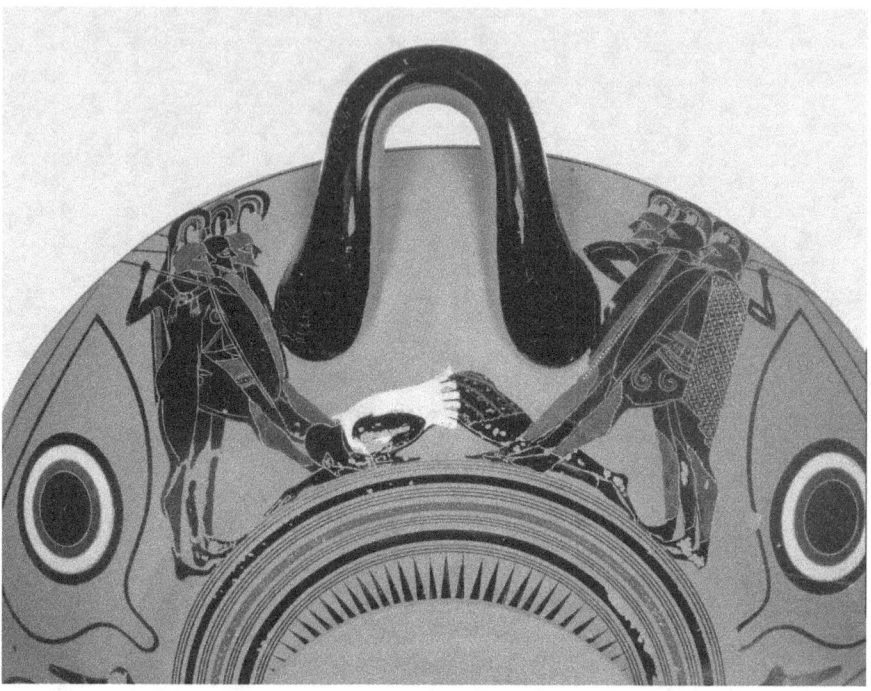

Fig. 5 Exterior of black-figure cup, attributed to Exekias, found in Vulci (Etruria), c. 530 BC. © Staatliche Antikensammlungen und Glyptothek München / Renate Kühling.

is firmly on the corpse, which occupies the centre of the composition on both sides. On one side of the cup, the fallen is distinguished by his armour, in particular the bright-white corselet, but also helmet and greaves; on the other, the body is already despoiled and dragged back to safety by one of the warriors, presumably a comrade of the fallen warrior. The contrast between the two images is striking, emphasizing not only the successful retrieval of the dead, but also the significance of the arms of the deceased. Such strong emphasis on the latter is comparatively unusual in other black-figure depictions, which tend to focus on the obligation to rescue the fallen and not on the practice of despoliation.[50] But there is little doubt that the cup provided the viewer with successive stages of a single combat encounter. The message was loud and clear: the war dead were to be fought over, either to be rescued or to be despoiled.[51]

In addition, the combat scenes of Exekias' cup demonstrate that within the composition of fights over the dead, the fallen warriors could be depicted as either wearing their panoply (full or partial) or be completely naked. An example

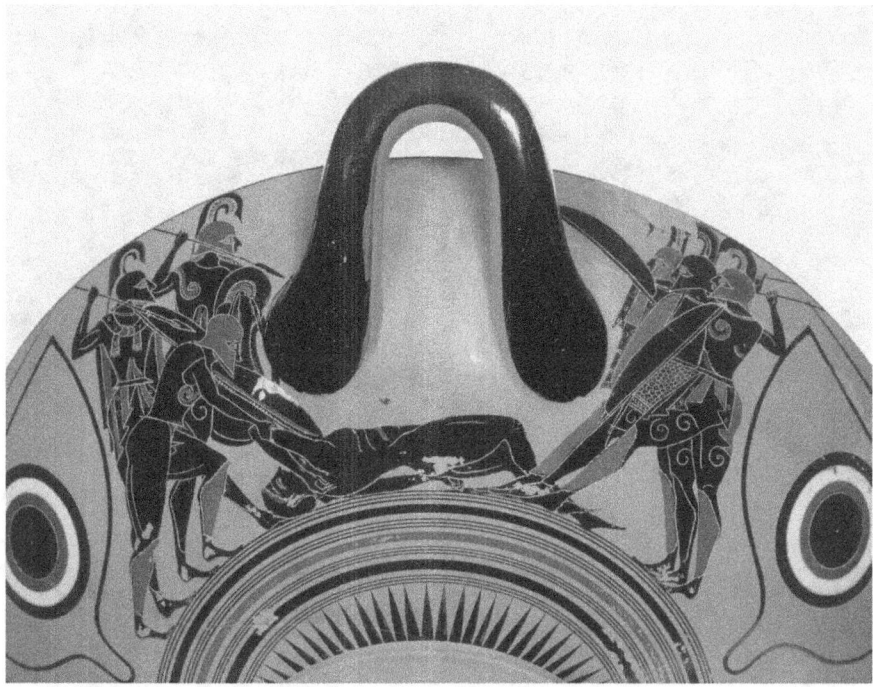

Fig. 6 Exterior of black-figure cup, attributed to Exekias, found in Vulci (Etruria), c. 530 BC. © Staatliche Antikensammlungen und Glyptothek München / Renate Kühling.

of a naked corpse placed in the middle of a hoplite encounter is provided by a red-figure cup from Berlin attributed to Oltos (Fig. 7). In the scene, the body of a naked, beardless youth is flanked by two warriors on each side, preparing to attack their opponents and clad in full hoplite armour, including carefully rendered Argive shields. The depiction of the fallen youth, who looks almost serene with his head supported on his arm, and whose body is devoid of any wounds, imbues the scene with a sense of ennoblement and beauty, reminiscent of the epic model of *kalos thanatos*.[52] The latter ideal, a commonplace in the Homeric songs and Archaic Greek elegiac poetry, glorified the concept of heroic death in battle in one's physical prime, which made the fallen man a spectacle for all to watch and admire. The phenomenon of nudity in Attic war iconography was certainly a more complex issue.[53] Combat scenes between largely naked warriors were not uncommon and the use of the motif often relied on the preference of individual artists. And while it is usually best to judge each representation on its own merits, as Echeverria recommended in his study of early combat imagery, the rhetoric of *kalos thanatos* in the case of the naked bodies on the battlefield appears to have played an important part.[54]

Fig. 7 Exterior of red-figure cup, attributed to Oltos, found in Vulci (Etruria), c. 515–510 BC. © bpk / Antikensammlung, Staatliche Museen zu Berlin / Johannes Laurentius.

In most representations of fights over the dead, however, the fallen retain at least some of their armour (Fig. 4). The presence of hoplite panoply on the corpses emphasizes the potential for despoliation (and perhaps maltreatment) by the enemy warriors and the duty incumbent on the fallen's comrades to retrieve the body, and ensure proper burial later.[55] Accordingly, this heightened valuation of the dead warrior was even more apparent in the scenes where the body had been already stripped, such as the one depicted by Oltos; the rationale for fighting and risking one's life would in such cases be largely diminished. That it is not, provides a testimony to the ideological importance of combat retrieval and care for the immediate post-mortem fate of the individual. Unlike the Homeric episodes of *Leichenkämpfe*, the glory involved in obtaining the arms of a slain foe is here largely downplayed; the main focus is placed firmly on the heroic fight and the moral obligation, both collective and individual, of the fellow warriors to protect the dead.

The large number of late Archaic portrayals of fighting over the dead reflects the extent of the demand for such iconography in Athens throughout the sixth century BC. The sudden decline of these images in the fifth century BC is, therefore, noteworthy. The Beazley Archive records only two depictions in the first quarter of the fifth century BC, and no surviving representations thereafter; examples in red-figure style, such as the Oltos cup, are indeed rare.[56] This rapid decline is matched by a substantial decrease in the number of all combat representations in early Classical art. The disappearance of scenes of fighting over the fallen from the iconographic repertoire of the fifth century BC might be accordingly taken as reflective of bigger changes in the iconography of war in Classical Athens. It demonstrates, if nothing else, that the subject was less attractive to artists and presumably to purchasers. More importantly, it may also indicate that the theme of fighting over the dead was simply less relevant to the military reality of the Classical period and the procedures associated with the customs of *anairesis* and *patrios nomos* which governed the retrieval and treatment of the war dead in fifth-century BC Athens.

Artistic portrayals of carrying the dead away from combat were also common in Archaic Athenian art.[57] While the theme does not quite attain the same popularity that fights over the dead held for the Athenians, the Beazley Archive still records no fewer than 121 representations of the subject, the majority of them dating once more to the 550–500 BC period (Table 2). These scenes too decline in the early Classical period, with four depictions in the first quarter of the fifth century BC, and only one after 450 BC. The most popular pot shapes are again amphoras (59 per cent) and lekythoi (13 per cent).[58]

The first appearance of a warrior carrying a fallen comrade in Attic black-figure style comes from the aforementioned François vase by Kleitias, dated to *c.* 570 BC. Painted on the handles of the famous volute krater which depicts a number of mythological scenes are two images of Ajax carrying the body of Achilles.[59] Accompanying inscriptions identifying the figures make this our first definite example of the episode from the Trojan Cycle. The composition of the

Table 2 Images of carrying the dead in the online Beazley Archive

Date Range	600–550	575–525	550–500	525–475	500–450	475–425	450–400
Number of records	1	14	62	39	4	0	1
Number of all combat depictions	51	402	901	867	217	74	45
Number of all archive records	1,899	5,456	13,138	18,748	13,043	12,464	8,435

Fig. 8 Black-figure amphora, attributed to Exekias, found in Vulci (Etruria), c. 540–530 BC. © Staatliche Antikensammlungen und Glyptothek München / Renate Kühling.

scenes recalls the earlier instances of a warrior carrying a fallen comrade in Geometric art: Achilles is conspicuously naked in one image and is disproportionally larger than Ajax, with his long hair almost touching the ground. Kleitias' artistic scheme may have inspired a couple of other mid-sixth century BC depictions, but the most influential interpretations of the scene were painted around 540 BC by Exekias.[60] The latter portrayed the theme on three different vases (Fig. 8). Exekias does not identify the figures, but most scholars assume that the image shows Ajax and Achilles, which may be supported by the presence of a single woman in his earlier depiction of the episode, commonly interpreted as Thetis.[61] A number of innovations appear, among which the portrayal of Achilles is the most noticeable;[62] the hero is now the same size as Ajax and wears a full hoplite panoply, which includes a corselet, Boeotian shield, helmet, greaves, and an elaborate cloak.[63] Exekias' addition of the protagonists' armour becomes the standard in later black-figure representations of the scenes, all of which appear to follow his general model in their compositions.

From 530 BC onward the scene becomes very common in Attic black-figure art. A few vases provide inscriptions naming Ajax; otherwise we should assume that the subject matter would have been intelligible to the viewers.[64] As in the case with fights over the fallen, spectators are often present and consist mostly of women, and sometimes a single man and a woman. Other examples place the action within a battle context. Such a scene is provided already by Exekias, who depicts Ajax in the process of lifting the body of Achilles, while Menelaus covers him on the flank against the attack by Amasos, Memnon's attendant, armed with a club (Fig. 9).[65] Achilles wears elaborately detailed armour except for a shield; his head tilts back and the rest of his helmet touches the ground. A similar narrative occurs on an unattributed amphora from Munich, where Ajax is about to shoulder the body of Achilles, surrounded on each side by Menelaus and Neoptolemus each fighting off Paris and Aeneas respectively; on other vases the warriors can also feature Teucer and Odysseus, or indeed remain anonymous.[66]

While the inclusion of other warriors reminds us that the scene is taking place within a combat melee, the vases depicting civilian spectators accentuate the importance of the action for those not physically present on the battlefield. In some cases, the latter might be identified with Peleus and Thetis, displaying a

Fig. 9 Black-figure amphora, attributed to Exekias, found in Orvieto (Etruria), c. 540–530 BC / Courtesy of the Penn Museum, Image Number 160458 / Object Number MS3442.

highly emotional image of parents witnessing the death of their son. The composition of a single man and woman flanking the central group, according to some scholars, could have been derived from the numerous vases depicting the departure of a warrior, thus introducing a strong family aspect to early war iconography.[67] The potential significance of such messages for the viewers was explored by Clemente Marconi, who in his study of painted pots buried in a warrior-grave (cenotaph) in Sicily suggested that the portrayals of the war dead might have performed a specific function for the families of the deceased. Among the amphoras found in the grave, which included images of a departure scene and duel of warriors, one featured the Ajax with Achilles' body scene. The whole sequence, Marconi argued, 'moves from the departure to the duel to, finally, the rescue of the body (...) This is a eulogy, in painting, of the *arete* of the dead warrior: a visual pendant of verbal discourses such as the funeral oration that might have taken place at the time of the funeral'.[68] The depiction of the fallen warrior rescued from the battlefield – with his body and armour intact – reassured the viewer that 'his body and his belongings were still untouched and now in safe territory'.[69] Such images, in turn, provided a universal language to commemorate the Archaic war dead, which appealed not only to the Athenians but also to the wider Greek world.

According to Lise Hannestad, the large number of artistic depictions of warriors rescuing the dead in Attic black-figure art of the sixth century BC implies that the motif, 'in its mythological disguise (...) must have had a deeper significance for contemporary viewers than a story from an epic'.[70] Compared to the artistic representations of fights over the fallen, the mythological reference contained in the scenes of warriors carrying the dead over their shoulders appears to be more specific. An easier identification with an episode from the Trojan Cycle, however, does not necessarily imply that the images had no relation to the combat experiences of their users. Since there are no inscriptions on most vases depicting Ajax with Achilles' body, as Gloria Ferrari remarked, 'one is free to interpret the same figures either in reference to the heroic world or in reference to contemporary practice'.[71] We should also not exclude the possibility that one could interpret the scene with reference to both worlds; the episode, in effect, would serve as a prism from the heroic world to evaluate contemporary actions. Its function could have been, as we saw, to reassure families of fallen warriors that their sons' bodies were looked after by their comrades. It could, however, also provide a military ideal for young and older men alike, demonstrating a feat of heroism and solidarity in battle, to be pondered and talked about during drinking parties. The relevance of such scenes, as was the case with images of duels over the war dead, diminished dramatically in the fifth century BC, with very limited representation in red-figure and virtually no examples beyond 480 BC.[72] The sudden nature of this disappearance demands an explanation.

Iconography of change?

Archaic war iconography, with its many depictions of fighting over and carrying the dead, presented a memorable picture of the grim nature of early warfare in Greece. The fate of the fallen warriors, lying in the dust or pulled away simultaneously by their comrades and enemies, appear to have been of special importance to Archaic Athenian, and wider Greek audiences, forming a significant part of all early Greek vase imagery and the artistic discourses on war. Although many of the scenes depict heroic actions, often within the framework of a mythological narrative, the popularity of these themes in Archaic iconography suggests to some scholars that the motifs of fighting over and retrieving the dead were more than just mythical stories from the past; they must, in some way, have related to the contemporary experience of combat. The images provided a clear ideal and behavioural model for the viewers of the vases, who could, and no doubt did, equate their actions with the famous feats of epic heroes, who fought over and rescued their comrades in battle.[73] The heroic subject nature of such imagery should be accordingly seen as a deliberate artistic attempt to parallel relevant aspects of epic and contemporary battles.[74] These aspects, as our study has shown, were relevant only for Archaic audiences, as demonstrated by the sudden disappearance of images containing combat despoliation and recovery of the dead in the fifth century BC. But is the reason for the change confined only to the realm of art? Or does it reflect wider changes in the practice of war by the Athenians?

Scholarly explanations for the changes in the imagery of warfare occurring in Classical art, which also witnessed a general decline in the number of vases depicting combat scenes, have been surprisingly few.[75] The most comprehensive theory for the phenomenon has been offered by Osborne, who in his recent study analysed the subject matter of Attic red-figure vases in the late Archaic and early Classical eras. According to him, the transformation of war iconography should be understood in relation to the parallel changes occurring in other artistic scenes, such as those featuring athletics, drinking parties or religious activities, among others.[76] These changes, he argued, had no relation to changes in the actual practices, which in most cases remained essentially the same.

Instead of attributing the iconographic shifts to what actually happened on the battlefield or in the gymnasium, Osborne suggested that the new developments reflected the different ways in which the Athenians saw the world. The move away from images depicting combat toward scenes of arming and war departure provided one example of this:

> The changing representations of soldiers increasingly separate hoplites from other forms of military activity, take the soldier out of the allegorical and heroic battleground, become ever more reluctant to represent battle, and concentrate more and more exclusively on the moment at which the hoplite leaves the domestic context that is itself increasingly reduced to the single figure of the wife or mother.[77]

The new imagery, in effect, takes the focus away from personal achievement and offers a more civic orientated discourse on the importance of army service on behalf of the *polis*. This change, as Osborne concluded, consisted of a move away from 'individualism to corporate values', being ultimately 'a shift from a world dominated by competitive values to a world prepared to embrace collaboration, or indeed a shift from a world of action to one of contemplation'.[78] He explored the possible role of a number of factors, such as the introduction of democracy at Athens and the trauma of the Persian Wars, while emphasizing also the prominent role played by the Athenian artists in the process.

Osborne's theory raises many important points concerning the fifth-century BC changes in Athenian art; his observations on the disappearance of scenes highlighting individual achievements and the concurrent rise of civic ideology in war iconography are particularly useful and help us to understand the changing ideology in democratic Athens.[79] The main weakness of his argument, however, concerns his reluctance to accept that Archaic war imagery, especially in its black-figure representations, could have had some basis in historical reality. Osborne's decision to treat them all as 'allegorical' and 'heroic', which as we saw earlier follows a long line of scholarship, is based largely on the false premise that only phalanx warfare can depict reality; his claim that 'the additions of names or (for example) Boeotian shields, and the ease with which Amazons are introduced into scenes that might be taken as illustrations of contemporary warfare, should warn us against seeing representations of contemporary warfare' is a direct reflection of this.[80] Furthermore, while scenes of duels and group-fighting indeed disappear in the first quarter of the fifth century BC, the dramatic decrease in the depictions of fights over and retrievals of the war dead occurs towards the end of the sixth century BC. According to our survey, there are no less than 366 representations of the latter in Attic black-figure art, which account for nearly 17 per cent of all combat depictions in the sixth century BC, compared to a mere fifteen depictions in red-figure, accounting to 3 per cent of combat scenes in the fifth century BC. The disappearance of these themes occurs, therefore, earlier than the broader iconographic shifts observed by Osborne in red-figure art.[81] And while Osborne's explanation of the fifth-century BC changes remains persuasive, the decline in the imagery concerning the war dead might be better understood outside of his model, indicating instead a fundamental change in the ideology surrounding the recovery and commemoration of the war dead and potentially also in the experience of combat. This change, as we will see in the following chapters, was likely a response to the major restructuring of the citizen army at Athens associated with the reforms of Cleisthenes, which, among other areas, addressed also the customs related to the treatment and burial of the war dead.

The Archaic iconography of war brings Homeric battle and its customs much closer to how warfare was perceived and experienced in Archaic Athens. While there is no question that pot painters could and did refer to the epics, their consistent selection of specific themes and episodes suggests that these must have held special relevance to their customers, enabling them to reminisce about their own actions in war. Illustrations of the war dead, fiercely fought over and rescued, but also equated with an ideal of beauty available to those who heroically sacrificed their lives in combat, provided the Athenians with a powerful cultural discourse with which to think about and remember the fallen.[82] The relative simplicity of the composition of scenes depicting corpses highlighted the moral message of these pots: 'a comrade has died and his body needs to be rescued'. Such moral obligation was likely part of the heroic code inherited from the Homeric epics; the military and social ideals that it exalts are very much in line with the 'hierarchical' principles which characterize the poems, and were still dominant in the artistic discourses of war among the Greek elites of the Archaic period.[83] Due to the limited nature of literary sources for Archaic battles, the full significance of retrieving the dead during combat is, nonetheless, harder to grasp and has been dismissed or overlooked by the majority of scholars studying early Greek warfare.[84] Archaeological evidence for early war burials in Athens and Attica, as we find out in the following chapter, can provide another source which supports the ideals conveyed in iconography, indicating that the 'hierarchical' standards of the *Iliad* were not very distant from the early Athenian conventions regarding the recovery of the war dead.

4

Archaic Monuments for the War Dead

The 'hierarchical' standards that defined the treatment of fallen warriors in the Homeric poems made a clear mark on the artistic discourses of the war dead in early Greek iconography. As we saw in the previous chapter, the many scenes of fighting over and retrieving corpses adorning black-figure vases had a prominent place in the war imagery of the Archaic Athenians, suggesting that these actions could have portrayed and idealized practices familiar from early battlefields. According to the 'hierarchical' model enshrined in the epics, however, the numerous scenes of *Leichenkämpfe* tell only half of the story. The reason why Homeric warriors risked their lives trying to protect the bodies of the *aristoi* was to provide them with magnificent and highly conspicuous funerals. This, in turn, ensured the 'imperishable glory' of the latter, of which the physical embodiment were the mounds heaped over their graves. Hector, listing the terms of his duel with Ajax, highlights the significance of proper burial for any Homeric *aristos*; should he be victorious, he will strip his opponent of his armour:

> '... but his corpse I will give back among the strong-benched vessels so that the flowing-haired Achaeans may give him due burial and heap up a mound upon him beside the broad passage of Helle. And some day one of the men to come will say, as he sees it (...) 'This is the mound of a man who died long ago in battle, who was one of the bravest, and glorious Hector killed him'. So will he speak some day, and my glory will not be forgotten'.
>
> 7.84–91

The other half of the 'hierarchical' model of the epics, therefore, concerned burial, which distinguished the Homeric elites in death from rank-and-file warriors, buried in common graves on the battlefield. But were such customs representative of how the Archaic Greeks interred their war dead? Or were they entirely fictional? The answer, as ever, is not simple. The literary accounts of pre-Classical battles are vague at most and offer little information on what the armies did with their dead following a battle. Examples of any Archaic *polyandria* in the wider Greek world are similarly almost non-existent, which further complicates the matter.[1] As a result, what we are left with is the evidence of individual graves and cemeteries. These, despite being removed from the immediate vicinity of Archaic battlefields, appear to tell us that the elite Athenians were clearly distinguished in burial throughout the Archaic era. The impressive monuments which adorned their graves testified to the superior social status of the deceased, who, as we will find out in this chapter, included casualties of war.

Elite burials

In his influential 1987 book *Burial and Ancient Society: The Rise of the Greek City-State*, Ian Morris offered a broad survey of all archaeological evidence for burials in early Attica (1050–510 BC). The results of his study were striking, suggesting that, for the most part, formal burials in Attica were restricted only to people of high rank. According to Morris, the fluctuations in the number and sizes of adult graves in pre-Classical Attica reflected the subordination of the masses of poor, dependent peasants to the Attic elites, which can be first observed in the burial evidence for the 1050–750 BC period. This situation changed briefly around the middle of the eighth century BC, which witnessed a widening of the burying groups associated with the rise of the Athenian *polis*, part of a wider Panhellenic trend. Soon after, however, unlike most of the other early Greek states, Athens returned to the previous burying group pattern, labelled by Morris as a 'pre-political', 'non-polis state form', structured around the political supremacy of the Athenian leisure-class. From *c.* 700 until 510 BC, Attic cemeteries were again monopolized by the Athenian elites (*agathoi*), at the expense of the poor, non-elite masses (*kakoi*). Access to formal cemeteries was limited on the basis of rank, apparent in the relatively small number of adult burials in the Protoattic and Black-Figure periods, as well as the impressive size and grandeur of the surviving grave markers.[2] The burial evidence, as Morris concluded, echoed the relationship of economic and political dependency which permeated the social structure of Archaic Athens; the rich minority of citizens controlled most of the land, while the majority of the poor were largely confined to working for the rich, with little hope of social or economic progression. This relationship, nonetheless, changed towards the end of the sixth century BC, fostered most strongly by the democratic reforms of Cleisthenes in 508/7, which brought about the gradual transformation of the social order in Athens. The change was especially visible in the cemeteries, which around 510 BC opened their doors to all citizens, regardless of social rank.

The burial evidence increased considerably and elite grave markers gradually disappeared, as the reorganized cemeteries become 'powerful symbols of descent and citizenship' of the new democratic order.[3]

Morris' interpretation of Archaic burials and the development of the Athenian citizen cemeteries has had a major impact on the study of early Greek burial practices. His theories on the exclusion from formal burial on the basis of rank; the monopoly of the elites symbolized by conspicuous graves and tombstones; and the radical changes in the archaeological record around 700 BC and towards the end of the sixth century BC have influenced scholars from a variety of fields and disciplines.[4] Applying Morris' framework to our investigation of the early customs regarding the treatment of the war dead could be similarly productive. For if we assume that the Athenian elites monopolized the Attic cemeteries of the Archaic period, expressing their status and social standing by elaborate and highly conspicuous grave markers, we would expect that the same elite men who fought and died in early Athenian armies would require similar treatment. It is hardly likely that these men would have been buried in archaeologically invisible mass graves (*polyandria*) with the rest of the non-elite warriors. On the contrary, they would most likely expect, or indeed require, an impressive funeral, perhaps not unlike the ones given to Achilles, Hector or Patroclus in the epic songs. The recovery of any elite dead after a battle or campaign would be consequently of paramount importance, as the fallen warriors had to be given funerals befitting their social standing; these burials, however, may not have been on the battlefield, as most scholars assume, but *at home*, where commemorating the heroism of dying in battle affirmed the elite status of the deceased and his family within their community. And indeed a brief look at some Attic grave markers of the Archaic period confirms that the custom of bringing back the war dead was practised for most of the Archaic period in Athens.

In the Homeric epics, a grave normally consisted of a heaped burial mound (*tumbos*) and a simple marker, most commonly a large stone, placed on top of the mound. Such grave (*sema*) is described in the *Iliad* as the 'due of the dead' (*geras thanonton*), and in its basic form it matches the archaeological evidence for adult burials in Attica from the eighth century BC.[5] From 700 BC, the adult graves in Attica are marked by mounds of earth, which after 650 BC grow steadily in prominence and size. The graves are typically accompanied by another marker placed on top of the mound, which consists of a *stele*, an undecorated stone block set vertically over the grave, and/or a large clay vase, of which the most impressive examples come from the late Geometric period. The most common method of burial is primary cremation, which replaces the earlier practice of secondary cremation towards the end of the eighth century BC.[6] This change is also followed by a gradual move towards extra-mural cemeteries, as burials within settlement areas in Attica become increasingly rare from 700 BC onwards.[7]

The relatively small number of graves, combined with the impressive size of mounds, which must have required some effort to build, suggests that early Archaic graves in Attica belonged to the elites. In each case, the exact cause of death is almost impossible to determine, but the imagery on the grave-marker vases gives us some idea of the social persona and standing of the deceased.[8] The surviving depictions usually concern the various stages of the individual's funeral, including scenes of *prothesis* and *ekphora*, giving us an insight into the burial rituals and ceremonies performed by the elite Athenians.[9] In addition, a number of late Geometric kraters represent warriors and war-related activities, with a clear preference for scenes of fighting in or around ships.[10] The historical value of such imagery, as is usually the case with iconographical material, has been a matter of some debate among scholars, who view them as either mythological or idealized representations deliberately drawn from the epic tradition, or as realistic depictions of scenes from the deceased's life.[11] And although providing a definite answer may be beyond reach, since the imagery was likely inspired by both factors, it seems clear that the artistic scenes of war depicted on early grave-marker vases formed an important part of the deceased's social identity: they conferred on the dead the status of a warrior, together with the activities normally associated with it (sea-battles, raiding etc.), which may have been relevant to him, or something he aspired to, during his life. Whether such graves belonged specifically to those who died in war is unfortunately unclear and a matter of speculation, as the funerary markers bear no relief sculpture or inscriptions. These, however, appear towards the end of the seventh century BC, which witnesses a major change in the form of the grave monument in Attica.

In the last quarter of the seventh century BC, the great mounds of the preceding decades start to shrink in both size and number, as more graves come to consist of mudbrick tombs accompanied by elaborate funerary sculpture.[12] The latter consist of imposing statues of naked or draped youths, known as *kouroi* and *korai*, which appear in Attica from about *c.* 610 BC; and, from 570s BC, of stone *stelai* with relief decoration portraying the deceased. Many of the funerary monuments are now accompanied by epitaphs, inscribed most often on the base of the statue, and providing the name of the deceased, and occasionally a few more details on his/her life and the artist. The gravestones are found all over Attica, but almost none have been discovered in situ; in fact, the survival of some the finest gravestones of this period is solely due to their later incorporation into the Themistoclean wall, which according to Thucydides (1.93) was hastily built after the Persian Wars, in part by using fragments of Archaic tombstones.[13] Despite these problems, however, the number of known grave monuments is still relatively high, providing us with one of the richest sources for the cultural, social and religious life of Athens in the sixth century BC.[14]

Based on the sheer size and artistic quality of the Attic funerary monuments of the sixth century BC, there is no doubt that the graves which they stood over and commemorated belonged to the wealthiest members of Athenian communities. Both the *kouroi/korai* and the relief *stelai* were very costly to make and individually commissioned from the sculptors' workshops, even though their style and general themes are common for most of the Archaic period. By far the most popular themes on the grave reliefs associate the deceased with the activities of war and athletics, thus confirming the social and cultural significance of both areas for early Athenian elites.[15] While there are a few representations depicting the dead as mature (bearded) men, the majority of Attic *stelai* depict the dead as youths, which suggests that a large number of such monuments were erected for people who died in their youth. And as military attributes feature prominently in the iconography of the reliefs, it is not only clear that the wealthy families wished to commemorate their kin as warriors, but also that the deceased in question could have been casualties of war.[16] It might, on the other hand, be argued that the monuments simply signify the key elements of the Athenian elites' self-image, modelled on the ideals of war and military excellence enshrined in the epic songs.[17] Alternatively, such monuments may only indicate that the buried men were members of the city's army throughout, or at some point in their lives. The regularity of the combination of the 'youth' and 'warrior' schemes on Archaic gravestones, which fits very closely with the ideological model of *kalos thanatos*, implies, however, that the graves may have indeed belonged to young Athenian men who died in war. While either or all of these interpretations may be true, a number of inscriptions accompanying the Archaic gravestones show that some of the deceased undoubtedly lost their lives in battle.

The most iconic of all Archaic gravestones from Attica belonged to a man named Kroisos, whose funeral monument consisted of an inscribed base surmounted by a magnificent *kouros*, commonly identified by scholars with the famous Anavysos *kouros*.[18] Kroisos was buried at Phoinikia in south-western Attica, where both the base and statue were found;[19] his grave memorial was most likely set by the side of a highly frequented road, as was common for most tombs in Archaic Attica. The short epitaph written on the base suggests that he fell in battle, literally defeated by Ares: 'Stay and take pity by the marker of dead Kroisos, whom once in the front ranks destroyed raging Ares'.[20] The grave was initially dated to the 540s BC and it has, therefore, been assumed that Kroisos died in the battle of Pallene in 546 BC, where the Athenians were defeated by Peisistratus and his allies. More recent estimations, however, move the date down to c. 530–520 BC, making the link with Pallene untenable.[21] Kroisos, most likely named after the famous Lydian king, was a member of the elite Athenian family of the Alcmaeonids. His high social standing was certainly symbolized by the imposing marble *kouros*, whose valour and beauty, evident in the perfect proportions of the naked body and long hair, commemorated him using highly elitist visual discourse.[22] Such representation, which alludes to the heroic ideal of *kalos thanatos*, is further enhanced and completed by the epitaph, which presents Kroisos' death in terms clearly reminiscent of the Homeric epics: he fell after fighting among the *promachoi*, an unmistakable mark of his courage, and was destroyed by the god of war himself.[23] His death in battle, therefore, was what guaranteed his glory and best described his life, giving us both a glimpse into the values central to the self-identity of the Archaic Athenian elites, but also explicit evidence that the bodies of wealthy warriors who fell in battle could have been brought back home for burial. This custom of returning the dead was by no means limited to Kroisos.

Indeed, the earliest example of a sepulchral epigram in Attica commemorates a man who fell in combat: it comes from Sepolia and belongs to the grave of a certain Tettichos.[24] The inscription, written on the base which supported a sizeable monument which does not survive, has been dated to 575–550 BC. In a fashion similar to the epitaph commemorating Kroisos, it addresses the passer-by directly, asking him to stop and lament the death of Tettichos: 'Let each man, whether a citizen or foreigner coming from abroad, pass by only after mourning Tettichos, a good man, who perished in war and lost his tender youth. Once you have lamented this, proceed to a good deed'.[25] The epitaph does not provide us with much information about the deceased, describing him only as a young and good man. It places considerably more emphasis on the person reading and looking at the monument.[26] Despite the relative lack of details concerning Tettichos, his life and death are represented using notions familiar from epic poetry: he is an *aner agathos*, which carried clear military connotations; he died an ideal, beautiful death – in combat and at the height of his youth.[27] Tettichos' death, therefore, is conceptualized along the archetypal pattern of *kalos thanatos*, as the achievements of his life are encapsulated by his glorious sacrifice in battle. The heroic language used in the epigram further testifies to the elitist and individualistic nature of the discourse employed in the commemoration of the war dead in Archaic Athens.[28] But more importantly, from our perspective, we should presume that after his death in battle, Tettichos' body must have been transported from the battlefield back to his home in Sepolia.[29] While identifying the exact battle responsible for Tettichos' passing is beyond our scope, it has been suggested that he most likely fell in one of the mid-sixth-century BC encounters between Athens and Megara.[30] If this assumption is correct, bringing Tettichos' remains back to his family would not have been a logistical problem, providing us with another potential instance of an elite Athenian brought back home for burial.

The final example of a grave belonging to a fallen warrior comes from the epigram commemorating Xenokles.[31] The inscription, dated to *c.* 550–530 BC, was found on a stepped tomb base built into the Themistoclean wall, and has been reconstructed as: '[He who] pauses and behold[s] your marker, Xenokles, the marker of a spearman, will know your manliness'.[32] Xenokles' grave monument most likely consisted of a *kouros*, and although the language used in his epigram makes less use of heroic and epic elements than the tomb of Kroisos, the elitist and individualizing aspects remain largely consistent. He is defined by his manliness and his skill as a spearman, which combined with the imposing nature of his *kouros* statue, sends a powerful message about his social identity as a warrior, and as a member of the Athenian elite. His death in battle is not mentioned but, judging by the cases of Kroisos and Tettichos, we can suspect that he did meet his fate on the battlefield, and that his body was transported to his family for a funeral. The lack of any indication of the manner of Xenokles' death is, in fact, reflective of a wider feature of Archaic epigrams, which very rarely mention the specific causes of death for the commemorated deceased.[33] A few of them can certainly be thought to have died in war, including the ones we have considered so far, suggesting that individual war burials at home may have been the norm for elite members of Archaic Athenian armies.[34]

One feature which all Archaic epigrams for war casualties have in common is their highly individualizing, heroic and elitist rhetoric. The fallen men are remembered as young individuals whose bravery and excellence in battle ensured fame and renown for themselves and their families. Their death on the battlefield is presented as their central achievement, and although the loss of their youth is to be pitied and lamented, it is also meant to inspire the passer-by to emulate their valour. In this context, it is revealing that the surviving epigrams offer no references to the communities or the wider *polis* that these men were fighting and sacrificing their lives for.[35] But elegiac poetry of the period, which the epigrams in many ways adopt and resemble, strongly champions the notions of patriotism and self-sacrifice, alongside those more traditional ideals of individual prowess, honour and glory attainable through battle. The poems of Callinus and Tyrtaeus provide the best examples of such martial exhortations, which reflected the new values that became increasingly prominent with the rise of civic consciousness in Archaic Greece:

> For it is a splendid honour for man to fight on behalf of his land, children, and wedded wife against the foe (...) All the people miss a stout-hearted man when he dies and while he lives he is the equal of demigods. For in the eyes of the people he is like a tower, since single-handed he does the deeds of many.
>
> Callinus Fr. 1.6–8, 18–21

> It is a fine thing for a brave man to die when he has fallen among the front ranks while fighting for his homeland (...) But for the young everything is seemly, as long as he has the splendid prime of lovely youth; while alive, men marvel at the sight of him and women feel desire, and when he has fallen among the front ranks, he is fair.
>
> Tyrtaeus Fr. 10.1–2, 27–30

> And if he falls among the front ranks, pierced many times through his breast and bossed shield and corselet from the front, he loses his own dear life but brings glory to his city, to his people, and to his father. Young and old alike mourn him, all the city is distressed by the painful loss, and his tomb and children are pointed out among the people, and his children's children and his line after them. Never do his name and good fame perish, but even though he is beneath the earth he is immortal, whoever it is that furious Ares slays as he displays prowess by standing fast and fighting for land and children.
>
> Tyrtaeus Fr. 12.23–34

Such fragments are clearly inspired by the military values enshrined in the Homeric epics, but their consistent focus on the defence of the community, the land, the children and the wives, is in many ways an elaboration of themes which were of comparably lesser importance in the exhortations made by the Homeric *basileis*.[36] The ever-present ideal of *kalos thanatos* is vividly depicted by Tyrtaeus, who speaks of the fairness of 'lovely youths' falling 'among the front ranks', and promises the dead a conspicuous tomb and 'good fame' (*kleos esthlon*), which will never perish. The factors which make a battlefield death beautiful, however, are no longer just youth and courage, but now also a sacrifice of a life for one's community. And even though both Callinus and Tyrtaeus were not Athenian, the similarities between their elegies and the Attic epigrams of the Archaic period are many: the ideal of fighting among the front ranks; losing one's youth in battle; or facing and being slayed by furious Ares.[37] The lack of even a single reference to the defence of the country and community is, therefore, most revealing and must be seen as a deliberate choice on behalf of the Archaic elites in Athens; or as a separate artistic tradition, which despite drawing on a lot of material relevant to contemporary martial elegies, remained otherwise independent and separate. This divergence between the funerary epigram and elegiac poetry, as George Robertson concluded, highlights the individualizing nature of Attic grave monuments and inscriptions, in which the deceased's valour in battle 'is a more important consideration ... than the fact that he may have contributed to the salvation of his *polis*'. Consequently, the deceased warriors' status as citizens 'takes second place to their status as heroes'.[38] The inclusion of civic ideals and values in the discourses of the commemoration of the war dead in Athens indeed emerged only with the Classical funeral oration, as we will see in the following chapter.

But while patriotic considerations were absent from Archaic Athenian epigrams, we should not assume that the concept of citizen duty involved in defending one's community was entirely unfamiliar to those serving and dying in the Athenian army. Even though elite values and rhetoric dominated the funerary monuments of war casualties, like the *kouroi* of Kroisos or Xenokles, a large number of sculpted grave *stelai*, accompanied with often few or no inscribed words, may have commemorated the war dead in a different, more *polis*-orientated way. These *stelai*, which begin to appear in number from the second quarter of the sixth century BC in Attica, depict the deceased standing in profile as warriors, both young and mature, and usually holding a spear in one hand.[39] Other decoration may also be included, such as a sphinx or a subsidiary pictorial relief, but the imposing warrior figure claims the viewer's attention. Due to the lack of any inscriptions on most of the warrior *stelai* we cannot conclusively determine whether such graves belonged to men who fell in combat, but judging from the evidence of inscribed monuments of the period, it seems more than plausible that some, if not the majority of them, did commemorate war casualties.[40] Accepting this assumption would, in turn, significantly increase the number of individual warrior graves in Archaic Attica, especially towards the end of the sixth century BC which witnesses a rise in the number of all surviving funerary *stelai*.[41]

The visual rhetoric of Archaic warrior *stelai* was certainly influenced and dominated by the broader elite ideology expressed in the sepulchral monuments of the era. Their high quality and cost, combined with their focus on the individual, leaves us with no doubt that these graves belonged to the wealthiest members of Attic communities. Their difference from the statues of Kroisos and Xenokles is, nonetheless, significant and highlights a different approach, both artistic and social, to commemorating the war dead.[42] The funerary *kouroi* which adorned the graves of the wealthiest Athenians and were most often accompanied by a lengthy epigram, provided a highly conservative and elitist form to commemorate the fallen. The combination of an imposing human statue and text, as we saw, made a powerful ideological statement aimed to glorify the deceased in heroic and highly individualizing terms, which in the case of war casualties was often centred on the *kalos thanatos* ideal. The statue itself, however, made no reference to war or army service, maintaining instead a constant and universal pose which remained mostly unchanged during the Archaic period; although the inscription may occasionally state that the deceased man died in battle, any mentions of a communal service or patriotic duty are absent.[43] And while a similar discourse could also be employed in combination with a relief *stele*, as was the case with the tomb of Tettichos, the visual rhetoric employed by the Archaic warrior *stelai* exhibited a greater degree of interest in the communal aspect of military duty and a warrior's sacrifice in service to his community. In contrast to the *kouroi*, the prime focus of the Archaic *stelai* was to commemorate the dead as warriors and members of the Athenian army.

A famous example of the communal values idealized in a private grave monument is provided by the *stele* of Aristion, built by Aristokles in c. 510 BC and found in the east coast of Attica (Fig. 10).[44] The once-painted marble relief, inscribed only with the name of the deceased and the sculptor, depicts an armed and bearded Aristion, confidently holding an upward-facing spear. The laconic nature of the monument places Aristion's service in the army as central to his identity, removing the elements of heroism, pity and family grief which characterized the ideological message of the inscribed *kouroi*. Such focus, as Robin Osborne suggested, puts Aristion's public military service to the fore, reasserting 'that such service is, and continues to be, of the highest value' and thus anticipating 'the public memorials to the dead in war of the democratic Athens of the fifth century'.[45] Aristion's memorial, together with other Archaic warrior *stelai*, may consequently provide our first indication of the growing importance of public duty associated with military service, which had been traditionally structured around heroic notions of individual accomplishment and glory. As such, they offer a silent counterpart to the martial elegies of Callinus and Tyrtaeus, filling in the gap between the latter and the funerary epigrams inscribed on the Attic tombstones. Furthermore, they indicate the existence of a different discourse, parallel but also complementary to the highly individualizing

Fig. 10 Grave *stele* of Aristion. Plaster cast, Museum of Classical Archaeology, Cambridge, No. 43 (Original: National Museum, Athens, No. 29).

and elitist rhetoric of the inscribed grave monuments; this rhetoric, which idealized the notion of military service for the community, gradually began to permeate into Athenian social and political mentalities from the first half of the sixth century BC. In short, the Archaic warrior *stelai* provided a platform for a new visual and ideological discourse to emerge, grow and eventually overtake the more traditional elitist forms represented by the funerary *kouroi*. This discourse, in effect, set the ground for public burials of the war dead and the *patrios nomos* of the Classical period.

Despite the ideological differences between the inscribed monuments and the sculpted *stelai* of Archaic Athens, both commemorated the deceased as an individual: one, as member of the elite; the other, as member of the wider community. Each medium, in its own distinctive way, placed the death of the individual at the centre, which, from the perspective of our investigation, strongly indicates that fallen warriors belonging to the wealthiest strata of Archaic Athens received individual burials. As a result, we should suspect that it was imperative for their bodies to be removed from the battlefield, at all costs, in order to be transported back home to their families. The existence of such mentality is supported further by the iconography of the period, which as we saw in the previous chapter placed individual duels, fights over the fallen, and retrieving the dead during combat as central to the perception and experience of war in the Archaic era. The evidence for elite burials and commemoration of the war dead in sixth-century BC Athens confirms, therefore, that the central themes and ideals preserved in the iconographic record must have been drawn from the actual practice of war. As such, it brings the 'hierarchical' standards of the *Iliad* much closer to the realities of Archaic battlefields, where the importance of retrieving and burying the bodies of leading warriors was paramount.

The war dead and Archaic Greek warfare

The above conclusion, if correct, fundamentally challenges our understanding not only of the early customs of war burials in Athens (and possibly elsewhere) but also the wider practice and experience of war in Archaic Greece. And while a definite reconstruction of what happened to the bodies of fallen warriors cannot be offered due to the lack of literary accounts of Archaic battles, a tentative one can be built instead based on the pattern depicted in the Homeric poems. Upon the death of any prominent member of the Athenian army, his comrades would have attempted to remove his body from the battlefield, in order to bring it home to his family for a private burial, accompanied by the building of a highly conspicuous grave marker. The deceased would have been transported back home by carts following any military engagements carried out within or close to Attica. Since many conflicts in the sixth century BC took place fairly close to home, carting the bodies back to the hearth was relatively easy and did not pose any major logistical problems.[46] Alternatively, the corpses of the dead could have been cremated to facilitate transportation, which would have made more sense for any conflicts occurring at greater distances. Even though cremation was by far the more expedient method – bones obviously facilitating ease of transport – burning bodies was a timely and expensive operation; a recent study estimated that successful cremation of a single body takes 7–8 hours and around 500–600 kg of wood.[47] It seems more plausible to assume, therefore, that cremation was practised only for those men who died far away from Athens and whose families could afford to cover the necessary expenses. Carting the bodies back home would otherwise have remained the norm.

In addition, the relative ease with which the bodies of the fallen could have been brought back home suggests that Archaic tomb memorials for war casualties were not cenotaphs. Although most of the monuments were not found in situ, precluding any definite association with human remains, they carry no obvious signs indicating that they commemorated men buried elsewhere.[48] Despite their secondary findspots (e.g. the Themistoclean wall), there is little doubt that the monuments for the war dead were originally located alongside other tombs of elite Athenians in the cemetery areas of Archaic Attica. Kroisos' memorial in Phoinikia, for instance, was almost certainly placed next to a burial mound containing the remains of multiple people, leading scholars to suggest that he was buried in a family tomb.[49] And while the possibility of Archaic monuments for war casualties being cenotaphs cannot be entirely ruled out, especially in the absence of positive evidence for their use, the common scholarly interpretation of them as genuine graves continues to be the most plausible one. Considering the importance ascribed by the wealthy Athenians to funerary ceremonies and commemoration of the dead, the lack of any archaeological evidence for early battlefield burials of warriors (elite or not) in Archaic Athens, further goes against the possibility of the early warrior memorials being cenotaphs.

While the comrades of a deceased warrior were obliged to return their bodies, his enemies were eager to despoil his corpse, and were willing to risk their lives in the process. The weapons and armour of defeated elite warriors were still prized for their material and symbolic value, but they also continued to serve as physical testimony to the individual's bravery and martial prowess. Spoils of war, which featured so prominently in the *Iliad*, would have been dedicated to the gods in a sanctuary; this practice becomes increasingly common in the Archaic Greek world, as shown by a rich series of helmets and shields from Olympia from the seventh and sixth centuries BC. Captured arms were also just as likely to be displayed in a place of honour in one's household, where they would impress visitors and were often accompanied by inscriptions naming the warriors who took them.[50]

This model of early Greek combat highlights, first and foremost, the dominance of the elites over the Athenian armies of the Archaic period. Their superiority influenced the practice of combat and the norms regarding the treatment of the war dead. In addition, the style of fighting, which allowed the warriors to fight over and retrieve the fallen during the battle, must have involved a good deal of flexibility in formation, again probably similar to that depicted in Homeric accounts of combat and on Attic black-figure vases. Plundering the bodies of slain warriors in the midst of battle was, as Pamela Vaughn pointed out, 'simply not a practical endeavor during pitched hoplite battles' which were fought in phalanx formations, relying on the cohesiveness of the warriors, and the need for each individual to stay in rank.[51] The biggest danger for any phalanx was the creation of gaps in the shield-line, which would undoubtedly have been caused by warriors trying to snatch the armour of enemy corpses or to carry a slain comrade back to safety.[52] Such practices, as we have seen, were in all likelihood very common in the elite-dominated warfare of the Archaic period. This, in turn, suggests that early Greek phalanxes, if there ever were any, must have been relatively open and flexible formations, quite unlike the ones we know of from the Classical period.[53]

While our knowledge regarding the treatment of the elite fallen of Athens is fairly secure, the post-mortem fate of non-elite warriors is much harder to deduce. As we noted earlier, our sources for the period offer no explicit hints about the standard procedures for the disposal of the dead after a battle, and there are almost no surviving mass-burial mounds in Greece before the end of the sixth century BC. Most scholars assume that the majority of the dead were normally buried in a *polyandrion* on the battlefield, but the relative lack of any archaeologically visible mass graves may be an indication of the relative unimportance of such burials.[54] Alternatively, the lack of such graves, combined with the magnificence of the individual elite war burials in Attica, could suggest that early Athenian armies consisted primarily, if not exclusively, of the wealthiest citizens of the *polis*. The latter interpretation, which we will discuss at more length in the final part of this book, seems to find confirmation in the sudden disappearance of elite gravestones in Attica in the last years of the sixth century BC, paralleled by the first public burials of the war dead.

The final question that we should ask before we move on to the first examples of Athenian *polyandria*, is whether the elite custom of private repatriation of the war dead finds any parallels in other Greek *poleis* of the Archaic era. As usual, the scarcity of pre-Classical battle accounts, combined with virtually no examples of early *polyandria* in the Greek world, severely limits the potential for any comparisons. Our best case study is provided by Archaic Sparta. The Spartans, as shown in their famous epigram from Thermopylae and archaeological evidence from the Classical era, buried their dead on or near the battlefield.[55] Common burial 'on the spot' was emblematic of the egalitarian standing of the Spartan citizens (*homoioi*), conferring equal glory on those who sacrificed their lives in obedience to the *polis*. Furthermore, battlefield *polyandria* provided a relatively easy and cost-effective way to dispose of the dead, while also serving as physical reminders of past Spartan invasions for local communities.[56] But the origins of the custom in Sparta are mostly unclear and surrounded by the controversies of the so-called 'Spartan mirage' – a tendency of ancient authors to ascribe the ideal of an austere and militaristic society back to an immemorial past and the reforms of the legendary lawgiver Lycurgus. Some evidence, however, suggests that public burials on the battlefield were not always practised by the Spartans.

The key piece of evidence concerning the war dead in early Sparta is the aforementioned fragment of Tyrtaeus' martial elegy (12.23–34), associated with the Second Messenian War (*c.* 640–600 BC). According to Tyrtaeus, any Spartan who perishes in battle was to be granted 'good fame' (*kleos esthlon*) and respect for his family, along with a conspicuous tomb (*tumbos*). The latter, he adds, will be 'pointed out among the people' and successive generations, which clearly indicates that the tombs which Tyrtaeus had in mind were located in the city. This, in turn, has led some scholars to suspect that individual burials for the war dead at home were once practised in Sparta. Although archaeological evidence to support this notion is relatively scarce, a series of Archaic terracotta relief amphoras, which regularly depict scenes of warfare (including fights over the dead), has been viewed as funerary in purpose and potentially marking the individual graves of the Spartans who fell in battle.[57] Recent survey studies of Spartan burials, in addition, revealed a significant number of Archaic graves located along the central roads crossing through the urban centre, which stood in stark contrast to the more numerous burials in cemeteries on the margins of the city.[58] The resulting spatial differentiation, as Paul Christesen hypothesized, could have been driven by social factors: 'burial within the urban fabric of Sparta may have indicated that the individuals in question enjoyed elevated social standing'.[59] It is tempting to associate the graves with the tombs of the fallen warriors mentioned by Tyrtaeus, which, being 'pointed out among the people', must have been located in the most prestigious and visible areas of the city.

All this seems to imply that the custom of repatriation and individual burial was indeed practised by the Spartans in the days of Tyrtaeus and into the sixth century BC. The logistical and practical details behind it are beyond our reconstruction but we may assume that the system was not unlike the one prevalent in Archaic Athens: the bodies of the dead were carted back for burial at home whenever possible. Most importantly, however, the existence of a repatriation custom for the war dead in Sparta, centred around the idea of conspicuous burials for the individual fallen, lends major support to the assumption that similar arrangements were indeed in place at Athens (and potentially elsewhere). The evidence for pre-Classical burials in Sparta, despite its somewhat tentative nature, has led scholars to posit that a major change in the practice of war burials must have occurred at some point during the sixth century BC. Such change is often associated with the ephorate of Chilon in the 550s BC and the beginnings of the Spartan hegemony in the Peloponnese, which might have included a programme of reforms aiming to institutionalize the Spartan citizen army.[60] The earliest sign of the latter might have been the common burial of the fallen after the battle of Thyrea (c. 546 BC), seen by most scholars as the first instance of Spartans burying their war dead 'on the spot', which became the standard practice of their armies following the battle.[61]

Whether similar changes occurred in other Greek *poleis* towards the end of the Archaic era is harder to ascertain. A move towards more communal ways to commemorate citizens falling in battle is implied by an inscribed sepulchral monument from Ambrakia, discovered in 1986 and dated to around 550 BC. The inscription honours citizens killed in combat, four of whom are mentioned by name, who died while accompanying ambassadors from Corinth, therefore bringing grief to their 'lovely homeland' (*SEG* 41–540). It is difficult to tell anything about the historical circumstances behind the monument, or indeed whether it served as a cenotaph or was built over a *polyandrion*, but the surviving epigram does point to an early instance of a public war memorial commemorating fallen citizens.[62] Although similar monuments do not appear in Greece until the end of the sixth century BC, there are some indications that Archaic *poleis* were taking more control over post-battle procedures of their citizen armies. The practice of collective dedications of war spoils is one example of this, as weapons from Panhellenic sanctuaries begin to bear inscriptions naming the citizens of the donor *poleis* (in nominative plural; as opposed to private dedicants) from the second half of the sixth century BC onwards. In her recent study, Janett Schröder emphasized the dominance of such city-state dedications of weapons at Olympia, stressing the importance of the practice as part of the early war memory making process.[63] While the move towards public dedications highlights the growing importance of community spirit among Archaic militias, it also suggests an increased level of army organization, as control over the spoils of war became gradually more regulated by public measures.[64] It remains unclear whether the latter were also extended to other procedures, including those governing the internment of the war dead, but they herald a wider movement away from private modes of war making in the late Archaic period.

In Athens, one aspect of the move towards greater public control over battle procedures was the abandonment of the custom of private burials for fallen warriors. It transpired on both practical and ideological levels, as the Athenians put a stop to individual distinction in burial and shifted the emphasis to communal values associated with the democratic city. Accordingly, the war dead were no longer buried individually; the 'hierarchical' ideals enshrined in the Homeric epics lost their relevance and appeal, replaced with a new 'egalitarian' model, which made all warriors equal in death and burial. The evidence of iconography and archaeology discussed in this and the previous chapter reveals that the first signs of the new discourse on the war dead emerged in Athens towards the end of the sixth century BC. As artistic depictions of the combat fallen dramatically declined in number, so did the elite monuments which commemorated the deceased as warriors. These phenomena, as we will see in the following chapter, coincided with the appearance of the first Athenian *polyandria* in the wake of the democratic reforms of Cleisthenes. Taken altogether, they heralded the introduction of the Classical custom of *patrios nomos*.

5

Ancestral Customs in the Classical City

The institution of public burials for the war dead was deeply engrained in the collective consciousness of the Classical Athenians. Death in military service on behalf of the *polis* guaranteed 'a splendid and magnificent funeral' (Pl. *Menex.* 234c) in the Kerameikos, the 'most beautiful suburb of the city' (Thuc. 2.34.5). In the latter decades of the fifth century BC, the privilege of repatriation and burial was indeed ubiquitous, as shown by the variety of cultural discourses which engaged with the custom. One of these was comedy. A scene from Aristophanes' play *The Birds*, produced for the City Dionysia in 414 BC, features an exchange between Peisthetairos and Euelpides, two Athenian citizens who, tired of paying fines and the city's obsession with lawsuits, fled Athens in search of a more peaceful place. After finding their way to Tereus (turned hoopoe), they become involved in a skirmish with the chorus of birds. Having to defend themselves with kitchen utensils, the men anticipate the worst and discuss burial plans:

Euelpides   But tell me, if we do get killed, where on earth will we be buried?

Peisthetairos   Kerameikos will take us. You see, we'll get a state funeral by telling the generals that we died fighting the enemy at Orneae.

Av. 393–9

Orneae, a play on words (*orneon* – bird), refers to a town in the Argolid which the Athenians seized with minimal effort in the winter of 415 BC (Thuc. 6.7). The scene insinuates that the standards to secure a burial in the Kerameikos were comically low: a dubious story of an insignificant skirmish was enough. Although the passage parodies the custom of state funerals in Classical Athens, perhaps poking fun at the fact that dead men could not justify their right to such honour, as Peisthetairos absurdly suggests he and Euelpides will, it simultaneously highlights the absolute confidence which the Athenian public had in the institution no matter the circumstances.[1]

The institution of the public funeral for the war dead, taken for granted by Aristophanes' audience, was far removed from the realities of the Archaic

Athenians, who regarded home burials for war casualties as the sole privilege of the elites. Extending it to every casualty of war, regardless of social or economic status, demonstrates the extent of the change in the customs of the Classical era. In many ways, however, the decision to repatriate the remains of the fallen was not the obvious choice; common burial on the battlefield, practised by the Spartans, was certainly the simpler option.[2] The process of identification, cremation by tribe, repatriation, storage and burial was costly and complicated; casualties of major battles could have numbered in the hundreds and required transportation over considerable distances across the Athenian maritime empire.[3] The institution of public burial was, therefore, without doubt a true testimony to the administrative and financial infrastructure of the *polis*. But more importantly, it demonstrated the commitment of the state to those who sacrificed their lives on its behalf, while also providing an ever-present platform, both cultural and political, to perpetuate the democratic values held by the community.[4] The ideological language adopted by the institution to achieve this, as has long been recognized by scholars, merged the elite discourses of the past generations with the city's new self-image, centred on egalitarianism and equality in death. Evoking the Archaic concepts of glory and heroism in funeral monuments and speeches, the Athenians ascribed the institution with elements of timeless significance. The continuity with the past, as this chapter explores, extended also to the level of practice, which could have played an equally important role in the 'ancestral' status of public burial in Classical Athens.

Towards public burials

The second half of the sixth century BC witnessed some major changes in the burial evidence of Archaic Attica. First, the conspicuous grave markers of the elites, after reaching peak magnificence around 560–540 BC, begin to dwindle in size. The crowning element of the relief *stelai*, which consisted of a separate finial (such as a sphinx) attached to the monument, disappears from about 530 BC, and is replaced by simpler decoration carved on to the *stele*.[5] This less elaborate, and somewhat cheaper, form apparently allowed more people to afford them, because the number of adult burials rises in the last decades of the sixth century BC; an increase, according to Ian Morris, that may provide us with a glimpse of the social widening of the burial group in Attica.[6] The radical transformation, however, takes place only towards the very end of the century, when the number of graves undergoes a dramatic rise commonly associated with the establishment of the first 'citizen cemeteries' in Athens. Between 510 and 480 BC, the grave markers of Athenian elites that had dominated the funerary record of the Archaic period, including the *kouroi* and *stelai* commemorating war casualties, disappear. Equally, the familiar visual signs of high status and conspicuous consumption are completely banished from the cemeteries.[7] These developments are also accompanied by wider changes in burial customs, including the sudden rise in the number of small-child and infant burials, reflecting growing concerns about legitimacy and the concepts of family and infancy.[8] Taken together, the momentous changes in burial evidence which took place at the end of the Archaic period seem to accompany the new social values associated with Cleisthenes' reforms of 508/7 BC. It is, therefore, not surprising that the first instances of public *polyandria* built for the war dead appear around the very same time, just when the newly democratic Athenian *polis* began to take full control over its fallen citizens.

While the first Athenian public burials for war casualties are usually dated to the years immediately following the introduction of democracy, some communal graves of an earlier date have occasionally been identified as potential *polyandria*. One example is a fragment of a *stele* with two columns inscribed with names, dated to *c.* 550 BC and found close to the south-western gates of Athens.[9] Despite admitting uncertainty as to whether the name-list was a gravestone, Lilian Jeffery suggested that the *stele* could have been a cenotaph to commemorate men lost at sea or in combat, or a *polyandrion* made on the field of battle.[10] The evidence, however, is far too limited and fragmentary to confirm any such suggestion, and, as Clairmont pointed out, it is not entirely clear to which battle the *stele* would refer and why a casualty list would be erected by the city gate in the south-west.[11] Considering that the next casualty list does not appear in Athens until the end of the sixth century BC, the possibility of a *polyandrion* at such an early date is very slim and should be dismissed unless further evidence can be found. Another potential candidate for an early casualty list comes from a *stele* found in the Anavyssos area, also dated to around 550 BC.[12] The monument contained a list of names and perhaps the name of a dedicator (Oionichos?), which again led Jeffery to suspect that it was a *polyandrion* or a cenotaph erected for casualties of a battle or a shipwreck. She also speculated that there were columns missing, which led her to conclude that 'this is a casualty list arranged under the headings of the tribes.'[13] This interpretation is again problematic, since any arrangement of casualty names by tribe seems highly doubtful at such an early date. Furthermore, considering the location of the Anavyssos area – far removed from the political centre at Athens – it seems unlikely that the only example of an early Athenian public *polyandrion* would have been located there. The monument was, therefore, in all likelihood built by private means; and while it could have commemorated the casualties of war (Pallene?), the decision not to employ the traditional media of commemorating the war dead (*kouroi*, warrior *stelai*), which become widespread around 550s BC, suggests that its function lay elsewhere.[14] In general, the lack of any clear-cut evidence for communal warrior graves in pre-508 BC Attica makes any speculations concerning early casualty lists highly conjectural.[15]

Our only evidence for an early public burial of an Athenian comes from an anecdotal story told by Herodotus. According to him, when Solon visited the court of Croesus in Sardis, the Lydian king, who thought himself the happiest of all men, asked him if he ever met anyone happier. Solon, preferring truth to flattery, surprisingly named a certain Tellus of Athens, who lived a prosperous life, had many fine sons and: 'crowned his life with a most glorious death: for in a battle between the Athenians and their neighbours at Eleusis he attacked and routed the enemy and most nobly there died; and the Athenians gave him public burial where he fell and paid him great honour' (1.30). The story, if we can believe Herodotus, provides our earliest instance of a public (*demosie*) burial in Athens. In addition, it has also been taken by some scholars as evidence for the custom of burial on the battlefield being practised by the Athenians in the Archaic period.[16] It seems more likely, however, that the honours bestowed upon Tellus as a result of his deeds in the battle were exceptional; we should not, therefore, assume that such honours were normally extended to all Athenians who fell. The only information which Herodotus gives us is that Tellus was buried individually on the battlefield, and that his tomb, which perhaps resembled the monuments we discussed earlier, was paid for by the Athenians. Furthermore, the exceptional nature of Tellus' burial on the battlefield may indicate that the normal procedure was indeed to return the bodies of fallen warriors back home for burial.[17] As such, it would confirm our assumption that this was the standard practice following any military encounter in the Archaic period.

The first warrior grave which most historians associate with an Athenian *polyandrion* was located near the Euripus and commemorated the dead from the battle between the Athenians and the Chalcidians in 506 BC (Hdt. 5.77).[18] Our knowledge about it comes from an epigram ascribed traditionally to Simonides, which would have been inscribed on a monument set above the grave:

> We fell under the fold of Dirphys, and our funeral mound was raised near the Euripus by our country. And not undeservedly: for we lost our delightful youth facing the rugged cloud of battle.[19]

Planudean Anthology 26

The inscription states very clearly that the funeral mound was raised at public expense (*demosia*), and contained the bodies of all the warriors who fell in battle. As such, it provides us with arguably the first Greek communal tomb erected by the state, which contained the remains of all fallen, without any distinction for social class. The identity of the men buried in the *polyandrion*, however, was a subject of a scholarly debate.[20] According to Denys Page, the admission of defeat (*edmethemen*), combined with the lack of any references to defending the community, suggests that the tomb belonged to the defeated Euboeans.[21] His reading has been subsequently revised by Hugh Lloyd-Jones, who stated that *edmethemen* should be read instead as 'we were killed', and does not necessarily imply defeat.[22] In addition, the absence of any patriotic considerations should not be taken as particularly unusual; the general rhetoric of the epigram uses elements familiar from Archaic epigrams for the war dead, referring to the loss of 'delightful youth' and the 'rugged cloud of battle', so its failure to mention the community is entirely in line with Archaic Athenian discourse of praising the war dead.[23] The Euboean *polyandrion* is, therefore, widely assumed to belong to the Athenian dead and is our earliest evidence for a new burial practice for war casualties imposed and supervised by the state. Its uniqueness is twofold: first, it was the first mass burial on the battlefield, which broke with the custom of returning the fallen back to their families; second, it was public and in line with the new democratic regime introduced in Athens. The inclusion of the word *demosia*, as Clairmont summarized, 'is just what one expects the poet to have been 'dictated' by the officials of the Democracy which in its infant stage was proud to give Athens' casualties for a first time in its history public burial'.[24] And even though the wider discourse employed in the epigram was still based on the old values of the elites, the egalitarian spirit and the ideal behind the actual burial must have indeed been revolutionary.

That the new custom of common battlefield burials seen in the Euboean *polyandrion* was practised in early democratic Athens is confirmed subsequently by the earliest Athenian casualty list, which commemorated the dead who fell during the conquest of Lemnos in *c.* 498 BC (Hdt. 6.140).[25] The fragmentary list consists of a *stele* inscribed on three sides with fifteen names in total, and dated roughly to the period of Miltiades' conquest of Lemnos. The names are written by an Attic mason and are arranged according to Athenian tribes, which indicates that the commemorated men most likely came from the contingent sent from Athens to aid in the operation, and did not include any Athenian settlers from Chersonese, as suggested by Jeffery.[26] Similar *stelai*, according to Pausanias' account (1.32.3), were also erected a few years later over the grave of the Athenian dead who fell in the battle of Marathon.[27] This, in turn, lends further support to the thesis that the earliest Athenian casualty lists were built over battlefield *polyandria* which pre-dated those erected as part of the later state burials in the Kerameikos.[28] Other examples of battlefield burials of Athenians in this period, including the dead from Artemision, Salamis and Plataea, confirm that the custom was a relatively common feature in the early decades of the Athenian democracy.[29]

In addition to battlefield burials, however, some of the fallen Athenians could have been also brought back for a communal burial at home. One example of such a practice is provided by the tomb of the casualties from a series of naval engagements against Aegina which took place around 491/0 BC (Hdt. 6.90–3).[30] Pausanias' includes this *taphos* in his description of the war burials at Kerameikos, clearly stating that it referred to conflicts before the Persian invasions (1.29.7). This example may be taken as an indication that public burials in the Kerameikos, which formed an essential part of the later *patrios nomos* custom, were already a possibility in the 490s BC. Considering the silence of our main sources regarding other public burials in the period, including those from the Ionian revolt or Mycale, it seems plausible to assume that the example of the Aeginetan dead was not an exception and that the casualties of other conflicts could have been also brought back to Athens.[31] If so, the early coexistence of two modes of public burials (battlefield and home) may indicate that early battlefield burials, such as those in Chalcis, Marathon and Plataea, were seen as special distinction and honour, reminiscent of the case of Tellus, whom the Athenians paid 'great honour' by burying him where he fell.[32] Such burials, which feature more prominently in the surviving historical record, eventually ceased around the 460s BC, after which the Athenians adopted one standard practice of public burial at home for all casualties of war.

A *patrios nomos*

Abandoning the old private custom of bringing back individual fallen must have had a profound impact on the Athenian *polis* and its citizens. By taking sole control over the bodies of dead warriors, the newly democratic city adopted the role played previously by the family. Consequently, retrieving casualties during combat was no longer of paramount importance, as all Athenian dead were made equal in accordance with the egalitarian ideals championed by the new regime. The disappearance of images depicting fights over corpses, which we witness precisely in this period, provides a very clear indication of the declining importance of such motifs, both in the reality and ideology of combat; in a symbolic realm, the increasing absence of such scenes matches the absence of the physical bodies, taken away from their families and claimed by the city.³³ Once a symbol of individual heroism and beautiful death, the imagery on these vases was gradually replaced by a different artistic discourse associated with the war dead and their commemoration in Classical Athens.

In some cases, the new discourses in art continued to rely on elements drawn from the iconographical themes preserved in black-figure representations of combat. The main example of this is the series of red-figure vases known as the warrior *loutrophoroi*. Around forty pieces of these vases have been found, appearing first between 490–480 BC. Their close association with war is apparent both in their martial imagery and the fact that many were discovered in the Kerameikos among the offerings accompanying a public *polyandrion* dated to *c.* 430 BC.³⁴ The warrior *loutrophoroi* depict a variety of combat scenes, including duels, departures and the Amazonomachy (Fig. 11), featuring hoplites, light-armed troops and cavalry. Reaching up to a metre in height and decorated by leading painters, they might have provided the Athenian elites an alternative way, as Patricia Hannah speculated, 'for costly display outside the grave in the

Fig. 11 Fragmentary red-figure terracotta loutrophoros, attributed to a painter of the Group of Polygnotos, *c.* 440 BC. The Metropolitan Museum of Art, New York, No. 38.11.4a,b / Fletcher Fund, 1938.

absence of more extravagant stone monuments'.[35] Since traditional opportunities for honouring the war dead were no longer available around the time of the Persian Wars, Hannah proposed that the sudden addition of military themes to the *loutrophoroi*, otherwise associated with nuptial scenes, can be understood as a response to the institution of public funerals.[36] The high quality and relatively small number of these vases suggests that this response likely originated with the Athenian elites wishing to express their grief over the deaths of their sons but denied the usual means to do so.[37]

In most cases, however the new iconographic discourse on the war dead diverged from the past representations of heroic deeds on the battlefield. The key evidence is provided by the white-ground *lekythoi*, which the Athenians used in a funerary context from around the 460s BC. Their imagery, in particular scenes depicting Hypnos and Thanatos carrying dead warriors (Fig. 12), could still allude to episodes from the epic and the ideals of *kalos thanatos*, but their message no longer challenged the viewer to specific actions.[38] Instead, we are left

Fig. 12 White-ground lekythos, attributed to the Thanatos Painter, found in Athens, *c.* 435–425 BC. The British Museum, London, No. 1876,0328.1.

to contemplate the scene and the transition of the fallen warrior to the realm of the dead. The dead, often still wearing their armour, are not presented in the context of the battlefield; we now see them next to a tomb, where the presence of their shades (*eidola*) could be felt by their grieving relatives.[39] Such imagery enabled the families to commemorate their sons in a private and intimate way, juxtaposed to the new public modes associated with state burials. In effect, as Nathan Arrington observed, they 'questioned the commemorative sufficiency of the *patrios nomos*'[40]. Although employing a different discourse to the warrior *loutrophoroi*, the imagery of white-ground *lekythoi* also evoked the elite customs of the past, where corpses were brought back to their families for burial. The latter practices, however, were incompatible with the new civic ideology. With the rise of the egalitarian spirit in the first decades of democracy, the Archaic practices associated with the treatment of war casualties were abandoned – reflected in the profound changes in the war imagery concerning the war dead.[41] The old customs, nonetheless, were reembraced, albeit in a modified way, by the *polis* and the ideology behind the *patrios nomos*.

At what date the funeral ceremonies for the war dead were officially established at Athens has been a matter of much historical debate and speculation, beginning with Thucydides' famous statement about the supposed antiquity of the custom.[42] According to him, the Athenians always buried those who had fallen in war in the public cemetery, or *demosion sema*, except for 'those who fell at Marathon; for their valour the Athenians judged to be preeminent and they buried them on the spot where they fell' (2.34.5). His decision to omit the burial of the Athenians at Plataea, as well as some other early examples of battlefield *polyandria*, has confused scholars ever since antiquity. Conflicting dates are proposed by Diodorus, Dionysios of Halicarnassus and Pausanias, as they tried to untangle the origins of the custom and its various components, including the funeral oration and games.[43] Modern historians are in similar disagreement: some suggest Cleisthenes' reforms, others look towards the immediate aftermath of the Persian Wars, and most credit Cimon or Ephialtes for introducing the customs. And although establishing the precise date behind the *patrios nomos* in Athens is not imperative for the argument of this study, the investigation so far suggests that the most likely period for the emergence of an official policy which required the repatriation of all war dead, in *all* cases and circumstances, could not have been in place before the end of the Persian Wars. The repeated recurrence of Athenian battlefield burials before 480s BC, which appear to have coexisted with early public graves in the Kerameikos reported by Pausanias, strongly implies that the custom that we know from the Classical era was a product of a later date. This, however, does not mean that the full institution simply sprang from nowhere, or indeed from the head of Cimon or Ephialtes.

Instead, it seems far more likely to assume that the introduction of *patrios nomos* at Athens was a piecemeal process. The first and most important step consisted of transferring control of the war dead from private to public hands, signalled by the disappearance of individual warrior *stelai* in the last decade of the sixth century BC. As the Athenian *polis* found itself in full control of the dead, new forms of communal burial and commemoration were gradually formed and adopted, including mass *polyandria* on the battlefields and in the Kerameikos, casualty lists, and (eventually) funeral games and orations.[44] The process of crystallization of all these components began around the time of Cleisthenes' reforms and was later heavily influenced by the experience of the Persian Wars. The latter, as we saw earlier in this book, had a major impact on Athenian cultural and military self-identity, in which customs surrounding the proper burial of war casualties, together with the radical condemnation of the maltreatment of the dead, played an essential part. In the end, after years of development and readjustment, the separate components of these customs took on their final form under the official heading of the *patrios nomos*.[45]

But while the customs of state burial became quickly associated with the egalitarian spirit of Athenian democracy, the ideological discourse which they employed was heavily drawn from the older rhetoric used by the Athenian elites of the Archaic period. As Loraux demonstrated in her study of the Athenian funeral oration, the language used by the orators praising the war dead during the annual celebrations was marked by elite values and representations. By drawing on the concepts of heroic achievement, agonistic spirit and beautiful death, the city extended the domain of war, once monopolized by the elites, to all citizens, with no distinction of social or economic status: 'it promised its valorous citizens a fine tomb and a verse epigram, once the privilege of the aristocracy, now the reward for courage, and, for much of the fifth century, only for courage, as the prohibition on all luxurious appointments in private burial places suggests'.[46] The funeral oration was, therefore, for the first time able to combine the discourses behind the Archaic monuments of Kroisos, Tettichos and Xenokles, imbued with highly elitist and personalized values, with those represented by the warrior *stelai* of Aristion and others, emphasizing the communal aspects of serving in the Athenian army. This combination, which provides the Athenian counterpart to the martial elegies of Callinus and Tyrtaeus, redefined the existing concept of *kalos thanatos* by adding the patriotic aspects missing from the Archaic sepulchral epigrams.[47]

Similarities between the *patros nomos* and Archaic customs surrounding the war dead, nonetheless, extended beyond the funeral oration. As our investigation has shown, the principle of bringing home the remains of war casualties, once widespread in the elite-driven warfare of the Archaic period, despite being occasionally adopted in the first decades after Cleisthenes' reforms, was temporarily replaced by communal battlefield burials, treated as a mark of special honour and privilege for all regardless of status and social standing. The later establishment of repatriation as a crucial element of the institution of *patrios nomos* forms something of an ideological bridge with the old customs of the Archaic era. Naturally, the new procedures were significantly different from the Archaic rites, dictated by the democratic nature of the *polis*. All the dead had to be returned and buried in the same place with no input from families, and finances were provided by the state. But the principle of repatriation, common in the elite ideology which permeated Athenian warfare in the sixth century BC, remained unchanged. As such, the privilege available once only to the wealthiest was granted to all Athenians, as death for one's country raised the social status of the poorest citizens to that of the elite warriors of old, brought home and commemorated by elaborate tombstones and epigrams. To bestow upon these procedures the trappings of ancient legitimacy, the Athenian institution of state burial evoked a far older custom in its treatment of the war dead, one which existed – in all likelihood predated – the days of Solon. This custom, which Clairmont referred to as 'a *patrios nomos*', allowed the city to take full control over the commemoration of its fallen sons, and by extension, the ideology and practice of war.[48] And the significance of returning to a *patrios nomos*, or repatriating the bones of the dead, as part of the new state institution, certainly deserves no less consideration than the funeral oration.[49]

The continuity in the practice, however, worked not only on the level of ideology. Perhaps more importantly, the decision to bring back the remains of every last man who died on behalf of the city was mostly felt on a purely human level. The families of the fallen warriors, who once used to bury their sons in private, were denied the opportunity to do so with the advent of democracy in Athens. This absence of bodies to wash, grieve over, bury and commemorate, must have been profoundly felt. In this light, the city's decision to repatriate the remains of the war dead and provide them with a much celebrated home burial would have offered meaningful ways to compensate for this absence. As the symbolic and physical presence of the dead was re-established, new private discourses of mourning appeared, shown by the evidence of the warrior *loutrophoroi* and the white-ground *lekythoi*, which associate the departed souls of the fallen with public tombs in the Kerameikos. The custom of mass repatriation, as we saw at the beginning of this chapter, was no easy task. It required a robust administrative system and considerable financial input. Since the decision to adopt it was not immediately taken, we should suspect that the custom was under negotiation in the early decades of the democratic city. Its final establishment sometime after the Persian Wars was, accordingly, a powerful demonstration of the city's commitment to its citizens. And while it became fundamental within the larger institution of state burials for the war dead in Classical Athens, perhaps more so than scholars previously thought, the main reward was the citizens' commitment to the city.

*

In his *Agamemnon* of 458 BC, the first play of the *Oresteia* trilogy, Aeschylus provides us with a memorable description of the ashes of the war dead being returned home from Troy. The chorus, making a long speech on the terrible costs of war, contemplates the tragic fate of those who fell far from home:

> There is much, at any rate, that strikes deep into the soul: one knows the men one sent off, but instead of human beings urns and ashes arrive back at each man's home. Ares, the moneychanger of bodies, holding his scales in the battle of spears, sends back from Ilium to their dear ones heavy dust that has been through the fire, to be sadly wept over, filling easily-stowed urns with ash given in exchange for men.
>
> *Ag.* 432–444

The practice described here by Aeschylus in many ways resembles the Athenian customs which must still have been relatively new in Aeschylus' day. Some small divergences, however, suggest that the playwright was not referring to the state burials of the Classical period. The war dead in *Agamemnon* are not cremated communally but individually, and each man's ashes (*spodos*) are returned to his 'dear ones'.[50] While the passage has confused some scholars, it is clear that in writing the speech, Aeschylus, born of a wealthy family at Eleusis in 525 BC, had in mind a private custom followed by the Athenians in his youth.[51] The antiquity of this custom, which involved the return of individual warriors to their families for burial, was far more suitable for the subject matter of his play, and as such gives us a unique glimpse into the fate of the war dead in Archaic Athens.

The custom of repatriating the remains of the war dead, as we have observed in the second part of this book, was central to the practice of war in Archaic Athens. Its importance was reflected both on black-figure vases that depicted fights over the fallen and combat recoveries; and in the elaborate graves of the Athenian elites, which commemorated them as war casualties who died a heroic and beautiful death on the battlefield. The practice, despite some changes in the style of sepulchral monuments, continued unhindered throughout the Archaic period until the last years of the sixth century BC and the democratic reforms of Cleisthenes. The latter, which transferred control of the war dead from Athenian families to the newly democratic state, ended the custom of private retrieval and burial in favour of communal battlefield burials and public graves in the Kerameikos. In time, the principle of the repatriation of the war dead was officially reinstated in its new egalitarian guise as part of the institution of state burial for war casualties. Although in many ways strikingly innovative, the discourse of *patrios nomos* allowed the Athenians to forge commonalities between their democratic present and the Archaic past. This apparently unbroken legacy helps to explain why it was widely seen as 'ancestral' by later citizens. Since the Archaic age, the war dead had held a special place in the collective memory and culture of the Athenians, whether in epic songs, drama and art or indeed, in the absurd exploits of Euelpides and Peisthetaerus and their battle with the birds in Aristophanes' comedy. And as the final part of this book will show, studying their burials can tell us a lot about war, the state and society in early Athens.

Part Three

6

War, State and Society in Archaic Athens

In 506 BC, the newly democratic Athenian *polis* found itself in a near impossible position. According to a famous account by Herodotus (5.74–7), Attica was invaded on three different fronts. The Spartan king Cleomenes, in response to his unsuccessful attempt to install Isagoras as tyrant in Athens, rallied a large Peloponnesian army in the south and marched on Eleusis. At the same time the Boeotians attacked from the west, taking Oenoe and Hysiae, whilst the Chalcidians ravaged Attic villages in the north. Facing highly improbable odds and the possibility of total defeat and humiliation, the Athenians responded to the threat with extraordinary efficiency, defeating all of their enemies in just one day. After the Peloponnesian force disbanded due to internal disagreements, the Athenians first dealt with the Boeotian army, winning a major victory by the Euripus; later, 'on the very same day', they crossed the strait to Euboea and despatched the Chalcidians in a similarly decisive fashion.[1] The victories, which became a landmark moment for the newly established Athenian democracy, were commemorated on the Acropolis, where the Athenians hung up the chains used to shackle the many prisoners taken after the battles, accompanied by a celebratory inscription and a bronze four-horse chariot (Hdt. 5.77).[2] In Herodotus' estimation, the reason for this seemingly unlikely success was unmistakeably clear and had everything to do with the political system at Athens. Equality of rights and speech (*isegoria*), as he explains, had changed the face of the Athenian military:

> Now, the advantages of everyone having a voice in the political procedure are not restricted just to single instances, but are plain to see wherever one looks. For instance, while the Athenians were ruled by tyrants, they were no better at warfare than any of their neighbours, but once they had got rid of the tyrants they became vastly superior. This goes to show that while they were under an oppressive regime they fought below their best because they were working for a master, whereas as free men each individual wanted to achieve something for himself.[3]
>
> Hdt. 5.78

Despite the obvious problems with the plausibility of Herodotus' narrative of the events of 506 BC, many scholars have adopted his view on the correlation between the political and military developments of the Athenian *polis* in the late-sixth century BC. The main strength of this interpretation has been most commonly sought in the limited and relatively unsuccessful nature of Athenian military exploits in the Archaic period, which led to an influential scholarly belief that Athens had no official system or means to mobilize large, citizen armies prior to the reforms of Cleisthenes and the introduction of democracy in 508/7 BC.[4] Archaic warfare, according to this view, consisted primarily of small-scale raids, infrequent and most often private in character, carried out by bands of aristocratic warriors who mobilized their followers whenever a need or opportunity for profit presented itself. Such war-bands, being self-sufficient by nature, fell outside the control of any public institutions and normally consisted of tens or hundreds of men at best, all of whom provided their own equipment and belonged to the elite strata of Archaic societies. Due to the lack of efficient administrative and financial bodies, mobilization of large-scale, public forces was beyond the capabilities of Archaic *poleis*. As a result, as Frank Frost argued in his seminal article, 'no regular mobilization' took place in pre-Cleisthenic Athens.[5] Since it 'lacked an institutional mechanism for mustering soldiers', as David Pritchard posited in his recent study, Archaic Athens 'did not have a publicly controlled army or any institutional means for mobilising soldiers, while the small numbers of Athenians who bothered to march out for battle did so very infrequently'.[6]

The scholarly notion of decentralized and aristocratic war-bands of the Archaic period is foreshadowed by Thucydides, who stresses the prevalence of 'armed robbery', both by land and at sea, as a common form of warfare among the Hellenes. Piracy and plundering of unprotected cities and communities, he explains, instigated and led by powerful individuals, was widespread and once considered an honourable profession (1.5-6). Not unlike Herodotus, the Athenian historian argues that significant changes came only with the growth of public institutions and infrastructure, which he dates to the end of the Archaic period in Athens, which truly enabled Greek city-states to expand their territories and power within the Hellenic world.[7]

Such ancient accounts, however, are inevitably fraught with difficulties, as they tend to oversimplify the general narrative in pursuit of specific and often very tangible historical agendas. Both Herodotus and Thucydides had clear reasons to downplay the level of development of Archaic Athens, from both a political and social perspective, and in particular to emphasize the insignificant nature, compared to the Persian and later Peloponnesian Wars, of early Athenian military exploits.[8] Their accounts, nonetheless, highlight the importance of the relationship between political, economic and social factors, and their impact on the composition of the army and the practice of war in Archaic Greece. These ancient considerations have formed a large part of modern scholarly debates on early Greece, and especially theories concerning the growth of the Athenian state.[9]

In Book 7 of the *Politics* (1328b2–24), Aristotle provides a list of essential functions and services which comprise a *polis*, allowing it to achieve the ideal condition of self-sufficiency (*autarkeia*). Among the list of six different needs, military sufficiency in the form of possession of arms for citizen members, 'both to use among themselves and for purposes of government, in cases of insubordination, and to employ against those who try to molest them from without', together with a good supply of money, are taken as vital for the successful existence of any city-state. Maintaining and administering a reliable fighting force based on the citizen members of the community is, therefore, seen by Aristotle as a natural requirement, 'indispensable for the existence of a state' (1328b3).[10] The importance of such citizen militias in the emergence of first city-states in Greece during the eighth century BC has been a foundational assumption for the 'hoplite revolution' model, which as noted before in this book, follows Aristotle's account and sees the rise of small-scale, subsistence farmers as fundamental to the early development of the Greek *poleis* and the introduction of first hoplite armies. The seeming lack of any reliable evidence for publicly raised and controlled armies until the very end of the Archaic period, which one can glimpse from the accounts of Herodotus and Thucydides, does, however, put any such considerations into serious doubt. On the other hand, positing that all early war activities fell to the control of a handful of wealthy citizens, who carried on privately organized and largely unchecked military ventures – with little or no control from the often complex Archaic city-states – can be seen as equally questionable. The answer has to be more nuanced, taking a more critical approach to the generalizing statements of the ancient literary sources.

It is clear that the division between 'private' and 'public', 'pre-state' and 'state' methods of waging war in early Greece, recognized in Yvon Garlan's seminal *War in the Ancient World: A Social History*, has important ramifications for our understanding of war and society in Archaic Athens.[11] The treatment and burial of the war dead, which as we saw in the previous chapter, underwent a radical transformation from old 'hierarchical' to new 'egalitarian' ideals, underscores this division and hints at important changes which gradually permeated the ideology, social composition and organization of early Greek military forces throughout the period. Tracing the process by which the war dead fell from private to public hands can, therefore, provide important insights in to the shape and functioning of the Archaic Athenian state and society. The main challenge for such a study, however, concerns the shape and structure of the pre-Cleisthenic army at Athens, about which our sources tell us very little, leaving us, as Henk Singor concluded, 'completely in the dark'.[12]

The traditional way of approaching the subject of pre-Cleisthenic military organization has been to focus on the few Athenian military ventures of the period and draw conclusions based almost exclusively on the accounts of Herodotus, Aristotle and Plutarch.[13] These, however, are too often skewed, conflicted and hazy in their details, and cannot provide us with a full and reliable picture. A new range of source material is needed to evaluate critically the available literary evidence; and as we have seen throughout our investigation, some of the most abundant sources for studying the Archaic period – myths, burials and artistic depictions on pottery – happen to concern the war dead.[14] Our final task in this book, therefore, will be to look at early Athenian military and social history from a different angle, incorporating the insights we gained concerning the treatment of the war dead in the previous chapters, glimpsed from the mythological, archaeological and iconographic evidence of the period. These insights, I will argue, throw new light on the Athenian military developments of the Archaic period, suggesting that Herodotus' influential and all-encompassing explanation – that democracy drove the development of warfare and stood behind the extraordinary Athenian victory against Sparta, Thebes and Chalcis in 506 BC – may be a little too naive and simplistic.

Early Athens

Relatively little is known about the history of Athens prior to 600 BC, because most of our accounts consist of legendary stories about the unification (*synoikismos*) of Attica, supposedly orchestrated by Theseus; and occasional, vague mentions in later authors whose focus is usually on much later events.[15] Despite these difficulties, a common thread which runs through all literary sources describes a society rigidly divided into two classes: the wealthy notables (*gnorimoi*) or noblemen (*eupatridae*), who controlled all of the best agricultural land; and the poor dependants (*pelatai*), who worked the fields of the rich and were also referred to as the 'sixth-parters' (*hektemoroi*). In his account of seventh-century BC Athens, Aristotle described the pervading state of inequality, stating that the many were enslaved to the few, which led to long periods of strife (*stasis*) and political instability:[16]

> (...) there was strife between the notables and the multitude that lasted a long time. For the Athenian constitution was in all respects oligarchical, and in fact the poor themselves and also their wives and children were actually in slavery to the rich; and they were called dependants, and Sixth-part-tenants (for that was the rent they paid for the rich men's land which they farmed, and the whole of the country was in few hands), and if they ever failed to pay their rents, they themselves and their children were liable to arrest (...) Thus the most grievous and bitter thing in the state of public affairs for the masses was their slavery; not but what they were discontented also about everything, else, for they found themselves virtually without a share in anything.
>
> [*Ath. Pol.*] 2.1–3

In addition to having full control of agricultural land, the Athenian notables wielded exclusive power over the early political, legal and religious affairs of the city. Their leading roles in the early *polis*, according to Plutarch (*Thes.* 25), had been entrusted to them by the time of Theseus, who gave the noblemen (*eupatridae*) 'the care of religious rites, the supply of magistrates, the teaching of the laws, and the interpretation of the will of Heaven'. The nature of the Eupatrids' domination over the political affairs of the city has been traditionally understood to be based on their superior and noble birth. Their name – 'the sons of good fathers' – combined with the repeated mentions of birth and wealth as important factors in early Athenian politics in Aristotle's account, led many scholars to see the Eupatrids as a strictly aristocratic group.[17] Recent studies, however, have questioned this interpretation, stressing that the term was never mentioned in any early literary sources and was most likely a later Athenian invention.[18] Accordingly, the significance of birth as an important factor behind political power and elite membership in Athens was doubted, along with the existence of any aristocracies in the wider Greek world.[19] And while good birth may have played some role in early Athenian political history, our sources make it explicitly clear that it was wealth, defined primarily by land ownership and one's ability to live off the labour of others, that provided the main symbol and root of the social and economic inequality which permeated Archaic Athens. Possession of land, controlled and managed by the leisured elites who in turn rented it to the poor, stood at the heart of the division between the notables and the dependants in seventh-century BC Attica.

The dominance of the notables over the Athenian state was clearly reflected in their monopoly over political offices. According to Aristotle's account, the most important officials 'before the time of Draco' were appointed by birth and wealth, and consisted of: the *basileus*, responsible for traditional rituals and festivals; the *polemarchos*, who presided over the military activities of the state; and the *eponymos* archon, who gave his name to the year, held most executive powers and was the principal official of state ([*Ath. Pol.*] 3.1–3). Together with six other officials, known as the lawgivers (*thesmothetai*) because of their involvement in drafting and preserving the city's statutes, these men comprised the body of nine archons, each of whom held their office for one year, after which they joined the council of the Areopagus, in charge of watching over the laws and administering most of the public affairs of the *polis*. Membership in the Areopagus was restricted to previous archons and, as Aristotle states, remained 'tenable for life', assuring that all political offices were firmly in the hands of the Athenian elites (3.6).

In spite of our limited knowledge of early Athenian history, the existence and dominance of a small group of elite landowners, with full power in the political and economic spheres of the *polis*, has been taken for granted by most ancient and modern scholars alike. The general impression conveyed by our sources suggests that the supremacy of the notables, based on wealth and ownership of land, was maintained at the cost of the mass of poor dependants, who, oppressed by their landlords, struggled to make ends meet. This picture is further confirmed by the archaeological evidence of the period.

As we saw in Chapter 4, after an increase of burial groups around 750 BC, which Ian Morris associated with the rise of the *polis*, from c. 700 BC Attic cemeteries were monopolized by the Athenian elites (*agathoi*), at the expense of the poor, non-elite masses (*kakoi*). Access to formal cemeteries, now located outside of settlement areas, was limited on the basis of rank, which in turn explained the relatively small number of archaeologically visible adult burials throughout the Archaic period. The adult graves were initially marked by an imposing mound and a simple marker (stone slab or clay vase), later replaced by a mudbrick tomb. As the mounds decreased in size towards the end of the seventh century BC, the first examples of elaborate funerary sculpture began to appear by the main roads and cemeteries in Attica. This burial evidence, as Morris concluded, highlighted the dominance of the Athenian *agathoi* over the physical space and artistic discourses surrounding the dead, thus reflecting the wider relationship of economic and political dependency which defined the social landscape of early Athens. His theory of the denial of formal burial to the majority of the Athenian population posited, in effect, the existence of a major and strictly enforced social gulf between a privileged group of the wealthy and a mass of poor, subordinate *kakoi*, unable to afford the funerary monuments and confined to archaeologically invisible methods of burial and commemoration.

The burial evidence of the seventh century BC lends itself, therefore, to immediate comparisons with our literary sources for the period. The rich minority of citizens, the notables, who comprised perhaps no more than 10–20 per cent of the wealthiest members of Athenian society, controlled most of the land, as well as the political and economic affairs of the *polis*.[20] Burials provided them with a platform to display their wealth and status, as well as the exclusive nature of their social identity.[21] At the same time, the majority of the poor, the dependants or sixth-parters, were confined to working for the rich elites, with little hope of social or economic progression, and no access to formal cemeteries. Their burials consequently consisted of informal disposal, since costly tomb memorials were far beyond their means, which in turn symbolized their inferior social standing in their communities. And although there is little evidence for the burials of the war dead in Athens, or indeed elsewhere, in the seventh century BC, we should suspect that it followed similar, elite-driven principles.

In addition to the burial evidence of the period, the archaeological survey studies of the early rural settlement in Attica may lend further support to the notion of a societal division between the rich and the poor. Throughout most of the Geometric and Archaic periods, there is little evidence for land exploitation in Attica, especially when compared to later eras. The relative emptiness of the countryside, as Lin Foxhall observed, suggests that small isolated rural sites were not popular before the Classical period. Accordingly, exploitation of 'marginal' lands, which the proponents of the 'hoplite revolution' model claim was symptomatic of the rise of small, subsistence farmers, is not reflected in the survey record.[22] Although survey studies of early Attica remain relatively limited, the similarities with other Archaic *poleis* should imply that the few consistently exploited plots must have been located close to the best agricultural land.[23] It is plausible to assume, in turn, that such lands were monopolized by the elite notables, who employed and exploited a large workforce which consisted of the poorer members of their communities. The latter were not able to achieve economic independence, which in turn meant that most of the countryside remained relatively empty, while explaining also the lack of any overseas settlements by the Athenians in the period.[24]

The superior social, economic and political position of the early Athenian elites over the rest of the population is, therefore, reflected in both literary and archaeological evidence for the period. In the course of the seventh century BC, the most prominent members belonging to the leisure-classes of Attic communities established firm control over the political and social organization of the *polis*, at the expense of the rest of the population. But can any of this tell us something about the military composition and practice of the early Athenian *polis*?

The obvious place to start when looking at the shape of Athenian military organization before the sixth century BC would be to focus on the position of the *archon polemarchos*, who presided over the military affairs of the *polis*. The existence of such an office clearly points to some form of early public control over war-making.[25] Despite their undoubted military importance, the exact role and duties of the *polemarchos* remain highly speculative and in all likelihood cannot tell us much about the organization of early Athenian armed forces. According to some scholars, the latter may have been modelled on the system of four Attic Tribes (*phylai*), each subdivided into three Thirds (*trittyes*), as discussed by Aristotle in his account of Solon's reforms ([*Ath. Pol.*] 8.3).[26] Such a system, it has been argued, provided an early analogy of the later ten *taxeis* army structure of democratic Athens. Direct evidence for any such basis behind early Attic military organization is, however, lacking, leading a number of historians to turn their attention elsewhere.

The first clearly attested event in Athenian political history for which we have some reliable testimony was the unsuccessful attempt at tyranny by Cylon, sometime in the 630s BC.[27] Cylon, an Olympic victor and son-in-law of the Megarian tyrant Theagenes, seized the Acropolis with a small group of followers. His efforts were very quickly foiled and he found himself besieged by the Athenians who resisted tyrannical rule. The latter, in Thucydides' account of the story, grew tired of the siege and withdrew, 'committing the task of guarding to the nine archons, to whom they also gave full power to settle the whole matter as they might determine to be best; for at that time the nine archons transacted most of the public business' (1.126.8). The archons, most of whom came from the noble family of the Alcmaeonids, persuaded some of Cylon's supporters taking refuge at the altar of Athena to surrender, giving them assurances that they would not be put to death. Later, however, they went back on their promise and killed them all. As a result of this sacrilege, the Athenians banished all living Alcmaeonids and 'disinterred and cast out the bones of the dead' (1.126.12).

Thucydides offers us the most detailed account of the events concerning Cylon's failed *coup d'etat*; some details of his narrative, however, vary from the slightly earlier version given to us by Herodotus. According to Herodotus, the officials in charge of the besieged party were not the archons, but 'the presidents of the naucraries' (*prytaneis ton naukraron*), who 'constituted the governing body of Athens in those days' (5.71). It was these men who were responsible for butchering Cylon's supporters, even though in the end the blame fell unfairly on the Alcmaeonids. The inconsistencies between Thucydides' and Herodotus' stories concern, therefore, two separate factors: a) the chief officials in Athens (archons vs presidents of the naucraries); b) the Alcmaeonids' responsibility for the murder.[28] Despite many attempts by modern scholars to reconcile the contradictions between the historians, no convincing explanation has so far been offered, leading Antony Andrewes to conclude in his *CAH* chapter that, due to 'irremediably muddied' nature of the accounts, the conflict is 'beyond resolution'.[29] But a recent study has suggested that it is Herodotus' version which may hold the upper hand.

In his book on the fiscal history of Archaic Athens, Hans van Wees brought a different piece of evidence to bear on the discussion, which sheds light on the discrepancies concerning the Cylonian affair. An inscription from an early fifth-century BC *ostrakon* appears to name 'Xanthippus of the offending *prytaneis*', which in van Wees' reading refers to a member of the Alcmaeonid family, still known as 'the offenders' on the basis of their sacrilegious acts from over a century before.[30] The *ostrakon*, therefore, lends support to the tradition behind Herodotus' account of events, suggesting that the blame for the massacre of the supporters of Cylon was indeed ascribed to 'the presidents of the naucraries', and not to the archons.[31] This, as van Wees concluded, implies 'that there was a genuine early tradition which blamed the massacre of Cylon's supporters on the Alcmaeonids as "chiefs of the *naukraroi*"'.[32] Such an interpretation does not necessarily settle the account in Herodotus' favour; after all, the inscription on the *ostrakon* merely provides us with a fifth-century BC tradition that mentions an Archaic institution, obsolete at the time of writing. It does, nonetheless, confirm the existence of another board of officials going back to the second half of the seventh century BC, whose members played a leading role in the political affairs of early Athens. But who were the *naukraroi*, and what were their roles in the early Athenian *polis*?

Accepting the involvement of the presidents of the naucraries in the story of Cylon presupposes that the *naukraroi* were important officials in the city's governing body. Their authority, however, must have been less substantial than that belonging to the archons, who as we saw before were the chief governors of the early *polis*. In short, the leading role assumed by the presidents following Cylon's coup can either be explained by the fact the archons were not present in the city during the events;[33] or – far more likely – that their responsibilities included public emergencies which required an immediate military response. In Thucydides' account, we are specifically told that after discovering Cylon's attempt to seize power, the Athenians 'all came in from the country in full force (*pandemei*)' (1.126.7) to resist him. It seems natural to assume that their mobilization was orchestrated by the presidents of the naucraries, in whose hands the authority to carry on the siege and settle the affair was subsequently left.[34]

The military capacities of the *naukraroi* are, nevertheless, not mentioned in any of our main sources dealing with early Athenian history. In fact, our knowledge of any of their authorities and duties in general is very limited, giving modern scholars studying the *naukraroi* a lot of headaches.[35] The basic account concerning their official position is given to us by Aristotle, who in his section on Solon's reforms states that there were forty-eight naucraries in Attica, and that the officials in charge of them were responsible for income and expenditure:

> And there were four Tribes, as before, and four Tribal Kings. And from each Tribe there had been assigned three Thirds and twelve *naukrariai* to each, and over the *naukrariai* there was established the office of *naukraroi*, appointed for the levies and the expenditures that were made; because of which in the laws of Solon, which are no longer in force, the clauses frequently occur, 'the *naukraros* to levy' and 'to spend out of the naukraric Fund'.
>
> [*Ath. Pol.*] 8.3–4

The naucraries, according to Aristotle's account, were local administrative units which played some role in the public taxation process, each presided over by an official responsible for the levying of taxes and the spending of the 'naukraric Fund'. The etymology of the word *naukraros*, which means 'ship-head' or 'ship-captain', suggests, in addition, that the fiscal duties of these officials must have been in some way related to financing and operating a fleet.[36] And such a link is confirmed by a couple of later sources, especially the second-century BC Julius Pollux, who in his *Lexicon* entry under 'demarchs' states that:

> These men, who governed the demes, were for some time called *naukraroi*, when the demes too were known as *naukrariai*. A *naukraria* was for some time the twelfth part of a tribe, and there were twelve *naukraroi*, four in each 'third'. These men voted on the tax-levies in the demes and the expenditures from them. Each *naukraria* provided two horses and one ship, after which it was probably named.
>
> 8.108

Pollux's details are further supported by an anonymous lexicon which defines the *naukraroi* as 'those who provided the ships, acted as captains and were subordinate to the polemarch' (*Lexica Segueriana* 1.283.20).[37] The exact sources behind these lexica entries are unclear but considering that most of their details match what little we know about early Athens (i.e. the division into four tribes and three 'thirds', and the office of polemarch), it is tempting to assume that the information they provide is of genuine historical value. This, in turn, would helpfully supplement Aristotle's account and add a further military dimension to the duties of the *naukraroi*. Apart from levying taxes and being in charge of expenditures in their respective naucraries, the *naukraroi* were responsible for providing ships and cavalry; furthermore, all of them were ultimately accountable to the polemarch, who, as we noted earlier, was the chief military official. As such, the importance of the *naukraroi* for the functioning of the early Athenian *polis*, on both a local and wider level, becomes much easier to comprehend, explaining why they played such pivotal roles in Herodotus' account of the Cylonian affair.

The function of officials serving as *naukraroi* in early Athens can be best understood by their primary responsibility: providing ships, which based on the etymology of their name must have been associated with the office from the very beginning. In all likelihood, the ships supplied by the *naukraroi* were privately held pentecarters, whose owners belonged to the wealthiest strata of Athenian society.[38] Such men, who combined seafaring experience with the financial means to build, maintain, and man ships, were the most prominent members of Attic communities; among them, the aforementioned Alcmaeonids were no doubt represented and actively involved, despite Herodotus' assurances to the contrary in his account of Cylon's coup. The additional duty to provide two horsemen mentioned in the later sources further highlights the elite status of the *naukraroi*, since horses and ships were among the most costly military items to possess on a private basis. It may also, as some scholars have argued, hint at an original defensive function of repelling seaborne attacks, since horsemen would have been very efficient in dealing with scattered raiders and alerting neighbouring villages and *naukraroi*.[39]

One odd aspect of the ancient traditions concerning the Athenian *naukraroi* is the fact that the surviving accounts offer no mention of mustering infantry among their responsibilities.[40] Instead, the main military focus appears to be firmly on the provision of ships and horsemen. This omission, apart from potentially giving more support to the defensive origins of the institution, suggests that the duty of mobilizing troops rested either with the polemarch, who presided over the military affairs of the *polis*; or, more likely, with the *naukraroi*, despite the silence in our sources.[41] Considering that the latter were responsible for providing crews for their ships and cavalrymen, it seems far more plausible to assume that the same officials were in charge of recruiting men from their respective naucraries.[42] Thucydides' account of Cylon's coup would thus provide the earliest example of the *naukraroi* mobilizing the Athenians in response to a political/military crisis. The lack of any direct mentions confirming such a role could, in turn, hint at the largely informal and non-regulated nature of this process in early Athens. Taking into account the rigidly divided social and economic make-up of Athenian society in this period, one would assume that the only Athenians able to afford the necessary equipment and time to engage in military activities came from the wealthy notables, among whom a select few who owned ships played the leading roles of *naukraroi*.[43] Consequently, the available force in each naucrary would have been relatively small, and based predominantly on personal relationships that existed among members of the leisured elites. Any standardized or regulated methods to muster troops were, therefore, unnecessary, since most *naukraroi* were already associated with a socially exclusive group of men who served together in military operations; both, as we will see, public and private.

We can only speculate about the origins of the public institution of the *naukraroi*, but it is reasonable to assume that their authority to muster men and collect taxes for military purposes on behalf of the *polis* was granted to them before Cylon's attempt at tyranny, i.e. the middle of the seventh century BC. Maintaining a ship and its crew was a highly expensive business, and the expenses incurred during their public campaigns were covered by 'the naukraric fund' from the tax levies (*eisphorai*), referred to by both Aristotle and Pollux.[44] In later times, these levies developed into the irregular *ad hoc* war taxes, imposed in Classical Athens to cover any urgent military expenditure.[45] Such a system, in turn, implies relatively high levels of administrative and fiscal organization in the Athenian *polis* of the seventh century BC.[46] Although one should imagine that some sort of line between public and private military ventures must have been established, the wealthy men who served as the *naukraroi* in early Athens undoubtedly operated on both levels, using private vessels for their own activities, such as trading and/or raiding, as well as those on behalf of the *polis*, which included both defensive functions and occasional offensive expeditions. Playing prominent roles in the military structures of the city's forces allowed the early Athenian elites to exert and confirm their social and economic pre-eminence on both a local and wider political scale. Early military organization, therefore, reflected the agricultural and burial patterns of the period – as well as the social norms we find represented in the mythological tradition – centred almost entirely on a small group of the wealthiest members of Attic communities, excluding the vast majority of the Athenian population.

The type of warfare which such a system of military organization favoured combined occasional public campaigns with more frequent, private, freebooting expeditions.[47] Since both types of activity were in the exclusive control of the very wealthiest, who also enjoyed the political and economic profits of these ventures, the nature of early war activities was not always clear because the boundaries between public and private must have remained fluid. This picture of early warfare fits very well with the one sketched by Thucydides in his account of the old days of Greece, where piracy and plundering, organized and led by the most powerful men for the sole purpose of profit, was the most common form of military activity (1.5). Indeed, it also bears very close resemblance to the Homeric practice of raiding, both communally and privately organized, which was widespread in the heroic world and exemplified by Odysseus' tale of a Cretan raider, who carried out nine successful raids, obtaining much wealth and prestige in his community (XIV.222–34).[48] Despite the similarities, however, the main difference between the Homeric heroes and the Athenian *naukraroi* were the clearly delineated public duties of the latter, who had the authority to muster men and finance their activities from 'the naukraric fund', thus relying far less on the war spoils and booty crucial for the warriors of the epic world depicted by Homer.[49]

The symbiotic relationship between public and private modes of warfare in early Athens can be glimpsed from the few accounts concerning the city's military activity in the seventh century BC.[50] The Athenians conducted wars against Aegina, Megara and Mytilene, which for the most part consisted of naval raids carried out by the *naukraroi* and almost certainly funded from the naukraric levies.[51] In fact, it has been suggested that a series of defeats suffered by the Athenians at the hands of the Megarians following Cylon's coup was the result of the expulsion of the Alcmaeonids following their sacrilegious acts; the Alcmaeonids, as we noted earlier, played key roles among the *naukraroi* and their absence must have had a big impact on the military capabilities of their *polis*, allowing the Megarians to take the initiative and capture Nisaea and Salamis. At the same time, private raiding was also common among the Athenians, as indicated by a law of Solon referring to 'bands travelling in search of booty or for the sake of trade' (Fr. 76A R). The high frequency of images of ships and fighting on beaches on Attic late Geometric vases, of which some were used as grave markers, provides further evidence for the prevalence of raiding among the rich, who used their vessels both for private and public ventures, thus being in full control of the military affairs of their *polis*.

To sum up, the domination of the landowning elites over early Athens depicted in the literary accounts and confirmed in the burial evidence, is reflected also in the military organization of the Athenian *polis* in the seventh century BC. The city's armed forces, under the supreme command of the polemarch, relied on a system of naucraries and officials known as the *naukraroi*, whose main responsibility was to provide ships and horsemen from their respective administrative units. Mobilization of armed forces, which also fell within the remit of these officials, was less regulated and relied on informal bonds between the members of the leisure-class and the *naukraroi*. In general, such structure was based on both private and public principles, as the *naukraroi* used their own ships and horses in most of their military activities, but were able to recoup the expenses from the official naukraric fund, subsidized from occasional tax levies. The possession of ships by the *naukraroi*, who themselves comprised of the very wealthiest Athenians, reinforced the political, social and military pre-eminence of the notables in early Athens. As their numbers were small, most war activities consisted of small-scale campaigns and raids, often for the sole sake of economic profit. Warfare, its practice and ideology, was entirely and exclusively in the hands of the Athenian elites.

The nature of early Athenian practice of war was, therefore, defined by the values and principles of the social class in control of it. Apart from the relatively centralized system of financing the public activities of the *naukraroi*, the official regulations concerning other aspects of military practice must have been relatively limited. The reliance on private means and modes of war-making meant that any standardization of issues such as mobilization, army division or – most importantly for us – procedures regarding the treatment of the war dead, were not at the level familiar from Classical times. Our evidence concerning the early burials of the latter, although of a limited nature, confirms the significance of the private, individual and elite-driven factors which dominated the military ethos of the period. The conspicuous burial mounds raised over the graves of the rich, often adorned by vases depicting naval raids and battles, suggests that war casualties were treated and commemorated in ways similar to those enshrined in the Homeric epics, dominated, as we saw, by inherently 'hierarchical' principles. Conversely, the lack of any evidence for the burial of non-elite warriors goes hand in hand with the wider trend of the exclusion and subordination of the masses to the notables, visible in both the Athenian cemeteries and our literary sources. The shape of the Athenian military, we may conclude, mirrored the political, economic and social worlds of early Athens, reflecting the widespread dominance of the landowning elites over the masses of the poor. And although the system of naucraries provided the basic principles of military organization until the reforms of Cleisthenes, a number of important changes were introduced in Athens by Solon and later the Peisistratids, to which we now must turn.

Solon's reforms

The deep political and economic inequalities which permeated Athenian society for most of the seventh century BC provide the background to the constitutional and legislative reforms of Solon. As we saw in Aristotle's account, the conflict between the landowning notables and the majority of poor dependants led to periods of *stasis* and instability, as the people repeatedly rebelled against the rich. The violent party struggle persisted for a long time until 594/3 BC, when the notables and the masses 'jointly chose Solon as arbitrator and Archon, and entrusted the government to him' ([*Ath. Pol.*] 5.2). Being granted full powers to reform the Athenian *polis* and its laws, Solon enacted a number of political and economic measures, which, according to ancient and modern traditions alike, provided the foundation stone for the later democratic system in Athens.[52]

Solon's reforms addressed, first and foremost, the agrarian crisis which enveloped Athenian society at the beginning of the sixth century BC. The most important of these included the abolition of loans on the security of a person, a previously widespread practice which in the eyes of Aristotle enslaved many of the poor and their children to the landowners; and the cancellation of all private and public debts ([*Ath. Pol.*] 6; Plut. *Sol.* 15). But the key changes introduced by the lawgiver concerned the Athenian governing powers. In particular, he set up firm procedures for the access and appointment of political offices, and instituted a new council of four hundred. The sole basis for wielding the highest state offices, such as the archons, the treasurers, and the sellers, was possession of wealth, calculated in dry and liquid measures of goods (*medimnoi*), where any previous considerations of noble birth and privilege were discarded. Appointments were made by lot from lists of men elected from the eligible property classes in each of the four tribes. The system of property classes (*tele*), which Solon either inaugurated himself or reformed, provided clear economic criteria for office-holding powers and potentially other civic duties, including military service.

Our most detailed account concerning the property classes comes from Aristotle, who discusses them in his section on the Solonian constitution ([*Ath. Pol.*] 7.3–4). According to him, Solon divided the Athenian people into four property classes based on annual produce in dry and liquid measures. He then distributed the chief political offices among the top three classes: the five-hundred-measure men (*pentakosiomedimnoi*), the knights (*hippeis*) and the yoke-men (*zeugitai*).[53] The rest of the citizen body were assigned to the lowest class of labourers (*thetes*), who were only entitled to sit in the Assembly or on a jury. Basing the criteria for office-holding entirely on wealth calculated in annual produce, the system of *tele* regulated access to political power among the wealthiest Athenians, which led many scholars to claim that the main purpose of its introduction was to put a definite end to any other, non-economic factors, such as birth or family connections, previously exploited by the elites to monopolize political power.[54] Accordingly, Solon's reforms provided access to political offices for a growing class of *nouveaux riches*, who on the basis of their non-elite descent were previously excluded from the political affairs of the *polis*. As we saw, however, such an interpretation appears unlikely, since the importance of aristocratic and hereditary factors as the driving principles behind elite social status was far lower than once assumed. Most importantly, extending political rights to new social classes is never mentioned by any of the ancient sources dealing with Solon's reforms; indeed even Plutarch, who emphasized the role of the well-born Eupatrids in early Athenian history, asserts that Solon 'was anxious to leave all the offices of state as he found them, in the hands of the rich' (*Sol.* 18).[55] The system of *tele*, therefore, simply formalized the mechanism of political appointments and reinforced the significance of wealth in Archaic Athens. This, as a number of studies have demonstrated, is further reflected by the fact that the top three property classes, judging by the amount of produce specified in Aristotle's account, must all have been leisured landowners, comprising altogether no more than 15–20 per cent of the Athenian population.[56] By contrast, the non-leisured Athenians from the Labourer class, encompassing perhaps as much as 85 per cent of the population, were denied access to any real political power or privilege, accentuating their inferior social status and economic dependence on the rich.

Despite the failure to address the widespread economic disparities between the elites and the common people, the Solonian system of *tele* was among the most successful and lasting reforms introduced by the lawgiver; it remained in place, albeit with some changes, well into the fourth century BC in Athens.[57] Apart from providing an economic basis for office-holding, a number of later sources indicate that the *tele* had an additional military dimension in the Athenian *polis*, imposing an obligation to serve in the citizen militia on the highest three property classes.[58] The key evidence is provided by Thucydides in his account of the Sicilian expedition, where he states that the Athenian force consisted of 5,100 hoplites, 'and of these, fifteen hundred were Athenians from the muster-roll and seven hundred *thetes* serving as marines on the ships' (6.43).[59] The explicit exclusion of the *thetes* from the muster-roll clearly implies that they were not under legal obligation to serve in the army, while also indicating that the other three property classes, the *pentakosiomedimnoi*, the *hippeis* and the *zeugitai*, were required to serve in the citizen infantry. This implication, of course, may have been valid only for the military realities of fifth-century BC Athens, especially since the additional army duties are not mentioned in Aristotle's description of the Solonian *tele*. Most scholars, nonetheless, have assumed that the military dimension went back to the Archaic period and the original reforms of Solon, if not earlier.[60]

The military dimension of the Solonian system of property classes has traditionally been ascribed to the rise in political importance of the yoke-men, or *zeugitai*, whom scholars following the 'hoplite revolution' model equated with the middle-class, yeomen farmers.[61] According to this interpretation, the early Athenian armies consisted of the knights (*hippeis*), who formed the cavalry force of the *polis*, and the *zeugitai*, who ('yoked' together) provided the hoplites for citizen phalanxes.[62] The latter were, understandably, supposed to be much more numerous, and their growing numbers and military importance were eventually reflected in new political roles and powers, such as those ascribed to them by Solon. But while there may be some value in such etymological associations, the general model is largely untenable, since as we saw earlier both the *hippeis* and the *zeugitai* property classes were almost certainly composed of leisured elites of early Athenian communities, and their numbers must have been relatively small, comprising no more than 15 per cent of the population.[63] The middle-class farmers, by contrast, are never mentioned in our sources; if they did exist, as van Wees concluded, they were simply 'ignored, insultingly lumped together with the poorest, and granted no political role beyond attending assemblies, a privilege shared by all adult males'.[64] Considering the socioeconomic situation of early Athens, characterized by a rigid division between the elites and the common people, it seems in fact most plausible to assume that the total absence of small subsistence farmers from our records is indeed a genuine reflection of the social reality of Solon's age. So, if the aim of the reform was not to grant political privileges to middle-class hoplites, then what was the reason behind the military dimension of the Solonian *tele*?

Since any answer to such a question has to be based on a large amount of guessing and speculation, the safest way to approach the subject may be to see the military requirements of the *tele* system within the larger frame of Solon's reforms. Apart from addressing the agricultural crisis which led to the enslavement of the poorest Athenians to the rich landowners, the main brunt of the legislation introduced by Solon concerned the formalization of political and legal processes in early Athens. Clear criteria were set for the eligibility and appointment of state officials; new political bodies, such as the council of four hundred, were established; judiciary powers, including the authority to punish and chastise wrongdoers, were delineated and rested with the Areopagus, although all citizens had a right to seek retribution if wronged, and to appeal to the jury-court if needed.[65] Public regulation was also exerted over other areas of everyday life, as Solon issued a number of laws on private funerals and changed the standard of the measures, weights, and currency in Athens.[66] All new laws, furthermore, were made available for everyone to see and read. According to Aristotle, they were inscribed and set in the 'Portico of the Basileus, and everyone swore to observe them' ([*Ath. Pol.*] 7.1). As such, Solon's reforms aimed to establish more formal and centralized ways to govern the Athenian *polis*, bringing the most important aspects of early political and social life under the full control of the state. The property class structure was, in effect, one example of this initiative on a political level, and so we should imagine that the rationale behind the military dimension of the system was based on similar principles.

Warfare and army organization were undoubtedly seen as vital to the successful running of the state and, considering the scope of Solon's reforms, it is highly improbable that they would have remained unaffected by the centralising processes initiated by the lawgiver. Later authors, in fact, credit Solon with a number of military regulations, including a law against draft-evasion (*astrateia*), a pension for wounded soldiers and provisions for raising the sons of men killed in battle at state expense.[67] And while some of these are not entirely credible, falling into a larger tradition of attributing Athenian laws to Solon, the *astrateia*-law could have plausibly gone back to his original legislation, as van Wees argued in his most recent study.[68] Introducing measures against draft-evasion would make every sense as part of a wider reform to impose new military duties and obligations which, in turn, lends further support to the claim that these were indeed in place by Solon's time. The property classification system, introduced or reformed by Solon, provided arguably the first official requirements for military service, replacing the previous and largely informal system based on personal relationships and obligations. As such, it constituted an essential part of the wider initiative to establish more formal and centralized ways to govern the organization and social structure of citizen militia in Athens. The military duties were imposed on the top three property classes, which as we saw comprised the leisured landowners who could afford the time and equipment required for occasional public campaigns. The political privileges of the elites that were legitimized by Solon's reforms were, in effect, matched by their obligation to serve in the citizen army, the avoidance of which was punishable by law.

The actual mechanics of calling up citizens for service remain beyond reconstruction at this early period; the property census may, in fact, have been used only to exempt the lowest class of *thetes* from any compulsory military duties.[69] It does stand to reason, however, that the officials responsible for army recruitment, the *naukraroi*, were provided with access to a public register of the propertied classes. Such a register, as Martin Ostwald argued, might even have been kept by the *naukraroi* in relation to their duties for the provision of cavalry.[70] Considering the fact that the *naukraroi* were later supplanted by the demarchs, who maintained a written record of all the citizen belonging to each deme (*lexiarchikon grammateion*) and were responsible for keeping the muster roll for the Classical Athenian army, it seems quite likely that they inherited this role from the Archaic *naukraroi*, who would have been in possession of a similar register based on Solon's *tele* classification.[71] Alternatively, as Frost speculated, an early muster roll could have been based on the phratry registers (*phraterikon grammateion*), which were drawn upon in the event of any mass mobilization ordered, presumably, by the polemarch.[72] Whatever the exact method, we can suspect that it did not require any major changes to the existing military structure of the naucraries, apart from imposing compulsory army duties on every member of the leisure-class in each district. Consequently, the size of the citizen militia could have been somewhat increased, while retaining its elite character and status, which after Solon's reform was based exclusively on wealth and material possessions.

It is hard to assess whether the changes to compulsory army service had any demonstrable impact on the Athenian military ventures following Solon's reforms. Our sources indicate that the Athenians did enjoy some success around the beginning of the sixth century BC, taking back Salamis from the Megarians, supposedly encouraged and led by Solon himself.[73] The details concerning the war, which come primarily from Plutarch and other late historians, are, however, too garbled to give us any reliable information on the shape of the Athenian military, although it could be speculated that the difficulties encountered during the campaign may have provided an immediate stimulus for Solon to introduce firmer conscription rules for the citizen army.[74] Plutarch (*Sol.* 11) also tells us that the Athenians took part in the First Sacred War against the people of Cirrha; again, we do not know much about the campaign, apart from the fact that the Athenians were led by Alcmaeon, the head of the Alcmaeonid family, which suggests that the Alcmaeonids returned to Athens from their banishment before the start of war, further boosting the city's military strength.[75] All in all, while the impact of Solon's reforms is perhaps hard to witness in the Athenian campaigns of the time – which, considering the nature of our literary sources, should not surprise us – it may have left a more visible mark in another area.

The evidence for the war dead undergoes a major change in character from the beginning of the sixth century BC in Athens. As we saw in the previous chapter, the main development concerns the transformation of Attic grave monuments, as the sizeable earth mounds are gradually replaced by mudbrick tombs accompanied by elaborate funerary sculpture. The latter take the shape of either marble *kouroi* statues in the form of naked youths, or (slightly later) of stone *stelai* with relief decoration portraying the deceased. War and military service are among the most commonly represented themes within the new sepulchral monuments, which stresses the social and cultural significance of commemorating the fallen as warriors for the Athenian elites who commissioned the monuments, at undoubtedly considerable expense. The epigrams inscribed on some of the graves, such as the tombs of Tettichos or Kroisos, indicate that a large number of those buried died in battle, and were most likely members of the citizen militia; after perishing in combat, their bodies were brought back to their families for individual burials. Largely missing from the funerary evidence of the preceding period, the war dead therefore make a sudden appearance in Athens in the decades following Solon's reforms. A similar trend can be also witnessed in the artistic depictions on Attic vases. Coupled with the sudden rise of black-figure pottery, images of the war dead, most commonly in the context of fighting over and rescuing fallen comrades, were becoming increasingly prominent from the second quarter of the sixth century BC onward. And while both of these developments were no doubt the result of a number of factors, including the rapid growth of the Athenian market and trade, they clearly reveal the emergence of a new artistic discourse of war.[76] The images and epigrams which commemorated the monuments surmounting the conspicuous tombs, together with the artistic themes explored on the vases after 600 BC, can be read, therefore, as an expression of new social and military ideologies, shaped, engaged with and perpetuated by the Athenian elites.

Although the transformation of the artistic discourse of war in the Athenian art of the late seventh and early sixth century BC could be seen as perhaps the most noticeable military change around the reforms of Solon, we should understand it as a result of the wider movement towards a greater centralization of the Athenian state, of which tighter public control over the citizen army was just one part.[77] Extending the state's influence over the army, previously monopolized by powerful and wealthy individuals who combined private and public interests in their military operations, would have certainly had an impact, both practical and ideological, on how the Athenian elites perceived their role in the practice of war. Solon's interference in the key areas which defined their social identity, including warfare, but also private funerals, led to new forms of self-representation which took over Athenian art with remarkable speed following the reforms.

The effect of Solon's funerary legislation on the Athenian elites would certainly have been of some significance. According to several later authors, Solon issued regulations concerning the conduct of private funerals, formalizing the details regarding the *prothesis*, the participation of women, and restricting the lavishness of the funeral procession (*ekphora*), which had to be conducted before sunrise.[78] And while most scholars see the legislation as designed specifically to curb funerary extravagance and display by the elites, it has been suggested that the rationale behind the laws could have been to do with other factors, of which religious considerations were the most significant. As Josine Blok convincingly argued in her study, Solon's regulations placed almost no limit on the financial expense or the number of male participants, which suggests that curbing displays of wealth or political loyalty could not have been the sole focus of the laws. Their main purpose, as she concluded, was instead to address the growing concerns over death pollution, which began to emerge as a powerful belief in all Archaic *poleis*, and 'to regulate the relations between the living and the dead'.[79] As such, Solon's funerary legislation would fall within the wider frame of his reforms, introducing public regulation into key areas of the social life of the Athenians. This interference, however strong it might have been, did not put any limitations on the form and cost of the funerary monuments, which provided the wealthy Athenians with a different platform to express and advertise their social status.[80]

The importance of war and war-related themes on sepulchral monuments suggests, in turn, that the Athenian elites felt a clear need to appropriate and claim these areas for themselves in a new visual media. Their control over the military sphere of the *polis*, previously taken for granted, must have been seen as being in some way challenged; and Solon's efforts to regulate and standardize the citizen army appear to be the most likely candidate for such a challenge. In effect, the new artistic discourse surrounding the war dead should be understood as a reaction of the elite Athenians to the growing control exerted by the state over their military activities and duties.[81] These new forms of self-expression were quickly adopted and disseminated, leaving a mark on Athenian art until the end of the Archaic period.

The ideology expressed in the funerary monuments was, as we observed in Chapter 4, highly individualistic and elitist in character. Initially, the main form of sculpture chosen by the families of the men who fell in war consisted of an imposing *kouros* set on an inscribed base, the prime examples of which were the slightly later tombs of Kroisos and Xenokles. Such statues glorified the heroic deeds of the deceased and placed their deaths within the framework of the epic concept of 'beautiful death'. The sacrifice made on behalf of the state was never mentioned or hinted at, since private, individualizing aspects took full priority over any patriotic considerations. With the emergence of warrior grave *stelai*, which start to appear within a couple of decades of Solon's reforms, the sepulchral statues built for the war dead began to exhibit ideals reflective of the increasingly public nature of the army. While the dead were still depicted as elite individuals, their military service to the community was given increased prominence over personal achievements and glory. One early example of this was the grave of Tettichos, which most likely consisted of a *stele* and an inscribed base. The sculpted relief, now missing, would have depicted an armed warrior, holding a spear in obedient service to his *polis*; the epigram, on the other hand, spoke of his heroic death and tender youth, putting the loss of his life above the sacrifice made for the community. As such, Tettichos' grave may provide us with the best example of two different ideological discourses employed by the elites in the wake of Solon's reforms, which coexisted, complemented but also competed with each other, reflecting attempts to establish a new social identity in the face of the increased centralization of the Athenian citizen army.

The main achievement of Solon's 594/3 BC reforms was to impose clear regulations over key aspects of early political, social and military life, all of which considerably accelerated the process of state formation at Athens. The prime example of this process was the introduction, or restructuring, of the system of property classification, which divided the citizens into four groups, or *tele*, ascribing political powers to the top three classes, comprising the wealthiest Athenians according to possession of agricultural wealth. The potential for office-holding given to the *pentakosiomedimnoi*, the *hippeis* and the *zeugitai* was, in addition, accompanied by an obligation to serve in the citizen militia when called upon. And although initially these reforms had arguably little effect on the practice of war, the increased public control over the citizen army was reflected in the new artistic discourses which began to spread gradually across the funerary sculpture and pottery depictions of the period, influenced by two competing ideologies: one accentuating the heroic and highly elitist principles; the other highlighting the importance of the community and public service.

The general principles behind the activities and organization of the Athenian military, however, remained largely the same. Despite a certain formalization of muster-rolls, the citizen army consisted predominantly of the leisured landowners, able to afford both the arms and time required for occasional public campaigns. The military structure still relied upon the previous system of naucraries, dominated by rich ship-owners, and standard army procedures, which, despite becoming increasingly public, continued to rely on mechanisms drawn from the private mode of war-making. The treatment of the war dead, therefore, remained unaffected, as private burial and commemoration of fallen warriors took on a new significance for the Athenian elites, providing a platform to claim and display their supremacy in war. Any significant changes to the ideology and social make-up of the citizen army were still not possible as the overwhelming majority of Athenians fell within the lowest property class of *thetes*, politically and economically disadvantaged, and excluded from compulsory service. Solon's abolition of enslavement for debt, together with the cancellation of all private and public debts, did, however, help to improve the condition of the property-less dependants, enabling more and more people slowly to aspire to economic independence. Such changes were soon on the horizon as Athens approached the 'Golden Age' of Peisistratid tyranny.

Peisistratus' tyranny

Solon's constitutional reforms left a mark on the social and political structures of early Athens, setting in motion a number of processes which increased the public authority and control over its citizens, impacting the long-term growth of the Athenian state. His reforms, however, apparently did little to establish short-term peace in the *polis*, as conflicts among the elites brought the city to a renewed state of turmoil. According to Aristotle's account, in the years following Solon's reforms the Athenians twice failed to appoint an archon, and had to remove Damasias by force, on account of him keeping the office beyond his tenure ([*Ath. Pol.*] 13.1–3). In general, the city was in a state of continuous internal disorder, as the people 'were always engaging in party strife' for the office of the archon.

The party strife (*stasis*) which dominated in Athens in the early decades of the sixth century BC is indeed mentioned by a number of other sources, providing further testimony to the resentment which Solon's legislation must have evoked among the Athenian elites.[82] The subsequent division into three separate political factions according to geographical region: 'the men of the Coast', 'the men of the Plain' and 'the party of the Hillmen', has caused a lot of controversy among modern scholars trying to establish the political ideologies and social backing behind each party.[83] One thing which remains clear, however, is that there was a definite winner at the end of the conflict, namely Peisistratus, the leader of the Hillmen party, who seized power and became the tyrant of Athens. The tyrannical rule which he started and later passed on to his sons lasted for nearly half a century, stabilized the political situation in Athens and brought economic prosperity to the majority of citizens, leading Aristotle to describe it as 'the Golden Age of Cronus' in Athens ([*Ath. Pol.*] 16.7).

Peisistratus' early rise to power is vaguely documented by Herodotus, who mentions that he distinguished himself in the war against Megara, performing 'great deeds' during the Athenian capture of Nisaea (1.59).[84] The long conflict with the Megarians for the possession of Salamis and Eleusis began, as we have seen, in the second half of the seventh century BC and continued through the Cylonian affair and the reforms of Solon, with the initiative swinging repeatedly from one side to another. But taking control of the Megarian port of Nisaea sometime in the 560s BC, proved to be the final and decisive victory, ending the war in Athens' favour.[85] Both Herodotus and Aristotle indicate that the credit for the ultimate victory was given almost entirely to Peisistratus, who served as a military commander in the army, establishing himself as one of the most popular and widely respected men in Athens (Hdt. 1.59; [*Ath. Pol.*] 14.1).[86] It was on the back of his military success that Peisistratus twice attempted to seize tyrannical power: first, with the support of a small group of men carrying clubs who, through trickery, he persuaded the Athenians to grant him as personal guard; and then by making an alliance with Megacles, the head of the Alcmaeonid family.[87] After both attempts proved unsuccessful, he left Athens to gather wealth and allies among other Greek *poleis*, eventually coming back and defeating the Athenians in battle at Pallene in *c*. 546 BC, this time planting his 'tyranny firmly with the help of large numbers of mercenary troops and a substantial income' (Hdt. 1.62–4). Even though most of these events are described to us by Herodotus, whose bias and personal preferences are often all too apparent, it is clear to see that military factors played a key role in Peisistratus' rise to power and his ultimate success.[88]

The two military aspects which have traditionally drawn most scholarly attention in studies of early Athenian military organization concern the identity of the 'club-bearers', who helped Peisistratus in his first coup; and the tyrant's reliance upon mercenary forces, which enabled him to win the battle of Pallene and later might have formed a regular contingent in the Athenian army.[89] Regarding the first, according to a theory proposed by Henk Singor, the unusual name given to the men who seized the Acropolis with Peisistratus, the 'club-bearers' (*korunephoroi*), did not refer to the fact that they were armed with clubs, since they could have hardly resisted any Athenians determined to defend their *polis* from tyranny (not unlike those who resisted Cylon's coup a few decades before). Instead, the term *korunephoroi* referred to a class of people who must have come, like their namesakes from Sikyon, from the poorest members of Athenian society, unable to afford the military equipment associated with the upper-classes (shield and spear) and, therefore, identified socially by their clubs and stones. Peisistratus, as Singor argued, depicted in our sources as the champion of the people, found his initial military support among the members of the *thetes*, whom he armed, sponsored and no doubt promised a better future. Due to lack of money, however, he could not maintain their loyalty which led to the failure of his initial bids at tyranny.[90]

The financial problem, however, was solved during Peisistratus' exile, during which he managed to gather the wealth necessary to pay his Athenian *korunephoroi* (turned by him into *doruphoroi*, spear-bearers) and thus successfully maintain his army. In addition, Singor proposed that the mercenary force of Argives which joined Peisistratus' army at Pallene, was similarly composed of lower class citizens, enticed from their homelands with money and free military equipment. These men, also referred to as the 'white-feet' (*leukopodes*) based on a few lines from Aristophanes' *Lysistrata* and its scholia, stayed as permanent troops in Peisistratus' army following the battle; together with the *korunephoroi*, their Athenian social equivalents, they formed the core of the Peisistratid army until the end of the tyranny.[91] In effect, the strategy of raising lower classes to 'hoplite' status, as Singor concluded, transformed the face of the Athenian military during the reign of the Peisistratids, as hundreds of poor citizens were able to join the citizen army. All this, in Singor's view, demonstrated that it was political decisions from above, not 'individuals acquiring more property and being individually admitted to the socially higher circle of the hoplites' as had been previously thought, that gave rise to a new hoplite class in late Archaic Greece.[92] This theory, despite raising a number of interesting points (especially concerning Peisistratus and the *korunephoroi*), is based on too much speculation, as there is little tangible evidence for a radical transformation in the social make-up of the Athenian army under the Peisistratids.[93]

The second aspect that scholars have focused upon was the employment of mercenary troops by Peisistratus and later his sons. Our accounts on the battle of Pallene indicate that Peisistratus' force consisted almost entirely of allied soldiers and mercenaries, including the aforementioned Argives, Thracians, Thebans, cavalry from Eretria, and Lygdamis of Naxos.[94] In addition, Herodotus adds, he was joined by some Athenians 'who found the rule of a tyrant more pleasant than freedom' (1.62). It is impossible to tell how many of these troops were granted to Peisistratus as a political favour, but some scholars have assumed that a large number of them were permanently hired as mercenaries by the tyrant and remained in service after the battle.[95] This interpretation fits well with the wider trend of Archaic Greek tyrants, who relied upon mercenary forces for their bodyguards and often rewarded them with the rights of citizenship and agricultural land.[96] In Peisistratus' case, this would apply specifically to the body of Argives, whatever their social standing, and to the Thracians;[97] the importance of the latter would be further confirmed by the sudden appearance of Thracian peltasts, as well as Scythian archers, in the Athenian vase painting from *c.* 540 BC.[98] The continuing reliance on mercenaries by the Peisistratids has been also deduced from stories concerning the disarmament of Athenian citizens, ascribed either to Peisistratus ([*Ath. Pol.*] 15.4) or to his son Hippias (Thuc. 6.58); and the taking hostage of the children of Athenians who did not flee Athens after the battle of Pallene (Hdt. 1.64). Such, actions, it has been argued, rendered the existing Athenian army impotent, ensuring the safety and long-term success of Peisistratus' tyranny. Whatever the citizen army had been before, it was disbanded and kept under check by the tyrant, who as Frost emphatically stated, 'now ruled outright with the support of mercenary troops', allowing 'the farmers of Attica to live undisturbed by the uncertain glamour of military service'.[99]

While both approaches to the Athenian army under the Peisistratids have some strengths and advantages, their argument relies far too heavily on anecdotal stories and/or single phrases from ancient sources.[100] That Peisistratus won the battle of Pallene with the support of allies and mercenaries seems beyond doubt, but there is no particular reason to assume that the very same mercenaries stayed on and formed the backbone of the tyrant's army for the next three decades.[101] The resentment of the Athenian elites, who as we saw controlled and defined the military strength of their *polis*, must have been high in the immediate aftermath of the battle, but there is no evidence of widespread retaliation or reprisals on behalf of Peisistratus. Although Herodotus, our main source for the events, does mention hostages taken from the families of those Athenians who 'remained and did not at once leave the city', the general impression is that their number must have been very limited (1.64). More importantly, the historian also states that Peisistratus, after gaining the upper hand in battle, ordered his sons to ride ahead and tell any Athenian fugitives 'that they need not worry and that each man should return to his own home' (1.63). Similarly, the supposed exile of the entire Alcmaeonid family after Pallene, which according to Herodotus lasted for the entire duration of the Peisistratid tyranny, cannot be taken as indicative of wider reprisals against the elites: the Alcmaeonids, as later evidence from an archon list shows, were back in Athens in the 520s BC;[102] their exile (if indeed it ever happened) must have been only temporary. We should imagine, therefore, that the elite Athenians whom Peisistratus defeated at Pallene, after an initial period of inevitable hostility, remained in Athens and came to be reconciled with the tyrant. In time, as Aristotle states, some of them even became his supporters, having been 'won over' by Peisistratus' 'friendly dealings with them' ([*Ath. Pol.*] 16.9).[103]

Since our accounts of the military organization during the Peisistratid tyranny give us relatively little to work with, a far better way to approach the subject is to take a wider approach and place the army issue within the general scope of Peisistratus' political programme and policies. One aspect which all of the sources unanimously agree upon is that the tyrants left the Solonian constitution intact and did not modify any of its official institutions. Herodotus, for instance, states that Peisistratus 'did not interfere with the existing structures of offices or change the laws' (1.59); Aristotle says that he handled the affairs 'more like a citizen than like a tyrant' and 'was willing to administer everything according to the laws' ([*Ath. Pol.*] 16.2, 8). Thucydides similarly adds that his sons made sure that the city 'was still governed by the laws which have existed previously' (6.54), that is in the age of Solon.[104] If the Peisistratids indeed did not alter the constitutional structure of the *polis* and carried on with the political processes based on the Solonian system, then it becomes almost inevitable to assume that the existing military organization of the state (i.e. the naucraries and the *tele*) remained equally unaffected. Such an explanation makes much better sense of the available literary evidence and seems preferable to any theories which presuppose the existence of a standing mercenary army which the tyrants supposedly kept and financed throughout their reign. Accordingly, after his victory at Pallene, Peisistratus simply disbanded the majority of his troops, leaving only the Athenians loyal to him and perhaps a few hundred of mercenaries to form his bodyguard and maintain order in the city.[105] His actions following the battle allowed him to regain the trust of the leisured elites and the Athenian people in general, thus bringing the political affairs slowly back to normal, including the organization of the citizen militia. Consequently, the system of naucraries continued unchanged, as did the military obligations imposed on the richest citizens by the Solonian property classification.[106] The only office which may have been affected was the polemarch, who was likely selected annually from the close family or the associates of the Peisistratids.

Indeed, a quick survey of the Athenian military ventures during the Peisistratid tyranny suggests that the general mode of war-making was still based on the coexistence of public and private principles familiar from previous decades.[107] The expedition to Chersonese, led by Miltiades (the Elder), was an example of a private venture of an elite Athenian. We are told specifically that the force consisted of volunteers who later settled in the Hellespont and engaged in another war against Lampsacus. That the settlement there was soon to be regarded as an Athenian interest, however, is shown by the fact that after the death of Miltiades' successor, Stesagoras, the Peisistratids sent Miltiades (the Younger) in a public trireme to replace him (Hdt. 6.34–9).[108] A more concerted naval effort, which almost undoubtedly included some citizen militia, was needed for the Athenian retaking of Sigeum and its subsequent defence against the Mytileneans around the 540s BC (Hdt. 5.94–5).[109] But the main instance of the full citizen army in action came in 519 BC when the Athenians, acting in response to a Plataean plea for protection, defeated the Thebans in a pitched battle (Hdt. 6.108). Despite some scholarly attempts to push the date of this event forward, on the logic that Athens could not have mustered such a force under the tyrants, the dating is firmly backed by a passage from Thucydides (3.68.5).[110] It seems clear, therefore, that Athenian citizens were heavily involved in the military activities of their *polis* when called upon, forming the core of the citizen militia, most likely ordered along the principles set down by Solon.

Another factor which confirms the public military undertakings of the Peisistratids concerns their more regular taxation of Athenian citizens, which according to Thucydides took the form of a twentieth of annual produce, allowing the tyrants to improve the appearance of the city and 'carry through their wars successfully' (6.54).[111] It has been suggested that these funds were used partly to keep a standing force of Thracian peltasts and Scythian archers, who helped in some of the campaigns and maintained peace and order in the city.[112] Even though this force may have only supplemented the main Athenian army, the introduction of coinage at Athens around the 530s BC could be seen as an official way to facilitate the necessary payments.[113] In addition, it is also plausible that the Athenians acquired their first triremes under the rule of Hippias, an endeavour which would certainly require major financial effort and the establishment of a system of liturgy.[114] And while some scholarly controversy surrounds the subject, contemporary evidence from rival Eretria suggests the existence of public payments for naval personnel, which indicates that similar structures must have been in place in Athens at the time.[115] The level of administrative and fiscal organization behind such initiatives implies a further step towards the centralization of Athenian military organization in the second half of the sixth century BC; a process first started by Solon was, therefore, significantly accelerated by the Peisistratids.

Finally, our evidence regarding the war dead from the Peisistratid period seems to support the assumption that the Athenian citizen militia did not undergo any major structural changes in its composition during the tyranny. The funerary monuments, which began to appear all over Attica in the wake of Solon's reforms, continued to consist of elaborate grave *stelai* and imposing *kouroi* built over the tombs of the wealthiest Athenians. The inscriptions commemorating some of them (Xenokles, Kroisos) make it clear that the dead were casualties of war, brought home from the battlefields to their families for burial. But while the rhetoric behind such inscriptions continued to be highly elitist and individualizing, the marked rise in the number of warrior grave *stelai* from the second half of the sixth century BC onwards indicates that the communal aspects of military service for the *polis* were becoming increasingly dominant among the Athenian elites. Some of the finest examples of warrior *stelai*, including the grave of Aristion, belong in fact to the last two decades of tyrannical rule at Athens. Apart from confirming that the wealthiest citizens continued to fight in the army, obliged to serve whenever called upon since the days of Solon's reforms, the burial evidence of the war dead suggests that the general structure, organization and military procedures remained unchanged under the Peisistratids. Far from being diminished or halted, the ideal of public service on behalf of one's state and community, enshrined in the grave *stelai* of men who died in battle, continued to grow and flourish, becoming the dominant form of war dead commemoration in the years leading up to the overthrow of Hippias and the establishment of democracy.

While the increased prominence of those communal ideals associated with serving in the citizen army could indicate that the public control introduced into the military sphere by Solon was met with more acceptance by a new generation of Athenian elites, the practices concerning the treatment of the war dead remained the same. The artistic discourse surrounding the war dead continued to provide the wealthy Athenians with a space to express their social identity and status. For this reason, returning fallen warriors home to their families was still perceived to be of utmost importance. The latter is especially clear in the artistic evidence of images on the Athenian pots, as the depictions of fights over the dead and combat retrievals witness a substantial rise in numbers from around 550 BC, becoming a leading subject of combat depictions in the sixth century BC. This rise is partly symptomatic of the growing pottery industry in Athens, which gained monopoly of the whole Mediterranean market for black-figure, and later red-figure, vases; at the same time, however, it indicates that retrieving the war dead, and bringing them home to their families, was ascribed with an even greater importance by the wealthiest Athenians fighting in the citizen armies. Far from being excluded from the latter, we have every reason to believe that the elites continued to form the backbone of the military force under the Peisistratids.

Indeed, we should perhaps suspect that the number of those eligible to serve in the army (i.e. belonging to the top three property classes) *increased* in the second half of the sixth century BC. As we saw in the previous chapter, the archaeological evidence of Attic graves belonging to the wealthiest Athenians increases in number after Peisistratus' victory at Pallene. According to Morris' seminal study, the number of elite adult burials becomes markedly higher from around 540 BC, leading eventually to the meteoric rise associated with the establishment of democracy and first citizen cemeteries from 510 BC. The increase in evidence between 540 and 510 BC, according to Morris, can be ascribed to the growing economic prosperity among the non-leisured Athenians, as more citizens were able to afford costlier forms of burial, thus rising on the social ladder of their communities. The fact that the general artistic discourse remained centred on military themes is, therefore, very revealing and provides potentially new evidence for our understanding of the social composition of the Athenian army during the Peisistratid regime. For if we assume that the increase in the elite burials witnessed in the period, some of which were undoubtedly those of war casualties, signifies the expansion of the Athenian elites, we should expect to see a similar increase in the number of citizens eligible for military service; especially since, as we argued, the Solonian system of *tele* was not interrupted by the tyrants. But can we make such an assumption? Or, in other words, is there enough evidence to posit a rise of a new class of citizen soldiers in the Athenian army under Peisistratus?

Agricultural revolution?

According to an anecdote in Aristotle, when Peisistratus was out settling disputes in the Attic countryside as part of his Local Justices system, one day he encountered a farmer digging rocks on Mount Hymettus. Amazed at the scene, Peisistratus sent his servant to ask the farmer about the crop he was cultivating. The man, not knowing who the person asking the question was, answered: 'All the aches and pains that there are, and of these aches and pains Peisistratus has to get the tithe' ([*Ath. Pol.*] 16.6). On hearing this, the Athenian tyrant was pleased at the man's honesty and hard work, and decided to exempt him from all taxes.

Despite its anecdotal nature, the story belongs to a much larger ancient tradition that saw the Athenian tyrant as the champion of the poor, whose primary concern was the improvement of agriculture and the economic wellbeing of small farmers.[116] Our sources habitually present Peisistratus as the leader of the *thetes*, 'who felt deep grievances against the rich' (Plut. *Sol.* 29), and 'a man who seemed most inclined to democracy' ([*Ath. Pol.*] 13.4; 14.1). His care for agricultural industry is related to us by Aristotle, who after emphasizing the kind and mild nature of Peisistratus' character, moves on to his support for the poor:

> (...) and moreover he advanced loans of money to the poor for their industries, so that they might support themselves by farming. In doing this he had two objects, to prevent their stopping in the city and make them stay scattered about the country, and to cause them to have a moderate competence and be engaged in their private affairs, so as not to desire nor to have time to attend to public business. And also the land's being thoroughly cultivated resulted in increasing his revenues; for he levied a tithe from the produce.
>
> [*Ath. Pol.*] 16.2–4

Although Aristotle suggests that Peisistratus' geniality towards the poor had clear political and economic motivations, the rule of the tyrant overall was remembered by the Athenians as the time of great wealth and prosperity. Indeed, the long-term success of his rule, as Brian Lavelle pointed out, relied primarily on his partnership with the *demos*, which formed an 'economic and political symbiosis, that kept the tyranny going'.[117] A number of measures, such as the agricultural loans or the institution of 'travelling judges', were certainly instrumental in giving new opportunities to the less wealthy among the Athenians, who found themselves less reliant on the leisured landowners and increasingly free to pursue an independent living as small farmers.[118] The civil strife and instability which had plagued Athens since the Cylonian affair appears to have ended, as Peisistratus managed to maintain good relations across the full social stratum, helping the once oppressed and disadvantaged poor, and appeasing the leisure-classes, who may initially have opposed his populist initiatives. How he achieved the latter remains largely unknown, but there is no reason to assume, as some scholars do, that his programme of helping the poor and fostering a community of small farmers was initially achieved by confiscating and breaking up the large estates of the elites exiled after Pallene.[119] Since most of Attica was still relatively uncultivated and unoccupied, there was no urgent need to redistribute the land; it made far more sense, as we argued earlier, for Peisistratus to leave the properties of the wealthy intact, thus gaining their support and trust in the long run.[120] The archon list from 525/4 BC that includes names from the most powerful families, including the Alcmaeonids and the Philaids, provides clear testimony to the tyrants' good relationships and political alliances with the Athenian elites.[121]

Peisistratus' support for small agriculture, which features so prominently in literary accounts of the tyranny, finds further confirmation in the archaeological survey studies of Attica in the late sixth century BC. As we mentioned at the beginning of this chapter, levels of agricultural activity are generally low for most of the Late Geometric and Archaic periods with relatively little expansion, since the best lands were monopolized by the leisured elites. This picture, however, changes towards the end of the sixth century BC, when we witness a gradual filling-in of the Attic countryside, as new lands are cultivated and new patterns of landownership begin to emerge.[122] According to van Wees, who dates the beginning of this process to around 550 BC onwards for the wider Greek world (with the exception of Sparta), the sudden spread of rural settlements was indicative of the rise of 'country-dwelling small farmers', who eventually formed a new middle-class of yeoman farmers.[123] Such an interpretation, in turn, is certainly consistent with both the literary evidence for the agricultural initiatives of the Peisistratids, as well as the burial evidence which sees a similar rise in the number of archaeologically visible graves throughout the Attic countryside. The inevitable explanation, therefore, seems to be that a growing number of enterprising citizens, who previously belonged to the poorer echelons of their communities oppressed by the landowning notables, took advantage of the political developments taking place in Athens throughout the sixth century BC. Given a fresh start by Solon, who abolished the system of loan slavery and cancelled their debts, they pursued the agricultural opportunities offered to them by Peisistratus and turned to small-scale, independent farming. In time, the small farmers began to reap the economic reward of their endeavours, which allowed them to elevate their social status, symbolized in their participation in the elite practices of burial, traditionally dominated by a discourse centred on war. Their engagement with the latter, however, was not only a matter of artistic choice, but was also an important part of their public duties and social identity, as the advancement on the Solonian *tele* ladder came with new military obligations.

In addition to the agricultural policies which led to the rise of small farmers (and the gradual widening of the *zeugitai* property class), Peisistratus and his sons transformed the *polis* in a number of other important ways. The steady growth of trade and industry in Athens played a big part in the general rise of wealth and prosperity, reflected in a number of building projects, new road systems, public festivals and the extraordinary development of Attic vase painting, to name just a few.[124] All of this was facilitated by the introduction of coinage and greater control over public spending. Within a few years Athens became the cultural centre of the Hellenic world, setting the highest standards in architecture and art, and attracting skilled craftsmen from all over the Mediterranean; indeed, as one scholar has put it, living in Athens under the Peisistratids must have been 'like living in Florence during the early years of the Renaissance'.[125] The cumulative appeal and impact of all these initiatives on individual citizens must have been significant, affecting their *polis* identity and concept of citizenship.[126] As Philip Brook Manville concluded, 'each man's social membership matured as a share of a public, all-embracing corporation. Society became more centralized, and broader values emerged which transcended the plurality of regional and ethnic loyalties'.[127] The old, competitive values of the elites, which highlighted personal accomplishment and glory, were giving way to a civic ideology, which ever since the reforms of Solon gradually permeated Athenian society.

This continuing social and political centralization must also have had an impact on the Athenian military, as fighting for the *polis* became more than just an exclusive pastime of the elites. The citizen militias began to be joined by an increasing number of small, independent farmers, previously excluded from compulsory public service. Their new roles are marked in the archaeological record of their burials, as they engaged with the ideology and artistic rhetoric of war previously monopolized by the richest members of their communities. The increased prominence of communal ideals, represented in the sepulchral monuments of Aristion and other warrior *stelai* from the mid-sixth century BC onwards, can be seen as both a mark of a wider shift concerning the ideal of military service for one's country, but also as an indication of the changing social make-up of the Athenian army. This is perhaps best demonstrated by the marked rise in the number of surviving grave *stelai*, which reach their peak in the last quarter of the sixth century BC, considerably outnumbering the examples of surviving *kouroi* for the same period.[128]

In addition, the importance and appeal of public service was further enhanced by new opportunities to join the militia, as new forms of contractual service became available, perhaps beginning with the commission of the first public triremes.[129] Consequently, private forms of war-making, which had supplemented and coexisted with public military efforts for the last century, were increasingly less viable, as control over warfare shifted firmly from the hands of the elites to the state. All this, building on the constitutional and legislative processes set in motion by Solon, prepared the ground for the reforms of Cleisthenes in 508/7 BC.

To sum up, we may conclude that the literary and archaeological evidence does support the idea of a rise of small, independent farmers during the tyranny of the Peisistratids.[130] The occupation of the Attic countryside, combined with the discernible rise in burial evidence and the tradition concerning the agricultural policies of the tyrants, all point to an emergence of a new social class of people, who slowly began to fill the once yawning gap between the Athenian elites and the masses of the poor. These men were gradually able to join the citizen militia, bolstering its numbers and slowly redefining its social composition. Their presence among the fighting forces is reflected in the burial evidence, which symbolized their new social and military identities through an engagement with an artistic discourse traditionally associated with the leisured elites. The increased prominence of ideals concerning military service for the community conveyed in the sepulchral monuments for war casualties indicates, however, that the wider ideology of war was changing. The inscribed statues erected for Kroisos and Xenokles, which celebrated the individual and his personal glory, were gradually replaced with simpler warrior *stelai* depicting the deceased as proud members of the citizen militia. This process, began around the time of Peisistratus' final accession to power, continued throughout the whole of the Peisistratid regime in Athens.

In effect, the public army grew in numbers, as more men were able to afford the time and equipment to join the citizen militia, which in turn contributed to the many military successes of Athens under the Peisistratids.[131] The full show of strength of the citizen militia was provided by its crushing victory over the Thebans in 519 BC, which gave the Athenians a glimpse of their city's military strength and potential. Despite the continued political and economic centralization experienced during the 'Golden Age', which accelerated the growth of civic consciousness in Athens, the procedures surrounding the treatment of the war dead remained initially unchanged, following the elite-driven customs of previous decades. The reason for this might be sought in the importance ascribed to the ritual by the wealthy Athenians, unwilling to compromise on age-old tradition.[132] Bringing the bodies back home for burial was, therefore, still essential and widely practised, even though the ideology behind the sepulchral monuments was increasingly removed from the elitist and individualizing principles of the past. The practical and logistical difficulties imposed by the increase in size of the citizen militia, as well as the number of long-distance overseas campaigns, such as those in Hellespont or Sigeum, suggest, however, that the 'hierarchical' procedures of dealing with casualties of war may have been progressively abandoned. Any official standardization of alternative forms of public disposal of the dead required the state to take full and exclusive control over every aspect of war-making. This process, initiated by Solon and continued by the Peisistratids, was completed only with the establishment of democracy at Athens.

Cleisthenes and democracy

The 'Golden Age' at Athens came to an abrupt end with the assassination of Hipparchus in 514 BC. Following the event, as our sources unanimously tell us, the tyranny became much harsher. Hippias carried out a number of executions and expulsions, becoming increasingly 'suspicious of everybody and embittered'.[133] As a result, a number of leading Athenian families found themselves in exile, chief among them the Alcmaeonids. After initial unsuccessful attempts to overturn Hippias' rule, including the fortification of Leipsydrion, the Alcmaeonids managed to enlist the help of the Spartans using their influence at Delphi. The first expedition of the latter, carried by sea and led by Anchimolius, ended in disaster; Hippias, having been warned of the enemy's approach, summoned a sizeable cavalry force from his Thessalian allies and defeated the Spartans at Phalerum, killing Anchimolius and many others.[134] With their prestige on the line, the Spartans sent a much larger land army under King Cleomenes the following year, which first dispatched the Thessalian cavalry and then entered Athens, besieging Hippias on the Acropolis 'with the aid of the Athenians' ([*Ath. Pol.*] 19.5–6; Hdt. 5.64). With his sons caught attempting to escape, Hippias eventually surrendered and handed the Acropolis back to the Athenians, which marked the end of tyrannical rule at Athens.

The end of tyranny, however, did not bring immediate freedom, as strife broke out between political factions of Cleisthenes and Isagoras. The former belonged to the Alcmaeonids and obtained the support of the *demos*, but had to withdraw from Athens after Isagoras called Cleomenes and the Spartans back. The 'small' Spartan force rallied by Cleomenes took temporary control of affairs at Athens, expelling seven hundred Athenian families and attempting to set up an oligarchy. This, however, was met with immediate resistance from the Athenians, who 'gathered in force', defeated the Spartans, recalled Cleisthenes and other exiles and executed all those who sided with Isagoras and the Lacedaemonians.[135] Power was then given to Cleisthenes, 'who became leader and champion of the people', introducing a number of constitutional reforms which marked the official introduction of democracy at Athens ([Ath. Pol.] 20.4). Although the new political system faced the immediate danger of invasion on three different fronts, as we saw at the beginning of this chapter, the citizen army won the day, guaranteeing the survival and future success of democratic rule at Athens.

All these events suggest that the shape of the citizen militia was significantly affected by the political situation at Athens following Hipparchus' assassination. The initial expulsion of the Alcmaeonids and other wealthy Athenian families must have had a big impact on the public army, reducing its numbers and potentially removing some of the men in charge of local naucraries. Hippias' forces, however, were still large enough to deal with the expelled elites at Leipsydrion, and we should assume that he could still count on the remaining Athenians obliged to serve in the army. But it seems plausible that he was already forced to enlist the help of allies and mercenaries, such as the Thessalian cavalry used to repel the Spartan attack at Phalerum. According to Herodotus, the latter provided the sole resistance to the land offensive of Cleomenes in the following year, who entered the city supported by the Athenians who 'desired freedom' (5.64). The citizen militia, or whatever was left of it, was no longer under Hippias' control and was likely involved in his final deposition. Following the return of the exiled Alcmaeonids and others, we should assume that it simply reverted back to its previous numbers and shape.

The relative ease with which the small force of Cleomenes took control of Athens in his next intervention in support of Isagoras raises potential problems, and has been deemed by some scholars as a prime example of the military inefficiency of the public army before Cleisthenes.[136] This interpretation, however, considering the decisive victories of the citizen militia over the Thebans in 519 BC, and its later actions in 506 BC, is unlikely. Instead, the lack of any initial resistance to Cleomenes' second incursion could be explained by the fact that the Athenians had no tangible reason to oppose him. As Herodotus tells us, Cleomenes, urged by Isagoras, sent a messenger to Athens attempting to banish the Alcmaeonids and their supporters, on the basis of their ancestral curse linked to their involvement in the Cylonian affair (5.70). Cleisthenes, and most likely the rest of the Alcmaeonids, responded by 'slipping out' of Athens, presumably unsure of the support of the *demos* in light of the charges. Their departure, in turn, ensured that any potential political opposition to Isagoras was temporarily dealt with. The subsequent arrival of Cleomenes, who had recently liberated the Athenians from the Peisistratids, was met with no initial resistance and little suspicion. It was only after Cleomenes began his efforts to establish an oligarchy, banishing families and trying to disband the council, that the Athenians orchestrated a full-scale military response. The latter, in fact, would have most likely consisted of a general levy, perhaps similar to those raised in response to the previous *coups d'état* of Cylon and Peisistratus.[137] Far from viewing these events as evidence for a spontaneous mobilization of the people, indicative of the previous military incapacity of the city, we should instead see them as a continuation of mechanisms already in place at Athens.[138] With the final return of the Alcmaeonids and other banished families, the army was back to its usual strength, of which it made full use during the general levy in 506 BC for the campaign against the Boeotians and the Chalcidians.

Attempting to assess the impact of Cleisthenes' reforms on the structure of the Athenian army in the last decade of the sixth century BC is, as a result, not an easy task. The citizen militia inherited from the Peisistratids was already an efficient and sizeable force, with relatively high levels of fiscal and administrative organization. In light of this, it is highly doubtful that the main purpose of the reforms was to reinvent the whole military system of the *polis*, as a number of scholars have suggested.[139] It seems far more likely that Cleisthenes introduced measures designed simply to improve the existing military structure, modifying some areas, but also leaving some largely intact. His reorganization of the citizen body, for instance, was certainly an example of the former, as dividing citizens into smaller and more complex administrative units was instrumental in ensuring quicker and potentially larger levies.[140] A potential military rationale for the introduction of demes, which according to Aristotle replaced the old system of naucraries ([*Ath. Pol.*] 21.5), could be the need to cope with the growing number of citizens eligible for army service. Substituting the forty-eight naucraries with 139 demes would have provided a solution to this, allowing more control over the available manpower in each district.[141] Accordingly, the public duties of the *naukraroi* were handed over to the demarchs, who kept the local citizen registers (*lexiarchika grammateia*) of all men belonging to a deme, with details concerning their economic standing and their liability to pay taxes and serve in the militia. We should not assume, however, that the military duties of the *naukraroi* were altogether abolished; it is far more likely that they continued to play important roles in the army, which relied on their military experience in the initial public campaigns.[142] Other institutions which the Athenian militia relied upon throughout the Archaic period, such as the system of property classes, together with any regulations which accompanied it, remained unchanged by the democratic reforms.

Further changes to the military organization of the militia were introduced in the years following the reforms: in 501/0 BC a new hierarchy of ten tribal generals (*strategoi*) was introduced ([*Ath. Pol.*] 22.2), supplemented by the *taxiarchoi* and *lochagoi* on lower army levels, and the trierarchs who captained the publicly owned navy. The increasing demarcation of military roles provides us with clear testimony for the institutional growth of the democratic army at Athens, but it also suggests that such differentiation was not in place by 506 BC, when the Athenians presumably still relied upon the old command structures prevalent in the Archaic period. Crediting Cleisthenes with immediate, revolutionary measures which transformed the face of the citizen militia and won the double victory against the Boeotians and the Chalcidians is, therefore, mostly misleading. The wider transformation of army structure and organization was, in all likelihood, a gradual process, started by Cleisthenes and continued in the years and decades which followed his reforms. Far from reinventing the entire military system, Cleisthenes set in motion a number of mechanisms which improved the existing structures built by Solon and continued under the Peisistratids, and accommodated the growing manpower of the Athenians eligible for service. An equally important aspect of his reforms in the military area was, however, carried out on an ideological level, as the citizen army became symbolic of the new democracy and the principles of equality which came with it. The ideological change, most prominently articulated in Herodotus' passage quoted in the opening of this chapter, is especially visible in the evidence concerning the burials of the Athenian war dead, which undergo a radical transformation in this period.

In the years following Cleisthenes' reforms the number of adult and child burials in Attica rises at an astonishing rate. As we saw in the previous chapter, this phenomenon was associated by Morris with the new democratic spirit instigated by the legislation, as the city cemeteries were no longer monopolized by the *agathoi* and opened their doors to all citizens, regardless of social rank. Even more importantly, from our perspective, the sculpted markers which surmounted the graves of the elites disappear in the very same period. According to one estimate, about seventy of them survive for the period between 510 and 500 BC, but only nine are preserved from 500 to 480 BC.[143] After this, the building of decorated gravestones virtually ceases for half a century, limited only to a few examples of public monuments raised by the city for the war dead. The sudden decline in the number of funerary monuments has been traditionally ascribed to a sumptuary law mentioned by Cicero, which imposed restrictions on the size and style of grave markers, and was supposedly enacted 'somewhat later' (*post aliquanto*), after the funerary legislation of Solon.[144] Cicero's account of the law, which has caused some scholarly debate, reads as follows:

> But somewhat later, on account of the enormous size of the tombs which we now see in the Ceramicus, it was provided by law that no one should build one which required more than three days' work for ten men. Nor was it permitted to adorn a tomb with stucco-work nor to place upon it the Hermes-pillars, as they are called. Speeches in praise of the deceased were also forbidden except at public funerals, and then allowed to be made only by orators officially appointed for the purpose. The gathering of large numbers of men and women was also forbidden, in order to limit the cries of mourning; for a crowd increases grief.
>
> *Leg.* 2.64–6

The decree has been mostly seen as part of Cleisthenes' democratic enactments, but establishing its effect on the funerary monuments in Attica poses many problems. Some of its parts, like those concerning the size and style of the tombs, seemingly reflect the decrease and simplification of grave monuments which took place during the reign of the Peisistratids; while others, referring to praise spoken by state officials at public funerals, make far better sense in the context of public burials of the fifth century BC. As a result, the *post aliquanto* law could, and has been, ascribed to a number of figures, such as Peisistratus, Hippias, Cleisthenes, Themistocles or Cimon.[145] Others, by contrast, have rejected its authenticity, arguing that 'its existence is a historical anomaly, which only hinges on a quote within a quote in Cicero's text'.[146] And while uncovering the definite origin behind the law may be seemingly impossible, approaching it from the perspective of the parallel changes affecting the treatment of the war dead can shed a helpful light on the debate.

The first Athenian *polyandrion* that we know of was built in Euboea and commemorated the casualties of the conflict against the Thebans and the Chalcidians in 506 BC. This was almost certainly the first public military campaign of the newly established democracy and we should assume, therefore, that the mass battlefield burial of the Athenians, which broke with the Archaic practice of returning the bodies of the fallen home, was a new measure likely introduced as a part of Cleisthenes' reforms. Its ideological impact on the Athenian army and wider society must have been profound, as the business of dealing with the bodies of the fallen was taken away from families and claimed exclusively by the state and the commanders in charge of the army. The common burial of the war dead, in addition, declared all of them equal, granting every fallen warrior similar distinction for their sacrifice on behalf of the *polis*. This practice quickly became the norm, as proven by the other early *polyandria* for the dead of Lemnos, Aegina and Marathon, although the location of the burials (battlefield or home) initially varied, as we saw in the last chapter.

As the individual burials of the war dead since the day of Solon were replaced by common army burials introduced as part of the egalitarian ideology behind Cleisthenes' reforms, the number of sculpted grave markers began to drop. The dead were no longer brought home to their families, who consequently could no longer honour them in the once traditional way. That some funerary monuments were, nonetheless, built until *c.* 480 BC could indicate that a few wealthy Athenians resisted the new army procedures and continued to commemorate their dead with cenotaphs.[147] Alternatively, and perhaps more likely, the decrease in numbers could simply suggest that the remaining monuments were built only for rich citizens who did not die in war; the initial difference, accordingly, would reflect the removal of the private war dead from citizen cemeteries at Athens. In light of this, it seems far more plausible to place any potential funerary legislation, which extended to all Athenian citizens, to a date around 480 BC, when sculpted monuments raised for individual dead completely disappear. Such a theory, first proposed by Verena Zinserling, makes better sense of the available archaeological evidence, even though it does not entirely match the exact measure of the *post aliquanto* law described by Cicero, who may have conflated different traditions and reforms in his much later account.[148]

The process of the appropriation of the war dead by the Athenian state, on both practical and ideological levels, began with the emergence of democracy at Athens, as the public *polyandria* for all fallen men were symbolic of the new egalitarian character of the citizen militia. As such, the procedures could be seen as one of the most radical and revolutionary measures introduced in the military sphere by Cleisthenes' reforms. Their break with the elite practice of individual burials at home, which must have had a far-reaching impact on Athenian families, is confirmed by the reduction in the numbers of sculpted grave monuments for the elites, but also by the fundamental changes in the representations of the war dead on Athenian pottery. As the dead were no longer differentiated by their post-mortem treatment, the once imperative custom of combat retrieval decreased in importance, both on the battlefield and in Athenian art. The full institution of the public funeral, including an accompanying oration and casualty lists, took, however, a few more decades to become the norm, as the Thucydidean *patrios nomos* was not officially standardized until the second quarter of the fifth century BC.

The continued growth of the elements which comprised the Classical institution of *patrios nomos* is perhaps best evidenced by the varied practice of burials at home and on the battlefield between 506 and 470 BC. But a crucial part in its final crystallization was played by the experience of the Persian Wars which, as we saw in Chapter 2, were a defining event for the ideology and practice of war in Athens and the wider Greek world. Being instrumental in creating a new ideal surrounding the treatment of the war dead, which led to the introduction of the Panhellenic convention of *anairesis* and the rewriting of traditional myths containing mutilation episodes, the victories over the Persians were soon followed by the official regulation of all ceremonies accompanying the state funeral for fallen Athenians. This, in turn, marked the final step in the city's appropriation of the war dead, as the old elite symbols, practices and visual rhetoric were all usurped and reinvented by the state, which claimed full control over the practice and ideology of war at Athens.

*

The famous Athenian double victory over the Boeotians and the Chalcidians in 506 BC, which saved the newly established democracy and, according to Herodotus, demonstrated the military superiority which came with the equality of rights and speech, was not entirely the democratic miracle that the latter would have us believe. The victory, instead, was won by a well-organized and experienced public army, which developed over a century prior to Cleisthenes' reforms of 508/7 BC. Its structure and organization underwent a number of changes over the Archaic period, as informal and private mechanisms were increasingly replaced by public and formal institutions, which provides important insights into the long process of state formation in Archaic Athens. From the reforms of Solon, which provided official criteria for military service, to the 'Golden Age' of the Peisistratids, who encouraged the economic growth of independent, small-scale farmers who joined the ranks of its citizen militia, the Athenian army underwent gradual stages of centralization. Power shifted from the wealthy elites, who once monopolized the practice and ideology of war, to the Athenian state, which took over elite discourse and incorporated it within the egalitarian ideals of the Classical *polis*.[149] The public burial and commemoration of the war dead following the double victory of 506 BC was, in fact, one of the first symbols of the latter, setting the ground for the later institution of *patrios nomos*. In years to come, the victory became a paradigm of the democratic success of Athens, even though the army that won it was primarily structured and governed along the principles set out by the elites and tyrants of the Archaic era.

While the process of army formation at Athens has often been unclear and skewed by the later literary accounts, the various political, economic and social shifts which determined and influenced it left a clear mark on the archaeological record concerning the Archaic war dead. As we saw in this chapter, the elaborate grave monuments, decorated with sculpted reliefs and inscribed with epitaphs, together with the iconographic evidence of pottery, can serve as a useful platform to trace the development of the citizen militia in Archaic Athens. Their changing appearance, style and ideological message gives us an insight into the discourse which surrounded the practice of war and the social make-up of the army, as the tombs of Kroisos and Xenokles are first replaced by the warrior *stelai* of Aristion and others, and later by the public *polyandria* of the Classical period. The war dead, as such, provide us with a unique lens through which to view war, state and society in Archaic Athens.

Conclusion

The inevitable association of the war dead in ancient Athens with the institution of *patrios nomos* has left a clear mark in modern scholarship. As most studies have tended to focus upon the trappings of commemoration rather than the dead themselves, the context from which the customs emerged has been largely overlooked. Following Thucydides, many scholars have been content to suppose that these 'ancestral customs' originated at some undefined point in the distant past. This book has demonstrated that such assumptions cannot stand, precisely because the procedures and ideology that surrounded the treatment of the war dead in Archaic Athens had remarkably little in common with the much-celebrated institutions of the Classical era. Instead, Archaic norms were far closer to those enshrined in the Homeric epics, where the widespread practice of combat retrieval and the despoliation of the fallen was reflective of the status-driven values of the society depicted in the poems. It is in the differences between the post-mortem treatment of the elites and the common man that Homeric society was most clearly in opposition to the egalitarian customs of *patrios nomos*. Where the elites were instantly retrieved from the battlefield and later celebrated by highly conspicuous funerals, common warriors were left untended and exposed until a temporary truce was concluded to dispose of their bodies in mass graves. But perhaps the contrast between Archaic and Classical approaches to war is most striking in relation to the maltreatment and mutilation of the dead. These were procedures that were absolutely condemned by the Athenian authors of the Classical period. Somewhat ironically, then, it is significant to find that such practices were integral to Homeric systems of vengeance, status and honour. In short, what Herodotus claimed only the barbarians were capable of performing in the Classical period was committed only by the Greeks in the *Iliad*.

The main purpose of this book was to investigate the norms and discourses surrounding the treatment of the war dead in Archaic Athens, despite the seemingly scanty nature of the evidence that has traditionally deterred modern scholars. This difficulty was approached by turning to previously underutilized evidence in the form of early Greek mythology and the iconography of Attic pottery. Both source types confirmed that fights over the dead and mutilation remained prevalent themes in the artistic representations of the Archaic period. More importantly, however, they revealed that a significant cultural and ideological shift occurred in Athens towards the end of the sixth century BC. As the expectations of audiences changed, mutilation stories and iconographical depictions of *Leichenkämpfe* disappear from Athenian mythology and art, which reflected the wider efforts of the *polis* to establish a new self-identity, influenced in particular by the experience of the Persian Wars. The forging of this new identity, represented both in cultural and military spheres, led to the establishment of new customs and practices. The wider Hellenic convention of battlefield truces for the recovery of the dead, known as *anairesis* – which marked the official end of any battle in Classical Greece – most likely originated at some point in this period. In the imagination of the Athenians, however, the custom was presumed to reach back into the mythical past, where its establishment was credited to Theseus. His many civilizing reforms stood at the heart of Athens' self-image as the archetypal protector of the customs of both gods and Greeks.

The cultural genesis of the institution of *patrios nomos* followed similar principles. Much like *anairesis*, the Athenians looked towards the mythological past to legitimize the customs which defined the egalitarian character of their *polis*. The public burials in the Kerameikos, accompanied by casualty lists, funeral games and orations, were all products of the early years of democracy in Athens. The burial of the war dead in the Archaic period had been governed by different principles, which dominated early artistic discourses. Aside from mythological stories and iconographic depictions, these discourses consisted of funerary monuments that commemorated individual Athenians who fell in combat. Such monuments were dominated by an elite ideology of heroism, enshrined both in their physical form in the shape of imposing *kouroi*, inscribed with short epigrams focusing on the deceased's heroic achievements and glory; and in the practice of removing the bodies of fallen warriors from the battlefield and returning them home to their families for burial. At the same time, however, a different visual rhetoric began to emerge. This placed increasingly more emphasis on the concepts of public duty and sacrifice associated with service in the citizen army. Initially the rhetoric represented by the warrior *stelai* of the sixth century BC complemented and coexisted with the elite-driven principles accompanying the burial of individual war casualties, but it eventually became the prime form of commemoration of the dead in Archaic Athens. And while individual grave monuments for the war dead disappeared around the time of the reforms of Cleisthenes, mirroring the wider artistic shifts of the period, the community-driven discourse employed by the warrior *stelai* heralded the arrival of communal burials associated with *patrios nomos*.

The various components of the Classical institution of *patrios nomos* represented a clean break with the ideology and practices of the Archaic era. This shift was best characterized by the changes in values implicit in the new system, a move from private to public, hierarchical to egalitarian and individual to collective. But while the new customs were in many ways revolutionary and reflective of the wider spirit of the period, the Athenians attempted to bridge the rift they had created with their historical past by planting the roots of *patrios nomos* not only in the city's mythological past, but also in the practices and discourses of the Archaic elites. This process, most clearly visible in the rhetoric employed by the funeral oration, was also reflected in the return to the practice of bringing the remains of fallen warriors home. The principle of the latter, drawn from the Archaic custom of the Athenian elites, was adapted to suit the democratic needs of the city, and thus provided an ideological bridge in the imagination of the Athenians. In time, it became an essential component of an institution which came to be synonymous with the democratic identity of Athens in the wider Greek world.

While the main focus of this investigation was to broaden our understanding of the war dead in ancient Athens, it is hoped that the study also offers possibilities that go beyond this subject. The evidence of early Greek myths, artistic depictions on pottery, and the grave markers of the Archaic period provide many important insights into the wider cultural shifts which occurred in Athens towards the end of the Archaic era, but also into the shape and organization of the early citizen army. A natural continuation of this study would be to extend its scope towards other cities and regions of Greece, and to attempt to explore the extent to which Athenian responses to changes – in both the military and cultural sphere – towards the end of the Archaic period were a wider Greek phenomenon. Even more importantly, however, further study into the reception of early Greek myths in the authors and artists of the Classical world, holds the potential to deepen our understanding of the social and cultural history of the Archaic Greeks. Its significance, therefore, goes well beyond the purely military, as is clear from the examples of mutilation and burial truce stories traced in this book. And considering the lack of scholarly engagement with the large body of early myths and their immediate reception, further study of this nature has the potential to throw new and important light on a period which all too often suffers from a lack of evidence. As such, it is my hope that the contribution of this book will go beyond the field of ancient warfare, and pave the way for new areas of research into a period where many ancestral customs were thought to have their roots.

Notes

Introduction

1. It is perhaps most telling that Michael Sledge's book (2005) on the retrieval, burial and commemoration of American soldiers begins with a quote from Sophocles' *Antigone*, followed shortly afterwards with excerpts from Homer and Thucydides. The proper burial of the dead formed the basis of many Athenian plays, most famously Sophocles' *Antigone* and *Ajax*, and Euripides' *Suppliants* and *Trojan Women*. Not burying the dead was both a serious crime and an offence against the gods. For more, see Rosivach (1983).
2. Hanson (1989); (1995); (2013); Ober (1996), 53–71; Viggiano (2013).
3. Loraux (2006).
4. 'By repatriating the ashes of the dead', as Loraux (2006), 47, claimed, 'Athens broke with the Greek practice of burial on the field of battle'. In a footnote (p. 432 n. 9) attached to this statement she mentioned the works of Jacoby (1944), 42–4; Gomme (1962), 94; Kurtz and Boardman (1971), 246–7, 257.
5. Pritchett (1985), 94–259.
6. Ibid., 249–51.
7. Schröder (2020), 100: 'Die spätere athenische Tradition (πατρίος νόμος), die Asche der Kriegstoten nach Hause zu überführen und vor den Augen der Polisgemeinschaft im Demosion Sema beizusetzen, reicht also nicht bis in archaische Zeit zurück ... alle Zeugnisse dafür sprechen, dass auch die Polis Athen ihre Toten in archaischer Zeit auf dem Schlachtfeld beizusetzen pflegte'.
8. Clairmont (1983); Arrington (2015).

1 The Homeric War Dead

1. Stab wounds to the eyes: 14.493–5; mouth: 16.345–50; bladder: 5.65–7. Decapitations: 10.454–7; 11.261; 13.203; 14.497–8; 20.481–3.
2. Finley (1991), 118.
3. Van Wees (1996), 79 n. 146.
4. Vermeule (1979), 94.
5. Achilles: XXIV.35–94; Hector: 24.777–804; Patroclus: 23.127–257.

6 On the relation between the Homeric epics and early Greek burials, see Mylonas (1948); Kurtz and Boardman (1971), 186–7; Vermeule (1979); Morris (1987), 44–6; Sourvinou-Inwood (1983); (1995), 108–40; Walter-Karydi (2015), 17–48.

7 The trend to reconstruct Homeric battle scenes and examine their relation to historical warfare began with the seminal study by Joachim Latacz (1977), who placed Homer in the context of the mid-seventh century BC. While scholarly interpretations of Homeric warfare itself differ, especially on the issues of massed formations, chariots and armour, most of them identify the seventh century BC as the period which best corresponds to battles depicted in the *Iliad*. For recent discussions, see van Wees (2004), 249–52; Raaflaub (2008); Snodgrass (2013). *Cf.* Schwartz (2009), 105–15, who rejected any historical value for Homeric warfare.

8 By far the best account of the *Iliad*'s influence on the military history of ancient Greece is Lendon (2005), 15–161, who argued that the poem 'is the baseline for understanding the military ethos of the Greeks and important for understanding the military methods of historical Greeks' (p. 22). See also Sears (2019), 19–24.

9 There is a vast amount of scholarship on the subject of Homeric society, which cannot be fully referenced here. For an introduction with further bibliography, see Raaflaub (1997b); Osborne (2004a). A small selection of studies relevant for this chapter includes: Calhoun (1934); Rose (1975); (1997); (2012), 93–165; Adkins (1971); Donlan (1979); (1989b); (1991), 1–34, (1994); Qviller (1981); Geddes (1984); Halverson (1985); Rihll (1986); Andreev (1988); Thalmann (1988); Ulf (1990); Finley (1991); and van Wees (1992).

10 A model of class-division was famously provided by Finley (1991), 53, who in his *The World of Odysseus* spoke of 'a deep horizontal cleavage' which separated the Homeric nobles from the multitude: 'Above the line were the *aristoi*, literally the "best people", the hereditary nobles who held most of the wealth and all the power, in peace as in war. Below were all the others, for whom there was no collective technical term, the multitude. The gap between the two was rarely crossed, except by the inevitable accidents of wars and raids'.

11 I am aware that by using the notion of 'class', I am imposing a modern concept on a society structured and based on entirely different concepts and values. Ever since the works of Marx, however, studies of class-division and economic exploitation in pre-capitalist societies have contributed important insight to our understanding of ancient Greece and Rome (e.g. Ste Croix (1981); Thalmann (1998); Rose (2012), esp. 1–55). I believe that using a well-defined concept of class can, therefore, provide a useful tool for exploring the social, economic and cultural worlds of ancient societies, and especially those with a limited base of evidence, such as Archaic Greece. Throughout this chapter, I define 'class' broadly as a socially acknowledged division based on economic and social status. I understand economic division as a broad control of the means of production and agricultural land by a group of people,

which I will refer to as the elite (*aristoi*). Control of agricultural land was especially significant considering the largely mountainous landscape of Greece. Social division, on the other hand, will manifest itself by a general social awareness of divisions based on wealth and birth, in turn justifying the superior social and political position, or status, of the elite over the common people. Finally, following a recent line of scholarship (Osborne (2009), 209–10; Rose (2012), 52–3; van Wees and Fisher (2015), 1–57), I will avoid using the term 'aristocracy', which I believe inadequately describes the early Greek elite, whose internal structure, political stability and hereditary nature did not reach the sophistication of the aristocracies of subsequent historical periods. An excellent recent discussion on the subject of aristocracy in Homer is provided by van Wees and Fisher (2015), 16–25, who conclude that apart from a few hereditary honours derived from Zeus and symbolized by the use of staff, there are no meaningful aristocratic elements in the poems which set the *basileis* apart. The position of a *basileus*, as they argued, is a gift from the community, 'who will withhold their support if they see his power abused, and moreover contingent on recognition by peers, who may "drop" him if he loses his wealth' (p. 25).

12 Translation by A. T. Murray; revised by William F. Wyatt (Loeb).
13 For more on the Achaean assembly scene, also known as *The Test*, see Thalmann (1988), 10–14; van Wees (1992), 79–85.
14 Morris (1986), 123.
15 For more on the elite ideology of the Homeric poems, see van Wees (1992), 78–83; Raaflaub (1997b), 633–5; and van Wees and Fisher (2015), 16–25. A more general (and critical) discussion of ideology in the *Iliad* is provided by Rose (1997). On Homeric audiences, see Dalby (1995), who challenged the scholarly consensus regarding the exclusively aristocratic audience, arguing instead, based on the vagueness and inaccuracies in Homer's descriptions of noble houses and diet, that the poems were built on the perceptions of 'the poorest', and 'least aristocratic'. I am inclined to believe that early Homeric poems, especially in their oral forms, were enjoyed by the full social spectrum, as suggested by Kirk (1962), 274–81, and Thalmann (1988), 2–3. The main themes and heroes of the *Iliad* and *Odyssey* clearly reflect an elite ideology which, however, in itself, certainly does not necessitate an elite audience.
16 The amount of scholarship on Homeric *basileis* is again endless and cannot be fully referenced here. A small selection referenced throughout this chapter includes: Andreev (1979); Qviller (1981); Geddes (1984), 28–36; Halverson (1985), 133–6; Ulf (1990), 85–125; Finley (1991), 74–107; van Wees (1992), 78–152, 274–98. For a listing of the most important bibliography on Homeric *basileis*, see Rose (2012), 109 n. 46. On the physical beauty of Homeric princes, see van Wees (1992), 78–9, who stresses the supposedly hereditary aspect of good looks among the nobles, which sets them apart from the masses.

17 Every Homeric community consisted of a number of *basileis*, who acted as heads of their respective households. Collectively, they governed the larger community as leaders, councillors and elders (*archoi, medontes, gerontes*), under the rule of one supreme *basileus*, whose position was largely hereditary, though not unchallengeable. On the island of Phaeacia, for instance, there were thirteen men 'marked out as kings (*basileis*)' who acted 'as leaders (*archoi*)', according to Alkinoös, the supreme *basileus* (VIII.390–1). Similarly, Telemachus speaks of the 'many other Achaean princes (*basileis*), young and old, in seagirt Ithaca', any of whom can hold the supreme *basileus* position 'now that the great Odysseus has perished' (I.394–6). For more see Raaflaub (1997b), 633–4; van Wees (1992), 274–6.

18 The standing and position of the Homeric *basileis* is also given by Zeus, as indicated by Menelaus' speech in the *Iliad* (17.248–51). For more on the hereditary status claimed by the Homeric *basileis*, see van Wees (1992), 281–94.

19 The 'choice meats' and 'filled wine cups' are symbolic gifts given by the community to the princes, known as the 'wine of the elders' (*gerousion oinon*), referred to also in Menelaus' speech in the previous footnote. The orchard, vineyard and ploughland, mentioned by Sarpedon, are all part of the royal estate (*temenos*) appointed to a *basileus* by the community. For more on *gerousion oinon* and Homeric feasting, see van Wees (1995), 164–77. For more on Homeric *temenea*, see Donlan (1989a); van Wees (1992), 294–8.

20 Van Wees (1992), 79; Singor (1995), 189–90.

21 See Latacz (1977); Pritchett (1985), 7–33; van Wees (1988), 2–14; (1992), 352 n. 47; (1997), 692–3; (2004), 153–65; Raaflaub (1997b), 635; (2008); Rawlings (2007), 34–6. In his speech during the Achaean assembly, Thersites even suggests that the main brunt of the fighting, as well as the capture of the booty, was done by the rank-and-file soldiers (2.225–42). For more on Homeric *laoi*, see Haubold (2000).

22 E.g. 5.529–32; 14.368–9; 15.301–5, 561–4, 617–22; 17.364–5. For an overview of massed fighting, or *Massenkampf*, in the *Iliad*, see Latacz (1977), 178–209. For phalanx formation in the *Iliad*, see Bowden (1993), 52–4; Schwartz (2009), 108–15.

23 Calhoun (1934), 208.

24 Ibid., 308.

25 Geddes (1984); Halverson (1985); Rihll (1986); Stein-Hölkeskamp (1989); Ulf (1990); Donlan (1991), 1–34. For the initial negative reception of Calhoun's argument, see Geddes (1984), 19.

26 Geddes (1984), 27.

27 Halverson (1985), 129–36.

28 Rihll (1986), 91.

29 Ibid.

30 Qviller (1981); Geddes (1984), 28–36; Halverson (1985), 133–6; Stein-Hölkeskamp (1989), 15–56; Ulf (1990), 1–49, 85–125.

31 Van Wees (1992), 79–83, 352 n. 46–56, addressed most of the critique against the class-division model putting particular emphasis on the elite perspective, agenda and ideology of the poems. According to him, both the *Iliad* and *Odyssey* focus exclusively on the ruling elite; non-elites 'only enter the poets' field of vision insofar as they affect the princes' life... Thus, if the people lead a shadowy existence in the epics and are not often explicitly distinguished from the princes, this is because in the heroic world the social distance between prince and "common" man is such that personal contact between them is infrequent, or regarded as insignificant, or both, and deemed an unsuitable topic for a story' (p. 81). I am largely in agreement with van Wees' interpretation, as I maintain that the class-division model (elite vs commoners) provides an accurate framework for our understanding of Homeric society, as will become clear later in this chapter.

32 'The common people', as Donlan (1991), 19, argued, 'are not regarded as social inferiors – there is, in fact, no birth or class nomenclature in Homer. The role of the people, though passive for the most part, does not imply submissiveness to their leaders. It must be remembered that the rank and file are also given the epithet *aristoi* (best), and that they, too, are called "heroes"'. Homeric society, according to Donlan, never attained the level of a stratified or class society, but reflected instead a tribal and egalitarian chiefdom system, reminiscent of Dark Age societies.

33 Geddes (1984), 27. Van Wees (1992), 80, albeit from a different perspective, also mentioned the remarkable rarity of any episodes highlighting class-division in the *Iliad* and *Odyssey*.

34 Both Calhoun (1934), 305, and Geddes (1984), 22, point out that there is nothing in the *Iliad* to suggest that Thersites was a man of low birth. His ugly appearance, however, juxtaposed with that of the handsome and beautiful princes, combined with the violent rebuke – usually reserved for the rank-and-file soldiers – that he receives from Odysseus, suggests that he must be a commoner. For more on the episode, see Postlethwaite (1988); Thalmann (1988); van Wees (1992), 353–4 n. 58. Thersites appears also in the story of Penthesileia from the *Aethiopis* (Arg. 1d), where he is killed by Achilles because of his abusive comments; and in the hunt for the Calydonian boar (Pherecydes Fr. 123 Fowler). Later sources, such as Apollodorus and Quintus Smyrnaeus, assign clear noble lineage to Thersites, which almost certainly featured in early non-Homeric epics. For more, see Gantz (1993), 621–2; Elmer (2013), 93–7; West (2013), 140–2.

35 For more on fighting over and despoiling the dead in Homer, see Fenik (1968), 177–8; Singor (1995), 194–6; van Wees (1996), 25–6, 54–6.

36 Of a total of 274 men killed in the *Iliad*, van Wees (1996), 79 n. 146, counted sixty-six attempts at despoliation, including seven collective attempts.

37 The following account is heavily influenced by the works of van Wees (1988); (1994); (1996); (1997), who emphasized the fluid and open nature of Homeric battlefields.

Other scholars, including Latacz (1977); Pritchett (1985), 7–33; and Schwartz (2009), 108–15, stressed the significance of massed formations in the fighting episodes of the *Iliad*, which, to my mind, cannot be inferred from the overwhelming majority of combat scenes in the poem. For other recent studies of Homeric warfare, see Singor (1991); (1995); Lendon (2005), 20–38; Rawlings (2007), 28–39; Raaflaub (2008); Sears (2010).

38 The prevalence of the 'hit-and-run' tactics as the dominant form of attack is especially evident when one considers the duration of individual battlefield encounters. According to van Wees (1996), 38, 'from a total of 170 battlefield encounters described and further 130 referred to, only 18 involve more than one blow, and a mere 6 of these involve more than a single exchange of blows. The only fight to go beyond a second exchange of blows is not part of a battle, but a specially arranged formal duel'.

39 Ares, as Vermeule (1979), 110, observed, is too big to wear Periphas' armour himself, but stripping it 'will publicly signal his success in looting, like the other heroes'.

40 Warriors killed: 4.465–9, 491–3; 14.476–7; 16.577–80; 17.289–303; wounded: 11.246–61, 368–400, 579–84; 13.527–30. For a short discussion with references, see van Wees (1996), 54–5, 79 n. 147.

41 Finley (1991), 119: 'Among more primitive peoples the victim's head served that honorific purpose; in Homer's Greece armour replaced heads. That is why time after time, even at great personal peril, the heroes paused from their fighting in order to strip a slain opponent of his armour. In terms of the battle itself such a procedure was worse than absurd, it might jeopardize the whole expedition. It is a mistake in our judgment, however, to see the end of the battle as the goal, for victory without honour was unacceptable; there could be no honour without public proclamation, and there could be no publicity without the evidence of a trophy'. Van Wees (1996), 55–6, 69 n. 73, on the other hand, disagreed and argued that Homeric spoils are 'sought at least as much for their material and utilitarian value as for their symbolic significance as trophies' (p. 56). He stressed the fact that spoils are obtained both individually and collectively, and in most cases they fall into the 'wrong' hands, as men strip warriors whom they have not killed themselves, which in turn diminishes their 'trophy' value. It seems to me, however, based on Idomeneus' remarks, that spoils acquired during the fighting, which as I argue below belong only to the Homeric *aristoi*, are valued primarily as symbols of military success and fighting among the *promachoi*; obtaining them in the heat of battle provided a proof of courage in itself, irrelevant of whether the successful warrior killed his victim or not. The material aspect of other battlefield spoils is, nonetheless, certainly evident for armour plundered during a pursuit or after battle, which I discuss later.

42 The practice of despoliation, which highlighted individual accomplishment, was according to Udwin (1999), 127–8, one of the main features of an arranged duel in

epic culture. Homeric warriors, as he summarized, 'seem to be obsessed with stripping the armor from the corpses of those they have slain, even when this activity opens them to easy attack exposing their flanks to the enemy. Victory over the common enemy thus seems to hold less importance than the establishment of a reputation for having personally killed a notable warrior'.

43 One exception is Achilles, who before his fight with Hector famously rejects the latter's request to return the body of the vanquished for burial (22.256–72); their fight, however, is not an arranged duel. Udwin (1999), in his study of the institution of the duel in epic culture, emphasized the peculiar nature of the duel between Hector and Ajax. The terms of their duel, unlike the earlier one between Menelaus and Paris (3.84–120), did not include any stipulations regarding the outcome of the war and were not concerned with the preservation of lives, which according to Udwin was the fundamental principle of the epic institution of the duel. As a result, their duel is 'rendered meaningless because the terms do not provide any reference to future disposition of the armies. Instead, agreement between the parties is expressly limited to the treatment of the loser's corpse and armor' (p. 83).

44 The exception here is again Achilles, who as a mark of special respect did not strip the armour of Andromache's father, Eëtion, but 'burned the body in all its elaborate war-gear and piled a grave mound over it' (6.418–9).

45 The walls of Odysseus' *megaron* in Ithaca were covered with no less than seventeen shields and helmets, with an additional twenty spears in a rack by a column near the door (I.126–9; XVI.284; XXII.21–5). Although it is not explicitly stated, one may suspect that they are all spoils of war. For references, numbers and brief discussion on the weapons and armour on display in Odysseus' *megaron*, see van Wees (1995), 149.

46 These are, however, the only instances in the *Iliad* where the spoils are dedicated to the gods. Seaford (2004), 56, stresses the 'relative marginality, in the Homeric perspective, of the practice of dedication'.

47 Van Wees (1996), 55.

48 Homer's occasional mentions of marching warriors who glitter with shining armour (4.431–2), according to Singor (1995), 187, 'could conceivably be attributed to the poetic imagination'. Indeed, Singor (1991), 19–24; (1995), 186–9, maintains that the Homeric masses (*plethos, laoi*) were equipped primarily with long-distance weapons (*belea*) and otherwise little or no armour, similar to the Lokrians (13.713–8). By contrast, according to him, the *promachoi* were always heavy-armed and consisted exclusively of the poem's *basileis* and *aristoi*. I find this theory problematic on two levels: a) there is little evidence to assume that the *laoi* were not fighting among the *promachoi*; everyone was expected to spend some time in the frontline and the intermittent mentions of warriors coming to the front and joining ranks to protect a comrade must surely include both the *basileis* and *laoi*; consequently b) the latter

must have been in possession of more than just long-range weapons, which also, in turn, explains the practice of post-combat despoliation, as men would hardly scavenge for stones, arrows and javelins only after the battle. The armour of the masses was certainly cheaper and less impressive than that of the *basileis*, but there is no reason to suspect that it was limited to long-range weapons only. The unusual equipment of the Lokrians was surely due to the fact that they are explicitly described as archers, which Homer singles out as exceptional for a full contingent. For more on the social status of the *promachoi*, see van Wees (1997), 688–9.

49 As Donlan (1981), 113 n. 14, noted, the sale of battlefield spoils ('bronze', 'shining iron') is implied at 7.472–4.

50 Ready (2007), 17–22, argued that there are 'two economies of exchange when it comes to spoils obtained in [Homeric] war': (a) the long-term transactions, which include any spoils obtained through the (re)distribution of booty after the battle, given by the leader of the expedition or the community; and (b) the short-term transactions, which include any spoils seized during the battle from a defeated foe, which do not make it into the common pot for (re)distribution. The latter, as he explains, are 'deemed valuable contributions to a warrior's status ... integral to the creation and reaffirmation of the social order. Nevertheless they are not portrayed as contributing so explicitly and systematically to the perpetuation of the social and cosmic order as the (re)distribution.' For more on the Homeric distribution of booty, see van Wees (1992), 299–310.

51 For examples of warriors defending the corpses of the *aristoi*, see 4.531–5; 5.617–26; 13.550–5.

52 For more on the Homeric concept of shame, see Redfield (1975), 133–9; Scott (1980), 14–25; Cairns (1993), 48–146; van Wees (1996), 21–3.

53 Dodds (1951), 1–63.

54 E.g. 17.91–3; 17.254–5; 18.178–80. For more on *nemesis* in the Homeric poems, see Scott (1980), 25–31; Yamagata (1994), 149–56.

55 See also 16.544–7.

56 It is important to note, as van Wees (1996), 22–3, observed, that shame did not encourage Homeric warriors to perform heroic military deeds in order to win more glory but rather stimulated essentially defensive actions, such as protecting the corpse of a fallen comrade. Shame impels men, according to van Wees, 'individually or collectively, to preserve their reputation by fighting back when the Homeric code requires a response to an attack or challenge. It must be stressed that shame is *not* likely to drive people positively to enhance their reputations by performing outstanding feats of prowess'.

57 For more references, see van Wees (1996), 66 n. 52.

58 The term used to describe these war bands in the *Iliad* is the plural form of the word 'phalanx' (*phalanges*), which often led modern scholars to assume that the Classical

phalanx formation was already present on Homeric battlefields (see n. 22 above). The epic phalanges, however, as argued by Echeverria (2012), 311–2, are consistently described throughout the poem as mobile and highly flexible *units* of warriors, which act independently and can be separated if needed. As such, they bear no resemblance to the Classical *formation* of a phalanx. For more on phalanges in the *Iliad*, see Singor (1991), 24–33.

59 For more on Homeric army organization, see van Wees (1988), 4–7, (1996), 2–4; (1997), 670–3; Singor (1991), 33–50; (1995), 184–93; Kucewicz (forthcoming A).
60 Taking the spoils: 13.640–2; 17.580–1. Retrieving the dead from the field: 13.656–8; 17.722–34.
61 Van Wees (1996), 18.
62 The standard procedure for the distribution of booty is outlined by Odysseus' account of his sack of Ismaros: 'I sacked their city and killed their people, and out of their city taking their wives and many possessions we shared them out, so none might go cheated of his proper portion' (IX.40–3). The mutual trust between the warrior and his leader could be broken, especially when the former felt that his service was not fully appreciated or rewarded by the latter. There are some complaints about the lack of appropriate gratitude voiced throughout the *Iliad* (9.316; 17.144–8), which in some cases – most notably, Achilles' anger at Agamemnon – may lead a warrior to withdraw his services altogether. For more on Homeric distribution of booty, see n. 50 above.
63 For more on the social significance of Homeric funerals, see Redfield (1975), 167–210; Morris (1987), 46–7; Vernant (1991); Clarke (1999), 180–9.
64 The main symbol of the social status of the deceased was his grave mound and *stele*, which reflected the dead warrior's glory (*kleos*). A grave mound ensured that a man's 'glory will not be forgotten' (7.91) and that his 'memory might never die' (IV.584–5). For more on Homeric grave mounds, see Morris (1987), 46; Sourvinou-Inwood (1995), 108–40; Clarke (1999), 185.
65 Vernant (1991), 50–74.
66 Ibid., 64.
67 See also XIV.366–71.
68 The worst fate that Telemachus could imagine for his missing father Odysseus is that his 'white bones lie out in the rain and fester somewhere on the mainland, or roll in the wash of the breakers' (I.161–2). Similarly, the loyal swineherd Eumaios imagines the unburied body of his master: 'But, for him, the dogs and the flying birds must by now have worried the skin away from his bones, and the soul has left them; or else the fish have eaten him, out in the great sea, and his bones lie now on the mainland shore with the sand piled deeply upon them' (XIV.132–6). As Vermeule (1979), 12, summarized, 'the worst was not to be buried, not to be mourned by mother or wife, or to have your body dallied with by the careless dogs and birds on land and the fish at sea'.

69 See McClellan (2019), 31–3.
70 The Homeric gods often help mortals throughout the poems but, as Hector's and Sarpedon's burials show, they are especially intent on ensuring that their favourite *aristoi* are provided with full burial ceremonies (see p. 39 below). For more, see Adkins (1972), 14–15; Yamagata (1994), 16.
71 Battlefield truces and the convention of *anairesis* are discussed in Chapter 2. The only other mass burial scene in the *Iliad* concerns the cremation of the victims of the plague brought on the Achaean camp by Apollo (1.52). No details of what happened with the remains are offered but it seems plausible to assume that they were buried on the spot in a common grave, similar to 7.430–6.
72 In addition, as pointed out by Krentz (2002), 33, the Trojan herald Idaios clearly does not admit defeat and commits to fight again, contrary to the norms of the Classical procedures of *anairesis*. The scholiast (bT 1.4d), quoted and translated by Morrison (1992), 141 n. 30, notes that the lack of subsequent scenes of mass burial is the result of Trojan victories: 'As the Trojans set up camp by the ships, [the Greeks] no longer thought of burying the dead, but rather of their own safety'.
73 See Page (1963), 315–24; Garland (1982), 73.
74 Thucydides briefly mentions the building of the Achaean wall as part of his discussion on the size of the Achaean army and the reasons behind the unusual length of the campaign (1.10.3–11.2). The passage in question reads as follows: 'And when they arrived and had prevailed in battle—as evidently they did, for otherwise they could not have built the defence around their camp—even then they seem not to have used their whole force, but to have resorted to farming in the Chersonese and to pillaging, through lack of supplies' (1.11.1).
75 Page (1963), 316. *Cf.* Davison (1965), who tried to reconcile the conflicting traditions about the Achaean wall by emending ἂν ἐτειχίσαντο for ἀνετειχίσαντο in Thucydides, based on his somewhat questionable assumption that *not* building a wall would have been a mark of the Achaean victory upon landing in Troy.
76 The earliest source which alludes to the practice of bringing the ashes of the war dead back home is Aeschylus' *Agamemnon* (435–44). A discussion, with a specific reference to Nestor's proposal in the *Iliad*, is offered by Fraenkel (1950), 227 [also quoted in Pritchett (1985), 101]: 'In mentioning the transfer of the warriors' ashes to their own cities Aeschylus allows himself what the scholiasts on similar occasions (e.g. on *Sept.* 277 and *Eum.* 566ff.) call an anachronism, for the practice of collecting the bones and ashes for the purpose of taking them back to the homeland was unknown in the period of the epic poems: the lines *H* 334f. which were obelized by Aristarchus stand 'in glaring contradiction to the practice of the Homeric poems' (Wiliamowitz, *Des Ilias und Homer*, 55)'. Aeschylus' passage is discussed at more length at the end of Chapter 5.

77 Leaf (1900), 321; Mylonas (1948), 63–4; Page (1963), 322–4; West (1969); Kurtz and Boardman (1971), 187; Kirk (1990), 278–9. For a summary of the debate concerning the burial scene of Book 7, see Pritchett (1985), 100–2.

78 Page (1963), 321–4; *contra* West (1969); Willcock (1976), 81. Van Wees (2006b), 132, by contrast, rejected the interpolation theory, positing that the burial mound built over the common grave in Book 7 was a cenotaph, and the ashes of the anonymous multitudes were indeed returned back home. This practice, according to him, reinforced the distinction between the Homeric elites, buried in individual tombs near the battlefield, and the masses, denied the privilege and taken home for burial by relatives or comrades. This argument, however, seems too far-fetched, as there is nothing in the *Iliad* or *Odyssey* to confirm that repatriation of the ashes of the dead was a standard practice. The latter, moreover, would have posed a number of logistical and economic problems, as burning the dead and collecting their remains required considerable time and effort, as shown in the cases of the Homeric *aristoi*. It makes far more sense, therefore, to assume that the common dead were disposed of in the quickest and most efficient way, i.e. buried in a common grave on the battlefield.

79 As Garland (1982), 70, noted, 'it is also notable that Homer's warriors did not see it as their business at the end of a day's fighting to reclaim the bodies of ordinary, common soldiers, even those that were easily recoverable ... It is almost as if ordinary soldiers do not qualify as proper dead'. The motif of unburied and rotting corpses is also mentioned in the *Odyssey* at I.161–2; III.258–61; XIV.132–6. See also Morrison (1992), 84–5.

80 Demonstrated most clearly by Odysseus' boast over the dead Sokos: 'Wretch, since now your father and your honored mother will not be able to close your eyes in death, but the tearing birds will get you, with their wings close-beating about you. If I die, the brilliant Achaeans will bury me in honor' (11.452–5).

81 According to Griffin (1980), 47–9, the corpses of fallen warriors are also used by Homer to convey the full meaning of war and death in an environment dominated by the exploits of great warriors, which are easier to represent due to the subject nature of the poem. 'Mass fighting and slaughter', as he argued, 'is harder to represent in heroic style, but the poet uses similes for this purpose, and also he uses the bodies of the slain. Events happen 'in a clear place where the ground showed through the corpses', warriors go 'through the slaughter, through the corpses, among the weapons and the dark blood'. Their chariots pass over the bodies of the dead, 'and the axle beneath and the rail all round were all spattered with blood, sprinkled by the drops cast up from the horses' hooves and the wheels. ... The corpse both is and is not the man. It stands for him, and its treatment enables the poet to do full justice to war and death in ways which otherwise could not have been embodied in the epic'.

82 The most comprehensive study of the mutilation of the dead in the *Iliad* is provided by Segal (1971), who interpreted the mutilation scenes as part of a larger framework of escalating brutality and 'the poem's movement from intense violence to calm finale' (p. 72). Other scholarly treatments of the subject include Bassett (1933); Vermeule (1979), 94–108; Vernant (1991), 50–74; van Wees (1992), 129–30; (1996), 51–4; (2004), 162; Lendon (2000), 3–11; McClellan (2017); (2019), 27–41. The argument here is a shortened version of Kucewicz (2016).

83 'Indeed', as Rosivach (1983), 197, remarked, 'one gets the impression from reading the *Iliad* that the normal practice of Homeric warriors was to leave the enemy dead unburied as "prey for dogs and carrion birds", that actual mutilation of corpses (described notably by the verb *aeikizo*) was, if not the norm, at least a frequent occurrence, and that the only way the dead were buried was when their bodies were recovered by their compatriots, usually in the course of the combat itself'.

84 Vermeule (1979), 96.

85 The contrast between the Homeric poem and the standards of Classical Greece was first noted by Plato, who voices his indignation at Achilles' mistreatment of Hector's body in his discussion on an ideal education system in the *Republic* (3.391c). The passage is discussed at more length in the following chapter.

86 Rosivach (1983), 206; Vernant (1991), 74; van Wees (1996), 51–3; Lendon (2000), 3–11; Kucewicz (2016).

87 On bodily mutilations in the *Odyssey*, see Kucewicz (2016), 427 n. 13. According to McClellan (2017), 161–2, the only clear case of post-mortem mutilation in the *Iliad* is the decapitation of Imbrios' corpse by the Lokrian Ajax. The remaining cases of possible corpse mutilations are either not clear (Hippolochus, Koön, Ilioneus), or consist of post-mortem abuse (Hector), which he distinguishes from post-mortem mutilation. While McClellan is right to point out that the exact moments of death are not specified for Hippolochus and Ilioneus (as opposed to Koön, whose beheading clearly takes places after Agamemnon 'unstrung him' (λῦσε δὲ γυῖα) – a common term for death in the *Iliad*), it seems to me that the extreme level of brutality which characterizes these scenes is largely unaffected and plays a key role in the vengeance aspect of each killing and mutilation.

88 Agamemnon's *aristeia* was discussed by Whitman (1958), 158–60, who interpreted its intense brutality and grimness as part of the *Iliad*'s character sketch of the Achaean king. The scene, according to him, fit the larger portrayal of Agamemnon in the poem: 'As Homer makes Agamemnon, he is a magnificently dressed incompetence, without spirit or spiritual concern; his dignity is marred by pretension; his munificence by greed, and his prowess by a savagery which is the product of a deep uncertainty and fear' (pp. 162–3). King (1987), 14–15, following Fenik (1968), 85, emphasized the similarity between Agamemnon's and Achilles' *aristeiai*, adding that 'brutal and grisly slaying is associated most of the time with

warriors of the second rank ... of the major heroes only Achilles and Agamemnon ... kill horribly with any consistency'. As will become clear in the discussion below, brutal killings and post-mortem mutilations (successful and/or intended) are ascribed to other Homeric *aristoi*, especially in the context of vengeance or attempts to reinforce social standing.

89 For a detailed study of this episode, see McClellan (2017); (2019), 34–41, who saw it as the only successfully executed post-mortem mutilation in the *Iliad* and therefore conspicuous for its brutality (see n. 87 above). According to him, the scene was a nightmarish anticipation of Achilles' attempted mutilation of Hector's corpse which played an 'important structural and metapoetic role' in the poem; it was intentionally placed at the mid-point of the narrative when Zeus was temporarily absent, signalling 'that the mutilation of Imbrius is strangely out of place in this epic universe' (2017), 172. The parallels between Imbrios' and Hector's mutilation are certainly noteworthy, but McClellan's insistence on the uniqueness of Imbrios' beheading as the only successful instance of post-mortem mutilation in the *Iliad* seems to me misguided.

90 I briefly discussed other potential cases of successful corpse mutilations suggested by Segal (1971), 10, 20, 31, in Kucewicz (2016), 428 n. 14. None of them can be interpreted as post-mortem mutilations.

91 On Homeric vengeance, see Lendon (2000), 3–11.

92 Ibid., 5.

93 On Homeric *timē*, see Yamagata (1994), 121–44; Adkins (1997), 702–6.

94 The mechanics of vengeance feature prominently in the few instances of warriors vaunting over the slain, e.g. 13.445–7; 14.470–4, 82–5. On the concepts of status, honour and violence in Homeric society, see van Wees (1992).

95 Lendon (2000), 5.

96 It is certainly striking that successful post-mortem mutilations are committed only by the Achaeans, as the victims are either the non-Greek Trojans (Hippolochos, Koön, Ilioneus, Hector), or their allies (Imbrios). According to a number of scholars, however, the practice of mutilation is disapproved of by the poet and the gods. Segal (1971), 13, for instance, asserts that 'the exposure and mutilation of a dead warrior's corpse does indeed arouse in Homer repugnance and even some measure of moral outrage'. Similarly, Lendon (2000), 9, claims that Homeric mutilation 'crosses the line of proper behavior and offends the gods'; and Krentz (2007a), 174, adds that 'the gods disapprove' of the mutilation episodes in the *Iliad*. I disagreed with their interpretation in Kucewicz (2016), arguing instead that the practice of maltreating the dead was perfectly acceptable by the moral and ethical standards of the society depicted in the *Iliad* and *Odyssey*, and as such is *not* condemned in the poems. For more on the ethics of Homeric mutilation, see Bassett (1933); van Wees (1992), 129–30; (1996), 51–4.

97 As argued already by Bassett (1938), 203–4.
98 Kucewicz (2016), 432–5.
99 The most revealing passage here is Zeus' speech to Thetis in Book 24, where we are specifically told that the disagreement among the gods concerning Achilles' maltreatment of Hector began nine days ago, on the day of Patroclus' funeral (24.107–8): ἐννῆμαρ δὴ νεῖκος ἐν ἀθανάτοισιν ὄρωρεν | Ἕκτορος ἀμφὶ νέκυι καὶ Ἀχιλλῆϊ πτολιπόρθῳ: the two days of Achilles' *aeikea erga* before the funeral apparently did not cause any disapproval on Olympus. Achilles' fault, therefore, lay only in his excessive maltreatment of Hector after Patroclus' funeral.
100 As argued by Yamagata (1994), 3–101, the Homeric gods do not express much interest in morality or justice in the human world: 'unless what *moira* bids coincides with the moral virtue of men, the gods do not behave as, or rather do not appear to be, defenders of human morality' (p. 101). For more on the Homeric gods and their concern for morality and justice, see Lloyd-Jones (1971a); Adkins (1972); Gill (1980); Winterbottom (1989); Ahrensdorf (2014), esp. 46–57.
101 In his study of the *Iliad*'s proem, Redfield (1979), 104–5, highlighted the powerful effect of the word 'feast' (*daite*), suggesting that its use for 'the carrion meal of the beasts is … a strong and (as the ancient critics complained) rather repulsive metaphor'. The ascription of man-like things to beasts in the proem, as he suggested, served to emphasize the later reversal in the poem where men become like beasts: 'in the proem the carrion-eating beasts do a man-like thing. What is presented in the proem as an objective fact about beasts appears in the poem (where no bodies are ever eaten by the beasts) as a subjective tendency of men, who in battle become somewhat like predators or scavengers'.
102 Rosivach (1983), 197. A full list of references to all mentions of animal mutilation in the *Iliad* and *Odyssey* is provided in Kucewicz (2016), 430 n. 25. For more on animal mutilation in Homer, see Bassett (1933), 47–50; Redfield (1975), 168–9, 183–6, 199–200; Vermeule (1979), 103–9; Vernant (1991), 71–2; Clarke (1999), 170–2.
103 Vermeule (1979), 46–8, traces the motif of excarnation by predators back to the sixth millennium BC, mentioning in particular the reconstructed rites in the Neolithic Vulture Shrine of Çatal Hüyük, *c.* 6150 BC, in which the vultures devouring corpses were believed to act as instruments of cleansing. Scenes of birds and dogs eating the enemy dead on the battlefield were, as she observed, 'drawn into the conventional language of war art, and into the limited male repertory of boasting, millennia before the Greek epic singer flourishes them as malevolent threats on the plain of Troy'. The best example of this is the predynastic Vulture Stele of Lagash, *c.* 2500 BC, which depicts vultures picking at the dead enemy, bearing a very close resemblance to similar scenes described in the *Iliad*. Homer's

use of the animal mutilation theme was, therefore, a continuation of a much older tradition of associating scavengers with military defeat. The motif appears also in early Greek art, e.g. Walter-Karydi (2015), 45–6. For other representations of birds attacking dead bodies in Mediterranean art, see Saunders (2008b), 171 n. 60.

104 Vernant (1991), 67; Redfield (1975), 169.

105 The only exception is the fate of Asteropaios, the leader of the Paionians, who after getting killed by Achilles is left exposed in the river Skamandros, and about his body 'the eels and the other fish were busy tearing him and nibbling the fat that lay by his kidneys' (21.203–4). The episode, which as Segal (1971), 31, remarked 'brings the corpse theme to a new pitch of horror' as 'the mutilation is actually a fact, not just a remote threat', heightens the drama behind Achilles' vengeance, which shortly later culminates in his maltreatment of Hector's body. For more on the episode, see Redfield (1975), 169.

106 McClellan (2019), 31–2, emphasized the importance of divine intervention in the cases of corpse abuse in the *Iliad*, suggesting that the Homeric gods ensure that the acts and threats concerning post-mortem mutilations are 'unfulfilled or unsuccessful'. Homer, according to him, is never explicit about animal mutilations, which appear in the poem only in the form of fears and threats, therefore providing a 'sanitizing' effect for the reader. The proem of the *Iliad*, however, makes it sufficiently clear not only that corpse abuse is a common reality on the Homeric battlefields, but also that it forms part of Zeus' will. The latter fact has been noted already by Redfield (1979), 108, who argued that the 'association of Zeus with the carrion scavengers is reinforced by the aspect of the verbs. Ἔθηκε and προΐαψεν are aorists, while τεῦχε and ἐτελείετο are imperfects; we are thus led to associate the verbs in pairs, and to see, not the death of the heroes, but their defilement, as the special accomplishment of Zeus'. If Zeus 'leads the charge in keeping corpses safe from mutilation', as McClellan suggested, his protection applied only to the corpses of the Homeric *aristoi*, and not to the rank-and-file warriors. In his study of Homeric misdirection, Morrison (1992), 83–93, suggested that the final fate of Hector's corpse could have been different, since 'the audience is encouraged to believe ... that Achilles will mutilate – not ransom – Hector's body' (p. 92). According to him, the *Iliad*'s proem, which accurately anticipates the events of the poem, indicates 'that something other than respect for the Trojan dead will bring this poem to an end' – thus misleading the audience.

107 For an introduction to Homeric beliefs on death and the soul, see Bremmer (1983); Sourvinou-Inwood (1995), 10–107; Johnston (1999), 3–35.

108 Bremmer (1983), 89. See also Mylonas (1948), 61–2.

109 Since Elpenor's ghost is one of the first to approach Odysseus, some scholars assume that he has not been admitted to Hades because his body had not received burial, much like Patroclus' ghost scene from the *Iliad* (e.g. Johnston (1999), 9).

Clarke (1999), 188–9, however, points out that nothing in the text suggests that Elpenor's ghost is unable to enter Hades, as the latter's 'request for burial does not mention anything about its effect on his life in Hades, and the issue in the meaning is the code of mutual respect which gives every funeral its meaning'. The main purpose of the scene is undoubtedly to emphasize the moral obligation to provide one's companions with burial; Elpenor's plea to Odysseus, nonetheless, does suggest that his afterlife was at least in some way lacking because of his unburied body. The beliefs concerning the effects of burial on a soul's afterlife expressed in the *Odyssey* appear, in any case, to be different to those presented in the *Iliad*, most likely due to the later composition of the *Odyssey*. The most notable difference is Book 24, where the shades of the dead suitors are able to enter Hades and speak to the ghost of Agamemnon before they are buried (XXIV.186-90). The entire Book, however, is believed to be a later addition to the *Odyssey*, therefore reflecting the new religious beliefs of the late-seventh or early-sixth century BC. For more, see Sourvinou-Inwood (1995), 94–106; Johnston (1999), 14–15.

110 For more on this scene, see Bremmer (1983), 83; Clarke (1999), 191–2; Johnston (1999), 10 . 'Since,' as Bremmer (1983), 104, summarized, 'these persons were the first to be met in the underworld by Odysseus, at one time they may have been believed to reside at the outskirts of the underworld without actually entering it, and so to form a special category of the dead with an infranormal status'. The infranormal status of the dead warriors in the scene, according to Johnston (1999), 10, is most likely because their bodies are still unburied.

111 According to Mylonas (1948), 64, such a motivation may have stood behind Achilles' continuous mutilation of Hector following the burial of Patroclus, which 'could give no pleasure to the *psyche* of Patroklos since it had already been admitted to Hades, but it could be taken to mean that the dead Hektor was believed to feel the pain and the disgrace of the act'. The obscure Greek ritual of *maschalismos*, which involved cutting off the extremities of a victim and stringing them on a rope tied under the armpits and across the chest of the corpse, may have been similarly intended to harm the victim's soul in the afterlife and prevent his ghost from avenging himself. The practice, however, is mentioned in only two passages from the Classical period (Aesch. *Cho.* 439; Soph. *El.* 445) and its exact purpose and meaning are problematic. For more on *maschalismos*, see Rohde (1925), 582–6; Vermeule (1979), 49; Parker (1984), 138; Johnston (1999), 156–9; Hughes (2000), 194–6; Herman (2006), 308; Sommerstein (2006a), 83; Muller (2011).

112 Johnston (1999), 151.

113 See Yamagata (1994), 14–17.

114 For more on both scenes, see Parker (1983), 70; Yamagata (1994), 14–15; Johnston (1999), 10.

2 The War Dead in the Greek Mythological Tradition

1. On the *Iliad*'s influence on the Greek military ethos, see p. 182 n. 8 above.
2. For a summary of 'orthodox', 'gradualist' and 'revisionist' models for the study of early Greek warfare, see Kagan and Viggiano (2013).
3. This view was most fully expressed in the works of Hanson (1989); (1995); and Ober (1996), 53–71. For the retrieval of the war dead as part of early Greek conventions of war, see Adcock (1957), 1–13; Pritchett (1985), 97–100; Connor (1988), 8–18; Vaughn (1991); Tompkins (2013), 532.
4. Krentz (2002); (2007a); Dayton (2006); van Wees (2011); Lloyd (2017); Konijnendijk (2018). See also Kucewicz (2012).
5. In an influential article, Krentz (2002) challenged the existence of most of the 'agonistic' rules of war, and argued that the earliest attested examples of retrieving the dead as a concession of defeat do not appear until the 460s BC. His claim, however, was based not on actual instances of the *anairesis* procedure, but mainly on the dating of the first battlefield trophies in Greek art and literature. Van Wees (2006b), 132, simply states that 'the convention of a post-battle truce for the retrieval of the dead was apparently not yet established in Archaic Greece'.
6. The exact dating of the temple remains unclear but the strong focus on the recovery of the war dead featured in the friezes suggests that it was influenced by the events following the battle of Delium in 424 BC, where the Athenians were unable to bury their dead for seventeen days, denied by the victorious Thebans (Thuc. 4.97–101; see also p. 199 n. 32 below). For the friezes in general, see Harrison (1972); (1997); Pemberton (1972); Schultz (2009); Arrington (2015), 172–6.
7. See esp. Arrington (2015), 125–76, who discusses the temple along with other depictions of the war dead within the sacred space of Classical Athens.
8. The remaining eastern frieze depicts a gathering of gods, which, according to Harrison (1997), 110, 'symbolizes on a suprahuman level the victories that we see Athens winning in the battles depicted on the other three sides'. Specific deities represented in the frieze, she also argued, matched the gods named in the oath of the Athenian ephebes, thus bringing the youth pledging to fight for the city together with their ancestors, whose military victories were depicted on the temple.
9. Detienne (1986), 46–7; Calame (2007), 259; Clark (2012), 5. In Archaic Greece, the term *muthos* was used to refer to the stories sang by the poets, along with other terms such as *logos* and *epos*. Its meaning changed in the Classical period, when it became associated with false and fictitious speech, in direct opposition to *logos* – true speech. For a longer discussion, see Vernant (1988), 203–22.
10. Calame (2007), 259; Clark (2012), 2.
11. As Graf (1993), 3, summarized, myth's 'capacity to adapt to changing circumstances is a measure of its vitality'. On the relation between oral tradition and Greek myths,

see Buxton (1994), 45–52; Foley and Arft (2015); Nagy (2015). For more on the fluid character of Greek myths in general, see Bremmer (1987), 3–4; Buxton (1994); Hall (2007).

12. Hall (2007), 333.
13. Ibid., 333–8.
14. Griffiths (2011), 200. See also Boedeker (1993). A similar episode can be seen in the repatriation of Tisamenos (Paus. 7.1.8), another member of the Atreid dynasty, whose bones were supposedly returned to Sparta from Helice in the mid-550 BC, coinciding with Sparta's expansionist efforts in the northern Peloponnese. For more on Tisamenus' repatriation, see Leahy (1955).
15. See Connor (1970); Rausch (1999), 86–106; Anderson (2003), 134–46; Hall (2007), 338–46.
16. Parry (1930); (1932); Parry, Lord and Bynum (1954); Lord (1960).
17. For the most recent edition, see West (2003). Recent scholarly treatments of the Epic Cycle, which discuss dating and authorship, include Burgess (2001); (2015); Davies (2001); West (2013); (2015); Fantuzzi and Tsagalis (2015a); (2015b); Nagy (2015). I follow West's (2013), 25; (2015), 101, suggestion that most of the Cyclic poems attained their final written form sometime between 660 and 550 BC.
18. Burgess (2001), 15–16; Davies (2001), 1. West (2013), 21; (2015), 104–5, drawing on a passage from Aristotle's *Rhetoric* (1417a12), argued that the first full digest of the Cycle was compiled by Phayllos by the third quarter of the fourth century BC.
19. Preserved in a single manuscript (Venetus A), which did not include the *Cypria*, featured in other MSS of the *Iliad*. For more, see Fantuzzi and Tsagalis (2015b), 36–40. For more on Proclus, see Hillgruber (1990); West (2013), 7–11.
20. West (2013), 14.
21. For a general introduction to Apollodorus' *Bibliotheca*, see Robert (1873); Diller (1935); van der Valk (1958); Higbie (2007), 243–5; Scott Smith and Trzaskoma (2007); Dowden (2011), 66–72.
22. Van der Valk (1958), 117, 162. The author of the *Bibliotheca* was certainly not the famous Alexandrian scholar Apollodorus of Athens, but I shall nonetheless refer to him as 'Apollodorus' (and not 'pseudo-Apollodorus'), since we cannot tell whether his name was a case of mistaken attribution; the prominence of his work hardly credits its author to be called 'fake-Apollodorus', as pointed out by Robert Fowler in a recent BMCR review (2019.11.36).
23. Especially his *Epitome*. A list of Apollodorus' sources is provided by Higbie (2007), 245. For a recent work on Apollodorus' relationship to his sources, see Acerbo (2019).
24. The artistic inferiority of the Epic Cycle has been remarked on already by Aristotle (*Poet.* 1459a37–b16). For a discussion of Aristotle's views on the poetics of the Cyclic authors, see Fantuzzi (2015), 410–6.

25 Kakridis (1949); Willcock (1997); Kullmann (2015). The different scholarly models for approaching the Cyclic poems ('Homer-centric', 'Neoanalyst', 'Systemic') have been recently discussed by Burgess (2015), 43–7. For studies on the Epic Cycle and its relation to the Homeric epics, see Griffin (1977); Burgess (2001); Currie (2006); Finkelberg (2015).
26 See Snodgrass (1998); Burgess (2001); Carpenter (2015).
27 Burgess (2001), 21; (2015); Davies (2001), 6–8; West (2003), 12–13; (2013), 6–7; (2015), 101–7; Fantuzzi and Tsagalis (2015b), 36–40.
28 Fantuzzi and Tsagalis (2015b), 16–17.
29 For an excellent summary of the myth of Seven Against Thebes in ancient literary and artistic sources, see Gantz (1993), 510–22. For an extensive bibliography on the development of the myth in tragedy and funeral orations, see Steinbock (2013), 155 n. 1.
30 The tradition on Heracles being the first to restore the bodies of the dead to his enemies is reported only by Plutarch, Aelianus (*VH* 12.27), and a second century chrestomathy (*Pap. Oxy.* 1241). As Jacoby (*FGrH* 3b [Text] p. 448) observed, 'we do not know its origin, nor can we find a place for it in the history of Heracles'. The story must have been of little significance, especially compared to the popularity enjoyed by the tale of Theseus' recovery of the Seven.
31 The whole procedure was outlined by Plutarch in *Life of Nicias* (6.5). For post-battle customs in ancient Greek warfare, see Pritchett (1985); Vaughn (1991); van Wees (2004), 136–8; Rawlings (2007), 192–5; Krentz (2007a), 173–6; Konijnendijk (2018), 206–14.
32 Denial of burial, although uncommon in Classical warfare, is always regarded as punishment for a bigger sacrilege committed by the enemy. After the battle of Delium in 424 BC, the victorious Thebans forbade the Athenians to bury their dead, on the grounds that the latter were unlawfully occupying the sanctuary of Apollo (Thuc. 4.97–101). The corpses lay unburied until the Thebans recaptured the temple seventeen days later, after which the dead were duly returned to the Athenians. In 405 BC, according to Pausanias (9.32.9), the Spartan admiral Lysander refused burial of the vanquished Athenians after the battle of Aegospotami, thus adding to the 'long list of his disgraces'. He was motivated by revenge for the Athenian pre-battle threats to cut off the right hands of all captives, as well the execution of some prisoners from Corinth and Andros by the Athenian general Philocles during the battle (Xen. *Hell.* 2.1.31–2). Finally, the Lokrians did not permit the burial of the defeated Phocians in 355 BC, punishing the latter for robbing the temple of Delphi (Diod. 16.25.2). On unburied war dead, see Pritchett (1985), 235–41.
33 For burial truces, heralds and corpses in Thucydides, see Lateiner (1977). In fact, the first attested example of a truce for the recovery of the dead granted by the victorious army occurs following the battle of Potidaea (432 BC), after which, as

Thucydides recounts (1.63.3), 'the Athenians set up a trophy and gave up their dead under a truce (*hupospondos*) to the Potidaeans.' Such a late date does not, of course, imply that conventions of *anairesis* were formally introduced only in the 430s BC, but it is, nonetheless, worth noting that this is the first time we hear about the practice in our sources.

34 Of the twelve examples of Archaic war burials collected by Pritchett in the fourth volume of his *Greek State at War* (1985), 159–66, none involves the *anairesis* procedure as we know it from the Classical period. The only instance which mentions a battlefield truce for the recovery of the dead comes from the First Messenian War and is related by Pausanias (4.8.13). The details of Pausanias' account, however, are highly questionable; his story was heavily based on the work of a third century BC rhetorician Myron of Priene, whom Pausanias himself criticizes for lacking 'truth and credibility' (4.6.4). Myron' version most likely reflected the post-battle conventions of his own time, especially considering the mention of a battlefield trophy (*tropaion*), which became a standard feature of Greek battles only from the mid-fifth century BC. Pritchett, despite mentioning the influence of Myron on Pausanias' work, accepts the battlefield burial tradition as genuine, 'whatever its source', and states that the account 'refers to a battle of hoplites' (p. 159). For Pausanias' Hellenistic sources, see Luraghi (2008), 83–7. On *tropaia* in Greek warfare, see Schröder (2020), 86–91, 186–99, 242–9.

35 Pritchett (1985), 97–9: 'The antiquity of the maxim that, after a battle, the conquerors were bound to allow the vanquished to bury their dead is proved by the fact that it was ascribed either to Theseus or to Heracles'. Vaughn (1991), 41: '(...) respect [for the battle-dead] was predicated on the practice of mutually returning (and thereby distinguishing) enemy-dead for proper observances, a tradition first attributed variously to Theseus or Herakles, which attests to its antiquity'. Tompkins (2013), 532: 'The custom of returning enemy dead has a long history in Greek culture, going back to mythical figures such as Theseus or Heracles'.

36 Hdt. 9.27; Lys. 2.7–10; Isoc. 4.54–8; 10.31; 12.168–74; 14.53–5; Dem. 60.8. See also Pl. *Menex.* 239b; Xen. *Hell.* 6.5.46. Later works include: Paus. 1.39.2; Stat. *Theb.* 12.105–311, 464–809; Apollod. 3.7.1; Hyg. *Fab.* 70.2; Diod. Sic. 4.65.9. For an excellent discussion of Athens' intervention on behalf of the fallen Argives in Athenian public discourse, see Steinbock (2013), 155–210.

37 Gantz (1993), 295.

38 Steinbock (2013), 169–74.

39 Pausanias (8.25.8) mentions that Adrastus' escape from Thebes is depicted in the *Thebaid*, but offers no mention of Athenian involvement as part of the epic work. For the *Thebaid*, see West (2003), 6–9, 43–55; Torres-Guerra (2015). There is similarly no evidence that the episode was a part of the sixth-century BC *Theseid*. See Hubbard (1992), 98 n. 58.

40 Theseus' early absence from the story should perhaps not be surprising, considering that he was a relatively minor figure in Archaic epic poetry.
41 Steinbock (2013), 160–2, highlighted the excavations of nine Middle Helladic tombs at Eleusis conducted by Mylonas (1975), 2:153–4, 262–4, who suggested that the graves were identified by the locals as those belonging to the leaders of the Seven, based on the evidence of Late Geometric cult activity. According to Steinbock, a similar identification linking heroic tombs with the great epic story developed in Eleutherae.
42 Steinbock (2013), 164.
43 Gantz (1993), 296. Two of the seven leaders, Amphiaraus and Adrastus, could not have been cremated there (as opposed to the warriors fighting in their contingents). The first was famously swallowed by the earth in his retreat from the battlefield; the second survived the battle. See also Fowler (2013), 412–4.
44 As suggested by Hubbard (1992), 96 n. 49.
45 According to the Ambrosian scholiast (ΣO.6.23a Drachmann), Aristarchus posited that Pindar was the first and only author to suggest a peaceable burial at Thebes. Hubbard (1992), 94, disapproves on the basis of Aristarchus' general unreliability in historical and mythological matters.
46 Cited also by Pausanias (9.18.2). The Alexandrian editors of Homer Zenodotus and Aristophanes condemned the passage, claiming that it was incompatible with Athenian tragic versions. For more, see *FGrH* 3b [Supp.] 1.444 n. 24; and Levi (1985), 344 n. 87.
47 The conflicting traditions were much later reflected by Pausanias (1.39.2). In his guide to Eleusis, he claims to have seen the graves of the fallen Argives: 'A little farther on from the well is a sanctuary of Metaneira, and after it are graves of those who went against Thebes. For Creon, who at that time ruled in Thebes as guardian of Laodamas the son of Eteocles, refused to allow the relatives to take up and bury their dead. But Adrastus having supplicated Theseus, the Athenians fought with the Boeotians, and Theseus being victorious in the fight carried the dead to the Eleusinian territory and buried them here. The Thebans, however, say that they voluntarily gave up the dead for burial and deny that they engaged in battle.' As Steinbock (2013), 168–9, remarked, Pausanias' account indicates that the Thebans eventually lost the 'memory war' against Athens, as they acknowledged the Athenian intervention and burial in Eleusis, disputing only 'whether the recovery had been achieved by means of war or persuasion'.
48 Storey (2008), 13.
49 As Sommerstein (2015), 469, concluded, the Athenian dramatists 'may not only modify, sometimes drastically, the stories they find in the Cycle; they may introduce, within its framework, stories entirely unknown to the Cycle. Aeschylus seems to do this only in order to accommodate specifically Athenian versions of myths properly belonging to other cities – Theseus' intervention to secure the burial of the Seven against Thebes (*The Eleusinians*) ...'. See also Shapiro (2012).

50 Hauvette (1898), 170–3; Hubbard (1992), 99. Alternatively, as Steinbock (2013), 169–74, suggested, the motif of Theseus' intervention on behalf of Adrastus could have taken form in the last decade of the sixth century, when Theseus first emerged as a prominent figure in Athenian culture. The myth, according to him, attributed special prominence to Eleusis, which became an integral part of Attica after Cleisthenes' reforms, and depicts Theseus as a diplomat, and a civilizing force and unifier of Attica, thus reflecting the political situation of Athens around 510–500 BC.

51 The Argive dedications of statues of the Seven Against Thebes (and the Epigoni) at Delphi might perhaps be seen in the same light, as suggested by Hubbard (1992), 98 n. 55. Pausanias (10.10.2) relates that the statues were made from the spoils of the victory at Oinoe (c. 460 BC); Jeffery (1961), 161–3, disagreed, dating the surviving bases to the period 480–465 BC.

52 Storey (2008), 12.

53 This interpretation may be further confirmed by the famous myth of Antigone's heroic burial of her brother Polyneices against the orders of Creon, which might also have been an invention of the Athenian tragedians. The story, set in the aftermath of the invasion of the Seven, appears for the first time in Sophocles' *Antigone* (441 BC), with no mention in any source prior to the fifth century BC. The first appearance of Antigone is in Aeschylus' *Seven Against Thebes* (467 BC), where together with her sister Ismene she laments the loss of her brothers (957ff.), but the authenticity of the scene has been doubted. As Sommerstein (2015), 470, recently summarized: 'There is no evidence that the story of Antigone's defiance of an edict denying burial to Polynices existed before Sophocles (for the last scene of Aeschylus' *Seven against Thebes* is spurious). Sophocles has interpolated it into the story between the battle in which Eteocles and Polynices kill each other (which must have been the climax of the *Thebaid*) and the burial of the Seven through the intervention of Theseus (not in the *Thebaid* but well known to all Athenians and a great source of Athenian pride)'. For a more detailed study, see Gantz (1993), 519–20.

54 As argued by Steinbock (2013), 159, who states that the myth contains 'clues for continuous reshaping and reworking during the archaic and classical period, which led to a variety of different versions inside and outside of Attica and to a conglomerate of interrelated layers of meaning in the Athenian master narrative of the funeral orations'.

55 The construction of the temple, including the programme of friezes, was contemporary with Euripides' *Suppliants*, written and performed in the spring of 423 BC. The latter, which most likely introduced the bellicose element to the story of Theseus' intervention in Thebes, may have been the main source of inspiration behind the mythical scene on the west frieze. See also Harrison (1997), 121–2.

56 Due to the fragmentary nature of the frieze, a definitive reading of the scene may be impossible. I am convinced, nonetheless, by the arguments of Harrison (1997),

117–20; and Schultz (2009), who made a strong case for the fall of Eurystheus and the Athenian defeat of an invading Peloponnesian army as the central subjects of the frieze.

57 On the mutilation of the dead in ancient Greece, see Tritle (1997); (2013), 288–9; van Wees (2004), 135–6; Muller (2014); (2017).
58 Allan (2001), 24–5.
59 Translation from Celoria (1992), 92. For short commentary, see Fowler (2013), 342–4.
60 On Pherecydes and his work, see Jacoby (1947); Huxley (1973); Fowler (1999); Dowden (2011), 61–4; Pàmias (2014), 48–50. A full collection of his fragments is provided by Fowler (2000), 272–364; (2013), 706–27.
61 For the division of his books, see Dowden (2011), 61.
62 On Antoninus Liberalis, see Celoria (1992); Higbie (2007), 248–9.
63 One of the distinguishing features of Pherecydes' mythographical accounts was his particular interest in miraculous and supernatural stories. According to van der Valk (1958), 143, Pherecydes' style, words and representations were distinctively Archaic and, therefore, most likely to be based on the Epic Cycle accounts.
64 For more on the *Ninth Pythian* ode, see Farnell (1915); Rose (1931); Burton (1962), 36–59; Carne-Ross (1985), 91–101.
65 See Farnell (1921), 109–10. For possible political implications behind Pindar's use of Iolaus' myth, see Farnell (1915); Rose (1931).
66 Nagy (2007a), 19.
67 For Pindar, as Rutherford (2011), 122, has put it, myth was 'a tool to be used for a purpose: to glorify, to teach, to explain, and to some extent also to entertain … Pindar's attitude towards the traditions of mythology was critical: he seems to have seen it as one of his functions to sort myth out, eliminating false traditions and returning to the truth'. For more on Pindar's use of myth, see Bowra (1964), 278–316. For his editorial activity, see Huxley (1975), 15–22. For Pindar's use of the Epic Cycle poems, see King (1987), 56–66; Nagy (1990), 414–37; Rutherford (2015).
68 In the *Iliad*, and most likely in early Archaic warfare, beheading your enemy was a perfectly suitable way to exact revenge and to display your military prowess. Decapitation appears in many other episodes in Greek mythology, such as the beheading of Troilos by Achilles at the shrine of Apollo. The latter most likely featured in the *Cypria* and a poem by Ibycus (*SLG* 224) and was depicted on two Attic black-figure amphoras (BA 6894, BA 302023). Classical authors and artists did not cover the scene, except for Sophocles, who might have included it in his *Troilos*; the play, judging from a surviving fragment (L (623)) mentioning 'cut-off body parts' (*maschalismata*), likely introduced further mutilation in the practice of *maschalismos* (see p. 196 n. 111 above), significantly increasing the atrociousness of Achilles'

actions, as argued by Sommerstein (2006b), 205. The unusual brutality of the episode is somewhat problematised by the fact that Sophocles' treatment of Achilles in his other works tends to be favourable, but the fragmentary nature of the play prevents us from making any firm conclusions. For a full discussion of Troilos in Greek literary and artistic sources, see Gantz (1993), 597–603; on Sophocles' *Troilos*, see Sommerstein (2006b), 196–247. The general subject of decapitation was also depicted, albeit rarely, in Archaic Greek art, as demonstrated by a black-figure lekythos by the Beldam Painter (*c.* 490 BC; BA331227), which depicts three warriors, each carrying a severed head. The interpretation of the scene is difficult, although it has been unconvincingly suggested that it represented a triple repetition of Amphiaraus with the head of Melanippus, discussed later in this chapter. For beheading in Greek mythology and art, see Vermeule (1979), 236 n. 30; Saunders (2008a), 89.

69 Another tragedy that potentially dealt with the story was Aeschylus' *Children of Heracles*, from which only a few fragments have survived. Plutarch (*Mor.* 1057e-f) quotes a fragment of it concerning the rejuvenation of Iolaus (Fr. 361 R) but it is unclear whether Aeschylus' play dealt with the same subject as Euripides' *Heraclidae*. For more on this play, see Lloyd-Jones (1971b), 404–5. Euripides wrote his *Heraclidae* most likely after *Medea* (431 BC) and before *Hippolytus* (428 BC). For the dating of *Heraclidae*, see Decharme (1906), 134–6; Zuntz (1955), 81–8; Conacher (1967), 120–4; Wilkins (1993), xxxiii–xxxv; Allan (2001), 54–6.

70 Alcmene's initial proposal to kill Eurystheus and return his body to his relatives for burial meant that she would not disobey the laws of the city (1022–5). In response, Eurystheus promised to protect the city if buried, presumably intact, 'in front of the shrine of the divine maiden, Athena Pallenis' (1030–1).

71 See Zuntz (1947); Grube (1973), 174; Burian (1977), 19 n. 49; Kovacs (1995), 113; Wilkins (1993), 193; Allan (2001), 222–3.

72 Burian (1977), 1; Allan (2001), 29.

73 Aristophanes was especially critical of his works, as noted and explained by Allan (2001), 15 n. 37. For more on Euripides' supposed 'impiety' and 'atheism', see Lefkowitz (2003).

74 For an excellent discussion of the war elements in the *Heraclidae*, see Konstan (2007), 197–200.

75 Wilkins (1993), xi.

76 Allan (2001), 25.

77 Strabo (8.6.19): 'Now Eurystheus made an expedition to Marathon against Iolaus and the sons of Heracles, with the aid of the Athenians, as the story goes, and fell in the battle, and his body was buried at Gargettus, except his head, which was cut off by Iolaus, and was buried separately at Tricorynthus near the spring Macaria below the wagon road. And the place is called 'Eurystheus' Head'.

78 Zen. *Proverbs* (2.61): '... and the Athenians defeated Eurystheus in a battle, and as many fell Hyllus, son of Heracles, killed Eurystheus and brought his head back to Alcmene who gouged out his eyes with weaving pins'.
79 The practice of cannibalism, more widespread in Greek mythology, was hinted at in the *Iliad* with Achilles (22.346-7) and Hecuba (24.212-3) expressing the wish to eat the flesh of Hector and Achilles, respectively. For more on cannibalism in early Greek art, see Vermeule (1979), 91-4.
80 Τυδεὺς ὁ Οἰνέως ἐν τῶι Θηβαϊκῶι πολέμωι ὑπὸ Μελανίππου τοῦ Ἀστακοῦ ἐτρώθη, Ἀμφιάρεως δὲ κτείνας τὸν Μελάνιππον τὴν κεφαλὴν ἐκόμισεν. καὶ ἀνοίξας αὐτὴν ὁ Τυδεὺς τὸν ἐγκέφαλον ἐρρόφει ἀπὸ θυμοῦ. Ἀθηνᾶ δέ, κομίζουσα Τυδεῖ ἀθανασίαν, ἰδοῦσα τὸ μίασμα ἀπεστράφη αὐτόν. Τυδεὺς δὲ γνοὺς ἐδεήθη τῆς θεοῦ ἵνα κἂν τῶι παιδὶ αὐτοῦ παράσχηι τὴν ἀθανασίαν. West's apparatus adds: Similiter schol. (AbT), ubi additur ἱστορεῖ Φερεκύδης (3 F 97): ἡ ἱστορία παρὰ τοῖς κυκλικοῖς G m.rec. suo Marte ut videtur ('Some manuscripts add 'The story is in Pherecydes'; in one a late hand adds 'The story is in the Cyclic writers'). For more on the fragment, see Cingano (1987); Fowler (2013), 412; Torres-Guerra (2015), 233-4.
81 According to the scholiast on Pindar *Nem. X*, the immortalization of Diomedes was also mentioned in Ibycus (Fr. 294).
82 Rutherford (2015), 452.
83 Robertson (1940), 178. Pindar's mention of Athena granting immortality to Diomedes, along with his summary of the entire Seven Against Thebes campaign (*Nem. IX* 13-27), indicates that he was familiar with the stories of the Theban Cycle, but the full extent of their influence on his poems is harder to trace. For more on Pindar and the Epic Cycle, see p. 203 n. 67 above.
84 Furthermore, Amphiaraus' description in *Ol. VI* 17 might have been taken directly from the *Thebaid*, as suggested by a certain Asclepiades, cited by the scholiast. For more, see Rutherford (2015), 452-3, who provides further references to modern discussions of the passage. For Amphiaraus in Archaic and Classical art, see Vicaire (1979).
85 Hdt. 1.52; 8.134. On Amphiaraus' hero-cult, see Currie (2005), 212.
86 For an introduction to *Seven Against Thebes*, see Rosenmeyer (1962); Cameron (1971); Torrance (2007). For more on Amphiaraus in the play, see Dawson (1970), 15.
87 Hutchinson (1985), 112.
88 As also argued by Cingano (1987), 95, who stated that Amphiaraus' absolution from the 'bloody episode' has to be seen as part of the '"processo di progressiva idealizzazione e moralizzazione" cui la figura di Anfiarao andò soggetta in ambito greco a partire presumibilmente dal V sec. a.C. quando, sia nella tradizione letteraria che in quella iconografica, le qualità di saggio, di indovino e di buon parlatore vennero accentuate a scapito dei suoi tratti più bellicosi e cruenti'.

89 In the Loeb edition of Sophocles' fragments (1996), Lloyd-Jones notes that Welcker's attribution of the fragment to *The Laconian Women* 'seems likely to be right' (p. 361).
90 A discussion of the event's possible appearances in early poetry is provided by Cingano (1987), 96–9, who speculated that the innovation may have been introduced by Stesichorus in his lost poem *Eriphyle*, which likely focused on the events of Seven Against Thebes and the story of Eriphyle's husband, Amphiaraus.
91 According to schol. on Pindar *Nem.* X 7, Euripides' lost play *Meleager* featured a brief comment about Tydeus, who 'will come to cannibal pleasures and tear the head of Melanippus with gore-red jaws' (Fr. 537), which appears to follow the same tradition as Sophocles. Herodotus (5.67) tells us that the tyrant Cleisthenes instituted the worship of Melanippus at Sicyon, assigning him the honours previously enjoyed by his foe, the Argive king Adrastus. According to the story, the tyrant of Sicyon, shortly after his war with Argos, decided to cast out the cult of Adrastus from his land. In order to do so he carried back the body of Melanippus, the bravest of Theban defenders and a descendant of the legendary Sown Men (Aesch. *Sept.* 412–16), from Thebes (as Melanippus was Adrastus' great enemy, having killed both his brother, Mecistes, and his son-in-law, Tydeus) and instituted his worship in place of that of Adrastus. Herodotus, however, says nothing about the state of Melanippus' body or his killer. For more on the passage and its relation to the Epic Cycle, see Cingano (1985).
92 For more on the Pyrgi Columen Plaque, see Brendel (1978), 234–7; Krauskopf (1984), 954; Cingano (1987), 99–103; Simon and Lorenz (1997).
93 Robertson (1940), 178; Beazley (1947); Vermeule (1979), 133; Krauskopf (1984), 953–5; Shapiro (1993), 35–7; Neils (1994), 193–4; Simon and Lorenz (1997). Other potential representations of the scene include the so-called Rosi Krater (now lost), and an Etruscan mirror which shows Athena and Athanasia (but no Tydeus). For illustrations, see Beazley (1947).
94 On Statius' *Thebaid*, see Vessey (1973), esp. 283–94; Henderson (1993); Hershkowitz (1995).
95 For more on the *Little Iliad*, see Davies (2001), 60–70; West (2003), 15–16; (2013), 163–222; Kelly (2015). Although the evidence is largely inconclusive, Burgess (2001), 24, argued that the poem might have told the story of the entire Trojan War.
96 For the story of the return of Philoctetes and the death of Paris, see Gantz (1993), 635–9.
97 ἰαθεὶς δὲ οὗτος ὑπὸ Μαχάονος καὶ μονομαχήσας Ἀλεξάνδρωι κτείνει· καὶ τὸν νεκρὸν ὑπὸ Μενελάου καταικισθέντα ἀνελόμενοι θάπτουσιν οἱ Τρῶες. For a short commentary see West (2013), 187.
98 In his commentary on the fragment, Davies (2001), 64, stated that Menelaus' mutilation of Paris should be seen as one of the many examples of the un-Homeric character of the Epic Cycle poems: 'That Menelaus (a notably mild and humane character within the Homeric tradition) should have been portrayed as doing this to

his enemy's corpse speaks volumes for the difference in ethos between the *Iliad* and *Odyssey* and a poem like ours [*Little Iliad*]'. The numerous examples of mutilations vividly described in the *Iliad* make Davies' interpretation of the fragment untenable. His statement stems from a wider trend in scholarship, reflected in particular by Griffin (1977), to emphasize the Epic Cycle's supposed preference for any elements of the supernatural, the grotesque, the excessively brutal, or anything suggestive of folk-superstition. Considering the fragmentary nature of the surviving Cyclic material, as Foley and Arft (2015), 82, rightly pointed out, 'it seems nearly impossible to make an informed aesthetic comparison to the *Iliad* and *Odyssey* or, even more basically, to judge the quality of an entire tradition from a handful of secondary references and late summaries of that tradition'. For more references on Griffin's argument, see Foley and Arft (2015), 81 nos 15–17.

99 On the *First Pythian*, see Burton (1962), 91–110. The scholiast on this ode (1.52) adds that Hieron, the winner in the long-foot race, was at the time suffering with some physical pain himself, which might have led Pindar to change the myth (which has Philoctetes healed by Machaon) for the sake of a better analogy.

100 On Bacchylides, see Campbell (1992), 5–7.

101 On Sophocles' *Philoctetes*, see Webster (1970); Mandel (1981); Usher (2001); Jebb (2004). Sommerstein (2015), 467–8, provides an overview of the fetching of Philoctetes in Greek tragedy and the Epic Cycle.

102 For more on this play, see Mandel (1981), 33–4; Gantz (1993), 637; Lloyd-Jones (1996), 333–5.

103 On Aeschylus' and Euripides' lost plays, see Webster (1970), 3–5; Lloyd-Jones (1971b), 464–8; Gantz (1993), 635–6; Jebb (2004), xiv–xix; Collard and Cropp (2008), 368–403. Other playwrights of the fifth century BC, including Achaeus and Philocles, also wrote dramas entitled *Philoctetes* – our knowledge of them, however, is very scanty. For more, see Gantz (1993), 637

104 For Philoctetes in Greek and Roman art, see Pipili (1994), 376–85.

105 Translation by R. Hard (OUP 1997).

106 The artistic representations of Oenone are very limited, with only two potential early depictions (one of them with Paris). The main problem, as Kahil (1994), 25–6, noted in her study of Oenone in Greek and Roman art, is that there are no recognizable criteria associated with Oenone.

107 ὑ–] ψόθεν εὐειδὴς ἄλοχος Π[άριος τὰν] | λοισθίαν ὥρμασεν Οἰν[ώνα κέλευθον·

108 For more on this fragment, see Stinton (1990), 50; Brown (2002), 167.

109 On Hellanicus, see Dowden (2011), 64–6; Fowler (2013), 682–95. On Parthenius, see Lightfoot (1999).

110 Stinton (1990), 52; Lightfoot (1999), 391; Fowler (2013), 528–9.

111 Apart from Parthenius' *Erot. Path.*, the myth is also mentioned in Lycophron (57–68), Ovid's *Rem.* (457), Conon (N. 23 – Oinone), Lucan (9.972–3); Quintus

Smyrnaeus (10.253–489); and Dictys Cretensis (3.26; 4.21). Suetonius also relates that it was performed as a mime in the reign of Domitian (*Dom.* 10.4).

112 Another potential example of a mythical mutilation of the dead in the context of war concerns Peleus' dismemberment of Astydamia, the wife of Acastos, during his capture of Iolcos. The story, mentioned in full by Apollodorus (3.13.7), was most likely related by Pherecydes, as indicated by the scholion on Pindar's *Third Nemean* ode (Fr. 62 Fowler). In this ode, Pindar dealt with the myth of Peleus' attack on Iolcos (31–4), but did not mention the gruesome mutilation detail. According to Robertson (1923), 6; (1940), 179, Pindar deliberately chose to refute and supress the latter, as he did not want to discredit his hero – following a pattern similar to his treatment of Amphiaraus. On this fragment, see also Huxley (1975), 18–19; Rutherford (2011), 115.

113 The same applies to their pre-Homeric existence. Morrison (1992), 91, 143 n. 61, mentioned the suggestion of J. A. K. Thompson that in the pre-Iliadic tradition Achilles' mutilation of Hector did include decapitation, later purged from the poem. Such claims, however, are not backed by any literary or artistic evidence and remain purely speculative.

114 Gantz (1993), 617.

115 Curiously, the fight between Agamemnon and Koön over the corpse of Iphidamas, which in the *Iliad* culminates in the decapitation of the latter, was depicted on the famous Chest of Cypselus, as reported by Pausanias (5.19.4). Although the inscription accompanying the scene was not drawn from the *Iliad*, it is clear that the Homeric scene must have been the inspiration behind the image. To my knowledge no other ancient depiction, literary or artistic, of Koön and Iphidamas exists. For more the scene and the Chest of Cypselus, see Snodgrass (1998), 109–16; Borg (2010), 86–9.

116 Vermeule (1965), 40, 51 n. 8. For illustrated examples, see BA301780, BA302142, BA302338, BA302340, BA302372, BA351200, BA351201, BA390342.

117 For more on the lost plays and their potential plots, see Gantz (1993), 617–8.

118 Gantz (1993), 618.

119 Pindar and Sophocles, as King (1987), 50–109, observed in her survey of Achilles' portrayal in the Classical period, tend to 'evoke only the positive aspects of Achilles' epic career' (*cf.* pp. 203–4 n. 68 above). The former, as she concluded, avoided any potentially discreditable stories in his poems, such as the maltreatment of Hector's corpse or the sacrifice of the Trojan youths on Patroklos' pyre. This attitude changes with Euripides, who in his dramas questioned the integrity of Achilles (and the Homeric ethos in general), highlighting his destructive nature and constant obsession with honour. For the portrayal of Achilles in Euripides, see King (1980); (1985); (1987), 77–104.

120 For more on Plato's portrayal of Achilles, see King (1987), 104–9.

121 Athenian tragedy, according to a somewhat controversial theory suggested by Winkler (1990), was one of the tools that the city of Athens used to educate its young citizens and prepare them for their future roles in the citizen army. Winkler's argument was later picked up by Shay (1995) and Tritle (2007), who suggested that Athenian drama also served an important role in reintegrating the returning soldiers back into the world of civilian life.

122 *TrGF* 4 T 136 Radt.

123 The other tragedies are *Adjudication of Arms, Neoptolemus, Eurypylus, Beggary, Spartan Women, Putting to Sea* and *Sinon*. For more on this passage, see Young (1983), 165–6; Heath (1989), 49–50; Fantuzzi (2015), 412–14. Since the poems of the Epic Cycle covered a much larger span of mythical time and events than the *Iliad* and *Odyssey*, as observed by Aristotle, inevitably the Athenian playwrights engaged more frequently with the plots contained in the Epic Cycle (see discussion by Fantuzzi (2015), 405–10). As part of his recent study on Greek tragedy and the Epic Cycle, Sommerstein (2015), 462–3, 81–6, compiled a comprehensive list of Aeschylus', Sophocles' and Euripides' dramas based on the Cyclic epics, which came up to 92 plays in total. Moreover, as Fantuzzi and Tsagalis (2015b), 14–19, suggested, Cyclic poetry might have regularly featured as part of the Panathenaic festival, since the term 'Homeric poetry' was initially 'used for *any* kind of epic poetry attributed to Homer, which included not only the *Iliad* and the *Odyssey* but also the Theban epics and Cyclic poetry'. *Cf.* Nagy (2015), 62–3.

124 As observed and counted by Arrington (2015), 174.

125 Harrison (1997), 121.

126 See Hall (1989); Miller (1997); Harrison (2002); Cartledge (2002), 51–77. For the impact of the Persian Wars, and especially the battle of Marathon, on Greek tactics and warfare, see Krentz (2002), 35–7; (2007b), 80; (2010).

127 As hinted by van Wees (2004), 138. Arrington (2015), 26, similarly argued that 'the Persian treatment of their fallen provided a mirror in which the Athenian care for corpses appeared as a particularly Hellenic virtue'.

128 The maltreatment and mutilation of the dead feature prominently in Herodotus' accounts of non-Greek peoples, including: the Persians (3.16, 79, 125; 5.25; 7.39; 7.238); the Medes (1.119); the Scythians (4.62–5); the Massagetae (1.214); the Issedonians (4.26); the Taurians (4.103); and the Amathousians (5.114). The Persian burial practices are represented in particular opposition to Greek customs, as 'the dead bodies of Persians are not buried before they have been mangled by bird or dog' (1.140); and their war dead are left unburied and exposed even after victorious battles (3.12; 9.83). On the Persian practice of mutilation, see Muller (2016). On head-hunting practices as part of Herodotus' depiction of the 'other', see Hartog (1988), 156–72.

129 Apart from contrasting the Greeks and barbarians, the anecdote also displays a clear anti-Aeginetan bias of Herodotus (and/or his sources), which features in a

number of other passages (e.g. 5.81ff.; 6.87ff.; 9.80), echoing a wider Athenian sentiment towards Aegina at the time of Herodotus' writing. While this throws some doubt on the historicity of the episode, the story certainly reflects a post-Persian War attitude to the treatment of the war dead in Athens and Greece.

130 Translation from Rhodes and Osborne (2003), 443.

131 The Oath of Plataea, recorded on a fourth century BC *stele* from Acharnae, has been generally treated by scholars as a fabrication; some, nonetheless, suspect that it might have been based on an authentic oath sworn by the allied Greek forces before the battle of Plataea or Marathon. Literary sources, including Lycurgus (1.81) and Diodorus (11.29.3), suggest that similar oaths were sworn during the Persian Wars and all of them included a vow to bury the dead. For more, see Meiggs (1972), 504–7; Robert (1973); Pritchett (1985), 116–17; Rhodes and Osborne (2003), 440–8; Cartledge (2013), 12–58; *contra* Siewert (1972); Robertson (1983), 81–2; van Wees (2006b); Krentz (2007c). In addition, as argued by van Wees (2006b), the oath could have been based on a late-Archaic oath of the Spartan sworn bands (*enômotiai*), thus suggesting that the egalitarian ideals concerning the burial of the war dead were already present among the non-Athenian *poleis* fighting on the Greek side (see pp. 114–16 below).

132 On the paradigmatic role of myths in ancient Greece, see Buxton (1994), 193–8.

3 The War Dead in the Early Greek Iconographic Tradition

1 A different version of events is provided by Xenophon (*Hell.* 1.6.35–7.34), who reports that the main accusation against the Athenian generals was that they failed to rescue the shipwrecked; he does not mention the war dead. His narrative may be preferred to Diodorus', since Xenophon is thought to have taken part in the events, but Andrewes (1974) criticized his version and defended Diodorus. Both the accounts of Diodorus and Xenophon stress the role played by Theramenes and Thrasybulus, who bore the main brunt of responsibility for failing to pick up the dead/shipwrecked after the battle, but escaped punishment by stirring the people against the other generals. For more, see Pritchett (1985), 204–6.

2 The importance of retrieving the war dead is further demonstrated by the famous action of Nicias at Solygeia in 425 BC (Thuc. 4.44). Despite winning the battle and setting up a trophy, Nicias, realising that two bodies of the Athenian troops were missing, decided to return to the region and send heralds to the defeated Corinthians asking leave to take up the corpses. As Plutarch relates, he 'preferred to renounce the victory and his personal triumph rather than allow two of his fellow-countrymen to lie unburied' (*Nic.* 6). The story undoubtedly served to illustrate Nicias' extraordinary piety, but at the same time it also provides clear evidence for

the Athenian, and more broadly Greek, concern for the proper treatment of the war dead, as well as the precision involved in the reckoning of casualties by Classical Greek armies.

3 For more on the post-battle procedures in Greek warfare, including the identification of the war dead, see p. 199 n. 31 above. Although ancient sources offer no clues as to how naval casualties were retrieved, we should assume that recovering the fallen would have been considerably harder after sea battles; for more, see Strauss (2000).

4 On the format and iconography of Athenian casualty lists, see Arrington (2015), 95–104.

5 Loraux (2006).

6 For the impossible attribution to Solon, based on Diog. Laert. (1.7.55) and Plut. *Publ.* 9.11, see Clairmont (1983), 11; Loraux (2006), 58. I will return to the question of the origins of *patrios nomos* in Chapter 5.

7 See, for instance, Jacoby (1944), 42; Kurtz and Boardman (1971), 247; Page (1981), 269; Schröder (2020), 101. Pritchett (1985), 249–51, in his discussion of the issue, stated that the rule 'Athenians at home, others on the battlefield, is clearly an oversimplification'. He did maintain, however, using the example of Tellus (Hdt. 1.30), that the Archaic Athenian war dead 'were buried on the battlefield'. In an odd article on collective burials in Greece, Robertson (1983) argued that 'all Greeks brought home the remains of those killed in war whenever they could, except where special arrangements were made abroad for burial and grave service' (p. 80). The evidence he used to back up his claim, which included the mythical episode of Seven Against Thebes and *Il.* 7.334–5, is inadequate and was rightly criticized by Pritchett (1985), 94 n. 1. Robertson subsequently conceded that the Spartans alone followed a 'distinctive' custom of burying the war dead on the battlefield, but reasserted his claim that the custom of repatriation 'was nearly universal' for other Greeks (1992), 166.

8 Jacoby (1944), 42.

9 As Clairmont (1983), 7, concluded, 'actual remains of *polyandria* for the casualties in warfare' in Archaic Athens are 'totally lacking'. The few questionable instances, such as the burial of Tellus, the Copenhagen and [O]ionichos stelai, are discussed in Chapter 5. In the wider Greek world, the only pre-Classical burials identified as *polyandria* are the mass graves from Paroika on Paros, and Acragas in Sicily. The former contained 160 vases of the cremated remains of young men; the latter, 150 vases and many inhumed corpses. For more, see Kurtz and Boardman (1971), 257; Morgan (2001); 33; Zaphiropoulou (2002); Brouwers (2013), 43–4. Another possible candidate, discussed by Morgan (2001), 32–3, is the Karaeria tumulus in Thessaly, which contained 18 tombs (158 burials in total), a large number of weapons and wheel rims from wagons or chariots. Morris (1998a), 38, dismissed the idea of a *polyandrion*, arguing that the ground provided elite families with means 'to represent

their dead men as heroic warriors'. It is clear that further studies are needed before we can draw any general conclusions from these examples, as some of the *polyandrion* identifications are largely tentative, and as Morgan (2001), 33, remarked, 'rest on the apparently anomalous form or content of the burial(s) in question, rather than on physical anthropological evidence or any clear expectation of what a *polyandrion* of this period might look like'.

10 The scholarly literature on Archaic Athenian vases is understandably vast, but the standard introductory works continue to be the handbook collections by John Boardman (1974); (1975). For recent works on Athenian pottery and its place within Athenian culture, see Filser (2017); Osborne (2018).
11 For more on the distribution of Archaic Athenian pots in the Mediterranean, see Osborne (1996b).
12 Osborne (2018), 39–40, for the estimates proposed by Cook (1959) being of the right order of magnitude.
13 For more on Athenian vases in Etruria, see Hannestad (1988); (1991); Spivey (1991); Osborne (2001); (2018), 40–6, 251; Reusser (2002).
14 Boardman (1991).
15 Osborne (2018), 46–7.
16 A more 'pluralistic approach', as advocated by Marconi (2004) in his study of Attic black-figure pots from a warrior-grave in Acragas, can be certainly rewarding in small-scale studies of war imagery. Osborne's (2004b) response to Marconi in the same volume seems to me a better approach for larger-scale, quantitative studies.
17 Scholarly works on Greek war iconography: Lorimer (1947); Webster (1955); Ahlberg (1971a); Lissarrague (1990); van Wees (2000); Hannestad (2001); Recke (2002); Hölscher (2003); Muth (2008); Schwartz (2009), 123–35; Hannah (2010); Viggiano and van Wees (2013); Echeverria (2015); Osborne (2018), 93–121.
18 Lorimer (1947). See also Carter (1972).
19 E.g. Boardman (1991), 95–6: 'The fighting scenes are the most consistently dominated by heroic rather than contemporary behaviour since the hoplite battle, with ranks advancing shoulder to shoulder, was the typical scheme for Archaic Greece, and this is ignored in art in favour of individual duels. On the battlefield each man was his own Hector or Achilles, not number six from the left in the second rank. Indeed the only true scene of a hoplite fight in early Greek art is on the mid-seventh-century Corinthian Chigi vase...'; Marconi (1994), 32: 'The first element, of course, was the characterization of the actual battle as a duel... There are no references to the phalanx, or to the practices of hoplitic warfare, and instead the battle is condensed to a one-on-one confrontation that must have been strongly evocative of the epic tradition'; Osborne (2004b), 46: 'We do not have to emphasize ... the absence of the phalanx to know that we are not dealing with an image of the reality of sixth-century B.C. hoplite warfare'. The vases most often taken to represent

an early phalanx formation are the Chigi olpe, attributed to the Chigi/Macmillan Painter, c. 640–630 BC; and the Macmillan and Berlin Aryballoi, attributed to the same painter, c. 650 BC. For a recent, exhaustive study of the Chigi olpe, see D'Acunto (2013). For a discussion (with illustrations) of early phalanx-like formations in Greek art, see Viggiano and van Wees (2013).

20 Echeverria (2015), 59, who neatly summarized the problem of previous scholarship: 'if the scenes truly represented contemporary military practices, they would depict phalanx warfare, since the phalanx was the standard way of fighting at that time; the scenes do not represent phalanxes, but archers, chariots and isolated warriors utterly incompatible with closed formations, so they do not represent contemporary practices but either past or legendary – 'heroic' – ones … Everything that does not fit the phalanx becomes then 'heroic', and hence fictitious' (p. 39). On a theoretical level, the scholarly obsession with phalanx formations in early art leads to an essentially circular argument: only massed formations can represent reality, because reality is massed formations.

21 Beard (1991), 21, with original emphasis. See also Ferrari (2003). Such views have been increasingly adopted by military historians, e.g. Hannah (2010), 266: 'In Athenian art, for example, ordinary soldiers could be elevated to the status of heroes, while mythological heroes could be portrayed as regular hoplites, in a deliberate blurring of the real and the imaginary'.

22 Lissarrague (1990), whose method, known as iconology, assumed that the mythological scenes depicted in Athenian art presented important and recognizable elements of reality, designed to convey the social ideals and sentiments of contemporary citizens.

23 Hölscher (2003), 4, with original emphasis.

24 Hannestad (2001), 110–15; Hölscher (2003), 5.

25 Hölscher (2003), 5.

26 Ibid.

27 Van Wees (2000); Krentz (2007b), 75–6.

28 Echeverria (2015), 60. Stewart (1997), 89, 247, counted a total of eight representations of massed formations for the entire Archaic period. According to the Beazley Archive, in the sixth century BC alone there are over 2000 vases depicting combat (see Table 1 below). Echeverria (2015), 48–50, provides per centage splits for large- and small-group fighting in Archaic art, concluding that 'vases representing only *one* fighting group, whether infantrymen alone or combined with other troops, account to more than 80 per cent of the scenes in our catalogue'. In more complex combat scenes featuring more than one fighting group in action, actions are usually split into smaller units, which according to him emphasized the individuals and their exploits.

29 Echeverria (2015), 45.

30 As van Wees (2000), 125, observed, 'it is odd that a society in which participation in war was widespread and frequent should have produced only a few more-or-less realistic images of combat, and otherwise have confined itself to a repertoire of legendary images entirely divorced from reality'.

31 Osborne (2018), 118. Although Osborne's main concern is with the changes in Athenian war iconography, which I discuss at the end of this chapter, he still treated the black-figure representations of combat as allegorical scenes set against heroic background. According to him, the images 'constitute an exploration of the status of the heavily armed warrior that is independent of the particular realities of contemporary warfare, either in Athens or in Greece generally' (p. 97). Such exploration, he argued, is reflected particularly in the brief popularity of the Scythian archers around 520 BC, entirely fictional and depicted usually with heavy-armed hoplites. Their appearance, as Osborne proposed also in his earlier study (2004b), occurred when the Athenians were not involved in serious warfare and had limited experience of combat; their disappearance from Attic art within a couple of decades coincided with the creation of a democratic army and increased war activity: 'Come 510 BC ... Athens needed not a virtual but a real army' (2004b), 50. I find it difficult to believe, however, that the Athenians had no 'real army' under the Peisistratids and little experience of combat (see Chapter 6 – where it is suggested that some Scythian archers may have been permanently employed by the Peisistratids). For a different view on Scythian archers in black-figure art, see Echeverria (2015), 53–4.

32 Good examples of recent quantitative studies are Filser (2017); Osborne (2018); (forthcoming).

33 The earliest examples are East Greek (2) and Corinthian in style: Ahlberg-Cornell (1992), 35–8, Nos 10–12, Figs 44–6; see also Fittschen (1969), 179–81. For shorter discussions, see Carter (1972), 54; Moore (1980), 424; Woodford and Loudon (1980), 26; Snodgrass (1998), 36–7.

34 Woodford and Loudon (1980), 26, Nos 4–5, noted the general lack of scepticism regarding the identification of warriors by previous scholars. Achilles' armour becomes central in the story of Ajax's suicide, which could be why it becomes prominent in black-figure depictions of the scene (discussed below). The fallen warrior's lack of armour in Geometric depictions, however, does not necessarily imply a different episode. Proclus tells us that in the *Aethiopis* Ajax 'hands over Achilles' armor to be taken to the ships; as for the body, he takes it up and carries it towards the ships, with Odysseus fighting the Trojans off' (Arg. 3 West). For a short discussion of the *Aethiopis*' fragment and its relation to early art, see West (2013), 151–3

35 Kunze (1950), 151–4.

36 The four representations are Cretan, East Greek and North-east Peloponnesian (2): Ahlberg-Cornell (1992), 71–2, Nos 48–51, Figs 107–9.

37 The earliest example is a late Geometric stand in Munich, dated by Snodgrass (1980), Fig. 10, to c. 700 BC; its imagery was studied by Langdon (2008), 234–44. According to Lorimer (1947), 99, the motif of fighting over the dead is unknown in Geometric art. While duels over a fallen warrior may be absent in earlier art, group fighting over corpses was already present in the Geometric period. One example is a Middle Geometric skyphos from Eleusis, depicting two pairs of warriors in combat over two corpses in the centre (for an illustration and short discussion, see Stansbury-O'Donnell (1999), 48, Fig. 19). Another is a Late Geometric amphora from Paros, which features confronting groups of warriors, including horsemen, fighting over a fallen, naked warrior (for more see Zaphiropoulou (2006), 273–4, Figs 5–9). Furthermore, depictions of naked warriors are common in Geometric art; as Matthew Lloyd pointed out to me, most of the dead bodies in Geometric vase painting appear to have been stripped of their armour and weapons, even though the fighting continues. This, in turn, provides further evidence for the practice of combat despoliation. For more on corpses in Geometric fighting scenes and the Near East, see Ahlberg (1971a), 88–103.

38 For examples, see Johansen (1923), Pl. 34; Lorimer (1947), Fig. 9d; Vierneisel (1967), Figs 1–3; Snodgrass (1998), 78–80, Figs 27–9. For a short discussion of the earliest examples, see Saunders (2008b), 163.

39 Lorimer (1947), Fig. 9; Saunders (2008b), Fig. 9–3.

40 Lorimer (1947), 98–104. Such motifs, as she concluded, 'are incompatible with the hoplite tactics which the archaeological evidence has shown to be contemporary with proto-Corinthian figure-painting from its very beginning. The hoplite phalanx did not attempt to retrieve its dead in the course of the action; they were picked up afterwards, by the right of victory or the favour of the victor' (p. 104).

41 Van Wees (2000), 145–6.

42 Ibid., 155.

43 I conducted the online search in March 2020. The results are based on the decoration descriptions (the search terms were 'fallen', 'body', 'carrying', 'lifting', 'fight', 'fighting') and images offered by the Archive. I have made every effort to consult the publication records in cases where the relevant archive entry was not accompanied by an image. Despite its limitations, especially concerning the relatively small number of images, the Beazley Archive provides the most accessible and comprehensive tool for sampling and gathering data on Archaic Attic vases. For more on its main strengths and limitations, see Stansbury-O'Donnell (2006), 25–7; Osborne (forthcoming).

44 Muth (2008), 160–215, studied the images as part of the victim iconography ("der Opfer-Ikonographie") in Athenian art, which changes significantly around 550–530 BC. The fallen warriors, according to her, reflected a wider movement of 'Pathetisierung' in combat scenes in late Archaic iconography: the increased interest

in the depictions of the war dead served primarily to provide new ways to engage with an older discourse on 'ruhmvolles Kämpfen und kraftvolles Siegen ... in dem das unterliegende Opfer weiterhin vorrangig der Charakterisierung des siegreichen Hopliten dient' (p. 201). A good overview of the theme of the 'battle over a fallen warrior' in Athenian black-figure art is provided by Saunders (2008b).

45 The scene also features on cups (5 per cent), kraters (4 per cent), along with 9 other pot shapes (<2 per cent for each). Although the representations are largely confined to warriors fighting on foot, some examples depict horsemen fighting over the fallen (e.g. BA46954, BA301681), often in the context of Amazonomachy. Indeed, this composition scheme features also horses fighting over fallen warriors (BA6110, BA301503), or fallen horses (BA340553).

46 For other examples, see Stansbury-O'Donnell (2006), Figs 30, 44, 65–6, 72–3. According to Stansbury-O'Donnell, who conducted an extensive study on spectators in Archaic Athenian vase paintings, depictions of duels constituted the most popular scene for spectators to watch: 'Such pictures can include a supporting warrior who is part of the nucleus and not a spectator, and a dead warrior frequently lies on the ground between the fighting warriors. Such scenes are neither mythological nor real, and should be seen as representing the idea of fighting more broadly, whether in the heroic imagination or in the army of a polis' (p. 169).

47 Lissarrague (1989), 48; (1990), 138, 234–7, suggested that the presence of non-combatants in such representations is intentionally meant to reflect societal divisions, presenting a metaphorical 'image of the social body'. The inclusion of women, who had no legitimate role to play on the battlefield, might be understood, as hinted by Pritchard (1999), 129–30, as artists' acknowledgment of 'women's part in the bearing and raising the protectors for the city'. As we will see later, the addition of women spectators may have also signified their importance in the burial ceremonies, as the bodies of some fallen warriors were brought back home to be tended and prepared for burial by the female members of the household. Alternatively, as Stansbury-O'Donnell (2006), 126, suggested, spectators functioned like 'a chorus performing at a festival', directing 'the viewer's attention to the narrative example' and the message behind the scene. They introduced, therefore, an aura of a ritualistic occasion, providing 'models for the viewer of the vase in terms of social behavior and identification'.

48 E.g. BA965, BA340485, BA340555. Saunders (2008b), 164, notes that the Heraclean and Dionysiac scenes are also a popular accompaniment to battles over the fallen, along with 'other military-scenes', including departures.

49 E.g. BA1908, BA310396, BA310069, BA350442, BA301601, BA350848.

50 The only prominent feature which often accompanies the fallen in Archaic art is the shield (see Fig. 4), which as Saunders (2008b), 166, argued, provided both a symbol of elite status and wealth, but was also an indication that 'the body is yet to be

stripped'. Its absence on the combat scenes from the Exekias cup is, however, by no means unusual.
51 Moore (1980), 422–3, speculated that the Exekias cup scenes may either both depict the struggle over the body of Patroclus, or two separate fights: one over Patroclus; the other over Achilles. She based her identification on the cup's similarity to another pot by the same artist – the Agora calyx-krater (*ABV* 145.19 and 260.30) – depicting two groups of three warriors fighting for the possession of a body; the accompanying inscriptions identify Patroclus as the fallen warrior. While nothing necessarily precludes her argument, it seems more likely that both sides of the Exekias cup depict part of the same narrative and therefore cannot be referring to two separate mythical episodes. Ultimately, the fact remains that the Exekias cup contains no inscriptions identifying the figures; considering the prevalence of fights over the dead in the epic tradition, one could easily ascribe it to another mythical episode which features successful despoliation.
52 For more on the depiction of wounds on Athenian black-figure vases, see Saunders (2008a), who noted that the Archaic vase painters certainly had the skill to portray physical injuries but chose not to include them in battle scenes. That wounds could have been depicted on the war dead is shown by the famous red-figure krater by Euphronios (*c.* 515 BC) showing the recovery of Sarpedon's body by Hypnos and Thanatos (*Il.* 16.479–81). In her study of the scene, Neils (2009) argued that the addition of wounds was used intentionally to heighten the sense of Sarpedon's defeat. Other examples of bleeding bodies in Attic art consist mainly of Trojan allies (e.g. Memnon, the Amazons) or mythological monsters (Kyknos). 'Clearly in these instances', Neils concluded, 'the viewer is not meant to empathize with them as fallen hero or heroine, but rather to view them as the deadly and barbaric opponents whom the mighty Greek hero has managed to slay'. Accordingly, Euphronios' Sarpedon should not be viewed as heroic, 'but rather as a desecrated or defiled corpse – stripped of its armor and displaying multiple wounds – although Patroklos delivered a single death blow to his abdomen . . .' (p. 215–6). Such an interpretation strengthens the notion that we should view the unharmed bodies in the anonymous battle scenes of Athenian art through the prism of their heroism and beauty. *Cf.* Walter-Karydi (2015), 87–8; Osborne (2018), 102–4. For more on the iconography of the corpse in Greek art, see Halm-Tisserant (1993).
53 See esp. Hurwit (2007), who in his study of the Dexileos relief argued that there was a 'wide variety of nudities in Greek art, with different (and sometimes contradictory) connotations' (p. 47).
54 Echeverria (2015), 54–6.
55 Argued also by Saunders (2008b), 169–70. Muth (2008), 179–80, speculated that the posture of the dead (e.g. lying on their back or stomach) might have also commented on the bravery of the fallen warrior. Considering the main ideological messages behind the theme (e.g. retrieval, heroic death), I find this less convincing.

56 According to Saunders (2008b), 164, the composition seems to be 'virtually absent' from Attic red-figure vases. The decline is best represented in the relative decrease of the scenes: in the sixth century BC they constitute 11.5 per cent of all combat depictions, compared to 1.5 per cent in the fifth century BC. Apart from the Oltos cup, there are only 10 other examples in red-figure; it is also notable that in the latest representations the focus of the scene is on the moment of dying, with some featuring Hypnos (BA200474), and others depicting warriors falling after the fatal blow (BA200479, BA202371, BA204360, BA205176). Osborne (2018), 106, noted that the decline applies to all representations of hoplite duels and group-fighting: 'Almost two-thirds of all such Attic red-figure scenes date to before circa 500, and a very large proportion of the rest were painted before 480'.

57 Discussed, with a comprehensive list, by Lissarrague (1990), 71–96. The scenes were also studied and catalogued by Woodford and Loudon (1980), 26–30, 36–8. I excluded the images featuring Hypnos and Thanatos carrying bodies of fallen warriors, which are discussed in Chapter 5.

58 The scene also features on cups (6 per cent), kraters (6 per cent), olpai (6 per cent), along with 6 other pot shapes (<3 per cent for each).

59 *ABV* 76.1; BA300000. The images, despite being almost identical, vary in tiny details; for brief discussions, see Woodford and Loudon (1980), 26; Marconi (2004), 35.

60 Other early depictions are by the Phrynos (inscribed; *ABV* 169.4) and Heidelberg Painters (uninscribed; *ABV* 64.26); see Moore (1980), 424 n. 64, who devoted a considerable part of her article to the theme of Ajax and the body of Achilles (pp. 424–31).

61 Earlier example: Woodford and Loudon (1980), Fig. 4; *ABV* 144.5. Since inscriptions identifying Ajax and Achilles appear in later black-figure examples inspired by Exekias' composition, it seems plausible to assume that Exekias indeed had the mythological scene in mind, especially given his penchant for scenes involving Ajax. The family context of the scene of Achilles' death is also strong on the François Vase, which on its main body features the wedding of Peleus and Thetis, among other scenes from the life of the hero; see Woodford and Loudon (1980), 26–7.

62 Other notable innovation is the fact that Ajax no longer moves right, which is the usual direction associated with the victors in Greek iconography. Moving left may offer a better view of Ajax's famous shield (Woodford and Loudon (1980), 27, 39–40), or be a hint to Ajax's 'dark future' following the episode (Moore (1980), 425).

63 The much-debated issue of the use of the Boeotian shields by artists to label their images as heroic stems from the fact that to date no extant archaeological examples of it have been found. The shields appear only in art, albeit rarely; in the survey of Echeverria (2015), 51–2, 'only one in ten heavy-armed warriors in the combat scenes . . . carries a Boeotian shield'. Considering that other kinds of shields (e.g. the *pelte*) have also left no trace in archaeological record, I share Echeverria's

scepticism about dismissing the Boeotian shields as non-historical pieces of equipment. For a good defence of the historicity of the Boeotian shields, see Boardman (1983), 27–33.

64 For a list of inscribed vases, see Woodford and Loudon (1980), 27 n. 14. Lissarrague (1990), 78–9, noted that the few inscriptions tend to accompany images in which Achilles is nude; the lack of inscriptions on other scenes, he suggested, might have been counterbalanced by the fact that the protagonists are usually armed with Boeotian shields, labelling the scene as heroic ('d'équivalence entre l'inscription et le bouclier béotien'). The motif of carrying a person can be also used to depict other episodes from the Trojan War, such as Aeneas' escape from Troy with Anchises, or Achilles' retrieval of the body of Penthesilea; these scenes, however, are easily distinguishable from the more popular images of Ajax with Achilles.

65 *ABV* 394.4; BA310396. Lissarrague (1990), 84, catalogued 7 battle and 9 warriors only scenes.

66 Munich: BA4652. Woodford and Loudon (1980), 29, included the vase in their non-standard category, since Achilles is exceptionally depicted nude; the latter, as Moore (1980), 430, added, is 'an oddity considering the importance attached to his armor'. Teucer and Odysseus: Moore (1980), 427–8.

67 Woodford and Loudon (1980), 28–9. See also Lissarrague (1990), 90. This is further accentuated by the departure scenes which accompany the images of warriors carrying the fallen, e.g. BA8689, BA19166, BA310387, BA331267, BA340498, BA351139.

68 Marconi (2004), 32.

69 Ibid., 36. The brunt of Marconi's argument was that such images would have spoken primarily to non-Athenian viewers, explaining why so many of the vases were found in Etruria and Sicily. Instead of interpreting the images as specific to Athens, where citizens fought and died for the *polis* and their bodies were 'retrieved to the civic space in order to receive the proper tribute from the community', Marconi rightly argued that the narrative 'focuses on the individualizing aspects of war, and on the way it affects family relationships' (p. 37). Lissarrague (1990), 81, was the first to remark on the incompatibility of the scenes with the Athenian practice of collective post-battle retrieval and burial, which he took to be the main argument against the 'realism' of the imagery. The fault in such reasoning, however, is that it backdates Classical customs to the Archaic era, thereby assuming that individualising modes of commemoration, and indeed repatriation, of the war dead should not be associated with Archaic Athens. The argument of this book, as will become clear in the next two chapters, is that such modes were central to the Athenian treatment of the war dead in the pre-Classical era.

70 Hannestad (2001), 114.

71 Ferrari (2003), 40.

72 According to Lissarague (1990), 71–2, 'les vases sont datables entre 570 et 480, en majorité entre 540–500; ils sont pour l'essentiel à figures noires, principalement des amphores'. His catalogue included 100 representations, of which only 10 are dated beyond 500 BC. The Beazley Archive contains four examples in red-figure.

73 This is perhaps best illustrated by pots which feature both scenes of fighting over and retrieving the dead (BA 4652, BA 7721, BA 45349, BA 360895). For more on the paradigmatic aspect of Athenian vases, see Schiebler (1987).

74 Suggested by Lissarrague (1989), 46; and Pritchard (1999), 127. *Cf.* Saunders (2008b), who in his study of the theme concluded that: 'far from illustrating reality, these images express elite (or elite-aspiring) ideals, and support the suggestion that the *battle over a fallen warrior* presents death on the battlefield in a positive fashion' (p. 174). Saunders, however, offers no reasons for rejecting the realistic aspect of the vases

75 The changes in war imagery were briefly analysed by Bažant (1985), 7–12. Muth (2008), esp. 215–38, 519–627, dealt with a variety of combat images but confined her study to the concept of violence. Filser (2017), 398–565, looked at chronological variations in the depictions of horses and horsemen (as well as symposia and athletics) in black- and red-figure Athenian pots, offering some historical explanations (pp. 566–80). For a study on the changes to the subject matter in early Attic black-figure, see Shapiro (1990).

76 Osborne (2018) also investigated the changes in the representations of sexual relations and satyrs.

77 Ibid., 117.

78 Ibid., 209.

79 There are, nevertheless, some exceptions to Osborne's model of change in Classical war imagery. These consist primarily of the red-figure warrior *loutrophoroi*, which appear around 490 BC and continue to depict combat scenes throughout the fifth century BC. Hannah (2010) catalogued forty examples, emphasizing their affinity to earlier art: 'The inspiration for these combat scenes involving heavily- and lightly-armed forces and cavalry need not lie in myth (though the heroic tone is manifest) or on the contemporary battlefield, but in the long artistic tradition of diversified military engagements going back through the archaic period in Attic art, and indeed in Greek art in general' (p. 284).

80 Osborne (2018), 94. See also pp. 212–3 n. 19 and p. 214 n. 31 above.

81 In his forthcoming study on the depictions of mythical episodes in Athenian sixth- and fifth-century BC pottery, Osborne notes that individual episodes (including Ajax carrying Achilles) enjoyed different periods of popularity, and that there is not the same marked shift in what is popular in the second quarter of the fifth century BC that is apparent in his broader model for non-mythological scenes; 'broad fashions' for types of stories, as he concludes, seem to have been more

important than any particular event or text. The decline in representations of Ajax carrying Achilles, according to Osborne's survey, matches a similar decline in scenes depicting Troilos and Achilles, Achilles and Memnon, and Ajax and Achilles dicing (among others), the relation of which to changes in warfare is less clear. While I cannot engage with the broader issue of changing popularity in the artistic representations of other mythical episodes here, I hope to discuss this further in a future study.

82 Painted pots were certainly a popular medium to commemorate the war dead in the Classical period, as shown by the white-ground *lekythoi* or red-figure warrior *loutrophoroi*, which will be discussed in Chapter 5.

83 The 'hierarchical' message of Archaic iconography was, in effect, conveyed primarily in the depiction of individual combat retrieval for the fallen, the exclusive privilege of the elites in Homer, which contrasted with the Classical 'egalitarian' custom of collective *post*-battle recovery of all casualties regardless of social standing.

84 Pausanias' description of the First Messenian War does suggest that the practice of stripping the enemy dead of their armour might have been prevalent on Archaic battlefields: 'The most remarkable was the death of those who tried to strip any of the fallen. For if they exposed any part of their bodies, they were struck with javelins or were struck down while intent on their present occupation, or were killed by those whom they were plundering who still lived' (4.8.7). In another passage, Pausanias relays the heroic fight over the fatally wounded Messenian king Euphaes (4.10.3–4), but the historical value of his battle accounts, which draw heavily on the work Myron of Priene, is to be doubted. Other examples of fighting over the fallen during combat come from Herodotus and his account of the second Persian invasion. The first one is the struggle over the body of Leonidas at Thermopylae (7.225); the second concerns the fight over the Persian general Masistius at Plataea (9.22–3). While both stories might be dismissed as heroic fiction, there is nothing to suggest that the incidents could not have taken place.

4 Archaic Monuments for the War Dead

1 The earliest *polyandria* referred to in literary sources come from Pausanias and concern a battle during the First Messenian War (4.8.13), the battle of Hysiae (2.24.7), and the Oresthasian *polyandrion* at Phigalia (8.41.1). The first example forms part of an implausible battle narrative (see p. 200 n. 34 above) and should be dismissed; the other two Pausanias claims to have seen, but we should be cautious about relying on local traditions he heard nearly 800 years after the events. The earliest battlefield burials in Herodotus are those of Tellus (1.30) and Anchimolius (5.63), both from the second half of the sixth century BC. The first *polyandria* may

date to the same period, as I argue later in this chapter. For a survey of Greek war burials in literary sources, see Pritchett (1985), 153–235. For archaeological evidence for pre-Classical *polyandria*, see pp. 211–12 n. 9 above.

2 The distinction that Morris draws is between formal and informal disposal, not between burial and non-burial. Informal disposal, as he explains, still constitutes 'a rite of passage for all the actors, but in a manner very different from that of the observed burials, and leaving little or no identifiable material residue' (p. 105).

3 Morris (1987), 210.

4 For criticism of Morris' model, see Osborne (1989), esp. 313–22; Humphreys (1990); Patterson (2006), esp. 49 n. 12. See also Morris (1998b), where he responds to some of the criticism and incorporates new archaeological finds to his model.

5 E.g. 16.457, 675. The marker on top of the mound may also consist of other objects, such as the oar fixed on Elpenor's grave by Odysseus (XI.75–8). For more on *geras thanonton* in Homer, see Garland (1982).

6 For more on the Attic Geometric and Protoattic burials, see Kurtz and Boardman (1971), 49–67; Morris (1987), 20–2, 125–130; Osborne (1989), 299–303; Houby-Nielsen (1992); Sourvinou-Inwood (1995), 109–47; Whitley (2001), 233–43; Walter-Karydi (2015), 17–48.

7 The movement towards extra-mural burials is generally ascribed to the growing concept of pollution associated with death and corpses, evidenced in the firmer physical delineation between sacred and living spaces introduced by the Greek *poleis* in the late-eighth century BC. For more, see Sourvinou-Inwood (1983), 43–4; Morris (1987), 192. For more on pollution (*miasma*) in general, see Parker (1983); and Osborne (2011), 158–84, who argued that pollution beliefs appear in Greece in parallel with the first legal codes, supplementing the latter in areas impossible to regulate by law.

8 A brief overview, with references, is provided by Sourvinou-Inwood (1995), 217–21.

9 Ahlberg (1971b).

10 Ahlberg (1971a). The central scene always focuses on the funeral (*prothesis* and/or *ekphora*), which may feature a procession of warriors as part of the composition; battle scenes, as Walter-Karydi (2015), 41, noted, are of secondary importance and 'nur auf der Rückseite'.

11 For a summary of the debate, see Whitley (1991), 48–53. Since most of the imagery depicted on the funeral vases concern funeral rituals, which were a part of everyday life in early Athenian communities, I believe that we can assume that scenes representing military activities were similarly drawn from real life experience. In a recent study, Walter-Karydi (2015), 41–3, stressed that the battle scenes represent a wider ideal of manhood; because of their anonymity, however, they cannot tell us anything about the dead: 'Am Grabmal geben denn auch solche anonyme Szenen keine Ereignisse aus der Biographie des Toten wieder; sie besagen nicht einmal, dass

er im Krieg fiel. Er ist nur in den *Prothesis-* und *Ekphoraszenen* zu erkennen: als der Leichnam, dem die rituelle Ehrung gilt'.

12 For more on Archaic burials in Attica, see Kurtz and Boardman (1971), 68–90; Schmaltz (1983), 149–89; Morris (1987), 22, 130–7; Houby-Nielsen (1995); Sourvinou-Inwood (1995), 140–297; Rausch (1999), 192–220; Walter-Karydi (2015), 49–118. Even though the earth mounds considerably reduced in size and were eventually replaced by mudbrick tombs, our largest examples, known as the *Grabhügel G* and *Südhügel*, come from the mid-sixth century BC. For more on these exceptional tumuli, which contained several graves each, see Houby-Nielsen (1995), 153–63, who argues that in their structure such common graves constituted the forerunners to public burials for the war dead of the Classical period.

13 For general works on Archaic gravestones of Attica, see Richter (1961); Jeffery (1962); Clairmont (1970), 3–22.

14 Clairmont (1970), 4 n. 5, estimated that the surviving number of Archaic Attic grave memorials is *c.* 167; the figure, however, represents all surviving grave elements (bases, *stelai*, sphinxes etc.) which in some cases may have belonged to the same monument; or in the cases of *kouroi/korai*, may have been used as dedications in sanctuaries. In his count, this figure constitutes about 30 per cent of the hypothetical total number of Archaic grave memorials, which he set to five hundred. Snodgrass (1983), 21, provides wider estimations for Archaic Greece.

15 For examples of warrior *stelai*, see Richter (1961), Nos 45–7, 65–8.

16 As argued by Schmaltz (1983), 173, who noted that the warrior *stelai* depict both bearded men and youths: 'Im ersten Fall dürfte es sich um Männer handeln, die vielleicht im besten Mannesalter im Kampf gefallen waren, womöglich aber noch zu Lebzeiten des Vaters, und die deshalb mit einem so aufwendigen Grabmal bedacht wurden. Die anderen Grabreliefs gelten dagegen wohl Epheben, jungen Männern, die gerade erst ihren Militärdienst abgeleistet hatten und dann als mutige „Vorkämpfer" in vorderster Reihe gefallen waren, wie es das Epigramm z. B. für Kroisos bezeugt'. See also Humphreys (1980), 104–5; Sourvinou-Inwood (1995), 221–97.

17 E.g. Meyer (1993), 107: 'Archaic monuments like *kouroi* or figured grave-*stelai* are thought to attempt a generic representation of the deceased – not a specific representation of a specific person but a representation of what type of person the deceased was, generally by giving him the attributes of the eternal and universal aristocracy of 'the best men''. It is important to note that warrior attributes, which featured heavily on the late Geometric funerary kraters, are not confined to all grave *stelai* of the Archaic period; the latter also depict athletes and clothed citizens, giving us more insight into the social persona of the deceased. This abandonment of anonymity, enabled also by the introduction of grave inscriptions from the mid-seventh century BC onward, contributed to what Walter-Karydi (2015), 58, referred to as 'die Entdeckung der Einzelperson' in Archaic funerary memorials.

18 Jeffery (1962), 143–4 (**57**); Clairmont (1970), 16–17; Richter (1970), 118–19 (**136**); Osborne (1988), 6–9; (2011), 108–11; Arrington (2015), 27–30; Tentori Montalto (2017), 35–8. For more on Attic Archaic *kouroi/korai* in general, see Richter (1970); Martini (1990); Sourvinou-Inwood (1995), 231–75; Lorenz (2010). The funerary use of *kouroi/korai* was limited almost exclusively to Archaic Attica; in the wider Greek world such statues were used primarily as dedications in sanctuaries.

19 Caskey (1977), 509–10. For more on the link between Kroisos' gravestone and the Anavysos *kouros*, see Robinson, Stevens, Vanderpool (1949); Neer (2010), 24–6.

20 *IG* i³ 1240; *CEG* 27: στέθι : καὶ οἴκτιρον : Κροίσο παρὰ σέμα θανόντος : hόν ποτ' ἐνὶ προμάχοις : ὄλεσε θόρος : Ἄρες.

21 The dating suggesting a link with the battle of Pallene has been proposed, for instance, by Richter (1970), 115–16; and Jeffery (1962), 144. This has been subsequently challenged (e.g. Clairmont (1970), 16) and a revised date in the 530–520s BC is now commonly accepted. Scholarly debates on the identity of Kroisos are summarized in Tentori Montalto (2017), 37–8, who concluded: 'chiaro che le fonti non sono sufficienti a rivelare con certezza né l'identità di Kroisos, né tantomeno l'evento bellico nel quale sarebbe caduto'.

22 The nudity of the *kouroi* statues has been traditionally interpreted as a heroic and purely symbolic feature, intended to represent paradigmatically the ideal of physical strength and beauty. Sourvinou-Inwood (1995), 235–40, argued, however, that the 'heroic nudity' of the statues was also meant to associate the deceased with the aristocratic world of the *gymnasion* and its notions of competition (*agon*), permeating the spheres of both athletics and warfare. Since all *kouroi* commemorated leisure-class youths, of which a large number fell in battle, she posited that their visual rhetoric should be taken, first and foremost, as a reflection of reality; this is further confirmed by the fact that nude figures are also found on some grave *stelai*, both those depicting athletes and warriors.

23 On the *kalos thanatos* ideal and Kroisos' tomb, see Arrington (2015), 27. The relation between the statue and the inscription on Kroisos' monument has been studied by Osborne (1988), 7–9, who suggested that the simplicity of the *kouros* elides the specific details of Kroisos' achievements mentioned in the inscription. As such, the statue and the inscription 'complement and undermine each other': one glorifies the deeds of the deceased, the other places him in the context of basic humanity in the face of death, familiar and equal to all viewers, whatever their social status. On the same subject, see also Sourvinou-Inwood (1995), 258–9, n. 642, who argued instead that Archaic funerary *kouroi* differentiated themselves from the viewer. According to her, the statue was intended to represent a particular person, usually a young athlete, and as such it spoke most strongly to young males of similar social standing and aspirations. The epigram and the statue, as she concluded, complemented 'each other by articulating different (complementary) aspects of the deceased's social persona'.

An altogether different reading of Kroisos' tomb was proposed by Lorenz (2010), who pointed out that the last two words of the inscription, 'furious Ares', are written in a separate line and stand out from the rest. And since these words may have attracted the reader's gaze first, he/she would initially associate the *kouros* with the god Ares, only later realising it depicts one of his victims. As such, the tomb granted Kroisos both the identity of a war god and of a pitiful victim, thus embodying him as an ideal of a 'generic powerful male'. While all interpretations provide plausible insights, I would stress that the ideological similarities between the epigram and the statue are usually far more apparent than the differences. In the case of Kroisos, the ideal of *kalos thanatos* was equally well expressed in both the inscription and the *kouros*, suggesting that both media were primarily intended to complement each other and express a similar, elite message: a youth frozen in his prime by a heroic death in battle. See also Bruss (2010), 389–91.

24 Richter (1961), 158–9, Fig. 203; Jeffery (1962), 133; Day (1989), 17–22; Arrington (2015), 27–30; Tentori Montalto (2017), 31–5. The earliest Greek epitaph which mentions the death of a warrior in battle is from the tomb of Arniadas in Corcyra, c. 600 BC. The inscription (*CEG* 145) reads as follows: 'This is the tomb of Arniadas. Him flashing-eyed Ares destroyed as he fought by the ships at the streams of Aratthus, displaying the highest valour amid the groans and shouts of war'. (σᾶμα τόδε Ἀρνιάδα. χαροπὸς τόνδ᾽ ὄ̄λεσεν Ἄρε̄ς βαρνάμενον παρὰ ναυσὶν ἐπ᾽ Ἀράθθοιο ῥοϝαῖσι πολλὸν ἀριστεύοντα κατὰ στονόϝεσ<σ>αν ἀϝυτάν). For more on early Greek sepulchral epigrams, see Trümpy (2010); Walter-Karydi (2015), 101–11.

25 *IG* i³ 1194; *CEG* 13: [εἴτε ἀστό]ς τις ἀνὲρ εἴτε χσένος | ἄλοθεν ἐλθόν ⁝ Τέτιχον οἰκτίρας ἀνδρ᾽ ἀγαθὸν παρίτο, ⁝ ἐν πολέμοι φθίμενον, νεαρὰν ἥβεν ὀλέσαντα. ⁝ ταῦτ᾽ ἀποδυράμενοι νέσθε ἐπὶ πρᾶγμ᾽ ἀγαθόν. Jeffery (1962), 133, speculated that Tettichos' monument consisted of a sculpted *stele*. Arrington (2015), 27, suggested that the latter most likely depicted a warrior carrying a spear, and could have resembled the monument for Aristion, discussed later in this chapter (Fig. 10).

26 For more on the interaction between epigram and passer-by, see Schmitz (2010); Tueller (2010); Vestrheim (2010).

27 The ideal of *kalos thanatos* in Tettichos' epigram is especially stressed by Day (1989), 17–22, who argued that instead of providing biographical information, the tomb symbolized an ideal state of death. On the similarities between epic poetry and early sepulchral epigram, see Trümpy (2010), 171–5, who goes as far as to argue that the latter were 'miniature epics'.

28 For more on the elite ideology of early sepulchral epigrams, see Sourvinou-Inwood (1995), 170–80.

29 Jacoby (1944), 44, includes the example of Tettichos in his list of all known Athenian casualties killed in service before 470 BC. He states that Tettichos was buried

privately in a family tomb but, rather confusingly, does not explain how this relates to his wider assumption that all Athenians were buried on the battlefield before the introduction of the *patrios nomos*, which he dated to 465/4 BC.

30 Richter (1961), 158. See also Tentori Montalto (2017), 34.
31 Jeffery (1962), 118–19; Tentori Montalto (2017), 77–8.
32 *IG* i³ 1200; *CEG* 19: [——τι]ς αἰχμετο͂, Χσενόκλεες, ἀνδρὸς [ἐπισ]τὰς ⁝ σε͂μα τὸ σὸν προσιδὸν γνό[σετ]αι ἐν[ορέαν]. Translation from Tueller (2010), 45.
33 The cause of death is mentioned only if it came by an illness or accident, or indeed by falling in battle. For more, see Clairmont (1970), 9.
34 For a full list of epigrams which mention death in warfare, see Clairmont (1970), 6 n. 24. In a recent work on Greek epigrams dedicated to the warrior dead, Tentori Montalto (2017) included four examples from Archaic Athens; apart from Tettichos, Kroisos and Xenokles, he also listed *CEG* 30 (*IG* i³ 1274ter), commemorating Spoud[——] (?). The latter, dated to 540–530 BC, is too fragmentary to draw any conclusions from. Tentori Montalto catalogued it under 'epigrammi privati geurrieri non caduti in guerra', along with Xenokles, stating that it is impossible to determine whether the epigrams commemorated casualties of war.
35 As argued by Robertson (1997); Morgan (2001), 38; Arrington (2015), 30; Walter-Karydi (2015), 104–11.
36 The motif of defending one's country is present in the *Iliad*, evidenced especially in the speeches made by Hector, who first exhorts his comrades 'to fight in defense of our country' (12.243); and later praises any man who dies in battle: 'He has no dishonor when he dies defending his country, for then his wife shall be saved and his children afterward, and his house and property shall not be damaged, if the Achaeans must go away with their ships to the beloved land of their fathers' (15.496–9). This ideal, however, is arguably less prominent in the poem, especially when compared to the martial elegies of the Archaic period, since the main motivation of Homeric *basileis* in battle, as we saw in Chapter 1, centres around concepts of personal gain and glory. For more on patriotism in Homer, see Greenhalgh (1972).
37 Robertson (1997), 150, argued that patriotic slogans reminiscent of those used by Callinus and Tyrtaeus were employed by Solon in his exhortations to the Athenians fighting for the possession of Salamis (Frs 1, 3), thus giving us an early example of an Athenian martial elegy.
38 Robertson (1997), 151. See also Walter-Karydi (2015), 107, who similarly concluded that 'die Gefallenen in den archaisch-attischen Grabepigrammen für ihre Tapferkeit gerühmt, aber ihr Tod wird nie auf die Polis bezogen, und sie werden nicht einmal als Athener ange sprochen'. For a survey study of Athenian epitaphs and their relation to changing concepts of citizenship, see Meyer (1993).
39 Archaic warrior *stelai* are discussed by Sourvinou-Inwood (1995), 223–7, who, in line with her wider argument that most Archaic grave memorials commemorated

youths, suggested that both beardless and bearded men depicted on the reliefs represented young male warriors.

40 Osborne (1988), 8–9, who looked as the *stele* of Aristion in particular, concluded that such monuments, first and foremost, chose to present the deceased as warriors, and 'it may or may not be' that they commemorated men who fell in battle. See also p. 223 n. 16 above.

41 Based on survey studies by Richter (1961) and Jeffery (1962), supplemented by Schmaltz (1983) and Kissas (2000), around 75 per cent of evidence for Archaic Attic grave *stelai* comes from the second half of the sixth century BC, with nearly 50 per cent belonging to the last quarter. All surviving warrior *stelai* are dated to the later sixth century BC, as noted by Walter-Karydi (2015), 69, who nonetheless points out that 'wird dieser Grabbildnistypus etwa gleichzeitig mit des Athleten im früheren 6. Jahrhundert aufgekommen sein'.

42 The ideological differences between the Attic funerary *kouroi/korai* and relief *stelai* have been a subject of some debate. Stewart (1986); (1990), 50, for instance, argued that the *kouroi* and *korai* were highly symbolic and elitist, recalling 'the splendor of Homer's heroes and heroines'; the *stelai*, by contrast, were more factual, representing the deceased 'as typical members of the polis community'. Osborne (1988), by contrast, spotted no indication of a difference based on class, and suggested that the monuments reflected different attitudes to death, with one contemplating the universality of death (*kouroi*), and the other celebrating life with its community duties (*stelai*). Finally, Sourvinou-Inwood (1995), 269–70, downplayed any dichotomies between the two forms, maintaining that they both drew from the same 'multidimensional spectrum' in order to represent the deceased's social persona. As will become clear from my argument below, I maintain that the clear visual contrast between the *kouroi* (naked youth) and *stelai* (warrior, athlete) reflected different ideological functions. While both forms were employed by the elites and commemorated the deceased as an individual, the latter invoked clear communal aspects absent from the *kouroi* statues.

43 On the conservative nature of the *kouroi*, see Osborne (1988), 6–9.

44 For more on the grave *stele* of Aristion, see Richter (1961), Nr 67; Jeffery (1962), 141 (**52**); Osborne (1988), 8–9.

45 Osborne (1988), 8.

46 As argued by Arrington (2015), 31–2, who emphasized that there were 'no restrictions on transporting the corpses of the dead from the battlefield and burying the body as a family' in sixth-century BC Athens.

47 The figures are provided by Rees (2018), who discussed the difficulties of cremation of the war dead in general. Secondary cremation for transport would have required less wood, especially for multiple bodies burned on the same pyre. Considering the importance placed on the return of the individual dead, it seems more likely to me

that bodies of the elite warriors would have been cremated individually. The main form of burial in Attica for most of the Archaic period, however, was primary cremation, which further suggests that corpses would have been carted back whenever possible. For more on cremation in ancient Greece, see Kurtz and Boardman (1971), 73–4, 98–9, 328; on cremation vs inhumation of the war dead, see Pritchett (1985), 251–7.

48 As opposed to, for instance, the memorial of Menekrates from Corcyra (c. 600 BC), accompanied by an epitaph stating that he was lost at sea, thus identifying the tomb as cenotaph (see Meiggs and Lewis (1969), 4–5).

49 For the archaeological report of Kroisos' tomb see Mastrokostas (1974), who concluded that: 'In dem Familienhügel dürfte neben und unter dem Bild auch die Knochenasche von Kroisos beigesetzt gewesen sein. Denn nach dem Wortlaut des Epigramms war Kroisos in einer Schlacht unter den Vorkämpfern gefallen. Und die Gefallenen oder überhaupt die in der Fremde Gestorbenen pflegten zumindest die Athener, indem sie die Urne mit der Asche überführten, im Land ihrer Väter zu bestatten ...'. (p. 228). Any assumptions that Kroisos' remains were buried in the family tomb must, however, remain conjectural. For late-fifth and early-fourth century relief *stelai* from Athens which did serve as cenotaphs for the war dead buried by the state, see Osborne (2010).

50 Olympia: Kunze (1958), 118–51; (1961), 56–137; (1967), 111–83. For more on the dedication of captured arms, see Pritchett (1979), 240–95; Snodgrass (1980), 105–7; (2006); Jackson (1991); Morgan (2001), 24–7; Baitinger (2011); Schröder (2020), 24–53. For spoils of war hung in Archaic households, see van Wees (1998), 363–6; (2007), Figs 9.2–3.

51 Vaughn (1991), 46–7.

52 In the early days of Greek warfare these gaps, as Jackson (1991), 240, observed, may have been constantly created by 'lone warriors who, ambitious for their own glory, might spring forth in the old way to challenge, kill and despoil (...) the fine arms of their social equals in the enemy phalanx'. This practice may have, in fact, carried on into the fifth century BC and possibly beyond (see p. 221 n. 84 above).

53 The existence of the phalanx formation in Archaic Greek warfare is a subject of a heated historical debate. Some associate its origins with the emergence of first citizen armies in the mid-eighth century BC, while others argue that it did not feature on the Greek battlefields until the fifth century BC. My preference leans strongly towards the second camp in this debate, represented by scholars such as Peter Krentz, Hans van Wees and Fernando Echeverria. For a recent summary of the debate, with references, see Kagan and Viggiano (2013).

54 Rausch (1999), 228–9, speculated that the Athenian war dead in the pre-Cleisthenic era were individually cremated on the battlefield and then either buried on the spot or returned home (e.g. Tettichos, Kroisos). Repatriation, according to him, was

dependent on the 'Finanzkraft und das Engagement der Angehörigen zu Hause bzw. der Kameraden im Kampfverband'. Considering the cost and difficulties of cremation, it is unlikely that the practice would have extended to all of the casualties.

55 Hdt. 7.228; Simon. 22b West = *AP* 7.249. The archaeological evidence consists of the Lacedaemonian *polyandrion* in the Kerameikos, which contained the bodies of 23 warriors who died during the 403 BC expedition to Athens (Xen. *Hell.* 2.4.31–4). For more on the tomb, see Hodkinson (2000), 252, 257–9; Stroszeck (2006). On the Thermopylae war dead, see Pritchett (1985), 168–73; Low (2006), 99–101.

56 See Low (2006), who also discussed the evidence of the so-called ΕΝ ΠΟΛΕΜΟΙ *stelai*. General studies on the Spartan war dead are otherwise rare and consist of mentions within larger works, e.g. Pritchett (1985), 241–6; Nafissi (1991), 290–309.

57 The amphoras are commonly dated to the period 625–550 BC, which further supports the case that they may have commemorated the war dead, buried collectively on the battlefield from the second half of the sixth century BC onward. Christou (1964) provided the main study of the amphoras (with illustrations); other discussions include Hodkinson (2000), 240–2; Förtsch (2001), 99–104. Funerary monuments comparable to those in Attica are rare in Archaic Sparta and the Peloponnese in general, as stressed recently by Kokkorou-Alevras (2010). Apart from the scenes on the terracotta amphoras, the war dead rarely feature in Laconian iconography. One notable example is a mid-sixth-century BC cup by the Hunt Painter (*CVA* Berlin 4, Deutschland 33, pl. 183.1), which according to Kurtz and Boardman (1971), 191, portrays 'warriors returning home bearing the bodies of the dead'. The vivid depiction of fresh wounds, combined with the fact that the fallen would not have been physically carried back to Sparta, suggest that the scene more likely presents the aftermath of a battle. For more on the cup, see Saunders (2008a), 85–6. On the Hunt Painter and Laconian pottery in general, see Pipili (2018).

58 See Christesen (2018), who catalogued 31 burials from the Archaic period, of which at least 12 were discovered alongside the Aphetaïs road, and a further 9 on the edges of the Gerokomeiou hill. For more on Spartan burial customs, see Cartledge (1987), 331–43; (2012); Nafissi (1991), 277–341; Toher (1991); Richer (1994); Hodkinson (2000), 237–70; Cavanagh, Cavanagh and Roy (2010).

59 Christesen (2018), 355.

60 See esp. Nafissi (1991); (2009). *Cf.* Van Wees (2018a); (2018b), who dated most of the institutional changes in Sparta to the end of the sixth century BC.

61 Thyrea: Paus. 2.38.5–6; Hdt. 1.82. Cartledge (1987), 337; Hodkinson (2000), 251; Christesen (2018), 314. *Cf.* Van Wees (2006b), 132–3, who posited that the Spartans initially buried only the most distinguished fallen on the battlefield, while taking the rest of the dead home. I disagree with this interpretation in my forthcoming article (*B*) on the Spartan war dead, where I further develop the arguments presented here.

62 As argued by Schröder (2020), 94–7, who provides further references.

63 Schröder (2020), 38, relying on data from Baitinger (2001), 239–46, stated that: 'Bei den beschrifteten Waffenweihungen in Olympia etwa steht den vereinzelten privaten Votiven (7) mehr als die sechsfache Anzahl an stadtstaatlichen Weihungen (46) gegenüber'. One example is Argos' dedication of 14 pieces of armour captured from the Corinthians; Jackson (2000) estimated that the inscriptions were made by 8 or 9 engravers, indicating a more substantial dedication than what has survived. Schröder's suggestion that late Archaic findings support the thesis that earlier, uninscribed dedications of arms and armour should be also seen as collective acts on behalf of Greek *poleis* is, however, problematic. The basis of this claim stems from the assumption that the origins of the practice of weapons dedications in the eighth century BC lie in the advent of the hoplite phalanx and the community values it promoted. Since recent studies convincingly downdate the latter to the end of the Archaic period (see p. 228 n. 53 above), the link with early weapons dedications is no longer tenable. For recent criticism of the traditional model of weapons dedications, see Lloyd (forthcoming).

64 The circumstances of this transferral undoubtedly varied from one polis to another; Sparta, for instance, did not dedicate captured weapons in sanctuaries at all (a phenomenon later enshrined by Plutarch in *Mor.* 224B, 224F, 228F–229A). Schröder (2020), 48, also noted that Archaic *poleis* ruled by tyrants began to dedicate weapons in Olympia only after their fall. For a full study of Greek *poleis* as dedicators of Waffenweihungen, see ibid., 37–53.

5 Ancestral Customs in the Classical City

1 Critical parody of the funeral oration for the war dead appears similarly in Plato's *Menexenus*.

2 For more on home vs battlefield burials, see Pritchett (1985), 249–51, who noted that the evidence from other Greek *poleis* is too scattered to offer any generalizations. Considering the sheer number of campaigns embarked on by the Athenians in the Classical period (on average one (or more) in two out of three years in the fifth century BC), their custom of repatriation was certainly exceptional. On the relation between Athenian democracy and war-making, see Pritchard (2010); (2018), who stressed the 'democratic bellicosity' of fifth-century BC Athens.

3 On the practical and logistical difficulties of the Athenian institution of public burials, see Rees (2018), whose study questioned the feasibility of many elements in the process, putting in doubt the traditional scholarly understanding of the custom based on Thucydides. Despite offering a number of insights, especially into cremation (see pp. 227–8 n. 47 above) and storage, Rees did not offer an alternative

solution to how the Athenians processed and buried their war dead. For more on casualties in hoplite battles, see Krentz (1985).
4 On a wider scale, this platform effectively contributed to what Pritchard (2018), 12–13, 109–37, referred to as the 'democratisation of traditional military virtues', making 'military service attractive to poor Athenians as a source of esteem' and therefore playing an important role in the city's pro-war culture.
5 For examples of the simpler types of decoration, see Richter (1961), 37–52; Kurtz and Boardman (1971), 85–6.
6 Morris (1987), 208.
7 The dramatic rise in the number of adult and child burials in Attica around 510 BC is well represented on a graph in Morris (1987), Fig. 22. For the disappearance of grave markers, see Stupperich (1977), 77–85; Morris (1992), 128–55; Rausch (1999), 206–8; Stears (2000), 27–31.
8 See Houby-Nielsen (1995), 147–50; (2000).
9 Jeffery (1962), 128 [20]; Clairmont (1983), 87–8.
10 Jeffery (1962), 128.
11 Clairmont (1983), 88.
12 Jeffery (1962), 143 [55].
13 Ibid.
14 Considering that the most obvious restoration of the lines contains the verb *anetheke*, it seems most plausible to treat the monument as a dedication, which had nothing to do with casualties of war. The list of names, as Jeffery pointed out, is harder to explain. Assuming that the monument was an unparalleled example of a practice later adopted by the state, based on a speculation concerning missing columns, is certainly taking it a step too far.
15 It is perhaps most revealing that Clairmont (1983), 87–94, who collected all available archaeological and literary evidence for pre-490 BC Athenian public burials, included only one example (mentioned above) predating the reforms of Cleisthenes. Notable exceptions to the general lack of Archaic mass burials for war-related casualties in Attica come from the cemetery on the Phalerum delta (see Papadopoulou (2017), 163–4). One consists of a late Archaic burial of 17 men, nailed to planks and stoned to death, before being thrown in a common pit. The men were likely pirates, punished by a practice known as *apotympanismos*; some of their bodies show signs of combat trauma. Recent excavations revealed another common grave from *c.* 650–625 BC, containing bodies of 78 captives, most in metal shackles, in 3 trenches; and a *polyandrion* (currently undated) for men killed or injured in battle, who, according to Papadopoulou's report, were 'unceremoniously thrown in a pit, while some were still alive'. While the graves may give us an indication of how the Athenians buried (and punished) foreign hostiles and/or criminals, we cannot draw any meaningful insights from them regarding burials for Athenian war dead.

16 Jacoby (1944), 44–5; Pritchett (1985), 161, 249; Schröder (2020), 98. Pritchett based his argument on a claim that any stories which only mention 'where a prominent participant in a battle is buried', such as Hermolykos' (Hdt. 9.105) or Anchimolius' (Hdt. 5.63) burials, indicate that the rest of the dead 'were buried at the same spot' (p. 161). Van Wees (2006b), 132 n. 25, rightly disagreed, stressing that the purpose of such stories was to demonstrate exceptional privilege.

17 As argued by van Wees (2006b), 132. The story, however, remains anecdotal and using it as the key piece of evidence for Archaic Athenian practice is highly problematic.

18 See Jacoby (1944), 45; Page (1981), 189–91; Clairmont (1983), 88–9; Robertson (1983), 88–9; Pritchett (1985), 164–5; Robertson (1997), 150–1; Rausch (1999), 226–7; Morgan (2001), 33; Arrington (2015), 42.

19 Δίρφυος ἐδμήθημεν ὑπὸ πτυχί· σῆμα δ' ἐφ' ἡμῖν ἐγγύθεν Εὐρίπου δημοσίᾳ κέχυται, οὐκ ἀδίκως· ἐρατὴν γὰρ ἀπωλέσαμεν νεότητα, τρηχεῖαν πολέμου δεξάμενοι νεφέλην.

20 For more on the debate, see Page (1981), 189–91; Pritchett (1985), 164–5; Robertson (1997), 150–1.

21 Page (1981), 189–91. Cf. Robertson (1983), 88–9, who argued that the tomb should be associated with an altogether different conflict between Chalcis and Eretria, of which we now have no record. This is highly unlikely, as there is no evidence for any early tradition of public commemoration of the war dead in either Chalcis or Eretria.

22 Lloyd-Jones (1982), 141.

23 This interpretation, as Robertson (1997), 151, noted, is further supported by an inscription accompanying a dedication made by the Athenians on the Acropolis following the victory. It is partially preserved on two stone bases (*IG* i^3 501; *CEG* 179), and mentioned also by Herodotus: 'Crushing the Boeotians and Chalcidians, the sons of Athens fought well, quenched their pride in grievous bondage of iron, and made these horses from a tenth of the spoils as an offering to Pallas Athena' (5.77). As Robertson concluded, no mention is made of defending the community or country, 'which is consistent with the spirit of other Archaic verse inscriptions relating to war'. For more on the dedicatory monument, see Schröder (2020), 74–9.

24 Clairmont (1983), 88–9.

25 See Jeffery (1961), 299–300; Clairmont (1983), 89–90; Pritchett (1985), 165; Rausch (1999), 224–5; Marchiandi (2008), 16 n. 35. Cf. Culasso Gastaldi (2010), 140–2, who dated the list to the 'età di Cimone'.

26 Jeffery (1961), 299–300. Frag. A mentions the Hippothontis tribe (*IG* XII suppl. 337).

27 For the so-called '*stele* of the Marathonomachoi' from Eua-Loukoi, which contained a casualty list of 22 names from the tribe of Erechtheis and a short epigram commemorating men who died fighting the Medes, see Proietti (2013); Tentori

Montalto (2013). A separate monument for men who 'kept all Greece from seeing the day of slavery' (*IG* I³ 503/4) was found in Athens, but its relation to a specific battle (Marathon or Salamis) has been debated; for more, see Rausch (1999), 234–41; Arrington (2015), 43–8; Schröder (2020), 179–81.

28 According to Clairmont (1983), 90, the practice 'was fully established' by 490 BC.
29 While there may be some doubt regarding the Athenian burials at Artemision and Salamis, I believe that the indirect evidence, including remarks from Plutarch (*Them.* 8.3) and a fragmentary inscription concerning Salamis (*IG* II² 1035), suggests that the Athenian dead were buried on the shore (Artemision) or the promontory (Salamis) nearby. Rausch (1999), 248, stressed the Panhellenic character of the burials at Plataea, inferring that similar arrangements would have followed other Panhellenic battles such as Salamis (citing also the destruction of the outer Kerameikos by the Persians as another reason for burial on the battlefield). *Cf.* Arrington (2015), 41–2. For more on Athenian burials during the Persian Wars, see Clairmont (1983), 95–123; Pritchett (1985), 166–78.
30 See Clairmont (1970), 6 n. 18; Pritchett (1985), 165–6; Arrington (2015), 40–1. Another potential example is a *stele* in Copenhagen, depicting two hoplites and dated to *c.* 500–475 BC. Based on the unusually wide width of the slab, it has been suggested that the monument could have stood over a *polyandrion*. For more, see Richter (1961), Nr. 77; Jeffery (1962), 149 [11]; Clairmont (1970), 6; Stupperich (1994), 101 n. 29.
31 As suggested by Arrington (2015), 40–2. *Cf.* Clairmont (1983), 101–2, and Pritchett (1985), 249, who argued that the apparent exception of the Aeginetan burial could be explained by practical considerations, as it 'seems natural for the Athenians to recover the bodies from the wrecks in the Saronic Gulf and to bury their ashes in their public cemetery rather than on some Attic headland'. If we accept that the dead from other naval conflicts such as Artemision and Salamis were buried close to the battlefield, which both Clairmont and Pritchett do, it would have made every sense for the Aeginetan dead to be treated in the same way. That they were not suggests that the casualties from Artemision and Salamis were treated differently and ascribed a special distinction by being buried 'on the spot'.
32 This interpretation is further supported by Thucydides' famous claim about the exceptional nature of the battlefield burial of the Marathon dead (2.34.5), echoed also by Pausanias (1.29.4).
33 Suggested also by Arrington (2015), 267.
34 On the *polyandrion*, see Hannah (2010), 273 n. 25, who also provides a full catalogue of the fifth-century BC warrior *loutrophoroi* in Athens. See also Arrington (2015), 208–17.
35 Hannah (2010), 289–90. The depictions of tombs on a number of warrior *loutrophoroi* confirms their funerary function (e.g. BA 12748, BA 217521). Arrington

(2015), 210–11, maintained that some of the *loutrophoroi* featured inscribed casualty lists, but the evidence is too speculative (or fragmentary) to confirm this.

36 Proposed also by Oakley (2004), 215–16; and Arrington (2015), 216–17.

37 Alternatively, though less likely, the warrior *loutrophoroi* may have been publicly commissioned to commemorate the war dead, as suggested by Kurtz (1984), 321. *Cf.* Hannah (2010), 273–6, who noted that 'it is just as likely that the warrior *loutrophoroi* were ordered privately by the grieving families'; Arrington (2015), 210, who stated that the *loutrophoroi* 'were probably private commissions, which could be deposited by families at both public graves and private cenotaphs'.

38 See Arrington (2015), 270–1, who also linked the scenes of Hypnos and Thanatos with the ideal of *kalos thanatos*. It is revealing that the fallen warriors in these scenes no longer feature any wounds, usually added in black-figure representations of Sarpedon's retrieval from the battlefield (see p. 217 n. 52 above). For more on white-ground *lekythoi*, see Oakley (2004); Arrington (2015), 239–74.

39 On the importance of visiting tombs in Classical Athens, see Garland (2001), 104–20. The tombs depicted on the *lekythoi* portraying the war dead might have been the public graves in the Kerameikos; as Arrington (2015), 264, noted, however, the lack of casualty lists in the images, which occasionally appear on other contemporary vases, suggests that 'tombs on lekythoi do not evoke in any systematic way the public cemetery'. *Cf.* Low (2010), 351, who speculated that the *lekythoi* portrayed the ways in which the Athenians made use of the public monuments as sites of private mourning.

40 Arrington (2015), 270.

41 These changes manifested themselves also in other areas of Athenian culture, such as architectural sculpture and, slightly later, votive and grave reliefs. An excellent study on the impact of the institution of public burial for the war dead on fifth-century BC Athens is provided by Arrington (2015).

42 The secondary literature on the subject is, unsurprisingly, considerable as both historians and archaeologists have attempted to solve the controversy. The following works provide a good starting point: Jacoby (1944); Clairmont (1983), 7–15; Pritchett (1985), 106–24; Rausch (1999), 230–48; Loraux (2006), 58–61, 94–117; Arrington (2015), 39–49.

43 Diodorus (11.33.3) says that after the battle of Plataea the Athenians held funeral games for the first time and passed a decree concerning funeral orations for war casualties who were buried at public expense. He does not specify where the dead were buried but one should assume that he envisions the whole custom being introduced at the same time (despite the fact that the Athenian dead at Plataea were buried on the battlefield). Dionysios of Halicarnassus (5.17.4) confirms that the funeral oration was added around the time of the Persian Wars, but cannot discern whether it was instituted in honour of the dead from Marathon, Artemision, Salamis

or Plataea. His statement, however, suggests that the basic custom was already in place before 490 BC. Finally, Pausanias (1.29.4), despite mentioning the graves of the Athenians who fought against Aegina in 491/0 BC (1.29.7) and at Eurymedon in *c.* 466 BC (1.29.14) in his survey of the Kerameikos, states that the first war casualties buried in the *demosion sema* were the fallen from Drabescus in 465 BC.

44 The earliest casualty list located in the Kerameikos is dated to 465/4 BC and commemorated the war dead from the conflicts at Drabescus, Thasos and Chersonese. Earlier casualty lists, as I argued above, were normally placed above the *polyandrion* on the battlefield, as was the case at Lemnos and Marathon. For more on the earliest list, see Braaden (1967); (1969). For recent works on the commemoration of the war dead in Classical Athens, see Low (2010); (2013); Osborne (2010); Yoshitake (2010); Arrington (2015).

45 To a greater or lesser extent, most scholars dealing with the subject of the origins of the *patrios nomos* adopt a piecemeal explanation; the main disagreement concerns the final mover behind the official establishment of the institution. My own preference is to credit Cimon, therefore placing the *patrios nomos* in the mid-470s BC. The traditions surrounding Cimon's ceremonial return of Theseus' bones to Athens (Plut. *Thes.* 36; *Cim.* 8.5-6), and his initiatives of beautifying the Academy, located at the end of the *demosion sema* (Plut. *Cim.* 13.8), clearly point to his interest, both symbolic and practical, for the Athenian commemoration of war casualties. For more on Cimon and the war dead, see Arrington (2015), 196-204.

46 Loraux (2006), 52. Rausch (1999), 229, similarly speaks of a 'kollektive "Aristokratisierung" der athenischen Kriegsgefallenen' in the wake of Cleisthenes' reforms.

47 For more on the relation between the funeral oration and the Archaic sepulchral epigrams, see Sourvinou-Inwood (1995), 191-5. On the ideal of *kalos thanatos* in the Athenian funeral oration, see Loraux (2006), 145-71; Yoshitake (2010).

48 Clairmont (1983), 11.

49 This link has been missed by Loraux (2006), 47, who following Jacoby assumed that repatriating the ashes of the dead broke with the universal Greek practice of burial on the battlefield (see p. 181 n. 4 (top) above). An important question for our understanding of the Classical Greek customs of burials for the war dead is how unique the Athenian practices were in the wider Greek world and to what extent was *patrios nomos* determined by the democratic *politeia* of Athens. In her survey of non-Athenian evidence from the fifth century BC, Low (2003) discussed other examples of casualty lists (Megara, Tanagra, Thespiae), noting similarities to Athenian commemorative practices. Schröder (2020), 200-30, revisited the evidence, concluding that other Classical Greek *poleis* adopted aspects of *patrios nomos* (e.g. casualty lists, repatriation) and that the 'Adaption der Praktiken war aber keineswegs

auf die Verbündeten Attikas oder auf Städte mit demokratischen Staatsordnungen beschränkt' (p. 229).

50 Rees (2018), 173–7, noted that Aeschylus' use of the word 'ashes' (σποδός) is unusual; Thucydides (2.34.3) refers to the cremated remains of warriors as 'the bones' (τὰ ὀστᾶ), as does Euripides (e.g. *Supp.* 949). In modern terminology the ashes are the ground up bones of the deceased returned to the family; the word used by the Greeks applied most likely to the bones of the deceased and/or the ashes produced by the pyre cremation wood. Since effective cremation of the bodies of the war dead required vast quantity of wood and constant supervision, Rees suspected that the remains of the Athenian war dead would have normally consisted of bones and soft tissue; in order to avoid mistranslation, he advocated the use of the word 'cremains'.

51 Jacoby (1944), 44, for instance, dismissed the passage on the basis of its exceptional nature, stating that 'nobody will seriously doubt that the singularity is due to a typical and deliberate anachronism after the Athenian custom which had been introduced but a few years earlier'. The anachronism employed by Aeschylus consisted, according to him, of projecting a contemporary custom (*public* repatriation) onto the mythical past. The custom alluded to by Aeschylus, however, more likely referred to the practice of *private* repatriation prevalent in Archaic Athens. For more on the passage, see Jacoby (1944), 44 n. 30; Pritchett (1985), 101; Garland (2001), 92; Arrington (2015), 34–5. See also p. 190 n. 76 above.

6 War, State and Society in Archaic Athens

1 Herodotus' account is, of course, problematic, as it is highly unlikely that the Athenian army would have first marched across Attica, fought a battle against the Boeotians, and then made a crossing to Euboea to take on the Chalcidians – all in a single day. As van Wees (2013b), 68, suggested, if Herodotus' narrative is to stand, it is far more plausible to assume that the Athenians used their fleet to transport the troops.

2 See p. 232 n. 23 above.

3 Translation by Robin Waterfield (OUP 1998).

4 As Frost (1984), 292, summarized in his survey of Archaic Athenian wars, the 'catalogue of Athenian military ventures for a period of something over a century is surprisingly modest for a people who were supposed to have been so fond of fighting and for whom the evolution of hoplite tactics was supposed to have been so politically significant'. Scholars who ascribe to the view of no public army in Athens prior to 508/7 BC include van Effenterre (1976); Frost (1984); Pritchard (2010); (2018), 5–6. The same view is also held for early Athenian naval organization: Haas (1985); Gabrielsen (1985); (1994), 19–26; Scott (2000), 93.

5 Frost (1984), 293.
6 Pritchard (2010), 8.
7 See also Gabrielsen (2007), 252–3.
8 Herodotus' statement on the Athenians being 'no better at warfare than any of their neighbours' is especially doubtful when one looks at his passage in Book 1, where he states that Athens and Sparta were the two most powerful states in Greece in the sixth century BC (1.56). Admittedly, as Bogdan Burliga pointed out to me, this did not necessarily imply military superiority. For a short discussion on the biased nature of Herodotus' and Thucydides' accounts of early Greek military development, see van Wees (2013b), 3–5.
9 For an introductory chapter on *Warfare and the State* in ancient Greece, see Gabrielsen (2007).
10 For a longer discussion on Aristotle's essential functions of the *polis*, see Manville (1990), 38–45.
11 Garlan (1975), 31–2, argued that Archaic Greek warfare consisted of 'private' wars and raids, which 'withdrew before natural principles of organisation' and were characteristic of pre-political, or pre-state, structures of early Greek communities, lacking any legal authority. This was opposed to later communal wars and campaigns, controlled and organized by the Greek *poleis* of the Classical period. For a short discussion, see Gabrielsen (2007), 248–9.
12 Singor (2000), 109.
13 E.g. Frost (1984); Pritchard (2010), 7–13; van Wees (2013b), 57–60.
14 This is not to say, however, that we should distance ourselves from written evidence; the latter remains indispensable for our general understanding of the Archaic era. The attempt here is rather to bring new art-historical material into discussion with what little we know about early military organization in Athens (mainly from Herodotus and Aristotle), in the hope the results, speculative as they might be, reinvigorate scholarly interest into a subject which many take to be beyond reconstruction.
15 On early Athenian history, see Jeffery (1976), 83–108; Andrewes (1982a); Manville (1990), 55–69; D'Onofrio (1997); Ste Croix (2004); Houby-Nielsen (2009).
16 I refer to the author of *Athenaion Politeia* as Aristotle in this chapter, but the work was more likely written by one of his students, which I indicate by putting the title in square brackets throughout (e.g. [*Ath. Pol.*]).
17 [*Ath. Pol.*] 1; 3.1, 6; 5.3.
18 According to Figueira (1984) and Duplouy (2003); (2015), 61–3, the term 'Eupatrids' was coined by an elite political group formed in opposition to Peisistratus and his sons; far from denoting an aristocracy, it served as a convenient slogan intended to stand for 'good for the fatherland', and not 'of good fathers'. Such interpretation is further supported by the fact the term does not appear in the surviving fragments of

Solon, and is indeed also absent from the whole of Archaic poetry. It similarly does not feature in Herodotus or Thucydides, and is mentioned only once by Aristotle ([*Ath. Pol.*] 13.2), by whose time the Eupatrids consisted of a group of families with hereditary priesthoods. Since most of our understanding of the Eupatrids' role in early Athenian history is based on Plutarch, it is best to approach the term, with its potential implications of noble birth, with caution. The comparative lack of any similar aristocracies of birth in ancient Greece and Rome, as observed by van Wees and Fisher (2015), certainly suggests that good birth was not as important a factor as has been assumed in previous scholarship. For a recent defence of the traditional view of the Eupatrids, see Pierrot (2015).

19 The good birth and reputation of one's family, according to such studies, provided a factor which did contribute to a person's social standing, but as van Wees and Fisher (2015), 33, argued, 'did not form the basis for any categorical claim to hereditary privilege'. Social status was not indefinitely ascribed, but achieved by adhering to an ideal of a lifestyle of leisure, culturally determined and under constant negotiation. Such lifestyle was in principle open to all who could afford it, and relied primarily on possession of property, and especially agricultural land. It is misleading, therefore, to treat the Athenian 'notables' as an aristocracy, since their good birth, despite providing some privileges, was not enough to achieve public recognition and esteem; the latter, as Duplouy (2015), 59, stated, were achievable only by a continuous investment in elite 'forms of behaviour which required a great deal of time, money and energy'. More recently, Filser (2017), 7–32, noted the lack of any 'aristocratic' elites in socioeconomical categories in early Athens, and emphasized the social importance of wealth in the form of landed property. On the use, or misuse, of the term 'aristocracy' in studying the ancient world, see also pp. 182–3 n. 11 above.

20 I follow here the estimate of Van Wees (2006a), 366. Blok (2006), 222, gives a similar figure of 25 per cent for the 'most prominent members of Athenian society' buried in the Kerameikos. Morris (1987), 94, suggested that the *agathoi* 'were quite a wide group', varying 'between 25% and 50% of the adult population' for the period from the eleventh to fifth centuries BC, although he added that 'actual proportions must have fluctuated considerably through time'. See also Filser (2017), 7–32.

21 See Richter (1961), 1; Morris (1987); Bintliff (2006), 325–7; Blok (2006), 222.

22 Foxhall (1997), 127, who drew her data from Lohmann (1985); (1992), concluded that 'between the eighth and sixth centuries settlement sizes gradually increased along with the general level of material prosperity, but were not yet at the high level attained in the fifth to fourth centuries' (p. 123). Foxhall, however, stressed the difficulties for multi-period survey studies of Attica, which remain relatively few.

23 For an overview of archaeological survey studies of other Archaic *poleis*, see Foxhall (2013).

24 Whitehead (1986), 8.

25 See Singor (2000), 109. Aristotle ([*Ath. Pol.*] 3.2) provides our only information about the office, stating that it was established 'because some of the Kings proved cowardly in warfare (which was the reason why the Athenians had summoned Ion to their aid in an emergency)'. For more on the *polemarchos*, see Rhodes (1981), 264–5.
26 Andrewes (1982a), 366; Siewert (1982), 154–5.
27 For more on Cylon's attempt at tyranny, see Andrewes (1982a), 368–70; Frost (1984), 286–7; Lavelle (2005), 36–41; van Wees (2013b), 49–52.
28 The Alcmaeonids' guilt is also suggested by Plutarch (*Sol.* 12) who states that the man behind the murder of Cylon's party was the archon Megacles, the head of the Alcmaeonid family. Plutarch's source for the story was also most likely followed by Aristotle in his account of the events in [*Ath. Pol.*] 1, of which only a few final lines survive.
29 Andrewes (1982a), 369–70.
30 Van Wees (2013b), 49–51.
31 Herodotus' assurance that the Alcmaeonids were wrongly blamed for the murders, which implies that they were *not* among 'the presidents of the naucraries', follows his general sympathy for the family, which he displays on numerous occasions throughout his work. For more on Herodotus and his Alcmaeonid bias, see Lavelle (2005), 9–11.
32 Van Wees (2013b), 50.
33 Especially if we read Herodotus' 'in those days' (*tote*) not as a general statement, but rather as referring more specifically to the events of Cylon's coup. Such a reading, argued Lambert (1986), would entail that the archons were away attending the Olympic Games, mentioned in Thucydides' account. Alternatively, as van Wees (2013b), 52, proposed, the supreme position of the *naukraroi* was 'merely Herodotus' best guess, an attempt to make sense of a tradition no longer fully understood'.
34 As argued by van Wees (2013b), 52.
35 For more on the *naukraroi*, see Billigmeier and Dusing (1981); Andrewes (1982a), 365–6; Gabrielsen (1985); (1994), 19–24; Haas (1985), 39–41; Lambert (1986), 110–12; Manville (1990), 75–6 n. 23; Ostwald (1995), 370–7; Wallinga (2000); Schubert (2008); Figueira (2011); van Wees (2013b), 44–61.
36 First proposed by Solmsen (1898). See also van Wees (2013b), 46–7. *Cf.* Billigmeier and Dusing (1981), who saw the etymological origins of the term in a Bronze Age office of temple officials; and Gabrielsen (1985), 44–9; (1994), 19–24, who stressed that the link between the *naukraroi* and ships appears only in later lexicographers.
37 Also quoted in van Wees (2013b), 48.
38 As argued by Ostwald (1995), 370–7; Wallinga (2000); Figueira (2011); van Wees (2013b), 44–61.
39 Greenhalgh (1973), 76; Wallinga (2000), 139–40.
40 The only possible exception, noted by van Wees (2013b), 162 n. 49, comes from Schol. Ald. on Ar. *Nub.* 37, which states that the *nauklaroi*, the predecessors of

demarchs of Classical Athens, were in charge of mobilizing citizens for the armed procession at the Panathenaic festival, which began sometime in the Archaic period.

41 Furthermore, one could also argue that it points to the insignificance of infantry troops compared to ships and cavalry. The notion of the military supremacy of hoplites has dominated much of our understanding of Greek warfare, but has been rightly questioned in recent scholarship e.g. Konijnendijk (2018), esp. 95–106; (forthcoming).

42 As argued by van Wees (2013b), 53–4.

43 This would certainly apply to any offensive expeditions, such as the wars against Megara, Aegina and Mytilene, and other small-scale raiding. In all such cases the wealthy warriors were likely accompanied by attendants, perhaps not unlike the mounted squires (*hippostrophoi*), popular across all Archaic Greek art (see Greenhalgh (1973), 58–61; Brouwers (2007)). The latter helped with the general day-to-day activities during a campaign; they could have assisted in the fighting (if needed) and, when necessary, facilitated the repatriation of bodies. On the other hand, mass mobilizations for defensive purposes would have involved larger sections of the population, as those unable to afford a full hoplite panoply could have fought as light-armed. The example of Cylon's coup is perhaps the best example of the latter, since Thucydides explicitly states the Athenians 'came in from the country in full force (*pandemei*)', implying that the force consisted of all available men. For more on attendants in Greek warfare, see van Wees (2004), 68–71.

44 The procurement of ships and cavalry, according to Ostwald (1995), 377, could be even seen as 'the earliest intelligible public expense in Athens. To defray it, a 'naukraric fund', raised from forty-eight *naukraries*, headed by one *naukraros* each, was created at some time before the middle of the seventh century to meet these irregular public expenses'.

45 Van Wees (2013b), 53. On early Athenian public expense and taxation, see Ostwald (1995); van Wees (2013b), 83–106.

46 This is the central notion behind van Wees' (2013b) book on early Athenian fiscal history. The existence of a number of other public administrative officials with clear financial functions, including the 'Treasurers' (*tamiai*), the 'Sellers' (*poletai*), and the 'Ham-Collectors' (*kolakretai*), mentioned in Aristotle's ([*Ath. Pol.*] 7.3) account of the Solonian constitution, adds further support to this view.

47 *Cf.* Pritchard (2018), 170, who asserted that Archaic Greeks in general 'did not depend on public finance for waging war'. His study did not, however, discuss the Athenian *naukraroi*.

48 For more on raiding in Homer, see Jackson (1993).

49 A good summary of heroic precedents for financing war is provided by van Wees (2013b), 17–23.

50 For more on the coexistence of private and communal modes of warfare in early Greece, see Raaflaub (1997a), 51–3; Gabrielsen (2007), 250–3.

51 Aegina: Hdt. 5.82–8; Megara: Plut. *Sol.* 12.3; Mytilene: Hdt. 5.95. On the earliest Athenian military ventures, see Andrewes (1982a), 372–5; Frost (1984), 285–90; Manville (1990), 86–7; Lavelle (2005), 34–44.
52 For an overview of Solon's reforms, see Jeffery (1976), 90–4; Andrewes (1982a), 375–91; Smith (1989), 18–22; Manville (1990), 124–56; Foxhall (1997); Ste Croix (2004), 73–128; Blok and Lardinois (2006).
53 For more on the Solonian *tele*, see Foxhall (1997); van Wees (2001); (2006a); Ste Croix (2004), 5–72; Valdés Guia and Gallego (2010).
54 E.g. Mitchell (1997).
55 Furthermore, Aristotle clearly states that a system based on the economic assessment of four classes was already in existence before Solon ([*Ath. Pol.*] 7.3), which implies that social divisions based on measurable wealth were the norm in the seventh century BC; Solon may have simply added new political and civic duties to each property class, without upsetting the general social and economic *status quo*.
56 Foxhall (1997); van Wees (2001); (2006a).
57 Rhodes (1981), 145–6.
58 For short discussions on the military dimension of the *tele* system, see Ste Croix (2004), 19–28; van Wees (2006a), 371–6. *Cf.* Rosivach (2002), 41 n. 21, who argued that the evidence for the military duties of the Solonian classes is too limited and ambiguous; the few mentions of the *thetes* were, according to him, 'most likely used to describe poor working folk, as it is used everywhere else in our ancient sources except in Aristotle's discussion of the Solonic classes and in later authors who draw on his discussion'. His dismissal of the muster-rolls mentioned by Thucydides (6.43), however, requires further explanation and so his argument remains unconvincing. More recently, Pritchard (2018), 39–46, challenged the military dimension of the Solonian *tele* and questioned van Wees' interpretation of the relevant passages from Thucydides. According to him, military service in Classical Athens was compulsory to all citizens, regardless of income class, who voluntarily chose the brand of the armed forces they wanted to serve in. In Archaic Athens, by extension, military service was not compulsory or regulated, which, considering the high administrative organization of the *polis*, I find highly implausible.
59 Other sources include fragments from Antiphon's speech *Against Philinos* and Aristophanes' play *The Banqueters*, both mentioned in Harpocration's *Lexicon* entries under '*thetes* and *thetikon*'. For more, see van Wees (2006a), 371.
60 Since the system of *tele* most likely predated Solon (see n. 55 above), it may be assumed that the lack of any mention of military duties in Aristotle's account, which focuses only on the political duties behind the Solonian *tele*, indicates that service in the citizen army had already been obligatory for the highest property classes. While this is in theory plausible, it seems more likely to me that the military duties were first introduced by Solon, who in later traditions is also credited with a number of

other military-related regulations (discussed below). See also van Wees (2013b), 86, 172 n. 15.
61 See, for instance, Hanson (1995), esp. 111–12; Valdés Guia and Gallego (2010), 265–71.
62 On the military etymology of the *zeugitai* class, see Whitehead (1981).
63 This applies specifically to the Archaic period, during which the *zeugitai* class was too small, as Foxhall (1997), 131, concluded, to provide 'a broadly based military force composed of sturdy yeoman peasants or free farmers'.
64 Van Wees (2013a), 232.
65 For more on Solonian laws, see chapters 7–12 in Blok and Lardinois (2006).
66 For Solon's reform of measures and coinage, see van Wees (2013b), 115–23. For his funerary legislation, see p. 243 n. 78 below.
67 Aesch. 3.175–6; Plut. *Sol.* 31.2; Diog. Laert. 1.7.55.
68 The law is mentioned by Aeschines: 'For Solon, the ancient lawgiver, thought it necessary to apply the same penalties to the coward as to the man who failed to take the field or the man who deserted his post. For there are such things as indictments for cowardice…Therefore the man who fails to take the field, and the coward, and the man who has deserted his post are excluded by the lawgiver from the purified precincts of the Agora, and may not be crowned, nor take part in the sacred rites of the people' (3.175–6). For more on this law and its possible connection to Solon's legislation, see van Wees (2018c).
69 As suggested by Frost (1984), 284. It is worth noting, though, that members of the thetic class were still able to join the citizen militia on a voluntary basis. The majority of them were normally excluded since they could not afford their own arms and armour, but serving as light-armed or manning the fleet provided alternative options. For more on *thetes* in Athenian armies, see van Wees (2006a), 371–6.
70 Ostwald (1995), 376.
71 Ostwald (1995), 376–9; Figueira (2011), 193.
72 Frost (1984), 284–5.
73 Plut. *Sol.* 8–9; Paus. 1.40.5; Polyaen. 1.20.2.
74 The campaign supposedly relied on a force of volunteers and a fleet of fishing-boats, which suggests that service in offensive military expeditions was not compulsory. For more on Solon and Salamis, see Frost (1984), 288–9; Lavelle (2005), 45–6; Pritchard (2010), 8–9; van Wees (2013b), 58–9.
75 For more on the First Sacred War, see Andrewes (1982a), 374–5; Frost (1984), 289–90; Lavelle (2005), 281 n. 58.
76 Alternatively, it could be argued that these developments reflected wider changes brought about with the 'the discovery of the individual' in Archaic funerary art, facilitated especially by the appearance of grave epigrams in the mid-seventh century BC (see p. 223 n. 17 above). Considering that clear military attributes in Attic

funerary monuments, whether in the form of *stelai* depicting warriors (as opposed to athletes or citizens) or epigrams for the dead, cannot be dated prior to Solon's reforms, the possibility of contemporary military changes having an impact on the emergence of new artistic discourses on war remains plausible.

77 The relation between the new developments in Athenian art around 600 BC and the reforms of Solon is briefly discussed by Snodgrass (1980), 145–6; and Osborne (1996a), 224–5. Other major changes in Athens which happen at the same time include, most importantly, the appearance of first public buildings in the Agora, which many scholars regard as the earliest sign of the city becoming a *polis*-state. For more, see Mersch (1997); Houby-Nielsen (2009), 206–10. The notion which holds Solon as key to the establishment of a true Athenian *polis* and early citizenship is presented most strongly by Manville (1990), 124–56.

78 [Demosthenes] 43.62; Cic. *De leg.* 2.59; Plut. *Sol.* 21. On Solon's funerary legislation, see Garland (1989); Toher (1991); Blok (2006).

79 Blok (2006), 199. Other early funerary regulations from Delphi, Gortyn and Ioulis, included measures similar to those introduced in Athens, suggesting that increasing public control over funeral rituals was a wider Greek phenomenon of the Archaic period. For more on the latter, see Garland (1989), 8–15; Toher (1991), 164–6; Blok (2006), 206–10.

80 As Snodgrass (1980), 146, concluded, the striking increase in expenditure on grave monuments following Solon's 'reputed legislation to limit expenditure at funerals, must mean that this kind of commemoration lay outside the scope of his law, and was maybe even stimulated by the wish to compensate for the ban on ostentation of a more ephemeral kind'. Sourvinou-Inwood (1983), 47–8, similarly doubted the supposed 'anti-elite' basis of the legislation, arguing that it was introduced as a response to the changing attitudes towards death pollution and memory-survival. She developed this premise in her later work (1995), arguing that the sudden emergence of inscribed grave monuments in Archaic Greece was 'a manifestation of a nexus of funerary attitudes which involved a greater concern for the survival of one's memory and a more anxious and emotionally intense perception of one's own death, and of the death of the important other' (p. 294). According to her, this phenomenon should be explained primarily in terms of the changing ideological attitudes towards death and eschatology, as socio-political factors, traditionally privileged by scholars, were far less relevant. This theory, however, was strongly challenged by Morris (1989), who convincingly argued that attitudes towards death in Archaic Greece remained largely unchanged.

81 A similar notion has also been put forward by Snodgrass (1980), 146, who saw the sudden appearance of conspicuous grave markers as 'a reaction to the new political situation' in Athens. The latter was, according to him, the result of Solon's efforts to substitute wealth for birth as the main criterion for political power. This interpretation,

as I argued above, has to be doubted as such a rationale is never mentioned by the ancient sources. It seems more likely, in my opinion, that the reaction of the elites was stimulated by the increasing centralization of the Athenian state, which brought a number of everyday practices and institutions, previously exclusively controlled by a select few of the wealthiest Athenians, under closer public control.

82 Hdt. 1.59; Plut. *Sol.* 13, 29; Arist. *Pol.* 1305a23–4. For more on the political unrest in early-sixth-century BC Athens, see Figueira (1984). On *stasis* in Archaic Greece, see van Wees (2008).
83 See Hopper (1961); Holladay (1977); Andrewes (1982b), 393–8; Manville (1990), 160 n. 7; Lavelle (2000); (2005), 67–89, 219–21.
84 Less reliable details concerning episodes from the campaign are also provided in later sources e.g. Aen. Tact. 4.8–12; Frontin. 2.9.9; Justin 2.8.
85 For a detailed study of the final stages of the Megarian conflict, with special emphasis on Peisistratus' involvement, see Lavelle (2005), 30–65.
86 The term used by Herodotus to describe Peisistratus' military leadership is *strategie*, which can imply one of three things: a) that he anachronized an office familiar from Classical times; b) that he referred to a genuine pre-Cleisthenic military office in Archaic Athenian army; or c) that he meant to use a generic term for general army leadership. Of these options, the final is most likely, as Herodotus uses the term *strategie* to describe other, non-Greek military positions (1.162; 5.26; 6.94), as pointed out by Lavelle (2005), 270 n. 133. It seems possible that Peisistratus served in the army as one of the *naukraroi*, assuming overall command over the campaign. It is also conceivable that he was the polemarch for one of the years during the conflict. For a longer discussion with references, see Lavelle (2005), 46–7, 269–70 nos 132–4.
87 Hdt. 1.59–61; [*Ath. Pol.*] 14.1–15.1; Plut. *Sol.* 30.
88 For Herodotus' biases in his account of sixth-century BC Athens, see p. 239 n. 31 above.
89 On the Peisistratid army, see Lavelle (1992); Singor (2000).
90 Singor (2000), 119–23.
91 Ibid., 123–8.
92 Ibid., 129.
93 Such a transformation would have surely left a significant mark in our records, including those concerning the burial and commemoration of the war dead. That it did not indicates that the nature of the citizen militia during the reign of the Peisistratids remained largely unchanged.
94 Hdt. 1.61; [*Ath. Pol.*] 15.2. For a detailed analysis of Peisistratus' force at Pallene, see Lavelle (2005), 139–42.
95 E.g. Frost (1984), 291–2; Rausch (1999), 250–2; Pritchard (2010), 12–13.
96 Polycrates of Samos, for instance, had 'vast numbers' of mercenaries at his disposal (Hdt. 3.45.3). For the link between Archaic tyrants and mercenaries, see Andrewes (1956); Trundle (2004), esp. 28–9.

97 See Ostwald (1969), 141.
98 For more on Thracian peltasts and Scythian archers in Athens, see Vos (1963); Best (1969); Singor (2000), 118. See also p. 214 n. 31 above.
99 Frost (1984), 291, 294. *Cf.* Rausch (1999), 250–1, who conceded that a complete exclusion of all Athenians from military service was unlikely, as some members of the elites (e.g. Kroisos) continued to serve in the Peisistratid army. Pritchard (2010), 12–13, echoed a similar sentiment.
100 Traditions concerning the disarming of the Athenians are certainly not to be believed; the accounts of Thucydides and Aristotle (also Polyaen. 1.21.2), despite bearing close resemblances, credit the stratagem to different people (Hippias in Thucydides; Peisistratus in Aristotle), and the absence of the story from Herodotus makes it even more suspicious. As Dover suggested (quoted in Holladay (1977), 52), the purpose of the story was to exonerate the Athenians who, deprived of their weapons, were not able to resist the tyrants. See also Pritchard (2010), 12–13 n. 62.
101 There is some disagreement about Herodotus' famous statement about Peisistratus' tyranny 'being rooted' with money and mercenaries, which follows his account of Pallene (1.64.1). The latter certainly helped him to win the battle and regain power in Athens, and he may have kept a small number of paid troops for some time after, but there is no reason to assume, as Singor (2000) did, that a large, standing army of mercenaries remained in the employ of the Peisistratids throughout their tyranny. It seems equally unlikely, however, that Peisistratus kept no mercenaries after Pallene, as Lavelle (1992) maintained. He most likely employed some, such as the Thracians and the Scythians, but the citizen army remained largely unaffected.
102 The 525/4 BC archon list was first published by Meritt (1939), with additional fragments added by Bradeen (1963). The archons mentioned on the list include Cleisthenes, son of Megacles, and Miltiades, a member of another noble Athenian family, the Philaids. The presence of the two most prominent families among the archons is a clear indication of the cooperation between the Athenian elites and the Peisistratids.
103 Lavelle (2005), 153, went further and doubted whether the Alcmaeonids were exiled at all. The 'perpetual exile' story related to us by Herodotus, whose bias towards the family is clear throughout his work, was most likely devised 'in order to bolster their image as tyrant haters'. While this is in theory plausible, I believe that a short exile was more likely, considering that the Alcmaeonids played key roles in the Athenian army at Pallene, with some of them possibly serving in their capacity as *naukraroi*.
104 See also Plut. *Sol.* 31.
105 As argued by Manville (1990), 162–3. It is possible that Peisistratus used some of his mercenaries from Pallene in his expedition to Naxos, where according to Herodotus, he put Lygdamis in charge 'by military means', sending him the child-hostages from the Athenian families (1.64). In the longer run, Peisistratus

most likely kept some Thracian peltasts and Scythian archers, who feature prominently in contemporary Athenian art. It is impossible, however, to determine their exact number and we should certainly not assume that they constituted the core of the Athenian military force during the tyranny.

106 That the native Athenian army remained more or less intact is also argued by Andrewes (1982b), 402–3. His claim that 'the army had somehow trained and kept in practice', however, is certainly taking it a step too far. Greek militias did not train for war, as convincingly argued by Konijnendijk (2018), 39–71.

107 For Peisistratus' foreign relations, see Andrewes (1982b), 402–5.

108 Andrewes (1982b), 404–5; Lewis (1988), 298; Manville (1990), 170 n. 48; Pritchard (2010), 9–10.

109 There is some chronological confusion regarding the episode in Herodotus which reflects earlier Athenian operations in the region. For more, see Andrewes (1982b), 403–4; Frost (1984), 287–8.

110 For more, see Frost (1984), 292, who, despite maintaining that no regular mobilization took place in Athens before Cleisthenes' reforms, was forced to admit that, although it is impossible to know 'how this particular force was raised', the Theban 'expedition was probably an official act of the Athenian people because the Plataeans had come as suppliants and begged for protection'. The public character of this venture is perhaps further emphasized by the fact that the Thebans were among the early allies of Peisistratus and did fight at his side at Pallene. See also Lewis (1988), 297–8; Manville (1990), 163 n. 17.

111 Aristotle says that Peisistratus levied a tithe on produce ([*Ath. Pol.*] 16.4), but his use of the word 'tithe' may have a more general meaning of 'levy', as argued by van Wees (2013b), 84, among others. For more on public taxation in Archaic Athens, see p. 240 n. 45 above.

112 See, for instance, Pritchard (2010), 12; van Wees (2013b), 71–2. They were also likely used to finance other big-scale military operations, including the activities in Sigeum and Chersonese, after Stesagoras' death.

113 On early Athenian coinage, see Price and Waggoner (1975); Kroll and Waggoner (1984); Kroll (1981); Andrewes (1982b), 408–9; van der Vin (2000); van Wees (2013b), 124–33.

114 Van Wees (2013b), 63–106.

115 For the inscription and an interpretation of the evidence from Eretria, see van Wees (2010). For more on early Athenian naval organization and warfare, see Gabrielsen (1985), (1994), 19–39; Haas (1985); Scott (2000); Wallinga (2000); Figueira (2011); van Wees (2013b).

116 As Frost (1984), 293, summarized, all the literary tradition 'seems to tell us is that Peisistratids found Attica a land of great estates and left it a land of many small landowners'.

117 Lavelle (2005), 159.
118 One way of achieving fairly quick independence, as Holladay (1977), 50, suggested, would have been to grow olives, a process which would require only the initial public support needed for the growth of trees. A switch from growing cereals to cultivating olives (and/or vines) would have also been more profitable in the long run, giving the Athenian farmers more freedom and perhaps even room to expand.
119 E.g. Lewis (1988), 302. Andrewes (1982b), 406 n. 61, provides some references.
120 As Holladay (1977), 56 n. 30, emphatically asserted, there is 'not a shred of evidence' for any confiscation or redistribution of the lands belonging to the elites, 'and it is difficult to see how all trace of it should have disappeared. Nor is it easy to reconcile such an action with the willingness of aristocrats to cooperate with the regime until the murder of Hipparchus changed their position'.
121 See p. 245 n. 102 above.
122 Foxhall (1997), 122–9; this trend can be also observed in other regions in Greece, as discussed by Foxhall (2013). See also van Wees (2013a), 235–6.
123 Van Wees (2013a), 236.
124 For more on the industrial and cultural dimensions of the Peisistratid tyranny, see Andrewes (1982b), 410–15; Smith (1989), 53–79; Manville (1990), 164–72; Neils (1992); Boersma (2000); Sancisi-Weerdenburg (2000).
125 Smith (1989), 3.
126 On citizenship in Archaic Athens, see Manville (1990); Frost (1994); Dmitriev (2018).
127 Manville (1990), 171.
128 See p. 227 n. 41 above. As noted before, most of the surviving warrior *stelai* come from the 530–500 BC period; e.g. Richter (1961), Nos 65–8. The decreased significance of *kouroi* is demonstrated in Rausch (1999), 207, whose survey of late Archaic funerary monuments revealed that Grabplastik comprised only 10 per cent of the data, compared to the more common grave *stelai* and bases.
129 See p. 246 n. 115 above.
130 This interpretation, briefly hinted at by Greenhalgh (1973), 153–5, follows the one proposed by van Wees (2013a), 236–45.
131 The new recruits consisted most likely of men who joined the property class of the *zeugitai*, who were obliged to serve in the citizen army, but also some members of the lowest thetic class, who became wealthy enough to fight in general levies and occasional foreign campaigns in which they served as volunteers.
132 The lack of public regulations for post-battle processes might be also implied by the absence of collective dedications of captured weapons by the Athenians under the Peisistratids. Such dedications, as we saw in Chapter 4 (p. 116), begin to appear in Panhellenic sanctuaries from the mid-sixth century BC onward, indicating the increased community spirit and institutionalization of public

militias in Greece. According to Schröder (2020), 48–53, Greek *poleis* ruled by tyrants engaged in the practice of 'stadtstaatlichen Waffenweihungen' only after their fall; the first collective dedications by the Athenians followed their victory over the Boeotians and Chalcidians (Athens; p. 232 n. 23 above), the conquest of Lemnos and the battle of Marathon (both Olympia).

133 [*Ath. Pol.*] 19.1; Hdt. 5.55, 62; Thuc. 6.59.
134 Hdt. 5.63; [*Ath. Pol.*] 19.5.
135 Hdt. 5.72–3; [*Ath. Pol.*] 20.
136 E.g. Pritchard (2010), 12–13.
137 As argued by van Wees (2008), 23–4.
138 The revolutionary impact of the general mobilization raised in opposition to Isagoras and Cleomenes is especially stressed by Ober (1993); (1998); (2007), who hailed it as the official start of democracy at Athens. See also van Wees (2008), 24 n. 40.
139 French (1960); van Effenterre (1976); Siewert (1982); Stahl and Walter (2009), 157; Osborne (2018), 88–93; Pritchard (2018), 4–9. *Cf.* Manville (1990), 203–4, who pointed out that Cleisthenes' legislation could not have been fully implemented in time to respond to the military challenges which the Athenians immediately had to face. Rausch (1999), 249–70, recognized the problem of the double victory in 506 BC won by a (supposedly) inexperienced army of citizens and suggested that the Athenians engaged in individual and group military training following the reforms of 508/7 BC. This, he argued, took the form of the *hoplitodromos*, as well as archery, slinging, and phalanx formation training supervised by the mercenaries who served under the Peisistratids. The evidence for such training programmes is, however, highly speculative, undermined further by the fact that Greek (let alone Athenian) militias did not train for war (see p. 246 n. 106 above).
140 On the conscription of hoplites in Classical Athens, see Christ (2001); Crowley (2012), 22–39; Pritchard (2018), 46–52.
141 For more on demes in Attica, see Whitehead (1986), who provided a good overview of their Archaic origins (pp. 3–38), and briefly discussed their supersession of the naucraries, including their role in levying troops.
142 Accordingly, the main purpose of transferring the previous public duties of the *naukraroi* to the demarchs was to separate their administrative and fiscal responsibilities (levying troops and taxes) from the purely military roles that the *naukraroi* played in the army command structure. For more on the division between the administrative, financial and military functions of the citizen army began by Cleisthenes, see van Wees (2013b), 60–1.
143 Rausch (1999), 207.
144 A comprehensive bibliography on the subject is given by Arrington (2015), 51 n. 151.

145 For different scholarly dating of the *post aliquanto* law, see Blok (2006), 240–1 n. 167. The less likely association with Cimon ('an act of crypto-philolakonism') was proposed by Stears (2000).
146 Blok (2006), 242.
147 This has been proposed by Arrington (2015), 52, who argued that the delay between the establishment of state burials for the war dead and 'the termination of private grave markers' should be seen as an indication of the 'contested and punctuated development of the new institution' of common public burials.
148 Zinserling (1965); supported by Clairmont (1970), 11–12. According to both of them, Cleisthenes was the originator of the decree, which was nonetheless properly enforced only by Themistocles in connection with the 'Demokratisierungsmassnahmen' of 487 BC. While the introduction of a sumptuary decree concerning funerary monuments in the 480s BC seems to me beyond question, its association with Cleisthenes is less plausible. Considering the immediate effect of the latter's measures to change the treatment of the war dead, one would expect that any similar reforms to private burials in citizen cemeteries would have been enacted with similar efficiency. That they were not suggests that no such regulations were imposed by Cleisthenes. The new treatment of the war dead already broke with an age-old tradition and must have had a significant effect on the wealthy Athenians; adding further sumptuary measures for private burials *at the same time*, seems hardly likely.
149 This is not to suggest, however, that the main developments of the period were solely due to the actions of Solon, Peisistratus and Cleisthenes – which is a popular and all too simplistic understanding of the Archaic period at Athens. The significance of trading, cultural exchange and openness to new ideas was perhaps even more important to the developments of the era, as Houby-Nielsen (2009), 208–10, rightly observed.

Bibliography

Acerbo, S. 2019. *Le tradizioni mitiche nella Biblioteca dello Ps. Apollodoro: percorsi nella mitografia di età imperiale*, Amsterdam.
Adcock, F. E. 1957. *The Greek and Macedonian Art of War*, Berkeley.
Adkins, A. W. H. 1971. 'Homeric Values and Homeric Society', *JHS* 91, pp. 1–14.
Adkins, A. W. H. 1972. 'Homeric Gods and the Values of Homeric Society', *JHS* 92, pp. 1–19.
Adkins, A. W. H. 1997. 'Homeric Ethics', in *A New Companion to Homer*, I. Morris and B. P. Powell, eds, Leiden, pp. 694–713.
Ahlberg, G. 1971a. *Fighting on Land and Sea in Greek Geometric Art*, Stockholm.
Ahlberg, G. 1971b. *Prothesis and Ekphora in Greek Geometric Art*, Göteborg.
Ahlberg-Cornell, G. 1992. *Myth and Epos in Early Greek Art: Representation and Interpretation*, Jonsered.
Ahrensdorf, P. J. 2014. *Homer on the Gods and Human Virtue: Creating the Foundations of Classical Civilization*, Cambridge.
Allan, W. 2001. *Euripides: The Children of Heracles – with an introduction, translation and commentary*, Warminster.
Anderson, G. 2003. *The Athenian Experiment: Building an Imagined Political Community in Ancient Attica, 508 – 490 B.C.*, Ann Arbor.
Andreev, J. V. 1979. 'Könige und Königsherrschaft in den Epen Homers', *Klio* 61, pp. 361–84.
Andreev, J. V. 1988. 'Die homerische Gesellschaft', *Klio* 70, pp. 5–85.
Andrewes, A. 1956. *The Greek Tyrants*, London.
Andrewes, A. 1974. 'The Arginousai Trial', *Phoenix* 26 (1), pp. 112–22.
Andrewes, A. 1982a. 'The Growth of the Athenian State', in *CAH Vol. 3: Part 3*, J. Boardman and N. G. L. Hammond, eds, Cambridge, pp. 360–91.
Andrewes, A. 1982b. 'The Tyranny of Pisistratus', in *CAH Vol. 3: Part 3*, J. Boardman and N. G. L. Hammond, eds, Cambridge, pp. 392–416.
Arrington, N. T. 2015. *Ashes, Images, and Memories: The Presence of the War Dead in Fifth-Century Athens*, Oxford.
Baitinger, H. 2001. *Die Angriffswaffen von Olympia (Olympische Forschungen 29)*, Berlin.
Baitinger, H. 2011. *Waffenweihungen in griechischen Heiligtümern*, Mainz.
Bassett, S. E. 1933. 'Achilles' Treatment of Hector's Body', *TAPA* 64, pp. 41–65.
Bassett, S. E. 1938. *The Poetry of Homer*, Berkeley.
Bažant, J. 1985. *Les citoyens sur les vases athéniens du 6e au 4e siècle av. J.- C.*, Prague.

Beard, M. 1991. 'Adopting an Approach: II', in *Looking at Greek Vases*, T. Rasmussen and N. Spivey, eds, Cambridge, pp. 12–36.

Beazley, J. D. 1947. 'The Rosi Krater', *JHS* 67, pp. 1–9.

Best, J. G. P. 1969. *Thracian Peltasts and Their Influence on Greek Warfare*, Groningen.

Billigmeier, J.-C. and Dusing A. S. 1981. 'The Origin and Function of the *Naukraroi* at Athens: An Etymological and Historical Explanation', *TAPA* 111, pp. 11–16.

Bintliff, J. 2006. 'Solon's Reforms: An Archaeological Perspective', in *Solon of Athens: New Historical and Philological Approaches*, J. H. Blok and A. P. M. H. Lardinois, eds, Leiden, pp. 321–33.

Blok, J. H. 2006. 'Solon's Funerary Laws: Questions of Authenticity and Function', in *Solon of Athens: New Historical and Philological Approaches*, J. H. Blok and A. P. M. H. Lardinois, eds, Leiden, pp. 197–247.

Blok, J. H. and Lardinois, A. P. M. H., eds, 2006. *Solon of Athens: New Historical and Philological Approaches*, Leiden.

Boardman, J. 1974. *Athenian Black Figure Vases: A Handbook*, London.

Boardman, J. 1975. *Athenian Red Figure Vases: The Archaic Period. A Handbook*, London.

Boardman, J. 1983. 'Symbol and Story in Greek Geometric Art', in *Ancient Greek Art and Iconography*, W. G. Moon, ed., Madison, pp. 15–36.

Boardman, J. 1991. 'The Sixth-Century Potters and Painters of Athens and their Public', in *Looking at Greek Vases*, T. Rasmussen and N. Spivey, eds, Cambridge, pp. 79–102.

Boedeker, D. 1993. 'Hero Cult and Politics in Herodotus: The Bones of Orestes', in *Cultural Poetics in Archaic Greece*, C. Dougherty and L. Kurke, eds, Cambridge, pp. 164–77.

Boersma, J. 2000. 'Peisistratos' Building Activity Reconsidered', in *Peisistratos and the Tyranny: A Reappraisal of the Evidence*, H. Sancisi-Weerdenburg, ed., Amsterdam, pp. 49–56.

Borg, B. E. 2010. 'Epigrams in Archaic Art: The 'Chest of Kypselos'', in *Archaic and Classical Greek Epigram*, M. Baumbach, A. Petrovic and I. Petrovic, eds, Cambridge, pp. 81–99.

Bowden, H. 1993. 'Hoplites and Homer: Warfare, Hero Cult, and the Ideology of the Polis', in *War and Society in the Greek World*, J. Rich and G. Shipley, eds, London, pp. 45–63.

Bowra, C. M. 1964. *Pindar*, Oxford.

Bradeen, D. W. 1963. 'The Fifth Century Archon List', *Hesp.* 32, pp. 187–208.

Bradeen, D. W. 1967. 'The Athenian Casualty List of 464 BC', *Hesp.* 36, pp. 321–8.

Bradeen, D. W. 1969. 'The Athenian Casualty Lists', *CQ* 19, pp. 145–59.

Bremmer, J. N. 1983. *The Early Greek Concept of the Soul*, Princeton.

Bremmeier, J. N. 1987. 'What is a Greek Myth?', in *Interpretations of Greek Mythology*, J. N. Bremmer, ed., London, pp. 1–9.

Brendel, O. J. 1978. *Etruscan Art*, Harmondsworth.

Brouwers, J. 2007. 'From Horsemen to Hoplites: Some Remarks on Archaic Greek Warfare', *BABesch* 82, pp. 305–19.

Brouwers, J. 2013. *Henchmen of Ares: Warriors and Warfare in Early Greece*, Rotterdam.
Brown, M. K. 2002. *The Narratives of Konon*, Leipzig.
Bruss, J. S. 2010. 'Ecphrasis in Fits and Starts? Down to 300 BC', in *Archaic and Classical Greek Epigram*, M. Baumbach, A. Petrovic and I. Petrovic, eds, Cambridge, pp. 385–403.
Burgess, J. S. 2001. *The Tradition of the Trojan War in Homer and the Epic Cycle*, Baltimore.
Burgess, J. S. 2015. 'Coming Adrift: The Limits of Reconstruction of the Cyclic Poems', in *The Greek Epic Cycle and Its Ancient Reception*, M. Fantuzzi and C. Tsagalis, eds, Cambridge, pp. 43–58.
Burian, P. 1977. 'Euripides' Heraclidae: An Interpretation', *CPhil.* 72 (1), pp. 1–21.
Burton, R. W. B. 1962. *Pindar's Pythian Odes: Essays in Interpretation*, Oxford.
Buxton, R. 1994. *Imaginary Greece: The Contexts of Mythology*, Cambridge.
Cairns, D. L. 1993. *Aidōs: The Psychology and Ethics of Honour and Shame in Ancient Greek Literature*, Oxford.
Calame, C. 2007. 'Greek Myth and Greek Religion', in *The Cambridge Companion to Greek Mythology*, R. D. Woodard, ed., Cambridge, pp. 259–85.
Calhoun, G. M. 1934. 'Classes and Masses in Homer. I & II', *CPhil.* 29 (3–4), pp. 192–208, 301–16.
Cameron, H. D. 1971. *Studies on the* Seven Against Thebes *of Aeschylus*, Paris.
Campbell, D. A. 1992. *Greek Lyric IV: Bacchylides, Corinna, and Others*, Cambridge.
Carne-Ross, D. S. 1985. *Pindar*, New Haven.
Carpenter, T. H. 2015. 'The Trojan War in early Greek art', in *The Greek Epic Cycle and Its Ancient Reception*, M. Fantuzzi and C. Tsagalis, eds, Cambridge, pp. 178–95.
Carter, J. 1972. 'The Beginning of Narrative Art in the Greek Geometric Period', *ABSA* 67, pp. 25–58.
Cartledge, P. 1987. *Agesilaos and the Crisis of Sparta*, London.
Cartledge, P. 2002. *The Greeks: A Portrait of Self and Others*, 2nd edition, Oxford.
Cartledge, P. 2012. 'Spartan Ways of Death', in *Salvare le poleis, costruire la concordia, progettare la pace*, S. Cataldi E. Bianco and G. Cuniberti, eds, Alessandria, pp. 21–38.
Cartledge, P. 2013. *After Thermopylae: The Oath of Plataea and the End of the Graeco-Persian Wars*, Oxford.
Caskey, M. E. 1977. 'News Letter from Greece', *AJArch.* 81 (4), pp. 507–22.
Cavanagh, H., Cavanagh, W. and Roy, J. eds, 2010. *Honouring the Dead in the Peloponnese: Proceedings of a Conference held at Sparta 23-25 April 2009*, CSPS Online Publication 2.
Celoria, F. 1992. *The Metamorphoses of Antoninus Liberalis: A Translation with a Commentary*, Abingdon.
Christ, M. 2001. 'Conscription of Hoplites in Classical Athens', *CQ* 51, pp. 398–422.
Christesen, P. 2018. 'The Typology and Topography of Spartan Burials from the Protogeometric to the Hellenistic Period: Rethinking Spartan Exceptionalism and the Ostensible Cessation of Adult Intramural Burials in the Greek World', *BSA* 113, pp. 307–63.

Christou, C. 1964. 'Ο ΝΕΟΣ ΑΜΦΟΡΕΥΣ ΤΗΣ ΣΠΑΡΤΗΣ: ΟΙ ΑΛΛΟΙ ΜΕΤ' ΑΝΑΓΛΥΦΩΝ ΑΜΦΟΡΕΙΣ ΤΟΥ ΛΑΚΩΝΙΚΟΥ ΕΡΓΑΣΤΗΡΙΟΥ', *AD* 19 A, pp. 164–265.

Cingano, E. 1985. 'Clistene di Sicione, Erodoto e i poemi del Ciclo tebano', *QUCC* 20 (2), pp. 31–40.

Cingano, E. 1987. 'Il duello tra Tideo e Melanippo nella *Biblioteca* della Ps.-Apollodoro e nell'altorilievo etrusco di Pyrgi. Un'ipotesi stesicorea', *QUCC* 25 (1), pp. 93–103.

Clairmont, C. W. 1970. *Gravestone and Epigram: Greek Memorials from the Archaic and Classical Period*, Mainz on Rhine.

Clairmont, C. W. 1983. *Patrios Nomos: Public Burial in Athens during the Fifth and Fourth Centuries B.C.: The Archaeological, Epigraphic-Literary, and Historical Evidence*, Oxford.

Clark, M. 2012. *Exploring Greek Myth*, Oxford.

Clarke, M. 1999. *Flesh and Spirit in the Songs of Homer: A Study of Words and Myths*, Oxford.

Collard, C. and Cropp, M. 2008. *Euripides: Fragments (Oedipus-Chrysippus, Other Fragments)*, Cambridge.

Conacher, D. J. 1967. *Euripidean Drama: Myth, Theme and Structure*, Toronto.

Connor, W. R. 1970. 'Theseus in Classical Athens', in *The Quest for Theseus*, A. G. Ward, ed., New York, pp. 143–74.

Connor, W. R. 1988. 'Early Greek Warfare as Symbolic Expression', *P&P* 119, pp. 3–29.

Cook, R. M. 1959. 'Die Bedeutung der bemalten Keramik für den griechischen Handel', *Jahrbuch des deutschen archäologischen Instituts* 74, pp. 114–23.

Crowley, J. 2012. *The Psychology of the Athenian Hoplite: The Culture of Combat in Classical Athens*, Cambridge.

Culasso Gastaldi, E. 2010. 'Lemnos e il V secolo', *ASAA* 88, pp. 135–47.

Currie, B. 2005. *Pindar and the Cult of Heroes*, Oxford.

Currie, B. 2006. 'Homer and the Early Epic Tradition', in *Epic Interactions: Perspectives on Homer, Virgil, and the Epic Tradition Presented to Jasper Griffin by Former Pupils*, M. J. Clarke, B. G. F. Currie and R. O. A. M. Lyne, eds, Oxford, pp. 1–46.

D'Acunto, M. 2013. *Il mondo del vaso Chigi: Pittura, guerra e società a Corinto alla metà del VII secolo a.C.*, Berlin.

D'Onofrio, A. M. 1997. 'The 7th Century BC in Attica: The Basis of Political Organization', in *Urbanization in the Mediterranean in the 9th to 6th Centuries BC*, H. Damgard Andersen et al., eds, Copenhagen, pp. 63–88.

Dalby, A. 1995. 'The *Iliad*, the *Odyssey* and Their Audiences', *CQ* 45 (2), pp. 269–79.

Davies, M. 2001. *The Greek Epic Cycle*, London.

Davison, J. A. 1965. 'Thucydides, Homer and the "Achaean Wall"', *GRBS* 6, pp. 5–28.

Dawson, C. M. 1970. *The Seven Against Thebes by Aeschylus*, Englewood Cliffs.

Day, J. W. 1989. 'Rituals in Stone: Early Greek Grave Epigrams and Monuments', *JHS* 109, pp. 16–28.

Dayton, J. C. 2006. *The Athletes of War: An Evaluation of the Agonistic Elements in Greek Warfare*, Toronto.
Decharme, P. 1906. *Euripides and the Spirit of His Dramas*, London.
Detienne, M. 1986. *The Creation of Mythology*, Chicago.
Diller, A. 1935. 'The Text History of the Bibliotheca of Pseudo-Apollodorus', *TAPA* 66, pp. 296–313.
Dmitriev, S. 2018. *The Birth of the Athenian Community: From Solon to Cleisthenes*, Oxon.
Dodds, E. R. 1951. *The Greeks and the Irrational*, Berkeley and Los Angeles.
Donlan, W. 1979. 'The Structure of Authority in the Iliad', *Arethusa* 12, pp. 51–70.
Donlan, W. 1981. 'Scale, Value and Function in the Homeric Economy', *AJAH* 6, pp. 101–17.
Donlan, W. 1989a. 'Homeric *Temenos* and Land Tenure in Dark Age Greece', *MH* 46, pp. 129–45.
Donlan, W. 1989b. 'The pre-state community in Greece', *Symb. Osl.* 64, pp. 5–29.
Donlan, W. 1991. *The Aristocratic Ideal and Selected Papers*, Wauconda.
Donlan, W. 1994. 'Chief and Followers in Pre-State Greece', in *From Political Economy to Anthropology: Situating Economic Life in Past Societies*, C. M. Duncan and D. W. Tandy, eds, Montreal, pp. 34–51.
Dowden, K. 2011. 'Telling the Mythology: From Hesiod to the Fifth Century', in *A Companion to Greek Mythology*, K. Dowden and N. Livingstone, eds, Oxford, pp. 47–72.
Duplouy, A. 2003. 'Les Eupatrides, "nobles défenseurs de leur patrie"', *Cahiers du Centre Glotz* 14, pp. 1–22.
Duplouy, A. 2015. 'Genealogical and Dynastic Behaviour in Archaic and Classical Greece: Two Gentilician Strategies', in *'Aristocracy' in Antiquity: Redefining Greek and Roman Elites*, N. Fisher and H. van Wees, eds, Swansea, pp. 59–84.
Echeverría, F. 2012. 'Hoplite and Phalanx in Archaic and Classical Greece: A Reassessment', *CPhil.* 107 (4), pp. 291–318.
Echeverría, F. 2015. 'Heroic Fiction, Combat Scenes, and the Scholarly Reconstruction of Archaic Greek Warfare', *BICS* 58 (1), pp. 33–60.
Elmer, D. F. 2013. *The Poetics of Consent: Collective Decision Making and the Iliad*, Baltimore.
Fantuzzi, M. 2015. 'The Aesthetics of Sequentiality and its Discontents', in *The Greek Epic Cycle and Its Ancient Reception*, M. Fantuzzi and C. Tsagalis, eds, Cambridge, pp. 405–29.
Fantuzzi, M. and Tsagalis, C., eds, 2015a. *The Greek Epic Cycle and Its Ancient Reception*, Cambridge.
Fantuzzi, M. and Tsagalis, C. 2015b. 'Introduction: *Kyklos*, the Epic Cycle and Cyclic poetry', in *The Greek Epic Cycle and Its Ancient Reception*, M. Fantuzzi and C. Tsagalis, eds, Cambridge, pp. 1–40.
Farnell, L. R. 1915. 'Pindar, Athens and Thebes: *Pyth*. IX. 151–170', *CQ* 9, pp. 193–200.

Farnell, L. R. 1921. *Greek Hero Cults and Ideas of Immortality*, Oxford.
Fenik, B. 1968. *Typical Battle Scenes in the Iliad: Studies in the Narrative Techniques of Homeric Battle Descriptions*, Wiesbaden.
Ferrari, G. 2003. 'Myth and Genre on Athenian Vases', *Cl. Ant.* 22, pp. 37–54.
Figueira, T. J. 1984. 'The Ten *archontes* of 579/8 at Athens', *Hesp.* 53, pp. 447–73.
Figueira, T. J. 2011. 'The Athenian *naukraroi* and Archaic Naval Warfare', *Cadmo* 21, pp. 183–210.
Filser, W. 2017. *Die Elite Athens auf der attischen Luxuskeramik*, Berlin.
Finkelberg, M. 2015. 'Meta-Cyclic Epic and Homeric Poetry', in *The Greek Epic Cycle and Its Ancient Reception*, M. Fantuzzi and C. Tsagalis, eds, Cambridge, pp. 126–38.
Finley, M. I. 1991. *The World of Odysseus*, 2nd edition, London.
Fittschen, K. 1969. *Untersuchungen zum Beginn der Sagendarstellungen bei den Griechen*, Berlin.
Förtsch, R. 2001. *Kunstverwendung und Kunstlegitimation im archaischen und frühklassischen Sparta*, Mainz.
Foley, J. M. and Arft, J. 2015. 'The Epic Cycle and oral tradition', in *The Greek Epic Cycle and Its Ancient Reception*, M. Fantuzzi and C. Tsagalis, eds, Cambridge, pp. 78–95.
Fowler, R. L. 1999. 'The Authors Named Pherecydes', *Mnemos.* 52 (1), pp. 1–15.
Fowler, R. L. 2000. *Early Greek Mythography Volume I: Text and Introduction*, Oxford.
Fowler, R. L. 2013. *Early Greek Mythography Volume II: Commentary*, Oxford.
Foxhall, L. 1997. 'A View from the Top: Evaluating the Solonian Property Classes', in *The Development of the* polis *in Archaic Greece*, L. G. Mitchell and P. J. Rhodes, eds, London, pp. 113–36.
Foxhall, L. 2013. 'Can We See the "Hoplite Revolution" on the Ground? Archaeological Landscapes, Material Culture, and Social Status in Early Greece', in *Men of Bronze: Hoplite Warfare in Ancient Greece*, D. Kagan and G. F. Viggiano, eds, Princeton, pp. 194–221.
Fraenkel, E. 1950. *Aeschylus Agamemnon II: Commentary on 1–1055*, Oxford.
French, A. 1960. 'A Note on Thucydides iii 68.5', *JHS* 80, p. 191.
Frost, F. J. 1984. 'The Athenian Military before Cleisthenes', *Hist.* 33 (3), pp. 283–94.
Frost, F. J. 1994. 'Aspects of early Athenian citizenship', in *Athenian Identity and Civic Ideology*, A. L. Boegehold and A. C. Scafuro, eds, Baltimore, pp. 45–56.
Gabrielsen, V. 1985. 'The *naukrariai* and the Athenian Navy', *C&M* 36, pp. 21–51.
Gabrielsen, V. 1994. *Financing the Athenian Fleet*, Baltimore.
Gabrielsen, V. 2007. 'Warfare and the State', in *The Cambridge History of Greek and Roman Warfare: Volume I*, P. Sabin, H. van Wees and M. Whitby, eds, Cambridge, pp. 248–72.
Gantz, T. 1993. *Early Greek Myth: A Guide to Literary and Artistic Sources*, Baltimore.
Garlan, Y. 1975. *War in the Ancient World: A Social History*, New York.
Garland, R. 1982. '*Geras Thanonton*: An Investigation into the Claims of the Homeric Dead', *BICS* 29, pp. 69–80.

Garland, R. 1989. 'The Well-Ordered Corpse: An Investigation into the Motives behind Greek Funerary Legislation', *BICS* 36, pp. 1–15.

Garland, R. 2001. *The Greek Way of Death*, 2nd edition, Ithaca.

Geddes, A. G. 1984. 'Who's Who in Homeric Society?', *CQ* 34 (1), pp. 17–36.

Gill, D. 1980. 'Aspects of Religious Morality in Early Greek Epic', *Harv. Theol. Rev.* 73 (3/4), pp. 373–418.

Gomme, A. W. 1962. *An Historical Commentary on Thucydides, Vol. 2*, Oxford.

Graf, F. 1993. *Greek Mythology: An Introduction*, Baltimore.

Greenhalgh, P. A. L. 1972. 'Patriotism in the Homeric World', *Hist.* 21, pp. 528–37.

Greenhalgh, P. A. L. 1973. *Early Greek Warfare: Horsemen and Chariots in the Homeric and Archaic Ages*, Cambridge.

Griffin, J. 1977. 'The Epic Cycle and the Uniqueness of Homer', *JHS* 97, pp. 39–53.

Griffin, J. 1980. *Homer on Life and Death*, Oxford.

Griffiths, A. 2011. 'Myth in History', in *A Companion to Greek Mythology*, K. Dowden and N. Livingstone, eds, Oxford, pp. 195–207.

Grube, G. M. A. 1973. *The Drama of Euripides*, London.

Haas, C. J. 1985. 'Athenian Naval Power before Themistocles', *Hist.* 34, pp. 29–46.

Hall, E. 1989. *Inventing the Barbarian: Greek Self-Definition through Tragedy*, Oxford.

Hall, J. M. 2007. 'Politics and Greek Myth', in *The Cambridge Companion to Greek Mythology*, R. D. Woodard, ed., Cambridge, pp. 331–54.

Halm-Tisserant, M. 1993. 'Iconographie et statut du cadaver', *Ktema* 18, pp. 215–26.

Halverson, J. 1985. 'Social Order in the *Odyssey*', *Hermes* 113, pp. 129–45.

Hannah, P. 2010. 'The Warrior *loutrophoroi* of Fifth-Century Athens', in *War, Democracy and Culture in Classical Athens*, D. M. Pritchard, ed., Cambridge, pp. 266–301.

Hannestad, L. 1988. 'Athenian Pottery in Etruria c. 550–470 BC', *Acta Archaeologica* 59, pp. 113–30.

Hannestad, L. 1991. 'Athenian pottery in Italy c. 550–470 BC: Beazley and quantitative studies', *Cronache di Archeologia e di Storia dell'Arte* 30, pp. 211–16.

Hannestad, L. 2001. 'War and Greek Art', in *War as a Cultural and Social Force*, T. Bekker-Nielsen and L. Hannestad, eds, Copenhagen, pp. 110–19.

Hanson, V. D. 1989. *The Western Way of War: Infantry Battle in Classical Greece*, Berkeley.

Hanson, V. D. 1995. *The Other Greeks: The Family Farm and the Agrarian Roots of Western Civilization*, New York.

Hanson, V. D. 2013. 'The Hoplite Narrative', in *Men of Bronze: Hoplite Warfare in Ancient Greece*, D. Kagan and G. F. Viggiano, eds, Princeton, pp. 256–75.

Harrison, E. B. 1972. 'The South Frieze of the Nike Temple and the Marathon Painting in the Painted Stoa', *AJArch.* 76, pp. 353–78.

Harrison, E. B. 1997. 'The Glories of the Athenians: Observations on the Program of the Frieze of the Temple of Athena Nike', in *Interpretation of Architectural Sculpture in Greece and Rome*, D. Buitron-Oliver, ed., Washington, pp. 109–25.

Harrison, T. ed. 2002. *Greeks and Barbarians*, New York.

Hartog, F. 1988. *The Mirror of Herodotus: The Representation of the Other in the Writing of History*, Berkeley and Los Angeles.
Haubold, J. 2000. *Homer's People: Epic Poetry and Social Formation*, Cambridge.
Hauvette, A. 1898. 'Les Eleusinies d'Eschyle', in *Mélanges Henri Weil*, Paris, pp. 159–78.
Heath, M. 1989. *Unity in Greek Poetics*, Oxford.
Henderson, J. 1993. 'Form Remade / Statius' Thebaid', in *Roman Epic*, A. J. Boyle, ed., London, pp. 162–91.
Herman, G. 2006. *Morality and Behaviour in Democratic Athens: A Social History*, Cambridge.
Hershkowitz, D. 1995. 'Patterns of Madness in Statius' Thebaid', *JRS* 85, pp. 52–64.
Higbie, C. 2007. 'Hellenistic Mythographers', in *The Cambridge Companion to Greek Mythology*, R. D. Woodard, ed., Cambridge, pp. 237–54.
Hillgruber, M. 1990. 'Zur Zeitbestimmung der Chrestomathie des Proklos', *Rh. Mus.* 3/4, pp. 397–404.
Hodkinson, S. 2000. *Property and Wealth in Classical Sparta*, Swansea.
Hölscher, T. 2003. 'Images of War in Greece and Rome: Between Military Practice, Public Memory, and Cultural Symbolism', *JRS* 93, pp. 1–17.
Holladay, J. 1977. 'The Followers of Peisistratus', *G&R* 24 (1), pp. 40–56.
Hopper, R. J. 1961. '"Plain", "Shore", and "Hill" in Early Athens', *BSA* 56, pp. 189–219.
Houby-Nielsen, S. 1992. 'Interaction between Chieftains and Citizens?', *Acta Hyperborea* 4, pp. 343–74.
Houby-Nielsen, S. 1995. 'Burial language in Archaic and Classical Kerameikos', *Proceedings of the Danish Institute* 1, pp. 129–91.
Houby-Nielsen, S. 2000. 'Child Burials in Athens', in *Children and Material Culture*, J. Sofaer Derevenski, ed., London, pp. 151–66.
Houby-Nielsen, S. 2009. 'Attica: A View from the Sea', in *A Companion to Archaic Greece*, K. A. Raaflaub and H. van Wees, eds, Malden, pp. 189–211.
Hubbard, T. K. 1992. 'Remaking Myth and Rewriting History: Cult Tradition in Pindar's Ninth Nemean', *Harv. Stud.* 94, pp. 77–111.
Hughes, D. D. 2000. *Human Sacrifice in Ancient Greece*, London.
Humphreys, S. C. 1980. 'Family Tombs and Tomb Cult in Ancient Athens: Tradition or Traditionalism?', *JHS* 100, pp. 96–126.
Humphreys, S. C. 1990. Review of I. Morris 1987, *Helios* 17, pp. 263–8.
Hurwit, J. M. 2007. 'The Problem with Dexileos: Heroic and other Nudities in Greek Art', *AJArch.* 111, pp. 35–60.
Hutchinson, G. O. 1985. *Aeschylus* Septem Contra Thebas, Oxford.
Huxley, G. 1973. 'The Date of Pherekydes of Athens', *GRBS* 15, pp. 127–43.
Huxley, G. 1975. *Pindar's Vision of the Past*, Belfast.
Jackson, A. H. 1991. 'Hoplites and the Gods: The Dedication of Captured Arms and Armour', in *Hoplites: The Classical Greek Battle Experience*, V. D. Hanson, ed., London, pp. 228–49.
Jackson, A. H. 1993. 'War and Raids for Booty in the World of Odysseus', in *War and Society in the Greek World*, J. Rich and G. Shipley, eds, London, pp. 64–76.

Jackson, A. H. 2000. 'Argos' Victory over Corinth: ΑΡΓΕΙΟΙ ΑΝΕΘΕΝ ΤΟΙ ΔΙϜΙ ΤΟΝ ΦΟΡΙΝΘΟΘΕΝ', *ZPE* 132, pp. 295–311.
Jacoby, F. 1944. 'Patrios Nomos: State Burial in Athens and the Public Cemetery in the Kerameikos', *JHS* 64, pp. 37–66.
Jacoby, F. 1947. 'The First Athenian Prose Writer', *Mnemos.* 13 (1), pp. 13–64.
Jebb, R. C. 2004. *Sophocles: Plays – Philoctetes*, London.
Jeffery, L. H. 1961. *The Local Scripts of Archaic Greece: A Study of the Origin of the Greek Alphabet and its Development from the Eighth to the Fifth Centuries B.C.*, Oxford.
Jeffery, L. H. 1962. 'The Inscribed Gravestones of Archaic Attica', *BSA* 57, pp. 115–53.
Jeffery, L. H. 1976. *Archaic Greece: The City-States c. 700–500 B.C.*, London.
Johansen, K. F. 1923. *Les vases sicyoniens*, Paris and Copenhagen.
Johnston, S. I. 1999. *Restless Dead: Encounters Between the Living and the Dead in Ancient Greece*, Berkeley.
Kagan, D. and Viggiano, G. F. 2013. 'The Hoplite Debate', in *Men of Bronze: Hoplite Warfare in Ancient Greece*, D. Kagan and G. F. Viggiano, eds, Princeton, pp. 1–56.
Kahil, L. 1994. 'Oinone', *LIMC* VII (1), pp. 23–26.
Kakridis, J. T. 1949. *Homeric Researches*, Lund.
Kelly, A. 2015. 'Ilias parva', in *The Greek Epic Cycle and Its Ancient Reception*, M. Fantuzzi and C. Tsagalis, eds, Cambridge, pp. 319–43.
King, K. C. 1980. 'The Force of Tradition: The Achilles Ode in Euripides' *Electra*', *TAPA* 110, pp. 195–212.
King, K. C. 1985. 'The Politics of Imitation: Euripides' *Hekabe* and the Homeric Achilles', *Arethusa* 18, pp. 47–66.
King, K. C. 1987. *Achilles: Paradigms of the War Hero from Homer to the Middle Ages*, Berkeley.
Kirk, G. S. 1962. *The Songs of Homer*, Cambridge.
Kirk, G. S. 1990. *The Iliad: A Commentary II*, Cambridge.
Kissas, K. 2000. *Die attischen Statuen- und Stelenbasen archaischer Zeit*, Bonn.
Kokkorou-Alevras, G. 2010. 'Funerary Statuary of the Archaic Period in the Peloponnese', in *Honouring the Dead in the Peloponnese: Proceedings of a Conference held at Sparta 23–25 April 2009*, H. Cavanagh, W. Cavanagh and J. Roy, eds, CSPS Online Publication 2, pp. 269–88.
Konijnendijk, R. 2018. *Classical Greek Tactics: A Cultural History*, Leiden.
Konijnendijk, R. forthcoming. 'Worthless Hoplites: Cavalry and the Character of Classical Warfare', in *Beyond the Phalanx: Greek Warfare and the Mediterranean*, R. Konijnendijk, C. Kucewicz and M. Lloyd, eds.
Konstan, D. 2007. 'War and Reconciliation in Greek Literature', in *War and Peace in the Ancient World*, K. A. Raaflaub, ed., Oxford, pp. 191–205.
Kovacs, D. 1995. *Euripides: Children of Heracles, Hippolytus, Andromache, Hecuba*, Cambridge.
Krauskopf, I. 1984. 'Athanasia', *LIMC* II (1), pp. 953–5.
Krentz, P. 1985. 'Casualties in hoplite battles', *GRBS* 26, pp. 13–20.

Krentz, P. 2002. 'Fighting by the Rules: The Invention of the Hoplite Agôn', *Hesp.* 71 (1), pp. 23–39.

Krentz, P. 2007a. 'War', in *The Cambridge History of Greek and Roman Warfare* I, P. Sabin, H. van Wees and M. Whitby, eds, Cambridge, pp. 147–85.

Krentz, P. 2007b. 'Warfare and Hoplites', in *The Cambridge Companion to Archaic Greece*, H. A. Shapiro, ed., Cambridge, pp. 61–84.

Krentz, P. 2007c. 'The Oath of Marathon, not Plataea', *Hesp.* 76, pp. 731–42.

Krentz, P. 2010. *The Battle of Marathon*, New Haven.

Kroll, J. H. 1981. 'From Wappenmünzen to Gorgoneia to Owls', *American Numismatic Society Museum Notes* 26, pp. 1–32.

Kroll, J. H. and Waggoner, N. M. 1984. 'Dating the Earliest Coins of Athens, Corinth and Aegina', *AJArch.* 88 (3), pp. 325–40.

Kucewicz, C. 2012. 'Age of 'Heroes'? The Rules of War in Archaic Greece', *Ancient Warfare* 6 (1), pp. 14–19.

Kucewicz, C. 2016. 'Mutilation of the Dead and the Homeric Gods', *CQ* 66 (2), pp. 425–36.

Kucewicz, C. forthcoming A. 'Kings, Tyrants and Bandy-Legged Men: Generalship in Archaic Greece', in *Military Leadership from Ancient Greece to Byzantium: The Art of Generalship*, R. Evans and S. Tougher, eds, Edinburgh.

Kucewicz, C. forthcoming B. '"Either This or Upon This"': The War Dead in Archaic Sparta', in *Beyond the Phalanx: Greek Warfare and the Mediterranean*, R. Konijnendijk, C. Kucewicz and M. Lloyd, eds.

Kullmann, W. 2015. 'Motif and Source Research: Neoanalysis, Homer, and Cyclic Epic', in *The Greek Epic Cycle and Its Ancient Reception*, M. Fantuzzi and C. Tsagalis, eds, Cambridge, pp. 108–25.

Kunze, E. 1950. *Archaische Schildbänder (Olympische Forschungen*, Bd. 2), Berlin.

Kunze, E. 1958. *6. Bericht über die Ausgrabungen in Olympia*, Berlin.

Kunze, E. 1961. *7. Bericht über die Ausgrabungen in Olympia*, Berlin.

Kunze, E. 1967. *8. Bericht über die Ausgrabungen in Olympia*, Berlin.

Kurtz, D. C. 1984. 'Vases for the Dead, an Attic Selection, 750–400 BC', in *Ancient Greek and Related Pottery: Proceedings of the International Vase Symposium in Amsterdam, 12–15 April 1984*, H. A. G. Brijder, ed., Amsterdam, pp. 314–28.

Kurtz, D. C. and Boardman, J. 1971. *Greek Burial Customs*, Ithaca.

Lambert, S. D. 1986. 'Herodotus, the Cylonian Conspiracy and the ΠΡΥΤΑΝΙΕΣ ΤΩΝ ΝΑΥΚΡΑΡΩΝ', *Hist.* 35 (1), pp. 105–12.

Langdon, S. 2008. *Art and Identity in Dark Age Greece, 1100– 700 B.C.E.*, Cambridge.

Latacz, J. 1977. *Kampfparänese, Kampfdarstellung und Kampfwirklichkeit in der Ilias, bei Kallinos und Tyrtaios*, Munich.

Lateiner, D. 1977. 'Heralds and Corpses in Thucydides', *CW* 71 (2), pp. 97–106.

Lavelle, B. M. 1992. 'Herodotos, Skythian archers and the *doryphoroi* of the Peisistratids', *Klio* 74, pp. 78–97.

Lavelle, B. M. 2000. 'Herodotos and the "Parties" of Attika', *C&M* 51, pp. 51–102.

Lavelle, B. M. 2005. *Fame, Money, and Power: The rise of Peisistratos and "Democratic" Tyranny at Athens*, Ann Arbor.
Leaf, W. 1900. *The Iliad I: Books I–XII*, New York.
Leahy, D. M. 1955. 'The Bones of Tisamenus', *Hist.* 4 (1), pp. 26–38.
Lefkowitz, M. R. 2003. '"Impiety" and "Atheism" in Euripides' Dramas', in *Oxford Readings in Classical Studies: Euripides*, J. Mossman, ed., Oxford, pp. 102–21.
Lendon, J. E. 2000. 'Homeric Vengeance and the Outbreak of Greek Wars', in *War and Violence in Ancient Greece*, H. van Wees, ed., Swansea, pp. 1–30.
Lendon, J. E. 2005. *Soldiers & Ghosts: A History of Battle in Classical Antiquity*, New Haven.
Levi, P. 1985. *The Pelican History of Greek Literature*, Harmondsworth.
Lewis, D. M. 1988. 'The Tyranny of the Pisistratidae', in *CAH Vol. 4*, J. Boardman et al., eds, Cambridge, pp. 287–302.
Lightfoot, J. L. 1999. *Parthenius of Nicaea: The Poetical Fragments and the Erotika Pathemata*, Oxford.
Lissarrague, F. 1989. 'The World of the Warrior', in *A City of Images: Iconography and Society in Ancient Greece*, C. Bérard et al., eds, Princeton, pp. 39–52.
Lissarrague, F. 1990. *L'autre Guerrier: archers, peltastes, cavaliers dans l'imagerie attique*, Paris.
Lloyd, M. 2017. 'Unorthodox Warfare? Variety and Change in Archaic Greek Warfare (ca. 700–ca. 480 BCE)', in *Unconventional Warfare from Antiquity to the Present Day*, B. Hughes and F. Robson, eds, Cham, pp. 231–52.
Lloyd, M. forthcoming. 'An Eighth-Century Revolution? Pre-Archaic Greek Warfare in Context', in *Beyond the Phalanx: Greek Warfare and the Mediterranean*, R. Konijnendijk, C. Kucewicz and M. Lloyd, eds.
Lloyd-Jones, H. 1971a. *The Justice of Zeus*, Berkeley.
Lloyd-Jones, H. 1971b. *Aeschylus: Agamemnon, Libation-Bearers, Eumenides, Fragments*, Cambridge.
Lloyd-Jones, H. 1982. Review of D. L. Page 1981, *CR* 32 (2), pp. 139–44.
Lloyd-Jones, H. 1996. *Sophocles: Fragments*, Cambridge.
Lohmann, H. 1985. 'Landleben in klassischen Attika', *Jahrbuch Ruhr-Universität Bochum*, pp. 71–96.
Lohmann, H. 1993. *Atene: Forschungen zu Siedlungs- und Wirtschaftsstruktur des klassischen Attika*, 2 vols, Cologne.
Loraux, N. 2006. *The Invention of Athens: The Funeral Oration in the Classical City*, 2nd edition, New York.
Lord, A. B. 1960. *The Singer of Tales*, 2nd edition, Cambridge.
Lorenz, K. 2010. '"Dialectics at a Standstill": Archaic *kouroi*-Cum-Epigram as *I-Box*', in *Archaic and Classical Greek Epigram*, M. Baumbach, A. Petrovic and I. Petrovic, eds, Cambridge, pp. 131–48.
Lorimer, H. L. 1947. 'The Hoplite Phalanx with Special Reference to the Poems of Archilochus and Tyrtaeus', *BSA* 42, pp. 76–138.

Low, P. 2003. 'Remembering War in Fifth-Century Greece: Ideologies, Societies, and Commemoration beyond Democratic Athens', *World Archaeology* 35 (1), pp. 98–111.

Low, P. 2006. 'Commemorating the Spartan War-Dead', in *Sparta & War*, S. Hodkinson and A. Powell, eds, Swansea, pp. 85–109.

Low, P. 2010. 'Commemoration of the War Dead in Classical Athens: Remembering Defeat and Victory', in *War, Democracy and Culture in Classical Athens*, D. M. Pritchard, ed., Cambridge, pp. 341–58.

Low, P. 2013. 'The Monuments to the War-Dead in Classical Athens: Form, Contexts, Meanings', in *Cultures of Commemoration: War Memorials, Ancient and Modern*, P. Low, G. J. Oliver and P. J. Rhodes, eds, Oxford, pp. 13–39.

Luraghi, N. 2008. *The Ancient Messenians: Constructions of Ethnicity and Memory*, Cambridge.

Mandel, O. 1981. *Philoctetes and the Fall of Troy*, Lincoln.

Manville, P. B. 1990. *The Origins of Citizenship in Ancient Athens*, Princeton.

Marchiandi, D. 2008. 'Riflessioni in merito allo statuto giuridico di Lemno nel V secolo A.C. La ragnatela bibliografica e l'evidenza archeologica: Un dialogo possibile?', *ASAA* 86, pp. 11–39.

Marconi, C. 2004. 'Images for a Warrior. On a Group of Athenian Vases and their Public', in *Greek Vases: Images, Contexts and Controversies*, C. Marconi, ed., Leiden, pp. 27–40.

Martini, W. 1990. *Die archaische Plastik der Griechen*, Darmstadt.

Mastrokostas, E. I. 1974. 'ΕΙΣ ΑΝΑΖΗΤΗΣΙΝ ΕΛΛΕΙΠΟΝΤΩΝ ΜΕΛΩΝ ΕΠΙΤΥΜΒΙΩΝ ΑΡΧΑΪΚΩΝ ΓΛΥΠΤΩΝ ΠΑΡΑ ΤΗΝ ΑΝΑΒΥΣΣΟΝ. ΤΟ ΚΛΙΜΑΚΩΤΟΝ ΒΑΘΡΟΝ ΤΟΥ ΚΟΥΡΟΥ ΚΡΟΙΣΟΥ', *AAA* 7, pp. 215–28.

McClellan, A. M. 2017. 'The Death and Mutilation of Imbrius in *Iliad* 13', in *Yearbook in Ancient Greek Epic: Volume I*, J. L. Ready and C. C. Tsagalis, eds, Leiden, pp. 159–74.

McClellan, A. M. 2019. *Abused Bodies in Roman Epic*, Cambridge.

Meiggs, R. 1972. *The Athenian Empire*, Oxford.

Meiggs, R. and Lewis, D. 1969. *A Selection of Greek Historical Inscriptions: To the End of the Fifth Century BC*, Oxford.

Meritt, B. D. et al. 1939–53. *The Athenian Tribute Lists, Vol. 1–4*, Cambridge and Princeton.

Mersch, A. 1997. 'Urbanization of the Attic Countryside from the late 8th Century to the 6th Century BC', in *Urbanization in the Mediterranean in the 9th to 6th Centuries BC*, H. Damgard Andersen et al., eds, Copenhagen, pp. 45–62.

Meyer, E. A. 1993. 'Epitaphs and Citizenship in Classical Athens', *JHS* 113, pp. 99–121.

Miller, M. 1997. *Athens and Persia in the Fifth Century BC: A Study in Cultural Receptivity*, Cambridge.

Mitchell, L. G. 1997. 'New Wine in Old Wineskins: Solon, *arete* and the *agathos*', in *The Development of the polis in Archaic Greece*, L. G. Mitchell and P. J. Rhodes, eds, London, pp. 137–47.

Moore, M. B. 1980. 'Exekias and Telamonian Ajax', *AJArch*. 84 (4), pp. 417–34.

Morgan, C. 2001. 'Symbolic and Pragmatic Aspects of Warfare in the Greek World of the 8th to 6th Centuries BC', in *War as a Cultural and Social Force*, T. Bekker-Nielsen and L. Hannestad, eds, Copenhagen, pp. 20–44.
Morris, I. 1986. 'The Use and Abuse of Homer', *Cl. Ant.* 5 (1), pp. 81–138.
Morris, I. 1987. *Burial and Ancient Society: The Rise of the Greek City-State*, Cambridge.
Morris, I. 1989. 'Attitudes Toward Death in Archaic Greece', *Cl. Ant.* 8 (2), pp. 296–320.
Morris, I. 1992. *Death-Ritual and Social Structure in Classical Antiquity*, Cambridge.
Morris, I. 1998a. 'Archaeology and Archaic Greek History', in *Archaic Greece: New Approaches and New Evidence*, N. Fisher and H. van Wees, eds, Swansea, pp. 1–91.
Morris, I. 1998b. 'Burial and Ancient Society after ten years', in *Nécropoles et Pouvoir. Idéologies, pratiques et interprétations. Actes du colloque* Théories de la nécropole antique, *Lyon 21–25 janvier 1995*, S. Marchegay et al., eds, Lyon, pp. 21–36.
Morrison, J. V. 1992. *Homeric Misdirection: False Predictions in the* Iliad, Ann Arbor.
Muller, Y. 2011. 'Le *maschalismos*, une mutilation rituelle en Grèce ancienne?', *Ktèma* 26, pp. 269–96.
Muller, Y. 2014. 'La mutilation de l'ennemi en Grèce classique: pratique barbare ou préjugé grec?', in *Corps au supplice et violence de guerre dans l'Antiquité*, A. Allély, ed., Bordeaux, pp. 41–72.
Muller, Y. 2016. '"Religion, Empire and Mutilation": A Cross-Religious Perspective on Achaemenid Mutilation Practices', in *Religion in the Achaemenid Persian Empire: Emerging Judaism and Trends*, D. Edelman, A. Fitzpatrick-McKinley and P. Guillaume, eds, Tübingen, pp. 197–227.
Muller, Y. 2017. 'Le sang dans les récits de mutilation corporelle en Grèce ancienne d'Homère à Diodore de Sicile', in *L'Antiquité écarlate: Le sang des Anciens*, L. Bodiou and V. Mehl, eds, Rennes, pp. 207–34.
Muth, S. 2008. *Gewalt im Bild: Das Phänomen der medialen Gewalt im Athen des 6. und 5. Jahrhunderts v. Chr.*, Berlin.
Mylonas, G. E. 1948. 'Homeric and Mycenaean Burial Customs', *AJArch.* 52 (1), pp. 56–81.
Mylonas, G. E. 1975. *Τὸ δυτικὸν νεκροταφεῖον τῆς Ἐλευσῖνος* II, Athens.
Nagy, G. 1990. *Pindar's Homer: The Lyric Possession of an Epic Past*, Baltimore.
Nagy, G. 2007a. 'Lyric and Greek Myth', in *The Cambridge Companion to Greek Mythology*, R. D. Woodard, ed., Cambridge, pp. 19–51.
Nagy, G. 2007b. 'Homer and Greek Myth', in *The Cambridge Companion to Greek Mythology*, R. D. Woodard, ed., Cambridge, pp. 52–82.
Nagy, G. 2015. 'Oral Traditions, Written Texts, and Questions of Authorship', in *The Greek Epic Cycle and Its Ancient Reception*, M. Fantuzzi and C. Tsagalis, eds, Cambridge, pp. 59–77.
Nafissi, M. 1991. *La nascita del kosmos: studi sulla storia e la società di Sparta*, Naples.
Nafissi, M. 2009. 'Sparta', in *A Companion to Archaic Greece*, K. A Raaflaub and H. van Wees, eds, Chichester, pp. 117–37.
Neer, R. T. 2010. *The Emergence of the Classical Style in Greek Sculpture*, Chicago.

Neils, J. 1992. *Goddess and Polis: The Panathenaic Festival in Ancient Athens*, Princeton.
Neils, J. 1994. 'Reflections of Immortality: The Myth of Jason on Etruscan Mirrors', in *Murlo and the Etruscans: Art and Society in Ancient Etruria*, R. D. De Puma and J. P. Small, eds, Madison, pp. 190–5.
Neils, J. 2009. 'The 'Unheroic' Corpse: Re-reading the Sarpedon Krater', in *Athenian Potters and Painters: Volume II*, J. H. Oakley and O. Palagia, eds, Oxford, pp. 212–19.
Oakley, J. H. 2004. *Picturing Death in Classical Athens: The Evidence of the White Lekythoi*, Cambridge.
Ober, J. 1993. 'The Athenian Revolution of 508/7 BCE', in *Cultural Poetics in Archaic Greece*, C. Dougherty and L. Kurke, eds, Cambridge, pp. 215–32.
Ober, J. 1996. *The Athenian Revolution: Essays on Ancient Greek Democracy and Political Theory*, Princeton.
Ober, J. 1998. 'Revolution Matters: Democracy as Demotic Action', in *Democracy 2500?: Questions and Challenges*, I. Morris and K. Raaflaub, eds, Dubuque, pp. 67–85.
Ober, J. 2007. '"I Besieged that Man": Democracy's Revolutionary Start', in *Origins of Democracy in Ancient Greece*, K. A. Raaflaub, J. Ober and R. Wallace, eds, Berkeley, pp. 83–104.
Osborne, R. 1988. 'Death Revisited, Death Revised: The Death of the Artist in Archaic and Classical Greece', *Art History* 11, pp. 1–16.
Osborne, R. 1989. 'A Crisis in Archaeological History? The Seventh Century B.C. in Attica', *ABSA* 84, pp. 297–322.
Osborne, R. 1996a. *Greece in the Making, 1200–479 BC*, London.
Osborne, R. 1996b. 'Pots, Trade and the Archaic Greek Economy', *Antiquity* 70, pp. 31–44.
Osborne, R. 2001. 'Why did Athenian Pots Appeal to the Etruscans?', *World Archaeology* 33 (2), pp. 277–95.
Osborne, R. 2004a. 'Homer's society', in *The Cambridge Companion to Homer*, R. Fowler, ed., Cambridge, pp. 206–19.
Osborne, R. 2004b. 'Images of a Warrior: On a Group of Athenian Vases and Their Public', in *Greek Vases: Images, Contexts and Controversies*, C. Marconi, ed., Leiden, pp. 41–54.
Osborne, R. 2009. *Greece in the Making, 1200–479 BC*, 2nd edition, London.
Osborne, R. 2010. 'Democratic Ideology, the Events of War and the Iconography of Attic Funerary Sculpture', in *War, Democracy and Culture in Classical Athens*, D. M. Pritchard, ed., Cambridge, pp. 245–65.
Osborne, R. 2011. *The History Written on the Classical Greek Body*, Cambridge.
Osborne, R. 2018. *The Transformation of Athens: Painted Pottery and the Creation of Classical Greece*, Princeton.
Osborne, R. forthcoming. 'How, any Why, the Athenians Painted Different Myths at Different Times', in *Texts and Intertexts in Archaic and Classical Greece*, A. Kelly and H. Spelman, Cambridge.
Ostwald, M. 1969. *Nomos and the Beginnings of Athenian Democracy*, Oxford.

Ostwald, M. 1995. 'Public Expense: Whose Obligation? Athens 600–454 B.C.E.', *Proceedings of the American Philosophical Society* 139 (4), pp. 368–79.
Page, D. 1963. *History and the Homeric Iliad*, 2nd edition, Berkeley and Los Angeles.
Page, D. 1981. *Further Greek Epigrams: Epigrams before A.D. 50 from the Greek Anthology and Other Sources, Not Included in Hellenistic Epigrams or the Garland of Philip*, Cambridge.
Pàmias, J. 2014. 'The Reception of Greek Myth', in *Approaches to Greek Myth*, 2nd edition, L. Edmunds, ed., Baltimore, pp. 44–83.
Papadopoulou, C. 2017. 'The Living and their Dead in Classical Athens: New Evidence from Acharnai, Halai Aixonidai & Phaleron', *Arch. Rep.* 63, pp. 151–66.
Parker, R. 1983. *Miasma: Pollution and Purification in early Greek Religion*, Oxford.
Parker, R. 1984. 'A Note on phonos, thysia and maschalismos', *LCM* 9 (9), p. 138.
Parry, M. 1930. 'Studies in the Epic Technique of Oral Verse-Making: I. Homer and Homeric Style', *HSCPh* 41, pp. 73–148.
Parry, M. 1932. 'Studies in the Epic Technique of Oral Verse-Making: II. The Homeric Language as the Language of an Oral Poetry', *HSCPh* 43, pp. 1–50.
Parry, M., Lord, A. B. and Bynum, D., eds, 1954. *Serbocroatian Heroic Songs*, Cambridge.
Patterson, C. 2006. "Citizen Cemeteries' in Classical Athens?', *CQ* 56 (1), pp. 48–56.
Pemberton, E. G. 1972. 'The East and West Friezes of the Temple of Athena Nike', *AJArch.* 76, pp. 303–10.
Pierrot, A. 2015. 'Who Were the *Eupatrids* in Archaic Athens?', in *'Aristocracy' in Antiquity: Redefining Greek and Roman Elites*, N. Fisher and H. van Wees, eds, Swansea, pp. 147–68.
Pipili, M. 1994. 'Philoctetes', *LIMC* VII (1), pp. 376–85.
Pipili, M. 2018. 'Laconian Pottery', in *A Companion to Sparta Vol. I: Blackwell Companions to the Ancient World*, in A. Powell, ed., Hoboken, pp. 124–53.
Postlethwaite, N. 1988. 'Thersites in the *Iliad*', *G&R* 35, pp. 123–36.
Price, M. J. and Waggoner, N. 1975. *Archaic Silver Coinage: The Asyut Hoard*, London.
Pritchard, D. M. 1999. *The Fractured Imaginary: Popular Thinking on Citizen Soldiers and Warfare in Fifth-Century Athens*, PhD Thesis, Macquarie University (Sydney).
Pritchard, D. M. 2010. 'The Symbiosis between Democracy and War: The Case of Ancient Athens', in *War, Democracy and Culture in Classical Athens*, D. M. Pritchard, ed., Cambridge, pp. 1–62.
Pritchard, D. M. 2018. *Athenian Democracy at War*, Cambridge.
Pritchett, W. K. 1979. *The Greek State at War* III, Berkeley.
Pritchett, W. K. 1985. *The Greek State at War* IV, Berkeley.
Proietti, G. 2013. 'The Marathon Epitaph from Eua-Loukou: Some Notes about Its Text and Historical Context', *ZPE* 185, pp. 24–30.
Qviller, B. 1981. 'The Dynamics of the Homeric Society', *Symb. Osl.* 56, pp. 109–55.
Raaflaub, K. A. 1997a. 'Soldiers, Citizens and the Evolution of the Early Greek *Polis*', in *The Development of the* polis *in Archaic Greece*, L. G. Mitchell and P. J. Rhodes, eds, London, pp. 49–59.

Raaflaub, K. A. 1997b. 'Homeric Society', in *A New Companion to Homer*, I. Morris and B. P. Powell, eds, Leiden, pp. 624–48.

Raaflaub, K. A. 2008. 'Homeric Warriors and Battles: Trying to Resolve Old Problems', *CW* 101 (4), pp. 469–83.

Rausch, M. 1999. *Isonomia in Athen: Veränderungen des öffentlichen Lebens vom Sturz der Tyrannis bis zur zweiten Perserabwehr*, Frankfurt am Main.

Rawlings, L. 2007. *The Ancient Greeks at War*, Manchester.

Ready, J. 2007. 'Toil and Trouble: The Acquisition of Spoils in the *Iliad*', *TAPA* 137 (1), pp. 3–43.

Recke, M 2002. *Gewalt und Leid: Das Bild des Krieges bei den Athenern im 6. und 5. Jh. v. Chr.*, Istanbul.

Redfield, J. M. 1975. *Nature and Culture in the* Iliad: *The Tragedy of Hector*, Chicago.

Redfield, J. M. 1979. 'The Proem of the *Iliad*: Homer's Art', *CPhil.* 74 (2), pp. 95–110.

Rees, O. 2018. 'Picking over the Bones: The Practicalities of Processing the Athenian War Dead', *Journal of Ancient History* 6 (2), pp. 167–84.

Reusser, C. 2002. *Vasen für Etrurien: Verbreitung und Funktionen attischer Keramik im Etrurien des 6. un 5. Jahrhunderts vor Christus*, Zürich.

Rhodes, P. J. 1981. *A Commentary on the Aristotelian* Athenaion Politeia, Oxford.

Rhodes, P. J. and Osborne, R., eds, 2003. *Greek Historical Inscriptions 404–323 BC*, Oxford.

Richer, N. 1994. 'Aspects des funérailles à Sparte', *Cahiers du Centre Gustave-Glotz* 5, pp. 51–96.

Richter, G. M. A. 1961. *The Archaic Gravestones of Attica*, New York.

Richter, G. M. A. 1970. *Kouroi – Archaic Greek Youths. A Study of the Development of the Kouros Type in Greek Sculpture*, 3rd edition, London.

Rihll, T. 1986. "Kings' and 'Commoners' in Homeric Society', *LCM* 11 (6), pp. 86–91.

Robert, C. 1873. *De Apollodori Bibliotheca*, Berlin.

Robert, L. 1973. *Bulletin épigraphique* (supplement to *Rev. Ét. Grec.* 86).

Robertson, D. S. 1923. 'Pindarica', *CR* 37 (1/2), pp. 5–7.

Robertson, D. S. 1940. 'The Food of Achilles', *CR* 54 (4), pp. 177–80.

Robertson, G. I. C. 1997. 'Evaluating the Citizen in Archaic Greek Lyric, Elegy and Inscribed Epigram', in *The Development of the Polis in Archaic Greece*, L. G. Mitchell and P. J. Rhodes, eds, London, pp. 148–57.

Robertson, N. 1983. 'The Collective Burial of Fallen Soldiers at Athens, Sparta and Elsewhere', *Echos du monde classique* 27, pp. 78–92.

Robertson, N. 1992. *Festivals and Legends: The Formation of Greek Cities in the Light of Public Ritual*, Toronto.

Robinson, D. M., Stevens, G. P., Vanderpool, E. 1949. 'An Inscribed Kouros Base', *Hesp. Supplements* 8, pp. 361–64.

Rohde, E. 1925. *Psyche: The Cult of Souls and Belief in Immortality among the Ancient Greeks*, London.

Rose, H. J. 1931. 'Iolaos and the Ninth Pythian Ode', *CQ* 25, pp. 156–61.

Rose, P. W. 1975. 'Class Ambivalence in the "Odyssey"', *Hist.* 24 (2), pp. 129-49.
Rose, P. W. 1997. 'Ideology in the *Iliad*: Polis, *Basileus, Theoi*', *Arethusa* 30 (2), pp. 151-99.
Rose, P. W. 2012. *Class in Archaic Greece*, Cambridge.
Rosenmeyer, T. 1962. 'Seven Against Thebes. The Tragedy of War', *Arion* 1 (1), pp. 48-78.
Rosivach, V. J. 1983. 'On Creon, *Antigone* and Not Burying the Dead', *Rh. Mus.* 126, pp. 193-211.
Rosivach, V. J. 2002. 'The Requirements for the Solonic classes in Aristotle, AP 7.4', *Hermes* 130 (1), pp. 36-47.
Rutherford, I. 2011. 'Singing Myth: Pindar', in *A Companion to Greek Mythology*, K. Dowden and N. Livingstone, eds, Oxford, pp. 109-23.
Rutherford, I. 2015. 'Pindar's Cycle', in *The Greek Epic Cycle and Its Ancient Reception*, M. Fantuzzi and C. Tsagalis, eds, Cambridge, pp. 450-60.
Sancisi-Weerdenburg, H. 2000. 'Cultural Politics and Chronology', in *Peisistratos and the Tyranny: A Reappraisal of the Evidence*, H. Sancisi-Weerdenburg, ed., Amsterdam, pp. 79-106.
Saunders, D. 2008a. 'Dead Warriors and Their Wounds on Athenian Black-Figure Vases', in *Essays in Classical Archaeology for Eleni Hatzivassiliou 1977-2007*, D. Kurtz, ed., Oxford, pp. 85-94.
Saunders, D. 2008b. 'Mourning Glory? The Depiction of Fallen Warriors in Athenian Black-Figure Vase-Painting', in *Beyond the Battlefields: New Perspectives on Warfare and Society in the Graeco-Roman World*, E. Bragg, L. I. Hau and E. Macaulay-Lewis, eds, Newcastle, pp. 161-83.
Schiebler, L. 1987. 'Bild und Gefäss: Zur ikonographischen und funktionalen Bedeutung der attischen Bildfeldamphoren', *JdI* 102, pp. 57-118.
Schmaltz, B. 1983. *Griechische Grabreliefs*, Darmstadt.
Schmitz, T. A. 2010. 'Speaker and Addressee in Early Greek Epigram and Lyric', in *Archaic and Classical Greek Epigram*, M. Baumbach, A. Petrovic and I. Petrovic, eds, Cambridge, pp. 25-41.
Schröder, J. 2020. *Die Polis als Sieger: Kriegsdenkmäler im archaisch-klassischen Griechenland*, Berlin.
Schubert, C. 2008. 'Die Naukrarien: Zur Entwicklung der attischen Finanz-administration', *Hist.* 57 (1), pp. 38-64.
Schultz, P. 2009. 'The North Frieze of the Temple of Athena Nike', in *Art in Athens during the Peloponnesian War*, O. Palagia, ed., Cambridge, pp. 128-67.
Schwartz, A. 2009. *Reinstating the Hoplite: Arms, Armour and Phalanx Fighting in Archaic and Classical Greece*, Stuttgart.
Scott, L. 2000. 'Were there polis navies in Archaic Greece?', in *The Sea in Antiquity*, G. J. Oliver et al., eds, Oxford, pp. 93-115.
Scott, M. 1980. 'Aidos and Nemesis in the Works of Homer, and their Relevance to Social and Co-operative Values', *AC* 23, pp. 13-35.
Scott Smith, R. and Trzaskoma, S. M. 2007. *Apollodorus' Library and Hyginus' Fabulae: Two Handbooks of Greek Mythology*, Indianapolis.

Seaford, R. 2004. *Money and the Early Greek Mind: Homer, Philosophy, Tragedy*, Cambridge.
Sears, M. 2010. 'Warriors Ants: Elite Troops in the *Iliad*', *CW* 103 (2), pp. 139–55.
Sears, M. 2019. *Understanding Greek Warfare*, Abingdon.
Segal, C. 1971. *The Theme of the Mutilation of the Corpse in the Iliad*, Leiden.
Shapiro, H. A. 1990. 'Old and New Heroes: Narrative, Composition, and Subject in Attic Black-Figure', *Cl. Ant.* 9, pp. 114–48.
Shapiro, H. A. 1993. *Personifications in Greek Art: The Representation of Abstract Concepts 600 – 400 B.C*, Zürich.
Shapiro, H. A. 2012. 'Attic Heroes and the Construction of the Athenian Past in the Fifth Century', in *Greek Notions of the Past in the Archaic and Classical Eras: History without Historians*, J. Marincola, L. Llewellyn-Jones and C. Maciver, eds, Edinburgh, pp. 160–82.
Shay, J. 1995. 'The Birth of Tragedy – Out of the Needs of Democracy', *Didaskalia: Ancient Theatre Today* [online journal] 2 (2).
Siewert, P. 1972. *Der Eid von Plataiai* (Vestigia 16), Munich.
Siewert, P. 1982. *Die Trittyen Attikas und die Heeresreform des Kleisthenes*, Munich.
Simon, E. and Lorenz, S. 1997. 'Tydeus', *LIMC* VIII (1), pp. 142–5.
Singor, H. W. 1991. 'Nine against Troy: On Epic ΦΑΛΛΑΓΓΕΣ, ΠΡΟΜΑΧΟΙ, and an Old Structure in the Story of the *Iliad*', *Mnemos.* 44 (1/2), pp. 17–62.
Singor, H. W. 1995. '*Eni Prôtoisi Machesthai*: Some Remarks on the Iliadic Image of the Battlefield', in *Homeric Questions: Essays in Philology, Ancient History and Archaeology, Including the Papers of a Conference Organized by the Netherlands Institute at Athens (15 May 1993)*, J. P. Crielaard, ed., Amsterdam, pp. 183–200.
Singor, H. W. 2000. 'The Military Side of the Peisistratean Tyranny', in *Peisistratos and the Tyranny: A Reappraisal of the Evidence*, H. Sancisi-Weerdenburg, ed., Amsterdam, pp. 107–29.
Sledge, M. 2005. *Soldier Dead: How We Recover, Identify, Bury, and Honor our Military Fallen*, New York.
Smith, J. A. 1989. *Athens Under the Tyrants*, Bristol.
Snodgrass, A. M. 1980. *Archaic Greece: The Age of Experiment*, Berkeley.
Snodgrass, A. M. 1983. 'Heavy Freight in Archaic Greece', in *Trade in the Ancient Economy*, P. Garnsey, K. Hopkins and C. R. Whittaker, eds, London, pp. 16–26.
Snodgrass, A. M. 1998. *Homer and the Artists: Text and Picture in Early Greek Art*, Cambridge.
Snodgrass, A. M. 2006. 'The Economics of Dedication at Greek Sanctuaries', in *Archaeology and the Emergence of Greece*, A. M. Snodgrass, ed., Ithaca, pp. 258–68.
Snodgrass, A. M. 2013. 'Setting the Frame Chronologically', in *Men of Bronze: Hoplite Warfare in Ancient Greece*, D. Kagan and G. F. Viggiano, eds, Princeton, pp. 85–94.
Solmsen, F. 1898. 'Ναύκραρος ναύκλαρος ναύκληρος', *Rh. Mus.* 53, pp. 151–8.
Sommerstein, A. H. 2006a. '*Polyxene*', in *Sophocles: Selected Fragmentary Plays Vol. I*, A. H. Sommerstein, D. Fitzpatrick and T. Talboy, eds, Oxford, pp. 41–83.

Sommerstein, A. H. 2006b. 'Troilus', in *Sophocles: Selected Fragmentary Plays Vol. I*, A. H. Sommerstein, D. Fitzpatrick and T. Talboy, eds, Oxford, pp. 196–247.

Sommerstein, A. H. 2015. 'Tragedy and the Epic Cycle', in *The Greek Epic Cycle and Its Ancient Reception*, M. Fantuzzi and C. Tsagalis, eds, Cambridge, pp. 461–86.

Sourvinou-Inwood, C. 1983. 'A Trauma in Flux: Death in the 8th Century and After', in *The Greek Renaissance of the Eighth Century B.C.: Tradition and Innovation*, R. Hägg, ed., Stockholm, pp. 33–49.

Sourvinou-Inwood, C. 1995. *'Reading' Greek Death: To the End of the Classical Period*, Oxford.

Spivey, N. 1991. 'Greek Vases in Etruria', in *Looking at Greek Vases*, T. Rasmussen and N. Spivey, eds, Cambridge, pp. 131–50.

Stahl, M. and Walter, U. 2009. 'Athens', in *A Companion to Archaic Greece*, K. A Raaflaub and H. van Wees, eds, Chichester, pp. 138–61.

Stansbury-O'Donnell, M. D. 1999. *Pictorial Narrative in Ancient Greek Art*, Cambridge.

Stansbury-O'Donnell, M. D. 2006. *Vase Painting, Gender, and Social Identity in Archaic Athens*, Cambridge.

Stears, K. 2000. 'The Times They Are A'Changing: Developments in Fifth-Century Funerary Sculpture', in *The Epigraphy of Death: Studies in the History and Society of Greece and Rome*, G. J. Oliver, ed., Liverpool, pp. 25–58.

Ste Croix, G. E. M. de. 1981. *The Class Struggle in the Ancient Greek World from the Archaic Age to the Arab Conquests*, Ithaca.

Ste Croix, G. E. M. de. 2004. *Athenian Democratic Origins and Other Essays*, Oxford.

Stein-Hölkeskamp, E. 1989. *Adelskultur und Polisgesellschaft: Studien zum griechischen Adel in archaischer und klassischer Zeit*, Stuttgart.

Steinbock, B. 2013. *Social Memory in Athenian Public Discourse: Uses and Meanings of the Past*, Ann Arbor.

Stewart, A. 1986. 'When is a Kouros Not an Apollo? The Tenea "Apollo" Revisited', in *Corinthiaca: Studies in Honor of Darrell A. Amyx*, M. A. Del Chiaro, ed., Columbia, pp. 54–70.

Stewart, A. 1990. *Greek Sculpture: An Exploration*, New Haven.

Stewart, A. 1997. *Art, Desire, and the Body in Ancient Greece*, Berkeley.

Stinton, T. C. W. 1990. *Collected Papers on Greek Tragedy*, Oxford.

Storey, I. 2008. *Euripides: Suppliant Women*, London.

Strauss, B. S. 2000. 'Perspectives on the Death of Fifth-Century Athenian Seamen', in *War and Violence in Ancient Greece*, H. van Wees, ed., London, pp. 261–83.

Stroszeck, J. 2006. 'Lakonisch-rotfigurige Keramik aus den Lakedaimoniergräbern am Kerameikos von Athen (403 v. Chr.)', *AA*, pp. 101–20.

Stupperich, R. 1977. *Staatsbegräbnis und Privatgrabmal im Klassischen Athen*, Münster.

Stupperich, R. 1994. 'The Iconography of Athenian State Burials in the Classical Period', in *The Archaeology of Athens and Attica under the Democracy*, W. D. E Coulson, O. Palagia, T. L. Shear, Jr., H. A. Shapiro and F. J. Frost, eds, Oxford, pp. 93–103.

Tentori Montalto, M. 2013. 'Nuove considerazioni sulla stele della tribù Erechtheis dalla villa di Erode Attico a Loukou-Eva Kynourias', *ZPE* 185, pp. 31–52.

Tentori Montalto, M. 2017. *Essere primi per il valore: gli epigrammi funerari greci su pietra per i caduti in guerra (VII–V sec. a.C.). Quaderni della rivista di cultura classica e medioevale 16*, Pisa.

Thalmann, W. G. 1988. 'Thersites: Comedy, Scapegoats, and Heroic Ideology in the Iliad', *TAPA* 118, pp. 1–28.

Thalmann, W. G. 1998. *The Swineherd and the Bow: Representations of Class in the Odyssey*, Ithaca and London.

Toher, M. 1991. 'Greek Funerary Legislation and the two Spartan Funerals', in *Georgica: Greek Studies in the Honour of George Cawkwell*, M. Flower and M. Toher, eds, London, pp. 159–75.

Tompkins, D. P. 2013. 'Greek Rituals of War', in *The Oxford Handbook of Warfare in the Classical World*, B. Campbell and L. A. Tritle, eds, Oxford, pp. 527–41.

Torrance, I. 2007. *Aeschylus: Seven Against Thebes*, London.

Torres-Guerra, J. B. 2015. 'Thebaid', in *The Greek Epic Cycle and Its Ancient Reception*, M. Fantuzzi and C. Tsagalis, eds, Cambridge, pp. 227–43.

Tritle, L. A. 1997. 'Hector's Body: Mutilation of the Dead in Ancient Greece and Vietnam', *AHB* 11, pp. 123–36.

Tritle, L. A. 2007. "'Laughing for Joy': War and Peace among the Greeks', in *War and Peace in the Ancient World*, K. A. Raaflaub, ed., Oxford, pp. 172–90.

Tritle, L. A. 2013. 'Men at War', in *The Oxford Handbook of Warfare in the Classical World*, B. Campbell and L. A. Tritle, eds, Oxford, pp. 279–93.

Trümpy, C. 2010. 'Observations on the Dedicatory and Sepulchral Epigrams, and their Early History', in *Archaic and Classical Greek Epigram*, M. Baumbach, A. Petrovic and I. Petrovic, eds, Cambridge, pp. 167–79.

Trundle, M. 2004. *Greek Mercenaries: From the Late Archaic Period to Alexander*, London.

Tueller, M. A. 2010. 'The Passer-by in Archaic and Classical Epigram', in *Archaic and Classical Greek Epigram*, M. Baumbach, A. Petrovic and I. Petrovic, eds, Cambridge, pp. 42–60.

Udwin, V. M. 1999. *Between Two Armies: The Place of the Duel in Epic Culture*, Leiden.

Ulf, C. 1990. *Die homerische Gesellschaft: Materialien zur analytischen Beschreibung und historischen Lokalisierung*, München.

Usher, R. G. 2001. *Philoctetes*, Warminster.

Valdés Guía, M. and Gallego, J. 2010. 'Athenian *zeugitai* and the Solonian Census Classes: New Reflections and Perspectives', *Hist.* 59 (3), pp. 257–81.

Van der Valk, M. 1958. 'On Apollodori *Bibliotheca*', *Rev. Ét. Grec.* 71, pp. 100–168.

Van der Vin, J. P. A. 2000. 'Coins in Athens at the Time of Peisistratos', in *Peisistratos and the Tyranny: A Reappraisal of the Evidence*, H. Sancisi-Weerdenburg, ed., Amsterdam, pp. 147–53.

Van Effenterre, H. 1976. 'Clisthène et les mesures de mobilisation', *Rev. Ét. Grec.* 89, pp. 1–17.
Van Wees, H. 1988. 'Kings in Combat: Battles and Heroes in the *Iliad*', *CQ* 38 (1), pp. 1–24.
Van Wees, H. 1992. *Status Warriors: War, Violence and Society in Homer and History*, Amsterdam.
Van Wees, H. 1994. 'The Homeric Way of War: The *Iliad* and the Hoplite Phalanx', *G & R* 41 (1&2), pp. 1–18, 131–55.
Van Wees, H. 1995. 'Princes at Dinner: Social Event and Social Structure in Homer', in *Homeric Questions: Essays in Philology, Ancient History and Archaeology, Including the Papers of a Conference Organized by the Netherlands Institute at Athens (15 May 1993)*, J. P. Crielaard, ed., Amsterdam, pp. 147–79.
Van Wees, H. 1996. 'Heroes, Knights and Nutters: Warrior Mentality in Homer', in *Battle in Antiquity*, A. B. Lloyd, ed., London, pp. 1–86.
Van Wees, H. 1997. 'Homeric warfare', in *A New Companion to Homer*, I. Morris and B. Powell, eds, Leiden, pp. 668–93.
Van Wees, H. 1998. 'Greeks Bearing Arms: The State, the Leisure Class, and the Display of Weapons in Archaic Greece', in *Archaic Greece: New Approaches and New Evidence*, N. Fisher and H. van Wees, eds, Swansea, pp. 333–78.
Van Wees, H. 2000. 'The Development of the Hoplite Phalanx: Iconography and Reality in the Seventh Century', in *War and Violence in Ancient Greece*, H. van Wees, ed., London, pp. 125–66.
Van Wees, H. 2001. 'The Myth of the Middle-Class Army: Military and Social Status in Ancient Athens', in *War as a Cultural and Social Force*, T. Bekker-Nielsen and L. Hannestad, eds, Copenhagen, pp. 45–71.
Van Wees, H. 2004. *Greek Warfare: Myths and Realities*, London.
Van Wees, H. 2006a. 'Mass and Elite in Solon's Athens: The Property Classes Revisited', in *Solon of Athens: New Historical and Philological Approaches*, J. H. Blok and A. P. M. H. Lardinois, eds, Leiden, pp. 351–89.
Van Wees, H. 2006b. '"The Oath of the Sworn Bands": The Acharnae Stela, the Oath of Plataea and Archaic Spartan Warfare', in *Das Frühe Sparta*, A. Luther, M. Meier and L. Thommen, eds, Stuttgart, pp. 125–64.
Van Wees, H. 2007. 'War and Society', in *The Cambridge History of Greek and Roman Warfare* I, P. Sabin, H. van Wees and M. Whitby, eds, Cambridge, pp. 273–99.
Van Wees, H. 2008. '"Stasis, Destroyer of Men": Mass, Elite, Political Violence and Security in Archaic Greece', in *Sécurité collective et ordre public dans les societies anciennes*, C. Brélaz and P. Ducrey, eds, Vandoeuvres-Geneva, pp. 1–48.
Van Wees, H. 2010. '"Those who Sail must Receive a Wage": Naval Warfare and Finance in Archaic Eretria', in *New Perspectives on Ancient Warfare*, G. G. Fagan and M. Trundle, eds, Leiden and Boston, pp. 205–26.

Van Wees, H. 2011. 'Defeat and Destruction: The Ethics of Ancient Greek Warfare', in *Böser Krieg: exzessive Gewalt in der Antiken Kriegsführung und Strategien zu deren Vermeidung*, M. Linder and S. Tausend, eds, Graz, pp. 69–110.

Van Wees, H. 2013a. 'Farmers and Hoplites: Models of Historical Development', in *Men of Bronze: Hoplite Warfare in Ancient Greece*, D. Kagan and G. F. Viggiano, eds, Princeton, pp. 222–55.

Van Wees, H. 2013b. *Ships and Silver, Taxes and Tribute: A Fiscal History of Archaic Athens*, London.

Van Wees, H. 2018a. 'Luxury, Austerity and Equality in Sparta', in *A Companion to Sparta Vol. I: Blackwell Companions to the Ancient World*, A. Powell, ed., Hoboken, pp. 202–35.

Van Wees, H. 2018b. 'The Common Messes', in A. Powell (ed.), in *A Companion to Sparta Vol. I: Blackwell Companions to the Ancient World*, A. Powell, ed., Hoboken, pp. 236–68.

Van Wees, H. 2018c. 'Citizens and Soldiers in Archaic Athens', in *Defining Citizenship in Archaic Greece*, A. Duplouy and R. W. Brock, eds, Oxford, pp. 103–43.

Van Wees, H. and Fisher, N. 2015. 'The Trouble with 'Aristocracy'', in *'Aristocracy' in Antiquity: Redefining Greek and Roman Elites*, N. Fisher and H. van Wees, eds, Swansea, pp. 1–57.

Vaughn, P. 1991. 'The Identification and Retrieval of the Hoplite Battle-Dead', in *Hoplites: The Classical Greek Battle Experience*, V. D. Hanson, ed., London, pp. 38–62.

Vermeule, E. 1965. 'The Vengeance of Achilles', *Bulletin of the Museum of Fine Arts* 63, pp. 34–52.

Vermeule, E. 1979. *Aspects of Death in Early Greek Art and Poetry*, Berkeley.

Vernant, J.-P., ed. 1968. *Problèmes de la guerre en Grèce ancienne*, Paris.

Vernant, J.-P. 1988. *Myth and Society in Ancient Greece*, New York.

Vernant, J.-P. 1991. 'A "Beautiful Death" and the Disfigured Corpse in Homeric Epic', in *Mortals and Immortals: Collected Essays*, F. I. Zeitlin, ed., Princeton, pp. 50–74.

Vessey, D. 1973. *Statius and the Thebaid*, Cambridge.

Vestrheim, G. 2010. 'Voice in Sepulchral Epigrams: Some Remarks on the Use of First and Second Person in Sepulchral Epigrams, and a Comparison with Lyric Poetry', in *Archaic and Classical Greek Epigram*, M. Baumbach, A. Petrovic and I. Petrovic, eds, Cambridge, pp. 61–78.

Vicaire, P. 1979. 'Images d'Amphiaraos dans la Grèce archaïque et Classique', *Bulletin de l'Association Guillaume Budé* 1, pp. 2–45.

Vierneisel, K. 1967. 'Neuewerbungen Staatliche Antikensammlungen und Glyptothek', *Münchner Jahrbuch der bildenden Kunst* 18, pp. 241–5.

Viggiano, G. F. 2013. 'The Hoplite Revolution and the Rise of the Polis', in *Men of Bronze: Hoplite Warfare in Ancient Greece*, D. Kagan and G. F. Viggiano, eds, Princeton, pp. 112–33.

Viggiano, G. F. and Van Wees, H. 2013. 'The Arms, Armor, and Iconography of Early Greek Hoplite Warfare', in *Men of Bronze: Hoplite Warfare in Ancient Greece*, D. Kagan and G. F. Viggiano, eds, Princeton, pp. 57–73.

Vos, M. F. 1963. *Scythian Archers in Archaic Attic Vase-painting*, Groningen.
Wallinga, H. T. 2000. 'The Athenian *naukraroi*', in *Peisistratos and the Tyranny: A Reappraisal of the Evidence*, H. Sancisi-Weerdenburg, ed., Amsterdam, pp. 131–46.
Walter-Karydi, E. 2015. *Die Athener und ihre Gräber (1000–300 v. Chr.)*, Berlin.
Webster, T. B. L. 1955. 'Homer and Attic Geometric vases', *BSA* 50, pp. 38–50.
Webster, T. B. L. 1970. *Sophocles: Philoctetes*, Cambridge.
West, M. L. 1969. 'The Achaean Wall', *CR* 19 (3), pp. 255–60.
West, M. L. 2003. *Greek Epic Fragments: From the Seventh to the Fifth Centuries BC*, Cambridge.
West, M. L. 2013. *The Epic Cycle: A Commentary on the Lost Troy Epics*, Oxford.
West, M. L. 2015. 'The Formation of the Epic Cycle', in *The Greek Epic Cycle and Its Ancient Reception*, M. Fantuzzi and C. Tsagalis, eds, Cambridge, pp. 96–107.
Whitehead, D. 1981. 'The Archaic Athenian ΖΕΥΓΙΤΑΙ', *CQ* 31 (2), pp. 282–6.
Whitehead, D. 1986. *The Demes of Attica, 508/7–ca. 250 BC: A Political and Social Study*, Princeton.
Whitley, J. 1991. *Style and Society in Dark Age Greece: The Changing Face of a Pre-Literate Society 1100–700 BC*, Cambridge.
Whitley, J. 2001. *The Archaeology of Ancient Greece*, Cambridge.
Whitman, C. H. 1958. *Homer and the Heroic Tradition*, Cambridge, MA.
Wilkins, J. 1993. *Euripides* Heraclidae*: With Introduction and Commentary*, Oxford.
Willcock, M. M. 1976. *A Companion to the Iliad: Based on the Translation by Richmond Lattimore*, Chicago.
Willcock, M. M. 1997. 'Neoanalysis', in *A New Companion to Homer*, I. Morris and B. Powell, eds, Leiden, pp. 174–89.
Winkler, J. J. 1990. 'The Ephebes' Song: *Tragōidia* and *Polis*', in *Nothing to Do with Dionysos? Athenian Drama in Its Social Context*, J. J. Winkler and F. I. Zeitlin, eds, Princeton, pp. 20–62.
Winterbottom, M. 1989. 'Speaking of the Gods', *G&R* 36 (1), pp. 33–41.
Woodford, S. and Loudon, M. 1980. 'Two Trojan Themes: The Iconography of Ajax Carrying the Body of Achilles and of Aeneas Carrying Anchises in Black Figure Vase Painting', *AJArch.* 84 (1), pp. 25–40.
Yamagata, N. 1994. *Homeric Morality* [Mnemosyne Supplement 131], Leiden.
Yoshitake, S. 2010. '*Aretē* and the Achievements of the War Dead: the Logic of Praise in the Athenian Funeral Oration', in *War, Democracy and Culture in Classical Athens*, D. M. Pritchard, ed., Cambridge, pp. 359–77.
Young, D. C. 1983. 'Pindar, Aristotle, and Homer: A Study in Ancient Criticism', *Cl. Ant.* 2 (1), pp. 156–70.
Zaphiropoulou, P. N. 2002. 'Recent Finds from Paros', in *Excavating Classical Culture. Recent Archaeological Discoveries in Greece*, M. Stamatopoulou and M. Yeroulanou, eds, Oxford, pp. 281–4.

Zaphiropoulou, P. N. 2006. 'Geometric Battle Scenes on Vases from Paros', in *Pictorial Pursuits. Figurative Painting on Mycenaean and Geometric Pottery Papers from two seminars at the Swedish Institute at Athens in 1999 and 2001*, E. Rystedt and B. Wells, eds, Stockholm, pp. 271–7.

Zinserling, V. 1965. 'Das attische Grabluxusgesetz des frühen 5. Jahrhunderts', *Wissenschaftliche Zeitschrift der Friedrich-Schiller-Universität Jena* 14, pp. 29–34.

Zuntz, G. 1947. 'Is the *Heraclidae* Mutilated?', *CQ* 41 (1/2), pp. 46–52.

Zuntz, G. 1955. *The Political Plays of Euripides*, Manchester.

Index

Achilles 28
   and Ajax 86–7, 93–6
   armour 22, 95
   funeral 13, 103
   grief 26
   maltreatment of Hector 29, 35–7, 39, 70–2
Aegina 124, 147, 174
Aeneas 25, 95
Aeschylus 52–6, 63–4, 71–2, 74, 130
Aethiopis 86
afterlife 39–41
Agamemnon 15, 26, 28, 31–2
   aristeia 17, 35–6, 192–3 n.88
   and Sparta 46
Ahlberg-Cornell, Gudrun 86–7
Ajax 25, 35, 71
   and Achilles 86–7, 93–6
   duel with Hector 22–3, 101
Ajax, Locrian 35–6
Alcmaeonids 106, 145, 153, 158, 169–71
   Cylonian affair 142–3, 147
   exile after Pallene 160–1, 166
Alcmene 57–61
Allan, William 61
Ambrakia 116
Amphiaraus 62–6
Anavyssos stele 121–2
Anchimolius 169
Andrewes, Antony 143
Antigone 202 n.53
Antoninus Liberalis 58, 61
Apollo 37, 39
Apollodorus 47–8, 57–8, 61–3, 66, 69
Ares 21, 106, 109
Arginusae, battle of 79
Argos, Argives 159–60
   in myth 45, 49–50, 52–6, 59–63, 73
aristeia 17, 22, 33, 35, 192–3 n.88
Aristion 110–11, 128, 163, 167
aristocracy 139, 183 n.11
Aristophanes 119, 159

Aristotle 138–40, 142, 152, 157–8, 161, 164–5
   autarkeia 137
   and Epic Cycle 73
   naucraries 144–6, 171
   property classes 149–51
army
   elite character 113–14, 136–7
   in Homer (organization) 26–7
   and state-formation 137
army, Athenian
   in ancient accounts 135–7
   cavalry 145
   early history 142–8
   naval organization 145–8, 162, 168
   and Peisistratus 158–64, 167–9
   post-Cleisthenes 171–2, 175–6
   private vs public 145–8, 155–7, 167–8
   and Solon 152–7
   undeveloped/lack of 136–7, 170–1
Arrington, Nathan 3–4, 127
Artemision, battle of
   polyandrion 124
ashes 31–2, 80, 130, 191 n.78, 236 n.50
Asteropaios 23, 195 n.105
Athanasia 65
Athena 26, 62–3, 65–6
Athena Nike, Temple of 44–5, 49–50, 55–6, 60, 73–4, 76
Athens
   Acropolis 135, 142, 169
   early history 138–48
   early wars 147, 153–4, 158, 162
   self-image 74–6, 128, 178
attendants, war 240 n.43

Bacchylides 63, 66, 68–70
battlefield *see* burial, mass burials, repatriation
battlefield truce (*anairesis ton nekron*) 51, 79
   in Homer 30–1

origins of 43–4, 51–2, 56, 74–6,
    199–200 nn.33–4
Beard, Mary 84
beautiful death (*kalos thanatos*)
    and 'antifuneral' 28–9, 38–9
    in Archaic art 91
    in Archaic memorials 106, 110, 156,
        224–5 n.23
    in Classical art 126
    in elegiac poetry 108
    and funeral oration 128
    in Homer 27–9
Beazley Archive 82, 88, 92–3
Blok, Josine 155
Boardman, John 3
Boeotia, Boeotians 63, 135, 171–2, 175
    shields *see* iconography
burial
    Archaic era 104–12, 120–1, 140–1
    battlefield (exceptional) 122, 124,
        233 n.31
    elite vs common (Homer) 13–14
    Geometric era 103–4
    in Homer 27–9, 30–3
    legislation 155, 173–4, 249 n.148

Calhoun, George 17
Callinus 14, 108, 110, 128
cannibalism 62–6, 205 n.79
casualty lists 121–4, 128
cemeteries, Attica
    extra-mural 104
    Kerameikos 119, 124, 127–8, 130–1, 178
    monopolized by elites 102–3, 140
    public 120–1, 172
cenotaphs 113
Chalcis, Chalcidians 122–4, 135, 171–3,
    175
Chersonese 162
Chigi olpe 84
Chilon 116
Christesen, Paul 115
Cicero 173–4
Cimon 54, 80, 127–8, 173
Clairmont, Christoph 3–4, 121, 123, 129
class 182–3 n.11
class-division
    Archaic Athens 138–42, 148–51, 165
    in Homer 15–18, 33–4, 185 n.31

Cleisthenes 169–71
    army reorganization 171–2
    burial measures 172–4
    and *patrios nomos* 127–8
    reforms 80, 99, 102, 121, 136
Cleomenes 135, 169–71
coinage, introduction 162, 167
commemoration, war dead
    private 125–7
    public 116, 122–4, 128–9
    see also kouroi, stelai, epitaphs
comradeship 26–7
Conon 69
Corythus 70
cremation 103–4, 112–13, 130
    see also ashes
Creon 50, 52
Cylon 142–6, 170
Cypselus, chest of 208 n.115

decapitation 35–6, 75, 203–4 n.68
    of Eurystheus 45, 56–61
    of Melanippus 62–6
demarchs 144, 153, 171
democracy
    introduction 169–71
    military impact 135–6, 172, 175–6
    and *patrios nomos* 80, 123–4, 127–30,
        174–5, 178
despoiling the dead
    in Archaic art 87, 90, 92
    in Archaic warfare 113, 221 n.84
    in Homer 21–4
Dictys Cretensis 69
Diodorus 61, 79, 127
Diomedes 23, 25, 32, 62
Dionysios of Halicarnassus 127
Dodds, Eric 25
Dolon 23, 32
duel 22–3, 101

Echeverria, Fernando 84–5, 91
Elephenor 19, 21
Eleusis 122, 130, 135, 158
    in myth 50, 52–5
Eleutherae 50, 52–5
elites
    Archaic Athens 138–42, 238 n.19
    burial (in Homer) 27–9, 101, 103

burial (pre-Classical) 102–12
 distinguished by armour 21–3
 in Homer (*basileis, aristoi*) 16–18,
  184 n.17
 and Peisistratus 160–1, 165–6
Elpenor 40–1
Ephialtes 80, 127–8
Epic Cycle 47–9, 63
 brutality 206–7 n.98
 and Classical authors 73
 limitations 49
 survival 47–8
epitaphs
 Archaic memorials 104–9, 156
 and elegiac poetry 107–9
 public 122–3
 rhetoric of 107–9, 123
Eretria, Eretrians 159, 162
Etruria, Etruscans 64, 68, 82–3
Eupatrids 138–9, 150, 237–8 n.18
Euphorbos 36
Euripides 52, 59–60, 72
Eurystheus 45, 56–61
Exekias 89–91, 94–5

Fantuzzi, Marco 49
Ferrari, Gloria 96
fights, over the dead (Leichenkämpfe)
 in black-figure art 88–92
 in Corinthian art 87–8
 in Geometric art 215 n.37
 in Greek warfare 81, 99, 114, 221 n.84
 in Homer 18–20, 24–7, 29–30
 in red-figure art 91–3
Finley, Moses 13, 21
Foxhall, Lin 141
François Vase 87, 93–4
Frost, Frank 136, 153, 160
funeral oration (*epitaphios logos*) 1, 3, 109,
 128–9

Gantz, Timothy 52–3, 71
Garlan, Yvon 137
Geddes, Anne 18, 33
Glaukos 16, 26
glory (*kleos*) 38, 106, 114, 156, 167–8
 and captured armour 21–2, 87, 92
 imperishable (*aphthiton*) 27–30, 34,
  101

and *patrios nomos* 120
 in Tyrtaeus (*esthlon*) 108

Hades 28, 40–1
Hall, Jonathan 46
Hannah, Patricia 125–6
Hannestad, Lise 96
Hanson, Victor Davis 2
Harrison, Evelyn 73
head-hunting 21
Hector 22–3, 25, 35–6, 41
 duel with Ajax 22–3, 101
 funeral 13–14, 29, 103
 mistreatment of 29, 35, 37–9, 70–2
Hellanicus 70
Heraclidae 45, 56–61
Herodotus 51, 60, 122, 135–8, 158–61, 170,
  172, 175, 177
 Cylonian affair 142–3, 145
 and mutilation 42, 57, 75, 209–10 n.129
Hesiod 48–9
Hipparchus 169–70
Hippias 160, 162, 169–70, 173
Hippolochos 35–6, 192 n.87
Hölscher, Tonio 84–5
Homer, Homeric poems
 audience 16, 183 n.15
 battle narratives 19–20
 brutality 13, 34–5
 as historical source 5–6, 14–15, 43, 81
 interpolations 31–3
 oral transmission 47
 and patriotism 226 n.36
 psychological warfare 38
 and vengeance 35–6
honour (*timē*) 21, 25–7, 29–30, 35–6, 38
hoplite revolution, model 2, 44, 137, 141
Hutchinson, Gregory 64
Hyllus 57, 61
Hypnos and Thanatos 29, 126

iconography, war
 Boeotian shields 84–5, 94, 218–19 n.63
 changes in 93, 97–9, 220–1 n.81
 constructionist approach 84–5
 Geometric art 104, 147
 as historical source 83–6, 96–9
 and nudity 85, 91
 pot shapes 88, 93

Scythian archers 160, 214 n.31
and spectators 88–9, 95–6
quantitative approach 86
and wounds 91, 217 n.52
see also loutrophoroi
Idomeneus 21–2
Ilioneus 35–6, 192 n.87
Imbrius 35–6, 193 n.89
Iolaus 58–61
Ionian revolt 124
Isagoras 135, 169–71
Isocrates 2, 60–1

Jacoby, Felix 3
Jeffery, Lilian 121
Johnston, Sarah Iles 41

Kebriones 19
Koön 26, 35
kouroi, korai 104–7, 109–10, 156, 163
disappearance 121, 167
see also Kroisos, memorials, Xenokles
Krentz, Peter 85
Kroisos 3, 105–7, 109–10, 113, 128, 154, 156, 163, 168, 224–5 n.23
Kurtz, Donna 3

Lampon 75
Lampsacus 162
land exploitation, Attica 141, 166
Lavelle, Brian 165
Leipsydrion 169–70
lekythoi, white-ground 126–7
Lemnos 67–8, 123, 174
lexiarchikon grammateion 153, 171
Libanius 66
Lissarrague, François 84
Little Iliad 67, 69–70
Lloyd-Jones, Hugh 123
Loraux, Nicole 3, 80, 128
Lord, Albert 47
Lorimer, Hilda 83, 87
loutrophoroi, warrior 125–6
Lycophron 69
Lycurgus 115
Lygdamis 159
Lysias 60–1
Lysippides 89

Manville, Philip Brook 167
Marathon, battle of 45, 73
polyandrion 123–4, 174
Marconi, Clemente 96
maschalismos 196 n.111
mass burials (*polyandria*)
Athenian 121–5, 173–4
for criminals 231 n.15
in Homer 31–3
pre-Classical 80, 101–2, 114, 116, 211–12 n.9, 221–2 n.1
Megacles 158
Megara, Megarians 107, 147, 153, 158
Melanippus 62–6, 206 n.91
memorials, funerary
and army service 109–11
artistic rhetoric 105, 109–11, 227 n.42
cost 105, 109–10
disappearance 172–4
survival 105, 113
see also *kouroi*, stelai
Menelaus 36, 67, 69–70, 95
Messenian War, Second 115
Miltiades, the Elder 162
Miltiades, the Younger 123, 162
mobilization, war
Archaic Athens 145–6, 148, 150–1, 153
and Cleisthenes 171
lack of 136
pandemei 144, 170–1
property classes 150–1
Morris, Ian 16, 102–3, 120, 140–1, 164, 172
Muth, Susanne 88
mutilation of the dead
animals 37–9, 194–5 n.103
in Athenian art 70–2
condemned 42, 57, 72, 75, 193 n.96
in early mythology 56–70, 72–3, 208 n.112
in Homer 34–9, 192 n.87, 193 n.96, 195 n.106
impact on the soul 40–1, 195–6 n.109
and non-Greeks 75, 209 n.128
Mycale, battle of 124
myth, mythology
censored/reinterpreted 60–2, 64–6, 70–3
contested 53–6
definition, nature of 45–6

in iconographic art 65, 68–9, 71
paradigmatic character 76
political use 46, 54–5, 57–8, 76
Mytilene, Mytileneans 147, 162

naukrariai, naukraroi 143–8, 157, 161
and Cleisthenes' reforms 170–2
Cylonian affair 143–4
function of 144–8
and mobilization 153
Neoanalysis 48
Neoptolemus 68, 95
Nestor 22–3, 31–2
Nisaea 147, 158
non-elites
Archaic Athens 138, 140–2
armour (Homer) 23–4, 187–8 n.48
burial (Archaic era) 114
burial (in Homer) 30–3
burial (in myth) 56
in Homer (*laoi*) 17–18
and Peisistratus 165–6, 168

Ober, Josiah 2
Odysseus 28, 64, 67–8, 95
Achaean assembly 15
Cretan tale 147
Doloneia 23, 32
nekyia 40–1
Oenone 69–70
Oltos 91–3
Olympia, Temple of 87, 113, 116
Orestes 46
Osborne, Robin 83, 86, 97–9, 110
Ostwald, Martin 153
Ovid 66

Page, Denys 31–3, 123
Pallene, battle of 106, 122, 158–61
Paris 67–70, 95
Parry, Milman 47
Parthenius 69–70
patrios nomos 1–2, 79–80
Archaic roots of 127–31, 179
in cultural discourse 119, 124–7
historical origins 80, 127–8, 235 n.45
ideological language 3, 120, 128–9
impact on citizens 124–5, 129–30
mythical origins 55

Patroclus
death 13, 26, 37
fight over 19, 22, 25–6
funeral 13, 23, 103
ghost of 40
Pausanias 61, 66, 123–4, 127
Pausanias, Spartan regent 75
Peisistratus, Peisistratids
agricultural revolution 164–9
and civic ideology 167–8
disarmament tradition 160
and the elites 160–1
fall 169–70
and funerary evidence 163–4, 167–8, 173
Golden Age 167–8
and *korunephoroi* 158–9
and mercenaries 159–60
political programme 161
populism 159, 165
rise to power 158
taxation 162
Peloponnesian War 51, 137
Peneleos 35–6
Persian Wars 54, 73–6, 80, 98, 105, 137
Athena Nike, frieze 45, 73–4
and battlefield truces 75–6, 175
and military identity 74–5, 178
and *patrios nomos* 126–8, 130, 175
Persians 45, 73–4, 209 n.128
phalanx formation 2, 114, 151
Archaic art 84–6, 98
in Homer 17, 20, 188–9 n.58
Phalerum 169–70, 231 n.15
Pherecydes 48, 58, 61–3, 66, 72
Philaids 166
Philoctetes 67–9
Pindar 48, 53–4, 58–9, 63, 66–8, 72, 74
Plataea, Plataeans 162
battle of 45, 73, 75
Oath of 75–6
polyandrion 124
Plato 2, 15, 72
Plutarch 46, 50–2, 138–9, 150, 153
polemarchos 140, 142, 145, 153, 161
pollution (*miasma*) 155
Pollux, Julius 144, 146
polyandria see mass burials
Polygnotos Group 125

pottery
  distribution of 82–3
  as historical source 81–3
  see also iconography
Pritchard, David 136
Pritchett, William Kendrick 3, 52
Proclus 47–8
promachoi 20–1, 23–4, 27, 30, 106
property classes (*tele*) 149–53, 156, 161, 166, 172
Pyrgi columen 64–5

Quintus Smyrnaeus 69

raiding 145–8
Redfield, James 38
repatriation, war dead
  Archaic Athens 103, 106–7, 111–13
  vs battlefield burial 3–4, 120, 124, 211 n.7
  Classical Athens 79–80, 119–20, 124, 129–31
  in Homer 31–2, 191 n.78
  logistics 112–13, 120
  other *poleis* 114–16, 235–6 n.49
retrieving the dead
  in black-figure art 93–6
  'egalitarian' model 34
  in Geometric art 86–7
  'hierarchical' model 33–4, 101
  in Homer 24–9
  importance of 79, 210–11 n.2
  in red-figure art 97
  see also battlefield truce
Rihll, Tracey 18
Robertson, George 109
Rosivach, Vincent 38
Sacred War, First 153
Salamis 147, 153, 158
Salamis, battle of
  polyandrion 124
Sarpedon 16, 19, 26
  armour 23
  death 13, 26, 29, 39
Schröder, Janett 3, 116
Scythia, Scythians 162
  in Athenian art 160, 214 n.31
Seven Against Thebes 49–56, 62–6
shame (*aidos*) 25–6, 29–30, 36–7

shameful treatment (*aeikea erga*) 37, 194 n.99
shield bands 87
Sicilian expedition 150
Sicyon 206 n.91
Sigeum 162
Simonides 48, 122
Singor, Henk 138, 158–9
Solon 122
  army regulations 152
  funerary legislation 155
  new war discourse 154–6
  raiding legislation 147
  reforms of 149–57
Sophocles 64, 68, 71–3
soul (*psyche*) 39–41, 129–30
Sparta, Spartans 46, 135, 169–70
  war dead 114–16, 120
spoils of war 113, 116, 230 n.63
  in Homer 21–4, 186 n.41
  trophies (*tropaia*) 51
Statius 66
Steinbock, Bernd 52, 54
stelai, funerary 104–5, 109–11, 156, 163, 167–8
  disappearance 120–1, 128
  public 121, 123
  see also Aristion, memorials, Tettichos
Storey, Ian 54–5
Strabo 61
strife (*stasis*) 139, 149, 157, 165

taxation 144–6, 162
Telemachus 46
Tellus 122, 124
Tettichos 3, 106–7, 110, 128, 154, 156
Teucer 71, 95
Thanatos 126
Thebaid 52–3, 55–6, 62–4, 66
Thebes, Thebans 58–9, 74, 138, 159, 162, 168, 170, 173
  Athena Nike, frieze 45, 49–50
  in myth 45, 47, 49–56, 58–9, 62–6
  see also Seven Against Thebes
Themistocles 173
Thersites 15, 185 n.34
Theseus 45–6, 50–2, 56, 138–9, 178
Thessaly, Thessalians 169–70
Thetis 94–5

Thracia, Thracians 159–60, 162
Thucydides 31, 51, 105, 136–7, 147, 150, 161–2
    Cylonian affair 142–4, 146
    and *patrios nomos* 1, 79–80, 127, 177
Thyrea, battle of 116
Tsagalis, Christos 49
Tydeus 53–4, 62–6
tyrants, tyranny 160
    see also Peisistratus
Tyrtaeus 14, 108, 110, 115, 128

unburied dead
    in Greek warfare 51, 74, 79, 199 n.32
    in Homer 32–3, 40–1

Van Wees, Hans 21, 23, 27, 85, 87–8, 143, 151–2, 166
Vaughn, Pamela 113–14
Vermeule, Emily 13, 34, 71
Vernant, Jean-Pierre 27–8
Viggiano, Gregory 2

war dead
    in Archaic iconography 86–97
    and Archaic memorials 105–12
    and Cleisthenes' reforms 172–5
    equality of 1–2, 120, 124, 127–9, 174–5
    Geometric era 104
    and Peisistratids 163–4, 167–9
    pre-Classical warfare 112–17
    private vs public 116–17, 128, 131, 137–8
    and Solon 155–7
    see also mass burials, repatriation
warfare, Archaic 84–5, 114, 136–7, 147
    and Homer 14, 17
West, Martin 48

Xenokles 107, 109–10, 128, 156, 163, 168
Xenophon 44, 60, 210 n.1

Zenobius 61
Zinserling, Verena 174

www.ingramcontent.com/pod-product-compliance
Lightning Source LLC
Chambersburg PA
CBHW072127290426
44111CB00012B/1814